FARMWORKERS

Alan Armstrong

FARMWORKERS

A Social and Economic History
1770–1980

B.T. Batsford Ltd · *London*

For Heather

First published 1988

Typeset by Butler & Tanner Ltd
and printed in Great Britain by
Butler & Tanner Ltd
Frome and London
Published by B.T. Batsford Ltd
4 Fitzhardinge Street, London W1H 0AH

British Library Cataloguing in Publication Data
Armstrong, Alan, 1936–
Farmworkers: a social and economic history
1770–1980.
1. Agricultural laborers—England—
Social conditions
I. Title
305.9′631′0942 HD1532

ISBN 0–7134–4391–X

Contents

List of Tables

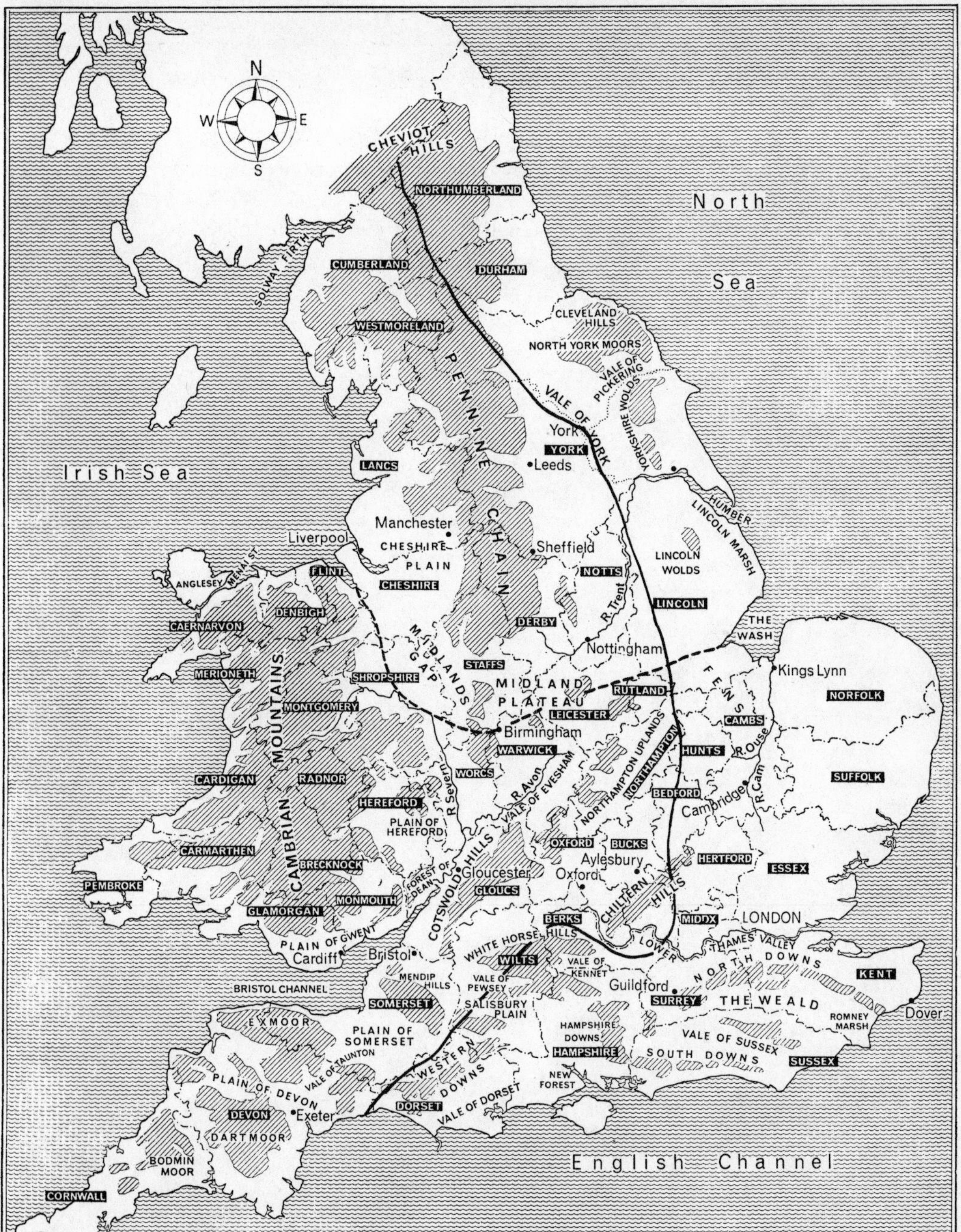

This map was originally drawn for J. D. Chambers and G. E. Mingay, eds., *The Agricultural Revolution, 1750–1880*, Batsford, 1966. Upon it have been superimposed the approximate boundaries of high and low wage districts (broken line) and the primarily corn-growing and grazing counties of England (black line), as identified in J. Caird, *English Agriculture in 1850–51*, 2nd edition, Cass, 1968.

Preface

This book examines the social history of a major element in the manual working population of England and Wales during two centuries of rapid economic change. It seeks to explore the characteristic experiences of some six or seven million persons – a minimum figure arrived at simply by summing estimates of the size of the agricultural labour force at thirty-year intervals between 1770 and 1980 – in four contextual settings: the home and the workplace, the local community and the wider social environment. There is a compelling case for a fresh overview at present, for nothing of the kind has been undertaken for many years. The last comprehensive attempt was made by a foreigner, Wilhelm Hasbach, whose *History of the English Agricultural Labourer* was first published in Germany in 1894, then by P. and S. King in England in 1908. Hasbach's study was impressive in its scale and conception, and still has considerable historiographical interest as one of the first books focused directly on the lives of the common people. His purpose was to trace the emergence of the rural proletariat ('a passive class') since the Middle Ages, and in successive chapters he sought to show how, following their achievement of personal freedom in the aftermath of the Black Death, large sections of the English peasantry came to lose their holdings as a consequence of enclosure and the engrossing of farms. However, the greater part of his book was concerned with illustrating the 'degradation' of the dispossessed labourers in the nineteenth century, and it concluded by advocating the multiplication of small holdings, a cry fashionable among radicals at the time he was writing. In his preface to the 1908 edition the Fabian, Sidney Webb, admitted that 'we shall not all concur with Professor Hasbach's political "values"', and among modern historians any reservations concerning its suitability as a textbook on that score are compounded by the fact that it was based almost exclusively on printed parliamentary papers and referred to nothing published after 1906. A new impression, without so much as a preface by the living authority, appeared in 1966. It was not reviewed in the leading scholarly journals, and W. E. Tate's opinion of the book expresses well the limited value that most historians would set on it: 'if only for its careful and compreshensive bibliographies . . . it is worth reading – or at any rate having at hand on one's bookshelf'.

In recent decades, agrarian historians have tended to concentrate their attentions elsewhere, for example upon the steps by which efficiency was raised in the agricultural sector (see, e.g. J. A. Yelling, *Common Field and Enclosure in England, 1450–1850*, Macmillan, 1977); on the contribution of agriculture to overall economic development (J. D. Chambers and G. E. Mingay, *The Agricultural Revolution 1750–1880*, Batsford, 1966; E. L. Jones, *Agriculture and Economic Growth, 1650–1815*, Methuen 1967); or on problems of practice and policy in agriculture in more recent times (C. S. Orwin and E. H. Whetham, *History of British Agriculture, 1846–1914*, Longmans, Green, 1964; E. Whetham, *The Agrarian History of England and Wales*, VIII, *1914–39*, Cambridge 1978). A clutch of excellent works dealing with the upper echelons of rural society has appeared and done much to stimulate further research founded on estate papers (D. Spring, *The English Landed Estate in the Nineteenth Century; its Administration*, Johns Hopkins University Press, Baltimore, 1963; G. E. Mingay, *English Landed Society in the Eighteenth Century*, Routledge and Kegan Paul 1963; F. M. L. Thompson, *English Landed Society in the Nineteenth Century*, Routledge and Kegan Paul 1963). However, the revival of social history since the 1960s has reawakened interest in the humble agricultural wage-earner and prompted much useful work, though not, so far, a survey capable of supplanting even Parts IV and V of Hasbach. At the present time university teachers need to refer their students to studies written from a variety of standpoints, which have never been brought together satisfactorily. What is available may be said to fall into six partially discrete categories, or traditions.

1. Studies written from the angle of vision of the labour economist, which closely examine wage-levels and the efficiency of labour use. Outstanding among recent work of this kind is E. H. Hunt, *Regional Wage Variations in Britain 1850–1914*, Oxford, 1974, in which the case of the farmworker looms large, while the same author set in train an interesting debate on agricultural labour productivity with an article in the *Economic History Review* in 1967. Other historians deeply engaged in studying the supply and use of farm labour include P. E. Dewey, whose work has concentrated chiefly on the period of the First World War, and E. J. T. Collins, who has published a number of articles in the academic journals and is currently working on a book dealing with the impact of technological changes on the use of labour in agriculture. As distinct from historical investigations, there exists a vast range of twentieth-century studies of labour in agriculture, in periodicals such as the *Farm Economist* and the *Journal of Agricultural Economics*, which were once of current interest and ought now to be drawn into the historical record.

2. Much more widely read by those with a general interest in the rural past are works which offer an insight into the social history of the farmworker viewed through particularly colourful and apparently significant episodes or events. Examples include A. J. Peacock, *Bread or Blood. The Agrarian Riots in East Anglia, 1816*, Gollancz, 1965 and especially E. J. Hobsbawm and G. Rudé, *Captain Swing*, Lawrence and Wishart, 1969 which superseded J. L. and B. Hammond, *The Village Labourer*, Longmans, Green, 1911 as the classic account of the 'last labourers' revolt' of 1830. Works such as these followed Hasbach in taking a gloomy view of the farmworker's situation and have stimulated a generation of students to write theses on the theme of rural social protest.

3. There is a body of trade union history mostly couched in terms of heroic struggles. Since the study of institutional labour history was itself a forerunner of the more broadly-based social history which has emerged during the last two decades, it is not surprising to find that the nearest approach to a general survey, R. Groves, *Sharpen the Sickle*, Porcupine Press, recently reissued by Merlin, was published as long ago as 1944. The foci of interest in this field continue to be the ill-starred attempts at unionization in the 1830s (J. Marlow, *The Tolpuddle Martyrs*, Andre Deutsch, 1971) and especially the saga of Joseph Arch and his union in the 1870s, which has engendered at least one substantial book (P. Horn, *Joseph Arch*, Roundwood Press, Kineton, 1971), along with a number of regional studies, one of the most useful being that of N. Scotland, *Methodism and the Revolt of the Field*, Alan Sutton, 1981.

4. In recent years a new style of social history has appeared which is not especially concerned with the elucidation of specific events and can be positively mistrustful of orthodox trade union history. A number of articles on rural topics may be found in the pages of *The History Workshop* (a 'journal of socialist historians') and, from the same stable, a number of monographs have emerged which include R. Samuel, ed., *Village Life and Labour*, 1981; D. H. Morgan, *Harvesters and Harvesting, 1840–1900. A Study of the Rural Proletariat*, 1982, and A. Howkins, *Poor Labouring Men. Rural Radicalism in Norfolk, 1870–1923*, 1985 (all published by Routledge and Kegan Paul). Meanwhile, K. D. M. Snell has produced *Annals of the Labouring Poor. Social Change and Agrarian England, 1660–1900*, Cambridge, 1985, a most substantial if controversial work which seeks to analyse the long term trends in employment patterns associated with the advance of capitalist agriculture. Works such as these are no less radical than anything that went before and are frequently more so. In particular, the approach taken in the majority of these publications is dominated by a conviction of the explanatory value of the concept of 'class', which, if not to the taste of all historians, is shared to a greater or lesser extent by writers in category 5.

5. Here we encounter studies which are written from a more consciously social scientific viewpoint, sometimes involving the fairly sophisticated use of statistics. A number of historical geographers have engaged in the task of wresting social meaning from spatial analyses of past historical situations: most noteworthy in this field is the work of Andrew Charlesworth on the distribution of the Swing riots in 1830 and, on a broader canvas, D. Mills's *Lord and Peasant in Nineteenth Century England*, Croom Helm, 1980 which probes the varying character of village communities. There is also a handful of works by anthropologists and sociologists focused on changes in rural society. W. M. Williams, with *The Sociology of an English Village: Gosforth*, Routledge and Kegan Paul, 1956 and *A West Country Village: Ashworthy*, Routledge and Kegan Paul, 1963, was perhaps the first post-war scholar to attempt to remedy the almost complete neglect of rural sociology in England, and J. Robin, *Elmdon. Continuity and Change in a North-West Essex Village, 1861–1964*, Cambridge, 1980, is the best recent book of this kind. However, few studies have been addressed directly to the farmworker. The outstanding exceptions to this generalization are A. Kussmaul's valuable study of a section of the agricultural labour force, *Servants in Husbandry in Early Modern England*, Cambridge, 1981, and H. Newby, *The Deferential Worker*, Allen Lane, 1977. This study is based on field researches in contemporary Suffolk and has the additional merit, rare among sociologists, of utilizing historical material very thoroughly. However, as the author very candidly admits, his findings for Suffolk cannot be taken as typical of the country as a whole, and in the last analysis, the object of his study is not a group of workers but the elucidation of a set of theoretical problems.

6. Any such intention is very far from the minds of those seeking a popular readership. My final category is inevitably a miscellany, springing from a range of authors with varying claims to scholarly expertise. At one end of the spectrum academic historians have occasionally set out to communicate the findings of scholarship vividly and readably to a wider audience. Recent examples would include various works of Pamela Horn, notably *Labouring Life in the Victorian Countryside*, Gill and Macmillan, Dublin, 1977 or G. E. Mingay, with *Rural Life in Victorian England*, Heinemann, 1977 and his sumptuous two-volume *The Victorian Countryside* (Routledge and Kegan Paul, 1981). The popular appeal of such works is matched, indeed exceeded by some of the fruits of a new *genre*, oral history, where the recollections of the aged are drawn on not only to entertain, but to illuminate aspects of the past. Since historians generally agree that what the actors in past social situations considered memorable and significant (rather than what they *ought* to have thought important!) is a valid area for investigation, oral history is well on the way to being accepted as an established branch of historical research. Outstanding examples include the various works of G. E. Evans, notably *Ask the Fellows who Cut the Hay*, 1956, and *Where Beards Wag All*, 1970, both published by Faber and Faber, along with R. Blythe, *Akenfield*, Allen Lane, 1969, which was subsequently broadcast on television. To a greater or lesser extent these books have succeeded in tapping a mood of nostalgia for the rural past which, though by no means without precedent, has made itself especially apparent since the 1960s, perhaps as an escapist reaction to the mounting problems of modern urban life, its pace, stresses, inner city decay, pollution problems and so on. Somewhat more deliberate attempts to exploit this mood include publications such as B. Winter, *A Country Camera*, David and Charles, 1971, whilst the Rabelaisian frolics described in G. Robinson, *Hedingham Harvest*, Constable, 1977 ('a cheerful, affectionate and often hilarious chronical of life and love in a Victorian village') have an obvious popular appeal. Studies such as R. Fletcher (ed.) *The Biography of a Victorian Village: Richard Cobbold's account of Wortham, Suffolk, 1860*, Batsford, 1977, and modern reprints of pre-1914 classics such as R. Jefferies, *Hodge and his Masters*, and G. Sturt, *Memorials of a Surrey Labourer* and *The Bettesworth Book* are presumably aimed at the same market. While most works in this category do not set out to minimize the hardships of rural life, in general they do not start, either, from the premise that the experience of rural workers was inevitably characterized by poverty, exploitation and tense class relationships. Indeed in some cases there is a perceptible tendency to emphasize the harmonies of rural life, with social conflict regarded as abnormal, often rooted in the quirks of individual behaviour rather than in the farmworker's fundamental situation, as it might be perceived by social scientists.

Any fresh attempt to write the history of the farmworker needs to start from the recognition that it cannot usefully be undertaken within a closed rural context. While as late as 1815 the importance of agriculture as the chief contributor to the national wealth and souce of employment was implicit in the high protection conferred by the revised Corn Law, the further advance of industry and the growth of towns worked progressively to weaken the basis of its case for special consideration from the legislature. Only in the trying circumstances of the 1914–18 war and during the Second World War and after did agriculture succeed in reviving these claims. However, it may be doubted whether the average farmworker had any clear appreciation of the changing position of agriculture in the national order of priorities, and even his self-interest was understandably difficult to determine. Radical and socialist theories seemed to suggest that so long as agriculture was run on capitalistic lines, there was a conflict of interest at its heart, making his employer essentially a class enemy. Certainly it would be foolish to deny that farmworkers as a body or as individuals endured many slights and indignities in the past, that they have grounds for resenting their lowly status, or to seek to minimize the depth of feeling that lay behind events such as the Swing riots in the 1830s, the labour troubles of the 1870s, or the remarkable Norfolk Strike of 1923. Yet the attachment of the union leadership to quasi-Marxist principles in the 1920s failed to establish any lasting degree of resolute class-consciousness. Never very far from the minds of many farmworkers at any time during the nineteenth and twentieth centuries was a sense of identity with the interests of their employers, derived in part from the intimacy of the work situation, and fortified by a strong suspicion that the true enemy of both was the anonymous urban consumer with his unthinking insistence on cheap food. Since the 1930s this point of view has been in the ascendancy, with farmers' and farmworkers' unions often prepared to act in concert as pressure groups to influence government in this country, and more recently in the European Economic Community. In short, the pre-industrial conception of an agricultural 'interest' may have been somewhat shaken during the Industrial Revolution, but in the long run proved to be very tenacious.

The mere mention of issues as broad as these would suggest that, from the social historian's point of view, something more than a narrow and austere analysis of labour as a factor of production is necessary, although we shall certainly have to accord centrality to supply and demand (including some significant demographic factors), on account of their obvious impact on the farm worker's material standard of life. I shall seek to supplement the economic approach by describing such elusive elements as beliefs, tastes and aspirations insofar as they can be imputed safely to a section of the community not given to expressing its innermost thoughts on paper. Regional and local variations capable of influencing all facets of the historical experiences of farmworkers will be given as much weight as space will allow. Naturally, the outcome of my labours cannot be expected to please everyone. However, my object will be achieved if I have succeeded in writing something which is widely read among devotees of all the traditions of rural social history mentioned above. For, at the present time, the great need is to mark out some common ground among the various competing approaches. In short, it is the object of this book to establish a point of convergence for existing studies, to essay a synthesis, and to provide a basis from which the merits and limitations of more exuberant adventures into this field of social history may be evaluated by those fresh to the study of the rural past. After due deliberation I decided that a primarily chronological treatment was best suited to the achievement of these aims.

In compiling this book I have run up a large number of debts. The first is to a number of academic colleagues who have read parts of the manuscript or given me much useful advice and encouragement. These include Professor G. E. Mingay whose knowledge of the rural history of the period is probably unrivalled, and Mr J. G. Oxborrow; and from universities other than Kent, Dr E. J. T. Collins, Dr B. A. Holderness, Dr P. E. Dewey and Professor F. M. L. Thompson. Going back a few years, the late Professor J. D. Chambers did much to reinforce my existing interest in population history, and unknowingly implanted the seeds of a new enthusiasm by the brilliance of his writings and discourses in the field of rural history. Next I must acknowledge sincerely my debt to the vast company of authors on whose works I have so freely drawn, and which have given me so much pleasure and instruction over recent years – even where I found myself disagreeing with their interpretations. While this is primarily a work of synthesis, to some extent I have sought to fill gaps in the existing literature and to locate new illustrative material from primary sources. Some of this was gathered locally, and I particularly remember the warm welcome received from Mr Tony Gould, District Organizer for the NUAAW, and his staff at the Maidstone Office. Other sources were consulted in locations well removed from Canterbury, and here I must record my appreciation of assistance in the form of a grant from the Trustees of the Wolfson Foundation. This was used chiefly for the purpose of visiting a large number of record offices during 1979 and 1980, selected on the basis of replies from County Archivists to a circular letter distributed in April 1979. Many took considerable pains in dealing with my initial enquiry, and to them also, my thanks are due. Next I should like to mention the assistance of librarians in a number of specialist institutions, apart from my own university. These have included the Museum of English Rural Life and the Institute of Agricultural History at Reading University, Wye College (University of London), the British Museum, the Public Record Office and the Ministry of Agriculture, Fisheries and Food. Acknowledgements are due to the Trustees of the Bedford Settled Estates for permission to publish correspondence held at the Bedfordshire County Record Office; and to Mrs Evans who allowed extracts from the Reminiscences of Frederick Swaffield at the Dorset County Record Office to be quoted. The editor and proprietors of *Punch* have permitted the reproduction of a number of cartoons still in copyright, and the Institute of Agricultural History supplied me with copies of similar material from *The Land Worker*. My thanks are due also to the Headmaster and the Head of History, Mr Shreeves, at Gillingham School, Dorset, who kindly agreed to allow the Swing letter on p. 74 which is in their possession, to appear. Finally, several members of the secretarial staff of this

College have assisted me by typing successive chapters over a period of years: I am grateful to all of them, but particularly to Mrs Jean Gil for putting the final version in order without the help, on this occasion, of her shiny new word processor.

Eliot College
University of Kent
at Canterbury

A.A.

January 1987

ONE

Introduction: the agricultural labour force in the later eighteenth century

Arthur Young, that eloquent and untiring apostle of the Agricultural Revolution,[1] did not achieve perfect consistency in his prolific writings; and his zeal for improvement led him to concentrate on what was exemplary rather than typical. Hence he cannot be regarded as a wholly objective observer of the agricultural practices or rural society of his day. Yet he had a keen sense of the value of numbers and, as it happens, collected the only reasonably reliable evidence on the structure of the agricultural labour force as it existed two centuries ago. From Bradmore Farm near North Mimms in Hertfordshire, Young set out during the summer of 1768 in a chaise, accompanied by his wife, on an extensive tour covering 2,500 miles, which took him northward to Drayton (Notts.), gathering observations on 16 holdings as he went. Yorkshire provided him with information on no fewer than 89 farms, Durham and Northumberland with 36 cases, Cumberland and Westmorland 28 and Lancashire and Cheshire another 22, before his homeward journey commenced. At Stone, Shenstone and Alston (Staffs.) Hagley, Bromsgrove and Pershore (Worcs.), Bensington and Henley (Oxon.), Maidenhead (Berks.) and Harmondsworth (Middx.), he collected details on another 57 farms. In all he had examined 250 holdings covering over 71,000 acres, and the geographical focus justified the title of his book, *A Six Months' Tour through the North of England* (1769). Scarcely had this impressive four-volume work left the presses when the intrepid traveller ventured forth once more, in 1770. On this occasion Mrs Young, described in Fanny Burney's diary as 'immoderately fat' and possessed of an 'overbearing temper' appears to have been left behind as Young once again struck northward, penetrating well into south Yorkshire before doubling back through the Fens, Norfolk, Suffolk and Essex. He then crossed into Kent and traversed the southern counties as far west as Axminster (Devon), whence he returned home via the Vale of Taunton, Bath, Reading and Beaconsfield (Bucks.). During the course of these journeys Young examined 92 farms, and another record of facts and impressions soon appeared under the title *The Farmer's Tour through the East of England* (1771).

Young did not gather information in a manner that would satisfy a modern statistician. Any systematization in his selection of farms was undermined from the outset by the fact that, on each occasion, he announced (in the newspapers) his intention of making a tour and invited readers who might allow him to see their experiments to make contact with him. Consequently he was able to take advantage of invitations from nobles such as the Marquis of Rockingham at Wentworth in Yorkshire and gentlemen such as Charles Turner of Kirkleatham and Simon Scroope Esq. of Danby, whose experiments with cabbages, it was said, conferred great honour on the family name; as well as from substantial improving farmers such as Robert Bakewell of Dishley, the noted stock breeder, and John Reynolds of Adisham in Kent. From this it might be presumed that Young took in a disproportionate number of farms which, by the standards of the day, would have been considered large (over about 300 acres) and indeed these did account for 24 per cent of his visits. But he did not neglect moderate-sized holdings and even those of 100 acres and less (respectively, 41 and 35 per cent). Indeed, he made a point of observing that his statistics refuted the notion of 'the whole kingdom being *monopolized* by *great farmers*'.[2]

Young used his material to strike many curious and not always illuminating averages; for example it emerged that, on the farms covered during the *Northern Tour*, there was one cow to each 24 acres surveyed, and rather over one acre to each sheep. Yet his extremely useful information on the employment of labour is capable of being analysed in such a way as to exhibit, with reasonable clarity, the chief influences on the size and composition of farm staffs. In the first place, the summary statistics for the two tours revealed a broad contrast between the predominantly arable south and east of England and the more pastoral north, in terms of average farm size and the provision of employment. The farms included on the *Eastern Tour* averaged 574 acres as against 286 for those covered on the *Northern Tour* and, correspondingly, they employed an average of 9.7 as against 5.1 adult farm servants and labourers.[3] This very broad regional contrast is one that many subsequent writers came to find convenient in the exposition of agricultural history, and it will be assumed quite frequently in this book. However, it must be understood as a necessary over-simplification. Young encountered farms in the north which included vast tracts of cultivated land, such as a 2,500 acre holding at Hetton (Northumberland) with 1,250 arable acres; while in the south his survey included farms as small as 42 acres (Leverington, Cambs.), 60 (Tring, Herts.), etc. Cutting across the gross regional contrast, critical factors determining the distribution of the labour force were the nature of the soil and the type of farming practised. By way of illustration we may note, at one extreme, a 2,000 acre holding at Penrith (Cumberland) running a similar number of sheep and rented at £200 per annum, which afforded employment to only one servant, four labourers, two maids and a boy; while by contrast a wholly arable farm of the same size at Bensington (Oxon.), where one day the skies would reverberate to the roar of American jets, was rented at £1,450 and employed no fewer than 17 servants, 20 labourers, five maids and five boys. Even quite a small arable holding of 70 acres at Risby (East Riding) was found to employ four servants and two labourers. The position is best summed up in a simple table, which, despite the small number of cases on which it has to be based, shows that, acre for acre, arable cultivation provided far more employment at all levels of farm size and especially for adult male servants and labourers; while grassland farms provided virtually none (except for maids and boys) until they rose above a hundred acres in size.

Table 1.1: Illustrations of the employment of labour on English farms *c.*1770

Farm size (acres)	*No. of farms*	*Average no. per farm of:* *Servants*	*Maids*	*Boys*	*Labourers*	*All employees*
A. 80% or more devoted to arable						
0–100	23	1.0	0.6	0.8	1.2	3.6
101–300	29	2.6	1.3	1.1	4.0	9.0
301–500	8	4.1	1.6	3.1	6.6	15.3
501–1,000	7	5.0	1.1	1.6	8.0	15.7
% of workers in each category (all sizes)		28.5	12.7	14.9	44.0	
B. Farms 75% or more devoted to grass						
0–100	13	0.3	0.8	0.0	1.9	3.0
101–300	6	1.3	1.3	0.3	0.8	3.8
301–500	3	3.0	1.7	1.0	3.3	9.0
501–1,000	3	1.0	1.3	0.7	4.7	7.7
% of workers in each category (all sizes)		24.5	28.6	17.3	29.6	

Source: Calculated from data in Young, *Northern Tour*, IV, tables A–E facing p. 343, and idem, *Eastern Tour*, IV, pp. 368–70. *N.B.* The table includes only farms where both acreage and full details of staff were given.

This takes us as far as we can go with respect to the influence of the size and type of holdings on the distribution of the labour force in the 1770s. From a social point of view, a re-arrangement of Young's material is necessary. In all, he noted the status of 2,688 workers, under four headings: servants (25.8 per cent), maids (13.1), boys (12.5), totalling to 51.4, and labourers (48.5). No account was taken of seasonal or casual employees. By examining these constituent elements of the labour force in turn, we may appraise their roles and at the same time bring out the element of fluidity which is too easily overlooked when we dwell on averages and 'structures', for it is clear that the extent of mobility was closely related to the life-cycle of the agricultural wage-earner.

Already in the late eighteenth century there were signs that the institution of farm service was coming under critical review by cost-conscious employers, particularly in the grain-growing regions of the south and east.[4] Even so, a striking feature of table 1.1 is the high proportion described as servants, maids and boys, who still accounted for over half the permanent farm staffs at this period. From an economic standpoint servants were simply wage-earning suppliers of labour on the land, yet in a social and demographic sense they were a distinctive category. For the great majority, service in husbandry was the institutionalization of a stage in life between childhood and adulthood. The boy or girl entering farm service for the first time characteristically did so between the ages of twelve and fifteen, by arrangement between his parents and the farmer. This usually entailed departure to board with the employer. We can sometimes trace such movements through the study of parish records. A comparison between two listings of labouring men and their sons at Terling (Essex) in May 1775 and July 1778 reveals that of 24 lads aged ten and over at the first date, only eleven remained in the village.[5] The others had disappeared, presumably into service in adjacent parishes. Not more than fifty miles from here lay Cardington (Beds.), remarkable in recent times for its conspicuous airship hangers visible from the former Midland Railway, and among demographic historians no less celebrated for its outstanding village census, made in 1782. Because this document gives details of all living children, whether or not at home, it has been used to show that virtually all children in the 0–9 age-group remained at home while at 10–14, some 16 per cent of males and 9 per cent of females had left to enter service. Thereafter, the chances of a son being away rose to 4 to 1 (at 15–19) with a 6 or 7 to 1 chance that, by his twenties, he would have left, being either in service or married. The proportion of boys living more than five miles from the parental home increased steeply with age, from about 20 per cent at 15–19 to 50 per cent from the age of 25.[6] The value of such arrangements to the parents is obvious. At a certain point it would be decided that a youth, or maid, ought to be earning his or her own keep, and the very restricted nature of accommodation in cottages would have been a further consideration: one bedroom would often have to serve the needs of boys and girls of all ages and in many cases the cradle would still be in use as the eldest children reached puberty. In return for a varied range of duties, the contractual arrangements entitled the young servant to food and lodging, as well as an annual lump sum which would increase as his experience and strength grew, particularly if he had the opportunity to develop specific skills with horses, cattle or sheep. It is clear that farm servants fared relatively well in the matter of diet. Writing of Hampshire at a slightly later period, Charles Vancouver described the ordinary breakfast of farm servants as bread and skimmed milk, with the remainder of the previous day's bacon. Lunch was bread and cheese with small beer, and dinner (prepared between three and four o'clock) consisted of pickled pork or bacon with potatoes, cabbages, turnips etc. There was bread and cheese for supper and fresh meat was usually served on Sundays. Somewhat similar dietary regimes were reported from Northamptonshire and Middlesex.[7] Doubtless the contrasts between one farmhouse and another were considerable and, along with the civility of the master and his wife, weighed heavily with their employees. Sometimes, in search of better conditions, farm servants would break their contracts and disappear; but for the most part they began and ended on a fixed day each year, usually Michaelmas, Martinmas or May-Day. Engagements were commonly, though not exclusively, entered into at statute fairs where, complained another prominent agrarian commentator, instancing the case of West Sussex, 'the roads were crowded with farm servants leaving their places and hying to the fair. It was a complete holiday: not a team to be seen, or a stroke of work going forward'.[8] Recent work has thrown further light on the frequency of moves (considerable) and the distances involved (small). In the case of 128 servants hired by a farmer at Tetney (Lincs.) between 1780 and 1830, 68 per cent stayed for only one year, while a scrutiny of 809 settlement examinations drawn from eight English counties from the seventeenth to the early nineteenth centuries suggests that 76 per cent stayed with the same master for only one year, and only nine per cent for more than two. After surveying the movements of some 1,500 male and female servants recorded at the Spalding Statute Sessions in 1767–85, Kussmaul has calculated that the mean distance for moves was 12.3 km. (men) and 10.8 km. (women), which may be somewhat higher than in other districts on account of the scattered nature of Fenland farms.[9]

With marriage this distinctive phase in the life of a farmworker came to an end. Men or women were unlikely to return to service except in the event of widowhood. This is not to say that the married labourer was reduced to a state of total immobility. Indeed, only 33 per cent of married men resident in Cardington had been born in the village, and 42 per cent (34 per cent among labourers) of those encountered in a group of parishes on the Vale of York in the period 1777–1812.[10] Nevertheless, the capricious exercise of their powers of removal by eighteenth-century parish overseers was often a factor for the poor man to reckon with, and many were reluctant to issue settlement certificates accepting responsibility for relief, except to unencumbered young men and women. For this and for other obvious reasons, there can be no doubt that, by comparison with farm servants, the married labourer was 'less mobile, more attached, even *adscriptus glebae*' in the words of a correspondent to the *Farmer's Magazine*.[11] In the case of Terling if we exclude the boys and youths already referred to, 72 from 90 adult males were still present after three years in 1775–8 (including seven out of ten described as 'non-settled'), which is an impressive rate of persistence, especially when we bear in mind that perhaps five or six would have died during the intervening period.

The situation of married labourers in the later eighteenth century defies adequate generalization. A minority worked on estates, which, though not normally paying more than the going rate of wages, offered solid advantages which probably made such positions eagerly sought after. Chief among these was the likelihood of more regular employment in winter, when the men could be occupied in such jobs as laying drains, carting dung, coal and timber, hedging, ditching and fencing; while maintaining the parks, extensive gardens, shrubberies and plantations of the grander establishments – 'part of the imposing fabric of the aristocratic presence' in the words of one authority[12] – was not directly a matter of profit and loss calculation. Elizabeth Gilboy found all these features when examining the account books of the Thornborough estate near Leyburn in Yorkshire, for the period 1749–53. Apparently the men did not participate to any significant extent in the rather sharp wage increases of the 1760s, and worked long hours, from daylight to dusk in winter, and 6 a.m. until 6 p.m. in summer. On the other hand, men such as William Glenton, who figured in the accounts throughout the period, received advances in wages and gifts from their employer in times of sickness and were assured of their position; she concludes, 'one is impressed with the atmosphere of stability running through the accounts'.[13] Some of the advantages for the estate labourer, notably greater regularity of employment, were enjoyed also by the more valued employees of farmers, particularly in the case of specialists working under yearly contracts such as shepherds and head ploughmen, with especially skilled and responsible tasks. These employees were often described as 'constant men', and in many respects their position resembled that of the farm servant except that, being

Shepherds about 1856. The man on the right is shearing while another sheep is brought to him. From a mid-eighteenth century print, artist unknown.

married, they lived out in cottages provided by the employer at 'free' or nominal rents.

However, the majority of those employed on farms were in a position which was less well-defined and often more precarious. Especially in the north-western counties and in Wales, many small occupiers worked regularly or occasionally for their neighbours and in these circumstances it was not always easy to draw a clear dividing line between employer and employee in terms of economic and social status. By degrees, they shaded over into the ranks of entirely wage-dependent labourers, who were particularly numerous in the south and east. Such men as these often lived in independently rented cottage accommodation, sometimes though not invariably with a garden or small piece of ground attached. They were likely to work not for one, but for several different masters during the course of a year, being hired by the week at best, more often by the day, or even on a piece-work basis. This practice was reckoned to be rapidly increasing during the closing decades of the eighteenth century in arable areas. 'I everywhere found that much work was done by the piece' commented Young in his *Southern Tour*; 'We do all the work we can by the piece' wrote the Revd J. Formby from Fincham in Norfolk in 1769, while an Essex correspondent remarked that 'the practice of letting work by the piece is rapidly increasing'.[14] Clearly, the practice did not lend itself to the management of cattle or sheep except in haytime, hence it was much less common in the dairying and breeding districts of the north and west. But elsewhere it became very general with the passage of time, and excited much the same controversies then as now. For all these reasons the independence of the labourer, such as it was, was bought at considerable cost. He was vulnerable to the whims of individual employers, to market forces and, especially, to the vagaries of the weather. 'As to the seasons' wrote John Howlett, the incumbent of Great Dunmow (Essex), in 1792, 'How amazing is the contrast to the poor labourer between a severe and frosty winter and a mild and open one? During the former the earth is fast bound in chains which defy the plough, the spade and the mattock, and trifling is the compensation he receives from voluntary bounty or parochial allowance; in the latter, he goes forth to his work with almost as little interruption as in the warmth of summer, or the mildness of Autumn'.[15] The ordinary labourer had no security against such hazards, for, unlike the farm servant, he could be laid off at any time without notice. Particularly in the case of elderly men or those unsound in mind, wind or limb, the work they were offered might well take on an intermittent character. Just as it is impossible to draw a very rigid distinction between servants and labourers because of the existence of 'constant men', so also the ranks of the labourers shaded over into casual workers whose contribution at certain times of the year was critical to the success of farming operations.

The overall demand for labour in agriculture varied on a seasonal basis, for natural reasons. Harvest-time saw a scramble for extra hands, which in abundant years became positively feverish. François de la Rochefoucauld, a young French nobleman directed to the study of English agriculture by his father, the duc de Liancourt, toured East Anglian farms early in the 1780s under the guidance of Arthur Young, and was impressed by the way in which the agricultural labour force expanded during the harvest months. One very large (3,000 acre) farm at Rougham (Norfolk), employing 14 servants, 3 maids and 30 regular day labourers, needed as many as 70 hands in harvest time. Another at Dunton in the same county (1,600 acres) had 14 servants and 12 day labourers and required 63 at harvest time. They were paid between 42 and 45 shillings for taking the harvest, as well as receiving food consisting of meat three times a day and strong and small beer in abundance. Farmer Glover, with 3,000 acres at South Creake, ordinarily employed 18 servants and the same number of day labourers, but his staff ran to 100, paid at about 2 guineas for the harvest period of 5–6 weeks, plus food and lodging. Although reticent in all other respects Glover waxed eloquent on the prodigious outlay involved: this swollen staff cost him three sheep a day and two bullocks a week, as well as three pints of strong beer each per day and as much small beer as they wanted. 'Nor is the supply of puddings any less lavish', marvelled de la Rochefoucauld, 'every weekday they have them made with dried raisins, on Sunday without raisins. The harvesters have something to eat five times a day: bread and cheese twice and meat three times. At one of these meals they have hot meat, which adds further to the expense.'[16] It is significant that the few recorded incidents of labour disputes in agriculture tended to occur under harvest conditions. Haymakers at Islington (Middlesex) were successful in securing wage increases in 1763 when the crop was unusually heavy, and again in 1795 when farmers were obliged to proffer 1s 6d against 1s a day: but similar efforts to exploit the bargaining position of labour were thwarted by an intense rainstorm in 1776, and in 1774 when the magistrates intervened to disperse a strike meeting which had become riotous.[17]

Among the Norfolk harvesters noticed by de la Rochefoucauld were Scotsmen, reputed good workers if inclined to be quarrelsome. They walked to Norfolk and back on foot, and on their return journeys consumed little but bread, small beer and milk, being anxious to take home their cash earnings untouched. Conspicuous in their dress ('jackets but no trousers having instead a cloth kilt which comes down to their knees') they were drawn, we presume, from among the ranks of crofters. From Herefordshire in 1794 it was likewise reported that the grain was cut by persons who came from the mountainous parts of Wales annually for that purpose, mostly it seemed from Cardiganshire; their descendants would increasingly find lucrative harvest work in the labour-starved Vale of Glamorgan by the 1830s.[18] But seasonal transfers of labour were also found within England itself, for example from the Yorkshire Dales to the East Riding and from the 'cheese' districts of north Wiltshire eastward and southward for the corn harvest on the southern chalklands. They were made possible by the different timings of the hay and corn harvests between hill and vale, heavy and light land, and north and south; and facilitated also by the fact that there were and would remain many districts where small farmers remained numerous. Especially in Cumberland, Westmorland and in Wales, critical periods in the year thus drew them into their neighbours' fields, sometimes on the footing of reciprocal co-operation designed to save one another the cost of hired labour but more often on a wage-paid basis which could, as we have seen, entail travelling considerable distances.

Another source of extra help was manufacturing industry. 'In hay and harvest time' observed the anonymous author of *An Inquiry into the Present Price of Provisions* (1773) 'it is inconceivable what numbers of tradesmen and handicraftsmen flock into the country'.[19] Thus we find a linen manufacturer, Henry Hindley of Mere in Wiltshire, countermanding an order for yarn on 19 June 1762, because it was then too late to turn it into cloth before the weavers abandoned their looms to work on the land. In the backward summer of 1770 he reported that the hay harvest had only just ended, and the corn harvest begun, with the consequence that his workmen were still in the fields in late September. As late as 26 October Hindley was unable to execute an order for cloth because, although the harvest had at last been reaped, 'a plenty of apples now imploys many workmen making syder'.[20] Other instances of the seasonal flow of labour out of manufacture abound in the literature. Arthur Young was informed by weavers and combers about Bocking and Braintree in Essex that 'in summer they did whatever husbandry work they were able, being better paid for it' and in the late eighteenth century West Riding manufacturers were to be found harvesting in the East Riding, West Country clothiers on the Wiltshire Downs, and the stocking makers of Leicester in Cambridgeshire.[21] The economic rationale of these flows is not far to seek; at this time the marginal productivity of labour employed in harvesting was probably higher than in many branches of manufacturing, and this was reflected in higher wages. Thus, according to Arthur Young's observations in 1768–70, average weekly wages were some 60–100 per cent higher in the harvest season than in the textile, pottery and lead-mining industries.[22] In the long run, flows out of manufacturing industry tended to diminish in importance as it was increasingly settled on a factory rather than a domestic basis and as industrial wages rose. Even so, throughout the nineteenth century and in some special cases well into the twentieth, harvesting was an attractive source of summer employment to those entrapped in monotonous work or the noxious environment of towns.[23]

The casual labour force included many female workers and adolescent children. They were to be found among the companies of migrating harvesters, for example on the Yorkshire Wolds in the 1790s. In the north and west generally, where women were accustomed to performing a great deal of agricultural work on small holdings, women shared the heaviest labours of the harvest fields. According to William Marshall it was rare in the North Riding 'to see a sickle in the hand of a man; reaping ... being almost entirely done by women' and in the Vale of Pickering in 1787 he found women earning 10d a day reaping, while a man's wage for binding the sheaves was 2s a day.[24] In the southern and eastern counties where females were more commonly engaged in domestic industries such as spinning, lace-making and straw plaiting, the majority took a less strenuous part at harvest time, and performed the lighter work of raking and gathering. Horticultural employment was another field of opportunity for female seasonal work, a particularly well-documented case being the migration of single women from Wales (especially Cardiganshire) to the Middlesex market gardens in the second half of the eighteenth century. The girls made their way on foot to Isleworth, Brentford and Hammersmith, where they set and tended crops from April onward and were employed to carry fruit and strawberries in baskets to customers in London. The close of the season would see them trudging back to Wales with their accumulated wages, which were very high by any Welsh standards.[25]

The seasonal involvement of unencumbered females and, locally, the wives of cottagers, is a feature which may be traced back as far as records will take us, and in the late eighteenth century the appearance of the larger farm, more extensive culture of new crops, and the wider adoption of improved methods encouraged a greater degree of neatness in agricultural practice, entailing hoeing and weeding which was capable of being performed as efficiently and more cheaply by women. In Northumberland, according to Bailey and Culley, 'the late ingenious Mr Ilderton' had first alighted on the idea of teaching women and children how to hoe, and within a few years virtually all the turnips of the county were tended at half the former expense.[26] However, such developments were by no means confined to the distant north, and in the south, recent research on seasonal patterns of unemployment derived from rural settlement examinations suggests that here also, women were increasingly finding employment in spring activities such as hoeing and weeding. These investigations also suggest that a degree of 'sexual specialization' in agricultural work may have been beginning to emerge, but unfortunately cannot tell us whether the aggregate volume of employment offered to females was tending to expand or to fall.[27] If contraction was the order of the day this would be unfortunate, for already in the late eighteenth century alternative sources of income for cottagers' wives were in some instances coming under pressure from the factory. This was at any rate true of hand-spinning. Sir F. M. Eden's sporadic observations made mention of the difficulty of procuring such work (e.g. at Seend, Wilts.) or the very inconsiderable, indeed declining wages of female spinners in such widely ranging localities as Kirkoswald (Cumberland), Brixworth (Northants.) and Swineshead (Lincs.) where they were so low that 'scarcely one person in ten will apply to it.'[28]

These were the characteristics of the labour force which served agriculture towards the close of the eighteenth century. The overall complexion of rural society, in which the wage-earner made up by far the largest constituent element, was decidedly different from that which obtained elsewhere in Europe at this period. To the east of the river Elbe lay the world of agrarian serfdom. Russia, Poland and Hungary contained estates sometimes running to hundreds of thousands of acres where the typical peasant still devoted a large part of the week to forced labour on his lord's land. In Western Europe the characteristic peasant had shed much of his servile status since the later middle ages, and in the main landlords had become merely collectors of rents and money dues. Thus in France, the forces of commercialization had brought into being a minority of wealthy peasants marketing their surplus produce and a majority of small and medium land-holders aiming for the most part to obtain self-sufficiency for their families. Serfdom had been a thing of the past in Britain for some three centuries, and it was becoming increasingly difficult to identify a counterpart to the peasant cultivators of France, the Low Countries and West Germany. It is true that the majority of Welsh upland farmers continued to follow a regime corresponding to the continental pattern of self-sufficiency, aiming to produce the basic requirements of life, in terms of food and clothing, and their equivalents could be found in outlying hilly districts of England itself – in Cumberland, Westmorland and the Yorkshire Dales for example. Yet elsewhere in England there had emerged, over many generations, the classic triad of the rentier landlord, the capitalist tenant farmer, and the virtually landless labourer, dependent on wages. Those regions which had advanced furthest along the path of modernity were also most closely associated with agrarian progress and with the image of English agriculture as the most efficient in the world, in the eyes of both home and foreign observers.

Historians of quite different persuasions agree that the emergence of a rural social structure of this kind made possible a more flexible and productive system of agriculture. Within the triad, the rentier landlord could play a vital role in encouraging agricultural progress. He was the provider of fixed capital and usually acknowledged the duty of standing by and supporting his tenants in difficult times. By virtue of his superior education and greater leisure, he might seek to disseminate new ideas among his tenants, and was usually very alive to the fact that, the greater the efficiency of land use, the fatter his rent-roll was likely to be. In a sense, the improving landlord might be seen as the strategist of agrarian progress. The role of the tenant farmer was entrepreneurial in nature; he furnished his own working capital in the form of stock and implements, and took the attendant chances of profit or loss. Both parties (though the farmer more directly) had an obvious interest in the productivity of the labour force and, during the eighteenth century, evinced an increasing interest in the efficient husbandry of time. The youthful French observer, de la Rochefoucauld, noticed much scope for improvement in this respect in East Anglia in 1784, noting that although the English working day ran from 6 a.m. until 6 p.m. (and longer in harvest), his fellow-countrymen worked longer, especially in summer. What was more, despite their 'enormous' wages, the Suffolk labourers did not perform 'nearly as much work as our people', taking frequent rests and talking a great deal.[29] Among English agricultural improvers there was a general sensitivity to this problem. On his very brief foray into Wales, Young was dismayed to observe the languid air of labourers in the district of Lanvachers; to him the self-evident need for greater regularity and work discipline suggested that farmers might consider (along with commendations and merit awards) instant dismissal in the case of poor service, since this would have a 'greater effect than all the hard words and scolding ... country fellows are so accustomed to this sort of correction that they are absolutely hardened to it'. He also recommended gentlemen to consider having their work people rung out and into home from the fields by means of a bell, fixed on top of one of the buildings.[30] Yet employers scarcely needed promptings from political economists to recognize what was needful. From Avebury in Wiltshire there survives an unusually interesting document of 1756 in which a group of farmers bound themselves formally in the sum of ten pounds to alter the hours of work of their 'Threshers, and other Daily Workmen and Servants', who had hitherto followed the 'very bad custom of going out of their Business two Hours every day at their Breakfast Time and one Hour at their Dinner-Time for the space of Nine Months in the year, and two Hours every Day all the other part of the year to our great detriment'. The signatories agreed to oblige their workers to labour from 6 until 10 a.m., 11 a.m. to 3 p.m., and 4 to 6 p.m. between mid-February and mid-November, and from daylight until 11 a.m., and 12 a.m. until nightfall during the remaining months. Any worker turned off for refusing to comply with these conditions would be denied employment by all the parties to the agreement.[31]

Such attempts to stiffen labour discipline, inculcate more regular patterns of work, and extend hours, reflected an increasing sense of time-thrift among employers and, it has been suggested, in the last analysis are explicable in terms of the character of the employer–employee relationship implicit in capitalist economic development.[32] Also, attitudes had been powerfully influenced by the pervasive ethic of Puritanism with its condemnation of sloth and constant admonitions to redeem the time, although the theme had long since ceased to be peculiar to employers of a specifically Puritan, or even Wesleyan or Evangelical persuasion. However, it is quite probable that the effort to inculcate a greater degree of work discipline in agriculture was slower to take effect on the land than in factories, mines and workshops, if the constant complaints of farmers (lasting well into the present century) give any indication. There are a number of possible reasons for this. It was simply impossible for labour to be monitored so closely on a farm as in a factory or workshop, owing to the greater dispersal of the workforce; the pace of work was not dictated by the machine and even when, many decades later, the use of machines became extensive, they were regulated by the operators. Moreover, the throughput of work in agriculture could never be executed as systematically as it was planned; and, even where hours of work were successfully extended, it was not obvious that more effort could be coaxed out of the labour force, because of the relatively low ceiling of their physical capabilities.[33] A more positive strategy for raising labour productivity was perceived as higher wages, at least among theoreticians. Economic writers after 1750 increasingly appreciated that high money wages did not necessarily spell high labour costs, and in the *Wealth of Nations* (1776) Adam Smith endorsed this view, arguing that 'the wages of labour are the encouragement of industry, which ... improves in proportion to the encouragement it receives ... where wages are high, accordingly, we shall always find the workman more active, diligent and expeditious than when they are low.'[34] This shift in the opinions of economic writers is, of course, an aspect of the transition from 'mercantilist' to 'classical' economic assumptions. To an increasing extent, it was appreciated that higher productivity might be engendered by the carrot as well as (or as an alternative to) the stick. However, during the closing decades of the eighteenth century there remained a notable gulf between theory and practice. For large sections of the agricultural labour force, wages appear to have failed to match price increases, and much of the remainder of this chapter will be concerned with tracing changes in wage levels and the underlying determinants of the economic return to labour.

There were, and would long remain, numerous difficulties in gauging the true remuneration of farm workers in cash terms. In the first place many men were paid by the day, or the piece, and the weekly wages which will be quoted are often derived from the usual daily wage multiplied by a factor of six. Consequently there is no way of taking account of the effect of under-employment upon total earnings. Secondly, they often include notional allowances for an enormous range of perquisites received in kind rather than cash. Beer, meals, special opportunities to buy meat or grain at advantageous prices, firing and sometimes rent commonly formed part of the labouring man's income. In the extreme case of west Wales it has been suggested that the rent of a cottage and some fields for corn-hire, besides the more general *hoglyn* or free buttermilk and potatoes may have made up the greater part of the wages of labourers about the middle of the eighteenth century.[35] Although there is reason to believe that payments in kind were coming under ever more careful scrutiny, they remained general to a greater or lesser extent. Thirdly, it is impossible to ascertain systematically the ancillary earnings of wives and children, or to take account of extra income derived from the cultivation of garden plots or the possession of animals in the case of better-off workers, or of charitable and parish funds. Ideally, one would wish to work with the gross annual earnings of the farm-workers' families from all these sources, although even then we should still face problems in drawing up a suitable index of consumer expenditure, with a view to assessing changes in their real value over time.

This is a formidable catalogue of difficulties, but does not preclude some limited conclusions from being drawn concerning the pattern of regional variations and the probable trends of real incomes in the closing decades of the eighteenth century. Once again, we may begin with the observations of Arthur Young, around 1770. Data culled from his various writings was collated many years ago by A. L. Bowley to yield an average wage for England of 7s 3d with significant variations by county.[36] In the *Southern Tour* Young set out a series of 'medium averages, which attempted to iron out seasonal variations and to include allowances for victuals, drink and board. Wages varied, it appeared, as follows:

20 miles around London	10s 9d
20–60 miles around London	7s 8d
60–110 miles around London	7s 4d
110–170 miles around London	6s 3d

Young noted the 'prodigious influence' of the capital but was vague about its nature. In any case, in wage-data from the ensuing *Northern Tour* the simplicity of the pattern was no longer apparent. Organizing his material in much the same way he found the general average of places from 100–200 and 200–300 miles from London (at 7s 2d and 7s respectively) was about equivalent to that obtaining within 50 miles of London (7s 1d) and actually exceeded wages found in the 50–100 mile range (6s 9d).[37] All that can be suggested with reasonable confidence is that about this time, in the early 1770s, an historic pattern which had once tended to yield higher wages in the south than in the north[38] was beginning to change under the influence of industrialization and provincial urban growth. This gave rise to a confused picture, of which Young could make very little sense. Twenty-five years later, the emergence of a differential in favour of the northern labourer was clearly apparent, and so also were its underlying causes. For the 1790s, the data founded by Bowley on wage statements drawn from Eden's *State of the Poor* suggests a 19 per cent advantage to the northern counties.[39] Lancashire affords a very good illustration of the trend. John Holt calculated that wages in the county had doubled within thirty years (1761–91) and noticed that they varied in inverse relationship to the distance from manufacturing or commercial centres. At Chorley, labourers earned 3s a day, with ale; at Euxton 2s or 2s 6d, at Ecclestone 1s or 1s 6d, while at outlying Mawdsley and Bispham labourers could be had, even at harvest time, for 1s 2d or 1s 4d. At Walton near Liverpool labourers' wages had risen from 10d per day in 1761 to 1s 8d in 1791.[40] Likewise in the West Riding wages were highest in the neighbourhood of the manufacturing towns and the same was reported true in Staffordshire. It is interesting to note that during his brief visit to South Wales in 1768 Young attached no significance to the existence of copper and tin works as a factor working to raise the price of labour: on the contrary he assumed that the cheapness of labour had favoured their establishment. But by the early nineteenth century it was clear that the profusion of Welsh collieries, limekilns, ironworks and canals had served to raise agricultural wages, which in future would be found to vary with conditions in industry rather than with the ebb and flow of agricultural prosperity.[41] Obviously the impact of competing forms of employment brought direct competition for labour in such districts; but the indirect influence of industrialization upon wages may have been just as important. Through the stimulation imparted by industrial and urban growth, enhanced agricultural production and land reclamation might serve to sustain the demand for labour at a high level across a wide area. Thus, wages in neighbouring counties virtually untouched by industrialization, tended to rise in sympathy. In the East Riding they were estimated by Young at 7s 6d in 1770 and by Eden at 11s 3d in 1795; and in Lincolnshire at 7s 0d (1770) and 9s 6d (1795). Meanwhile, in Bedfordshire they had remained unchanged at 7s 3d, and in Buckinghamshire, seemingly fell from 8s to 7s.[42]

As we have said, no sensitive and reliable cost of living index exists for these years. However, in a situation where some 70 per cent of household expenditure was commonly devoted to the purchase of foodstuffs[43] (and most of this on bread-grains and flour) we are justified in taking existing indexes of agricultural prices as a guide. On account of the low agricultural prices then prevailing, the second quarter of the eighteenth century has been described as a golden age for the labouring man; but after 1755 they began to ascend. An index of agricultural prices (bread, flour, oats, malt, peas) yields an average figure for 1775–89 of 142

(1720–44 = 100) whilst significantly, the indexes for dairy produce (butter, milk, cheese) and meat (beef, mutton, pork, bacon) rose by rather less (136 and 132 respectively). Increases of a similar, sometimes greater, order of magnitude were general across Europe and there is evidence of declining real wages from the Netherlands, France, Germany and Spain.[44] Did the English farmworker share in this decline, and was it the case, as might be anticipated from our wage figures, that the experience of the northern labourer was decidedly different from that of his counterpart in the relatively unchanging south?

Even among the best informed writers of the day, there was considerable disagreement on this point. Nathaniel Kent, the prominent Norfolk estate agent and agriculturalist, pointed out in 1796 that during the preceding forty or fifty years the price of provisions had risen by 60 per cent and wages by only 25 per cent in Norfolk. John Howlett concurred in the view that the price of labour had not increased in proportion to the advance in the cost of provisions, while the Revd David Davies, rector of Barkham (Berks.), whose arresting survey entitled *The Case of the Labourers in Husbandry Stated and Considered* (1795) was based on the study of a collection of household budgets, maintained that 'it is a fact, in which old people uniformly agree, that the joint earnings of a labouring man and his wife were sufficient to maintain themselves and three children, and in a better manner too, about the middle of this century'.[45] On the other hand, Thomas Ruggles of Spains Hall, Essex, an author of various works on the Poor Law, while conceding that the aggregate of misery was greater among the poor than before, was convinced that real wages had increased in the long term. Sir F. M. Eden, who emulated Davies in collecting household budgets (though in his case with a northern bias), was critical of simple comparisons between the relative movements of wheat prices and wages in his *State of the Poor*. 'It has, indeed, been very confidently asserted . . . that the industrious labourer is less able to support himself by his labour than formerly . . . this is a proposition which I am by no means prepared to assent to.'[46] Perhaps the most perceptive comment came from the great economist, Adam Smith. His *Wealth of Nations* appeared against a background of increasing prices during the preceding decade which had not, he believed, been accompanied by any noticeable rise in the money price of labour. Nevertheless, over a longer period, and as a consequence of overall price changes since the previous century, the 'real recompense of labour, the real quantity of the necessaries and conveniences of life which it can procure to the labourer . . . has augmented'.[47]

From this discussion of wages and prices in the 1770s and 1780s we can draw a number of tentative conclusions. Firstly, there is little evidence (except ambivalently, from increasing recourse to piece-rates) that employers were responding with any degree of enthusiasm to suggestions that labour productivity would be increased by offering higher wages. On the contrary, wages were settled according to the laws of the market.[48] Secondly, it is clear that the balance of supply and demand was coming to favour the northern labourer relatively, at any rate by the 1790's: the notable wage discrepancy which was opening up between the north and the south would, as we shall see, persist until the advent of statutory wage controls after the First World War. Thirdly, the answer to the question of what was happening to real wages in the second half of the eighteenth century depends entirely, as Smith perceived, upon the chosen baseline of comparison, and according to what part of the country is under consideration. If we were to focus primarily on the north, and compare the position of farmworkers *c.*1780 with that of their counterparts a century before, it would almost certainly be correct to infer a significant improvement in real incomes. On the other hand, in coming to an assessment of the position of the labourer during the closing decades of the eighteenth century, it is reasonable to make the kind of comparison that would have been available to workers within the terms of their own experience and childhood recollections. In the majority of cases these would not reach back much before about 1740, which is to say, squarely within the 'golden age' previously referred to. It should also be borne in mind that whilst the experience of the northern labourers during the second half of the century was decidedly more favourable, they were a minority, albeit a sizeable one.[49] The short and medium term experience of the majority of farmworkers alive in the 1780s was that of seeing wages failing to rise commensurately with prices, after 1755. Since at this period there is no likelihood that this adverse trend was fully compensated by a rise in other sources of income it would seem that we have to infer, for a majority of farmworkers, a perceptible trend towards a declining standard of living in the later eighteenth century.[50] At the same time we should not forget that the most startling contrasts were liable to occur from one year to the next, according to the vagaries of the weather and the harvest.

How should this adverse trend be explained? Tradition has it that the immiseration of the rural labour force was the inevitable outcome of the precocious capitalist development which England had undergone since the later Middle Ages. Although this had brought agriculture to a level of efficiency unmatched elsewhere in Europe, its social consequence had been 'the expropriation and expulsion of the agricultural population, intermittent but renewed again and again', in the words of Karl Marx, with enclosure identified as the main agency of proletarianization. Developing this theme, Hasbach argued, ninety years ago, that the fourteenth century demographic catastrophe of the Black Death had begun the metamorphosis of the medieval peasant village, engendering a decrease in villeinage and a rise in the number of free holdings and free men. The more vigorous elements pushed ahead in the fifteenth and sixteenth centuries with enclosures then aimed primarily at increasing the extent of pasture, and this, says Hasbach, 'almost always resulted in an increase in the number of free proletarians'. However, outside the districts most directly affected by enclosure labourers were not as yet entirely wage-dependent, since they were still likely to hold a house, garden, stock and rights of common.

In the seventeenth century enclosure progressed further, usually by simple agreement of the parties involved, but with the eighteenth came a vast increase in the number of enclosures by act of Parliament. These acts usually entailed the division of the common pasture and consolidation of scattered arable strips, and the process was also conducive to 'engrossing', or the amalgamation of farms. Small farmers, be they tenants or owners, were likely to lose their holdings at such times, and with loss of access to the commons the last shreds of independence among the cottagers disappeared, leading to their final proletarianization.[51] This classic institutional explanation of the emergence of the farm labourer is not, it is worth emphasizing, confined to historians of the left. On the contrary, it has long been accepted in its essentials by many historians of a moderate liberal persuasion. Thus, in the years immediately preceding the First World War, a majority of participants in the great debate about land monopoly, the plight of the labourer and the flight from the land accepted some variant of the theory of dispossession, and the school of thought produced at least one literary classic – J. L. and B. Hammond, *The Village Labourer* (1911). To them, and to a long line of successors, enclosure was a 'plain enough case of class robbery'.[52]

How much of this analysis holds up in the light of modern research? Since the Second World War hundreds of studies of enclosure have appeared and we can take up here only the issues most directly related to the concerns of this book, that is, the phasing and extent of the movement and its implications for village populations. To begin with, it is now generally agreed that a vast amount of enclosure had already been accomplished, usually by private agreement, before 1760. Indeed, one authority puts the proportion of English land enclosed as high as 75 per cent by this date.[53] This was accompanied by a tendency to the consolidation of or amalgamation of holdings (the two expressions are not synonymous), although the connection with enclosure was only a tenuous one. In numerous instances the passing of land into fewer hands preceded enclosure by many years, and the trend was observable in old-enclosed as well as in common field villages.[54] Among the influences which prompted such changes were shifts in the balance of farming activities, price levels and farming costs and the search for economies of scale. In particular, modern researchers have insisted that the major decline of small owners and minor farmers in general tended to occur during the century before 1760, when they had to contend with low agricultural prices.[55] Today, even Marxist writers accept that the British case was unique in that 'the peasantry' was 'virtually eliminated *before* the acceleration of economic growth that is associated with the development of industrial capitalism', and as Turner has pointed out, they are beginning to use the expression 'appropriation' (which allows for the buying out of smaller men) in preference to 'expropriation' with its connotations of dispossession by force or conspiracy.[56]

Despite this very important shift of emphasis, much attention continues to be paid to the era of George III when enclosure by act of parliament had become the dominant form. Between 1760 and 1829, according to one authoritative study, there were 3,724 such acts in England with two phases of brisk activity standing out clearly. These were 1765–79, when the movement was particularly noticeable in the heavier soiled counties of the Midland clay belt, notably Northamptonshire, Warwickshire and Leicestershire; and 1795–1814, the period of the French Wars, when lighter soils in East Anglia, Lincolnshire and the East Riding were the focus of attention, and in both England and Wales there was a notable assault on commons and wastes.[57] Even though Georgian parliamentary enclosure is now viewed widely as a 'mopping-up operation' its social effects continue to excite controversy and are particularly pertinent to the period covered in these early chapters. It is convenient to take each explicit charge in turn.

1. Enclosure acts were conducive to consolidation and amalgamation and further reduced the number of separate holdings

This, it is supposed, was so because small owners were unable to meet their share of the public costs and of fencing, and were obliged to sell; or, in the case of small tenants, because landlords were able to take advantage of the automatic extinguishing of existing leases when an enclosure act took effect, to form larger units. Most research has concentrated on the small landowners, and a number of studies have shown, on the basis of the Land Tax returns, that their numbers, far from falling, were actually increasing during the later eighteenth and nineteenth centuries.[58] Against this it has been argued that the extent to which the costs of enclosure rose during the later eighteenth century has been seriously underestimated;[59] that the Land Tax evidence is notoriously treacherous to handle, sometimes giving undependable results;[60] and that head-counts of the kind used, for example, by Johnson and Chambers obscure the point that the heads in question changed faces in quite large numbers at the time of enclosure.[61] With regard to small tenants less is known, but it has been pointed out that in the early nineteenth century there was no lack of small farms, those of under 100 acres still predominating in twelve English counties.[62] Taking the evidence in the round, it seems reasonable to conclude that in aggregate the number of small farmers bore up surprisingly well during the most active period of parliamentary enclosure, because they were cushioned to some extent by rising prices, and that dispossessed small farmers probably did not greatly augment the numbers competing for wage-paid employment in the agricultural sector.

2. Enclosure displaced the rural population, driving small farmers and labourers from the land

Some instances of declining numbers can of course be found. In Cambridgeshire, Longston (enclosed 1800) and Elsworth (1803) both lost population in 1801–11 with falls of one and eleven per cent respectively. In Leicestershire the recently enclosed townships of Shawston (1793) and Church Langton (1791) both declined between 1801 and 1811 while a fall of 20 per cent in the tiny township of Drayton between 1811 and 1821 was attributed to enclosure in the second of these censuses.[63] On the other hand the explanatory notes in this census linked enclosure with population *increases* in about forty instances, and historians have produced numerous illustrations of this trend. On the Yorkshire Wolds enclosure was often associated with substantial, even dramatic population increases in such parishes as East and West Lutton and Weaverthorpe, and at Raunds (Northants.), where the inhabitants had petitioned unsuccessfully against enclosure in 1797, fearing that its effect would be 'the almost total depopulation of their town . . . driving them from necessity and want of employ in vast crowds into manufacturing towns', the population grew from 890 in 1801 to 1,101 in 1811.[64] As early as 1912, in a work overlooked by the Hammonds, Gonner concluded that 'so far as the counties, or even large districts or portions of counties are concerned, there is really no evidence of depopulation . . .' Later, in a seminal article published in 1953, Chambers drew attention to the steady rise in the rural population down to the 1840s and the likelihood that improved agriculture worked to maintain a high level of employment both in enclosed and in open parishes where improvements in agriculture were adopted.[65]

In recent years, Chambers's conclusions have, in turn, been questioned. His remarkable qualities as an historian were perhaps not fully matched by commensurate skills in economics and as several commentators have pointed out, increases in the labour-land ratio do not necessarily signify that the changes associated with enclosure were labour-intensive in the economist's sense. The probability is, rather, that capital accumulation and the spread of innovation should be accorded primacy in accounting for increases in agricultural output during the period 1780–1850, and although the labour force continued to grow slowly until about 1850, agriculture was certainly releasing labour on a significant scale since the *proportion* working on the land approximately halved between 1760 and 1840.[66] Moreover Crafts has drawn attention to a small but positive correlation, at the county level, between enclosure and out-migration.[67] A second criticism of Chambers's position is that, inasfar as enclosure was associated with increased arable cultivation, insufficient attention was paid to the increased seasonality of employment, which is, of course, a matter of considerable social importance. Snell has concluded from the study of settlement papers that in a large number of southern counties and individual parishes, enclosure was associated with an exacerbation of existing patterns of seasonal unemployment which tended to fall increasingly into the winter months (though by the same token, to decline in the summer).[68] These various qualifications to Chambers's view that enclosure created more employment on the land must now be given due weight. But historians will need to guard against encouraging a reversion to the crude catastrophic views characteristic of the pre-Chambers period, well-exemplified in a passage from G. D. H. Cole who supposed that 'the peasants, during the Industrial Revolution, were torn from the land and driven into the noisome factory towns'.[69]

3. Labourers and cottagers were further proletarianized and their condition rendered more miserable, by loss of access to the commons

The traditional view is that the commons had once afforded an opportunity for members of the cottager class to keep a cow, pigs and some geese, as well as to gather wild fruit and firewood; but in the words of the Hammonds, after enclosure 'the anchorage of the poor was gone'.[70] Although it is now generally agreed that the appointed enclosure commissioners carried out their work with scrupulous attention to detail it may be held that their decisions were at once entirely legal respecting property rights, and yet inequitable. Allotments set aside in lieu of substantiated common rights were often inconsiderable in size and costly to fence, and in consequence were frequently sold shortly after the event to richer landholders. In any case, compensation was legally due to the owners, not the users of these rights: for example at Harston (Cambs.), although an acre was set aside for each cottage, 'as most of the cottages belonged to the owners of the large estates they laid the land to them instead of attaching it to the cottages'.[71] However, there was controversy as to the true economic value of such rights. Ardent agricultural improvers of the late eighteenth century such as John Billingsley and Eden maintained that the commons were a sorry sight, these 'pastures of geese, hogs, asses, half-grown horses and half-starved cattle';

while they had an injurious tendency to make the cottagers reliant on imaginary benefits, and in so doing, inculcated indolence. The Sutton Coldfield commons were reckoned a case in point, affording 'unequivocal proof that a right of common does not add, either to the comforts, or the happiness, of the Poor'.[72] Doubtless the improvers were right in their claims that many thousands of acres were capable of being put to more productive use, but achieving a general good can often involve losses to individuals. In the case of the enclosure of Skelton Common (Cumberland) in 1770 the local incumbent, Samuel Lewthwaite, ruminated on the failure of the population to increase (although there was no actual decrease to account for), and attributed this, in a letter to a Carlisle doctor, to the 'destruction' of cottagers who once had common rights and the opportunity to graze two or three cows and a few sheep, and could thereby 'make a shift to raise a family'. Even Arthur Young, after personal investigations in a number of parishes, eventually came round to the view that 'in many cases the poor had unquestionably been injured' and quoted the reflections of an experienced commissioner, Mr Forster of Norwich, who regretted that in twenty enclosures he had been an accessory to harming some two thousand poor people at the rate of twenty families per parish.[73] Two recent contributions have thrown further light on the matter. Firstly, Neeson has suggested on the basis of intensive work on Northamptonshire that most householders in unenclosed villages were beneficiaries of the commons to a greater or lesser extent, and also contends that opposition to enclosures was more widespread than is usually supposed, instancing such cases as Wellingborough, West Haddon and Wilbarston. However, resistance was more characteristic of villages containing numbers of artisans and mechanics, small shop-keepers, innkeepers and butchers: it was relatively uncommon in smaller, more purely agricultural villages, perhaps indicating that 'enclosure was less disruptive in such places and harder to resist too'.[74] Secondly, Snell has produced some fresh statistics to support the view, widely held among contemporaries, that enclosure was associated with a tendency for *per capita* expenditure on the poor to increase.[75] A word of caution is in order, however. While acknowledging that common rights were still important in eighteenth-century England (and thereby the point that their loss could be acutely felt), Malcolmson points out that at mid-century their economic value varied from place to place, sometimes to the point of irrelevance; that in some regions such rights had probably never existed or had long since been eliminated, and that elsewhere they had survived only in an attenuated form.[76] In addition, we should remember that like other forms of property, common rights could be freely bought and sold, and there are indications that, over a long period, they increasingly fell out of reach of the humbler cottagers. In the Feldon district of Warwickshire, for example, village trading and craft families were evidently the main beneficiaries on the eve of enclosure.[77] Finally, it is obvious that the resources of the commons were not capable of being stretched infinitely to meet the needs of an expanding rural population.

That the character of rural society had been shaped by the forces of emergent capitalism and by enclosure there is no doubt. However, in seeking to explain pressures on living standards in the later eighteenth and early nineteenth centuries, attention must also be paid to population growth. This phenomenon was almost entirely overlooked by early writers such as Hasbach and the Hammonds, and it was not until after the Second World War that its significance as an independent factor in social change was seriously discussed, notably by Chambers who, as well as illuminating many aspects of agrarian history, was one of the pioneers of demographic history in this country. The broad dimensions of the growth which resumed about 1750 are not in serious doubt. In England and Wales population rose by 127 per cent in the ensuing 80 years, and in 16 primarily agricultural counties by 88 per cent over the same period,[78] so raising the possibility that 'natural' growth was bringing into existence more hands than could readily be accommodated within even an improved agricultural system. Recent advances in our knowledge of demographic change, while far from providing a conclusive set of explanations, enable us to say more than was possible in Chambers's day.

The calculations of Wrigley and Schofield suggest that, at the national level, mortality was set on a declining trend with deaths per 1,000 at risk falling from 30.6 in 1720–50 to 22.9 in 1820–49.[79] There is no reason to suppose that rural areas were excluded from this favourable development and, indeed, it is probable that gains in life expectation were greater in the countryside than in the towns. A number of studies give useful local illustrations of the improvement. For example, a thorough and wide-ranging study of no fewer than 60 parishes in rural north Shropshire has reached the conclusion that infant (0–1) mortality stood at about 200 (again, per 1,000 at risk) between the mid-sixteenth and early eighteenth centuries; thereafter it fell to 160–70 by the mid-eighteenth century, 130 by its close, and 110 by the 1840s. Likewise infant mortality at Bottesford (Leics.) fell from 164 (1700–49) to 143 (1750–99) and 115 (1800–1) while in the age-group 1–4, mortality fell from 108 to 81 and 76. Here, adult mortality also improved. The population of survivors to 40, of those aged 25, moved from 786 (per 1,000) in 1700–49 to 861 (1750–99) and 924 (1800–24), and overall the crude mortality rate was reduced to only 18 by the period 1800–50.[80]

To a limited extent these favourable trends may have been a by-product of agrarian improvements. One argument suggests that enclosure was conducive to the reduction of animal diseases (notably brucellosis and bovine tuberculosis) and thus the frequency with which they were transmitted to human beings. However, its author has been criticized for failing to appreciate that the majority of land enclosed during the eighteenth century was open field and not the wastes upon which animals grazed indiscriminately, while drove roads and markets continued to offer ample opportunities for the transmission of disease.[81] A more promising hypothesis is connected with improvements in land drainage. There were numerous contemporary suggestions of this kind. For example, despite his reservations about the enclosure of Skelton Common, the Revd Lewthwaite opined that 'Inclosing and cultivating the ground has considerably meliorated the Quality of the Air in this neighbourhood . . . To this, and to a more nourishing mode of living, I suppose, we must attribute it that the Ague is so rare a Complaint, from which twenty years ago the poorer people were very seldom free.' In the same vein Edwin Chadwick's famous *Sanitary Report* of 1842 attributed a considerable decline of mortality around Wisbech (Cambs.) to drainage, and supporting evidence of the diminution of agues came from medical officers referring to improvements around Newhaven (Sussex), Ongar and

Dunmow (Essex) and in East Kent, where the marshy land bordering the Isle of Thanet had been effectively drained.[82] Recent research concludes that such districts did, indeed, exhibit all the signs of *vivax* malaria and that where its vector (the *Anopheles atroparvus* species of mosquito) bred freely, the toll of energy and life imposed on marshland communities was dramatic. However, the demise of malaria was a slow and sporadic process and improved drainage was but one factor among many working to reduce its frequency and severity.[83] Other explanations of reductions in rural mortality have been sought in improved standards of nutrition (which seems unlikely in the closing decades of the eighteenth century); advances in medical practice and facilities (here the relatively widespread practice of smallpox inoculation may have played a significant if not a decisive role); and the possibility of exogenous changes in the virulence of specific diseases or in the latent immunity of the human host. Indeed, recent discussions of the fall in mortality, which was European-wide, agree that improvements in death rates were at least in some measure autonomous in nature.[84]

However, in recent years changing levels of fertility have moved to the centre of the stage. In an ingenious argument published ten years ago, Anderson used data on the proportions ever-married in the 1861 census to show that in primarily agricultural registration districts where more than 75 and less than 45 per cent of the workforce consisted of labourers, the mean age at marriage was lower by 1.9 years (for males) and 1.8 (females) in the first category. From this it could be inferred that a shift involving only 20 per cent of the farm labour force (in effect, a change which replaced one farmer or farm servant in five by a labourer) could have produced as many as 6 per cent more births per marriage cohort. This strongly suggested that structural shift over several generations would have advanced birth rates markedly and made a major contribution to demographic growth.[85] Recently, Wrigley and Schofield have provided more direct evidence: the implication of their statistics is that only about one-third of the national population growth after 1751 should be apportioned to mortality reduction, and two-thirds to rising fertility. This, they show, was not primarily due to a shift of procreative behaviour within marriage, for age-specific marital fertility rates changed little. Rather, it reflected changes in marriage habits. Between the later seventeenth and the end of the eighteenth century, the proportion of females never-married is calculated to have fallen from 26 to 4–7 per cent, and the mean age at marriage sank from 26.2 in 1700–69 to 23.4 in 1800–39.[86] Whether this trend was more, or less marked in the countryside than in the towns we do not at present know: but the advent of the new data, and along with it a small number of independent studies showing a falling age at marriage in such villages as Napton and Bidford-on-Avon (Warwicks.) and Powick (Worcs.),[87] creates a strong presumption that fertility increases were at least as important as mortality decreases in generating rural population growth.

This shift in the balance of received opinion concerning the mechanisms of demographic change is, for obvious reasons, welcome to historians of a radical persuasion. For example Levine holds that the social impact of proletarianization over a lengthy period undermined the force of traditional sanctions against early marriage (at different dates according to local circumstances) and thus served to raise the average number of children per family, a trend subsequently fortified by structural shift. In one of the parishes he studied (Terling in Essex) 'economic polarization' from a very early date was accompanied by fairly low ages at marriage from as early as the seventeenth century, while comparable changes at Shepshed, a Leicestershire framework knitting village, occurred after 1750 and at Bottesford from about 1800. The mortality improvements which have already been alluded to played only a subsidiary role.[88] More recently Snell has argued that in the late eighteenth and early nineteenth centuries the new demographic evidence can best be explained in terms of adverse social trends eroding traditional restraints on marriage, instancing particularly the absence of incentives to thrift once the possibilities of partial independence or upward social mobility via the commons were curtailed; and two long term trends, namely the decline in farm service and declining female participation in the labour force, forcing women to marry earlier.[89]

However, there is a clear danger that Snell's arguments are pressed too far, in the present state of our knowledge. In the first place, he has very little direct evidence of the alleged links because he does not engage in the detailed parish-by-parish demographic analysis which would be necessary to establish them conclusively. Secondly, his case rests primarily on the experience of southern, particularly south-east, England. Thirdly, his caveats, though detectable, are often very subdued, and easily missed; they include one which is particularly significant. In the course of castigating Chambers for assuming that population growth was 'natural', Snell remarks that population growth could be explained '*with at least partial reference* [my italics] to institutional changes which ... had adversely affected the security of livelihood.'[90] Put this way, it is unlikely that Chambers would have disagreed with him, but it is improbable that the Nottinghamshire sage would have approved of Snell's virtually total disregard of the mortality factor. For even if, in the light of the new demographic knowledge, it has to be relegated to a secondary role in accounting for national population growth, falling mortality must have played *some* role in swelling the number of landless men and effecting structural change in the villages. In Europe, where a falling death rate is still considered to have been the chief mechanism involved, population growth certainly had an effect of that kind. For example, describing the implications of population growth in Sweden between 1700 and 1830, Utterstrom remarks that 'As the increase in the number of farms could not keep pace with the number of households, the numbers of the agrarian classes beneath that of the farmers naturally grew ... during the last two decades of the eighteenth century the increase in the number of wholly or almost propertyless households was particularly great ... from this time onward the greatest increase was among farm labourers living in (*inhyseshjon*) and cottars with little or no land (*backstugusittare*).'[91]

Of necessity these summaries of the modern literature on enclosures and rural demography have taken us far back in time, and forward into the nineteenth century. But where do they leave us? Probably with the impression that it is misleading to concentrate on either institutional or population changes as alternative but mutually exclusive agencies of social change in eighteenth- and early nineteenth-century villages. This, indeed, is suggested by a number of local studies which describe their changing configurations. At Moreton Say (Shropshire) the population doubled between 1780 and 1800 and the proportion of farmers sank from 58 per cent of the whole in 1700–5 to 16 in 1813–22, as well as halving absolutely as a result of the amalgamation of holdings. Meanwhile the number of labourers quadrupled, and came to account for 84 per cent of the village population. In the more populous parish of Ash in East Kent, the number of separate holdings shrank from 135 in 1705 to 79 in 1841. However, amalgamation was not the sole or even main cause of the rising proportion of labourers, for, despite emigration, the population of the village had about doubled.[92] In the Isle of Axholme (Lincs.), a district with something akin to a continental peasant structure, consolidation was not a problem, and the number of property-owners actually increased by 9 per cent between 1800 and 1829; but the population rose by 33 per cent, causing Chambers to remark, very aptly, that 'a proletariat was coming into being by the natural increase of the peasant population'.[93] It is also clear from these examples and from the foregoing discussion that there is no reason to expect that the demand for and potential supply of labour in rural England and Wales would balance neatly. As we shall see, the French Wars greatly complicated the picture and the pressure of oversupply in relation to market conditions came to be felt much more severely in the years after 1815. But the time has come to return to the specific historical *locale* of the later eighteenth century, where some ominous signs of stress were already making themselves apparent.

Apart from the wage-data which have already been reviewed, we may note the implications of the extensive series of household budgets collected in the early 1790s by Davies and Eden. In all, Davies collected 121 (mainly from the southern half of the country) covering 1788–94, and Eden 66 more (chiefly northern) in 1794–6.[94] A typical specimen is given below:

Crawley, Hants. Family No. 6
(Man, wife, four children, the eldest a boy of 14, the youngest an infant. Considered good managers, since they bought their flour by the bushel).

Expenses per week	£	s	d	*Earnings per week*	£	s	d
Bread or flour		5	10	The man			
Salt			1½	(harvest excepted)		7	0
Bacon			4				
Tea, sugar, butter		1	10	The woman			4
Cheese			4				
Beer			2	The children		2	0
Soap, starch, blue			2¼	Total		9	4
Candles			2¼				
Thread and worsted			2				
Total		9	2				

Expenses per annum	£ s d	*Earnings per annum*	£ s d
(9s 2d × 52)	23 16 8	(9s 4d × 52)	24 5 4
Add rent (£2), fuel (£1 10s), Clothing etc. (£4)	7 10 0	Add extra harvest earnings	1 10 0
Total	31 6 8		25 15 4

Deficiency of Earnings: £5 11s 4d

Because the great majority of these budgets registered similar annual deficits, the Hammonds concluded that they showed 'the normal labourer, even with constant employment, was no longer solvent'.[95] In fact, they need to be interpreted with greater care. In the first place, there are obvious signs of incompleteness on the side of expenditure in some budgets, while with regard to income Davies noted the occasional omission of harvest earnings and Eden thought the labouring men 'unchangeably mysterious and insincere', liable to confound all enquiries and in most instances likly to understate their annual incomes.[96] Secondly, when the budgets are considered as a whole there are clear relationships between the number of dependants at home and the average annual deficit, percentage of income spent on food, and proportion of food expenditure laid out on bread or grainstuffs.[97] In itself this is hardly surprising and lends credibility to the evidence; but it should be borne in mind that both authorities, consciously or otherwise, tended to collect a disproportionate number of cases where families were positioned at the stage of the life-cycle where the number of dependants was near its maximum, and the strain was correspondingly great.[98] Thirdly, a modern dietary study has shown that the calorific intake implied by the northern budgets was some 15 per cent higher than the southern ones within the Eden group or than the Davies budgets, and that the northern intake of protein, fats and carbohydrates was decisively higher.[99] This gives some backing to Eden's persistent references to the superior condition of the northern labourers who, he claimed, (along with the Scots and the Welsh) were able to regale themselves with more meat and a variety of dishes, notably porridges and broths, of a kind unknown in the south where 'the poorest labourers are habituated to the unvarying meal of dry bread and cheese from week's end to week's end'.[100] Thus, in a number of respects a closer scrutiny of these budgets reveals both rather less and rather more than the Hammonds assumed. Still, no-one would claim that they portray a situation which any modern reader would envy. The average calorific intakes in the Davies and Eden budgets were 1,990 and 2,170 respectively.[101] These estimates stand significantly below the present-day recommended range of 2,100 to 3,600 calories according to body size and type of activity; in fact they fall into line approximately with the intakes observed in various parts of the underdeveloped world in the 1960s, with similar characteristic deficiencies in proteins and fats. One would not wish to dissent from the cautious view, expressed by Davies, that a labourer's wage, together with that of his wife, was 'barely sufficient to maintain, in all necessaries, independent of parish relief, the man, his wife and two children'.[102]

Finally, we may take note of statistics of expenditure on the poor. From an outlay of £690,000 in the mid-eighteenth century, national annual expenditure rose to over £2m. by the mid 1780s, and *per capita* relief expenditure in 1780 stood at 6s 2d in those counties later to be designated by James Caird as the 'south', as against 3s 1d in the 'north'. Studies of the operation of the Poor Law in Berkshire, Cambridgeshire and Essex have called attention to the increasing frequency of casual relief among able-bodied men and women, especially in the 1770s,[103] and more thought was given to devising arrangements which would be at once more humane and more cost-effective. One manifestation of this was Gilbert's Act (1782) which encouraged and regularized outdoor relief and can be seen as a tacit recognition that the problem of labour was one of finding remedies for a periodic excess of supply.[104] The same act authorized groups of parishes to form themselves into unions. However, some districts of East Anglia scarcely needed this prompting. Parishes in the Suffolk hundreds of Carlford and Colneis joined together to set up a house of industry as early as 1756, and by 1779 similar incorporations covered half the parishes in the county. These developments were followed in Norfolk from 1764 in the Lodden and Clavering hundreds, followed by East and West Flegg in 1775, Forehoe (1776) and Tunstead and Happing (1785).[105] In Dorset, it has been pointed out, most large villages had established Houses for the Poor by the mid-century and already, in every parish, the community was 'pulling along landless labourers who could not find, or keep, regular employment'.[106]

TWO

The impact of war, 1793–1815

> Dinner today Souse, Veal Pye and Calfs Heart rosted. Billy Bidewells People brought our Newspapers from Norwich. The King of France Louis 16 inhumanly and unjustly beheaded on Monday last by his cruel blood-thirsty subjects. Dreadful times I am afraid are approaching to all Europe. France the foundation of all of it.

So reads the diary of Parson Woodforde of Weston Longueville, Norfolk, for 26 January 1793;[1] and his reaction typified that of most men of social standing in the English countryside. Though initially the Revolution had met with some sympathy – Wordsworth's 'Bliss was it in that dawn to be alive' summed up the early mood – the execution of the French monarch was widely seen as the culmination of a series of excesses perpetrated by the infant Republic. The French had proffered fraternity and help to all oppressed peoples who desired to obtain their liberty: in August 1792 they tore up existing treaty obligations by decreeing the re-opening of the river Scheldt, a move considered highly detrimental to British commercial interests. Realizing what must inevitably follow, France declared war on Britain on 1 February, apparently to the delight of George III. Hostilities between the two nations, which Napoleon was not alone in likening to the struggle between Rome and Carthage, continued until July 1815, broken only by two brief intermissions. The first of these was heralded by the Peace of Amiens (March 1802) which lasted only a year, while the second was the interlude between Napoleon's first abdication (April 1814) and his return from Elba in March 1815, setting in train the 'hundred days' which came to an end on the plain of Waterloo.

Popular impressions of the French wars tend to be coloured by successful British feats of arms fought abroad, which included Nelson's famous naval victory at Trafalgar and a series of actions fought at Corunna, Torres Vedras, Salamanca, Vittoria, etc., during the Peninsular campaign. It might be supposed that, safe behind the ring of squat martello towers designed to sweep the southern beaches with grapeshot, English rural society was scarcely ruffled by the war save where the appearance of red-coated militiamen set maidens' hearts fluttering, as in Jane Austen's best-loved novel, *Pride and Prejudice* (1797). However, it is easy to overlook the ideological element in the struggle and, what concerns us more, the extent to which the war approached total commitment. Average gross public expenditure has been put at £19.6m. for 1786–90, when more than half was spent on servicing the existing national debt and only some £6m. on the

Army, Navy and Ordnance; but by 1815 government expenditure had soared to £113m., a figure not exceeded before 1899. This included military expenditure amounting to £72m. which, in one authoritative calculation, was alone equivalent to no less than one-quarter of the gross national product.[2] There was an unprecedented diversion of manpower into the armed forces. In 1792 the British army numbered no more than 45,000 men, the majority manning foreign garrisons, and the navy was only 16,000 strong. Another 31,000, chosen in principle by ballot from among males aged 18–45, were attached to county militia regiments in England and Wales, ordinarily receiving 28 days training a year and capable of being drawn on in emergency to serve for indefinite periods. New categories of volunteer corps and local militiamen were created during the war, and by the early summer of 1809 the British economy was supporting armed forces comprising nearly 300,000 regular soldiers or embodied militia and 130,000 seamen and marines, a figure equivalent to roughly one man in every nine or ten of military age in Great Britain and Ireland. If local militiamen (199,000) and volunteers (189,000) are added, the proportion rises to about one in every six.[3]

All wars, when conducted on a large scale, tend to give rise to inflation and in this case wholesale prices rose by approximately 70 per cent.[4] The impact of rising prices was felt almost immediately, since the outbreak of war in 1793 coincided with the first of a series of poor harvests; in 1796 the overseas balance of payments came under particularly heavy strain owing to the need to meet the cost of large imports of corn and naval stores from the Baltic as well as major remittances to armies and allies abroad. While gold reserves were thus depleted, persistent rumours of a possible French invasion began to circulate at the turn of the year and timid persons everywhere began to demand guineas from their local banks. This developed into a panic run when news of a French landing at Fishguard became public on 25 January 1979, and two days later the Bank of England was relieved of its obligation to pay cash against its notes. Shortly afterwards the Bank began issuing notes of small denomination, and suspension of cash payments remained in force until 1821, with Bank of England paper circulating freely alongside the familiar notes issued by the country banks situated in every town with claims to modest commerical significance. The very existence of an inconvertible paper currency, so ran an argument accepted by many contemporaries, was conducive to over-issue, and hence to a decline in the value of the pound relative to commodities and to a fall in its standing on the foreign exchanges. However, it is now apparent that the inflation of the war years cannot simply be ascribed to monetary mismanagement or the shortcomings of the banking system; explanations need to take account of the overall financial strategies of the government of the day.[5] Vast government outlays increased personal incomes in the form of profits, salaries, commissions, interest and even wages, and tended to outrun the supplies of goods and services available. Taxes were indeed raised to the point where, towards the end of the war, they may have accounted for as much as one-sixth of the national income, and it is noteworthy that the exigencies of war finance drove William Pitt's government to take the momentous step of instituting an income tax which was levied from 1799 to 1816, with a short intermission following the Peace of Amiens. Although government revenue more nearly approached the extra expenditure than in the major wars of the present century, inflation was not avoided, and the government met the gap between its outlays and taxation by borrowing from the wealthier classes, with the result that the National Debt rose by a factor of some 3.5 as a consequence of the war.

On account of its centrality in the economy, agriculture could not fail to be profoundly affected during these years. Most striking was the impact of government contracts, which by 1813 necessitated in the west country alone 'nearly 400 fat bullocks per week for the victualling office, for the Royal Navy, the Prison ships and Garrisons at Plymouth, and the War Prison on Dartmoor', while in general military requirements boosted the demand for leather, tallow, timber, wool, horses and horsefeed.[6] Several adverse seasons and the continuing growth of the population also had their part to play in raising the prices of agricultural produce in Britain, while foreign supplies became awkward to obtain. These circumstances combined to give British agriculturalists the advantages of a near-monopoly situation. It is true, imports of wheat reached unprecedented levels in 1796 and 1800–1 and at first sight it is surprising to discover that in 1810 they included a quantity of French corn, the enemy having enjoyed a bumper harvest in 1809. Napoleon reasoned that this would raise prices and please French agricultural producers, while at the same time draining bullion from England, so weakening her ability to subsidize the allies. Yet the cost of imported grain was always high, for freight charges, insurance and license fees totalled to some 30–50s a quarter; and overall, even though imports ran higher than in the 1780s, they were always small in relation to home production.[7]

In response to high prices, so the traditional account goes, landlords and farmers were spurred to fresh exertions, particularly directed towards the arable side. It appears that about 43 per cent of all English enclosure acts of the period 1730–1844 were concentrated into 1795–1814, and the proportion involving only commons and waste increased significantly. Among the wildernesses brought into cultivation at this time were Sherwood Forest (Notts.), Enfield Close and Hampton Common (Middx.), Canford Heath (Dorset), Charnwood Forest (Leics.), Delamere Forest (Cheshire), Bere Forest (Hants.), Bexley Heath (Kent) and Alston Moor (Cumberland).[8] Though Wales was less affected by parliamentary enclosure, it has been calculated that in 1793–1815 some 200,000 acres, or roughly one-eighth of the land lying in common or waste was enclosed by act of parliament. Typical Welsh enclosures affected the upland fringes of established arable areas, the most spectacular example being 400,000 acres on Fforest Fawr (Brecon) in 1808; or coastal commons or waste, such as the sandy marsh and mud flats of Morfa Duffryn in Merioneth, lying below the walls of Harlech castle.[9] Another agrarian improvement involved increased attention to land drainage. Arthur Young found much to enthuse about around Market Deeping and South Holland in Lincolnshire, where 'fens of water, mud, wild fowl, frogs and agues have been converted to rich pasture and arable, worth from 20s to 40s an acre', pointing to 'health improved, morals corrected, and the community enriched'. Similar noteworthy if more limited improvements took place around Beverley and Barmston in the Hull valley, following an act of 1798, and in Somerset.[10]

In recent years historians have shown an increasing awareness of the complexities of agricultural adjustments during the war. It is pointed out that enclosure *per se* did not invariably lead to changes of the kind necessary to increase agricultural productivity, and certainly in the case of Welsh enclosures farming practices changed relatively little in these years. Some of the more ambitious drainage closures carried out in Lincolnshire and elsewhere were far from efficient, with extensive areas remaining liable to flooding.[11] It seems highly probable that, more than anything else, the mere extension of the cultivated acreage helped to raise the output of grainstuffs, and it is not obvious that this was achieved, as was once assumed, at the expense of the nation's meat supply. For during the war years the price of beef rose by more than that of mutton or pork, and in several years outpaced that of wheat, while there is some evidence that farmers responded to shifts in price relativities by adjusting their product mix. If a recent study of land-use patterns in Northumberland is any guide, many were wary of committing themselves to permanent changes. A common tactic was simply to switch some of their best land to convertible husbandry, permitting ready transfer from pastoral to arable use and vice-versa; or to adjust cropping ratios, for example by shifting from barley and oats to wheat.[12] From the standpoint of the social historian, however, the salient feature is that *all* farm product prices were swollen during the war to a greater or lesser extent. As a prominent Northumberland farmer remarked, '... we meet with much more money than expected. The farmers in ye district are full of money, and indeed it is not to be wondered at, as every thing the farmers have to sell are at a higher price than I ever knew before'. The prosperity of farmers was soon noticed in a myriad of small ways. Surveying his little flock one Sunday during the summer of 1796, Parson Woodforde made a mental note for his diary, and anticipated a flood of comment on the rising social pretensions of farmers. 'Mrs Howlett was at church and exhibited for the first time, a black vail over her face. Mem. Times must be good for Farmers when their Wives can dress in such stile'.[13]

Doubtless it is too facile to infer the existence of bloated profits from such reported changes in life-style. Almost the only piece of detailed work on this point suggests, in fact, that the percentage return on farming capital employed was not remarkably high. On nine southern farms giving rise to 92 observations in the years 1793–1815, it has been shown that only very occasionally did the rate of return rise above 14 per cent, while 35 instances fell in the range of 9–14 per cent, and 42 below that level.[14] One reason for this was that rent payments came under scrutiny by landlords, who were often fortified by the not implausible theory that the highly rented tenant was under more pressure to be enterprising. On the Fenlands, according to one authority, there were effectively two scales of rent for the same quality of land – that required by the 'reputable landlord' and that sought by jobbers or dealers in land.[15] Yet the social rank of the landlord offered no certain guarantee of a relaxed attitude, as the tenant of the 200-acre Knight's Place farm at Cobham (Kent) may have reflected when Lord Darnley's steward systematically raised his rent from £80 in 1788 to £100 (1790), £160 (1802), £180 (1803) and £230 in 1809, the point at which he began to run up arrears before being obliged to quit in 1814.[16] And if rents on the Earl of Darlington's estate moved up by only 62 per cent between 1790 and 1815, those on the Lancashire estates of the Blundell family at Little Crosby advanced from £1,650 (1795) to £4,000 in 1815, while on the Milton estates in Northamptonshire and Huntingdonshire they bounded upwards from £7,639 in 1792 to reach £21,000 by the end of the war. A survey of evidence of this kind points to the conclusion that rent increases averaged about 90 per cent, though with wide variations between different estates (50–175 per cent) and still more between individual farms (20–300 per cent).[17] While landlords in turn had to meet considerable taxes, it is clear that many were energetic in tapping the increased revenues of their tenants, especially after 1805. Their success in this regard undoubtedly played a part in shaping the thoughts of the wealthy Jewish radical, David Ricardo, whose theory of rent (that it represented the difference between the amount produced by a given piece of land and that which, at prevailing prices, would just fail to pay for the labour and capital put into it and hence would command no rent) was adumbrated in his *Principles of Political Economy* (1817). In practice, there was enough diversity to fuel suspicions that the landlord on the one hand, or the farmer on the other, was benefitting most from high prices.

Whatever the apportioning of income between landlords and farmers, traditional accounts of the experience of agricultural workers yield an impression that is almost wholly bleak. For example, J. L. and B. Hammond claimed that if the rent receiver took more than was needed to induce him to let his land, and the farmer made larger profits than were necessary to encourage him to apply his capital and ability, 'the labourer received less than was necessary to maintain him, the balance being made up out of the rates', a passage quoted with approval in a new work published in 1980.[18] Much of this chapter is addressed to gauging the impact of the war on farmworkers' living standards in an attempt to clarify such vague statements. Our starting point must lie in a close examination of the labour market, for it is clear that these years saw a relative shortage of male labour, particularly evident at critical seasons of the year. It is true, not all the forces of the Crown were drawn from England and Wales, many coming from the Highlands and Ireland; and among those who were, it is impossible to specify exactly what proportion came from the ranks of agricultural wage-earners. But sufficient young men were drawn away, against the background of a rising demand for agricultural labour, to significantly alter the relationship between supply and demand. Even before the war, the 1791–2 mania for canal building had diverted sufficient labour to engender a petition to Parliament suggesting that farm workers should be prohibited from cutting canals during the harvest months, and gave a foretaste of what was to come. By 1795 shortages had become a matter of regular complaint as a series of Quota Acts requiring local authorities to find stated numbers of soldiers began to bite. 'At present', wrote John Boys from Betteshanger in Kent in 1796, 'we have the greatest scarcity of labourers and ploughmen I ever remember, owing, probably, to the demand upon our population by the army and the navy', while a year later *The Times* drew attention to a general scarcity of harvest men 'severely felt in many parts of the country'. *The Farmer's Magazine* commented in 1803 on a shortage of hands in Essex ('in consequence of the drafts for the army') and Staffordshire and in Wales, while from Herefordshire in 1805 it was reported that the male population was 'so much thinned by the levies and operations of war that the farmer, in particular, has but little opportunity of selection'. Drainage work in

Lincolnshire was reported as being hampered by a scarcity of workmen in 1806; and in the same county, fears were expressed in 1808 that part of the harvest might be lost merely from a want of reapers.[19]

These circumstances almost certainly weakened the obligations and ties associated with farm service. The complaint by Francis Kinder of Kirkby in Ashfield (Notts.) that his serving man Robert Jackson had 'quitted his place without permission and without any just reason for so doing', laid on 13 January 1809, is by no means an isolated occurrence in the Quarter Sessions papers of this and presumably other counties; and there is a consensus in contemporary accounts that hiring agreements were frequently broken by youths who, having obtained the farmer's 'earnest money', would go off to take the King's shilling or seek a better-paid job with another farmer, or a non-farm occupation.[20] Married men as well as the single and footloose were sought for military service, and their apprehensions were played upon in patriotic effusions such as Hannah More's *Ploughman's Ditty*, 'being an answer to that foolish question what has the poor to lose' (1804):

> 'I've a dear little wife
> Whom I love as my life
> To leave her I should not much like Sir;
> And 'twould make me run wild,
> To see my sweet child
> With its head on the point of a pike, Sir'.[21]

One may doubt whether many mature farmworkers were moved by such persuasion, or attracted to join the regular army or navy even by the prospect of enrolment bounties equivalent to half a year's pay. However, they were liable for militia service on the same basis as others, by ballot. According to one gentlewoman at Brandsby, near York, these arrangements fell 'terribly hard on the poor ... nor do they submit with a perfect good grace even in these quiet parts', and in this district there were instances of the local gentry subscribing, as was possible under the regulations, for the cost of the poor's substitutes. In practice, it was from among the ranks of labouring men that the substitutes were most likely to be drawn. Of 45 men balloted at Bromley (Kent) in March 1897 only one, a labourer, agreed to serve on his own account, and among 44 substitutes were 21 labourers, six grooms and four indoor servants. Meanwhile, at nearby Gravesend, the substitutes for 22 persons unfortunate in the draw included 11 labourers and three husbandmen, including a nineteen-year-old farm servant sent up by Sir John Dixon Dyke, Bart. Significantly, among 736 men enrolled into the militia at Woodbridge, Suffolk, in 1814, no fewer than 402 were labourers and another 36 were servants.[22] Others sought immunity by joining local corps of volunteers. The implications of all this for the farm labour market were considerable. Although neither militia men nor volunteers were liable to foreign service, they could be 'embodied' or called up for periods of training sometimes for protracted period of weeks or even months at a time. Thus, complained a North Devon farmer in 1812, 'in the midst of summer when every nerve should be exerted in cleansing the soil and preparing for turnips, there are between 2,000 and 3,000 men (chiefly servants in husbandry or labourers) taken from their work for upwards of a fortnight, in this district alone'.[23] To conclude from all this that the war years gave rise to consistently full employment in agriculture would be to exaggerate the case, for there was undoubtedly considerable variation by locality and over time, and it is significant that the brief interlude of peace from March 1802 to May 1803 saw a 'backwash of servicemen seeking work' with complaints that even at harvest time farmers were unwilling to employ all the labour available.[24] As we shall see this was a harbinger of the future. Still, the grain of the evidence, though literary rather than statistical in nature, suggests that the war years saw a level of employment which was at any rate fuller than before the war; and unquestionably higher than that which would have obtained had the war not occurred.

As yet there was relatively limited scope for farmers to meet their labour problems through extending farm mechanization. Despite the anticipation of the engineer Richard Trevithick, that 'every part of agriculture might be performed by steam; carrying manure for the land, ploughing, harrowing, sowing, reaping, thrashing and grinding', proposals for steam tilling machinery seem to have made little progress beyond the drawing board.[25] The only major new equipment to make noticeable if patchy progress was the threshing machine, designed to economize on the labour employed in the drudgery of hand-flailing to separate the corn from its straw. Andrew Meikle of East Lothian in Scotland is usually credited with the design of the first successful threshing machine in 1786, and relatively complex and expensive fixed installations, usually powered by water or a horse-wheel, were quite common in the Scottish lowlands and on the large farms of Northumberland in 1794: by this date several had also appeared in Lancashire 'on account of labour being dear', even though it was not primarily a corn county. Although use of the threshing machine spread further during the war years, particularly in Yorkshire, across Wales and in Devon and Cornwall, its progress was far from all-conquering. Indeed, at first sight paradoxically, it failed to make the headway that might have been expected in the corn counties of south-east England, where farmers preferred either to continue hand-flailing or to deploy a cheaper, less bulky, but also less efficient 'portable' form of the threshing machine, often hired from contractors rather than purchased. The chief reasons for this relatively slow diffusion probably lie in the southern farmers' appreciation that, to them, the threshing machine could bring only marginal economic benefits. For notwithstanding that farm labour was scarce during the French wars, it remained generally cheaper than in the north, and was not difficult to come by in the winter months when threshing took place. Moreover, farmers were aware of the probable impact on the poor rates of the withdrawal of winter employment on any scale.[26] Various patents were taken out during the war years for a variety of drills, haymaking and winnowing machines, as well as horse rakes, scarifiers, chaff and turnip cutters and so on, while minor improvements in the design of ploughs, such as the application of a case-hardening process to cast-iron shares by Robert Ransome of Ipswich after 1803, may also be noted. Small gains in productivity may have accumulated as such patents were actually applied on the land, and it has been argued that these years also saw the 'early adoptive phase' of a shift in hand-tool technology involving the use of more efficient tools in the harvest fields. The heavier but more efficient bagging hook, or the scythe, it is thought, now began to make headway against the lighter sickle.[27] However, taken in the round, technological innovations were relatively unimportant during the war years. In the main, extensions in the cultivated acreage and increases in the output of the agricultural sector were dependent on the farmers' ability to assemble sufficient manual labour, working along traditional lines, to enable their objectives to be achieved.

As ever, the greatest problems were posed by getting in crop harvests. From the earliest years of the war men serving in home-based regular army units and the militia were made available to farmers at harvest time. When a company of Welsh militiamen quartered in Whitehaven was set to work it was found that, being mostly rural labourers in origin, they had providently brought their scythes to Cumberland with them. Yet these arrangements could be frustrating to employers, as for example during harvest time in Sussex in 1805, when the troops were ordered out of the fields and back to their barracks, to the considerable chagrin and bewilderment of the local farmers.[28] Employers therefore had to look elsewhere for alternative supplies of labour. Itinerant harvesters appeared in increasing numbers, notably on the newly cultivated fenlands. In 1800 Thomas Stone's early morning slumbers at Long Sutton (Lincs) were disturbed by 'assemblies of harvest men under my windows, talking as many different dialects as the builders of Babel, Irish, Scotch and Welch, upwards of fifty in a body, bargaining with the farmers for the work of the day'. The Irish, in particular, appear to have presented themselves in larger numbers than hitherto, and impressed employers to an increasing extent. 'Were it not for these seasonable and able assistants', commented a farming periodical in 1812, 'the work could not be performed in time, and the workmen of the county know no bounds to their demands, both as to price and to beer.'[29] Meanwhile, 'many women reapers' were doing a quarter of an acre a day in Cambridgeshire at the harvest of 1811, while on a Wiltshire farm, women harvesters outnumbered males by 3 to 1. Even a century later the recollection persisted on the Berkshire Downs of the 'petticoat harvests' of the Napoleonic Wars, when the women got in most of the harvest because the men had gone to war.[30] It is also probable that women workers increased their involvement at other seasons, which is consistent with Snell's suggestion that the war years saw 'relatively equal female employment in both the spring and the harvest'.[31] When the Sussex Agricultural Society published awards made to wives and widows who had performed the greatest amount of work during the year ending October 1798, the figures mentioned were above those which could have been run up over the hay and corn harvest seasons, viz.

Mary Blunt	185 days	(awarded £4 4s)
Mary Carver	124 days	(£3 3s)
Mary Taylor	112 days	(£2 2s)
Mary May (aged 75)	86 days	(£1 1s)

Similar awards were made by the Essex Society in 1801 to those who had worked 200, 163, 150 and 102 days respectively.[32]

Notwithstanding all such expedients the wages of farm workers rose significantly during the war years, though with considerable local and regional variation. It is true, some local investigations have revealed only very modest increases, as in the case of Sussex. Here, a careful examination of somewhat scanty data

'Lowkers', or women weeders, about 1814. This 'garrulous class of mortals' was said to require the frequent eye of the master, seen in the background. From G. Walker, *The Costume of Yorkshire*, Leeds, 1885.

suggests that the average wage, which stood at 8s 6d in about 1770 and 9s 6d in 1793, climbed by a shilling or so in 1794–5 but did not rise above 13s even at the height of the wartime scarcity in 1813.[33] However, if this was the experience of Sussex labourers, they appear to have been singularly unfortunate, for two of the more consistent series available suggest rises amounting to nearly a doubling over the war years (table 2.1).

The figures given in the table correspond approximately to the only available 'national' series for agricultural wages, calculated over eighty years ago by A. L. Bowley and G. H. Wood. Their index of 'average earnings in a normal week' moves from 57 in 1792 to 103 in 1814; or, to take the years directly comparable with table 2.1, from 61 (1794) to 105 (1812).[34] They also accord quite closely with those arrived at from the inspection of wage books from no fewer than 36 estates in five midland counties, which have been drawn together in an index of average daily remuneration moving from 100 (1790–1) or 116.5 (1793) to 200.5 (1814).[35] On the whole, historians have been prepared to accept that wage increases amounting to something just short of a doubling occurred during the war years, at least among day labourers, though the cash component of the incomes of farm servants probably did not increase to anything like this extent.[36]

Even so, many historians have been inclined to think that, once the cost of living is taken into account, real wages fell. Hasbach remarked, 'up to 1812 wages rose though not adequately' while Ernle declared, 'It is certain that a very important advance in agricultural wages was made during the period of the

Table 2.1: Examples of wage movements during the French Wars

	Cobham Hall, Kent (Daily wage)			*Cumberland* (Weekly wage)
	Winter	*Summer*	*Harvest*	
1794	1s 6d	1s 8d		8s 0d
5				8s 2d
6				8s 4d
7	2s 0d	2s 0d	2s 4d	9s 0d
8				10s 0d
9				10s 6d
1800	2s 0d	2s 0d	2s 6d	11s 0d
1				11s 6d
2				11s 9d
3	2s 0d	2s 0d	2s 6d	12s 0d
4				13s 6d
5				14s 6d
6	2s 6d	2s 6d	2s 6d	15s 0d
7				
8				
9	2s 6d	2s 6d	3s 0d	15s 6d
1810				
1				15s 3d
2	3s 0d	3s 0d	3s 0d	15s 0d

Sources: A. L. Bowley, *Wages in the United Kingdom in the Nineteenth Century*, Cambridge, 1900, pp. 33–4; H. G. Hunt, 'Agricultural Rent in South-East England, 1788–1825'. *Agricultural History Review*, 1959, vol. VII, p. 106. *N.B.* Hunt's figures exclude the value of the daily allowance of beer to labourers.

Napoleonic wars. Unfortunately it is equally certain that, even if wages had doubled, the price of provisions had trebled'. Recently, the Cobham Hall wage series has been set against a local cost of living index which moved upwards by 120 per cent between 1790 and 1812, leading to the conclusion that throughout the war real wages were usually below the 1790 level, and in the worst years, 1795, 1802 and 1812, stood at only 86, 85 and 85 (1790 = 100). Even T. S. Ashton, a major contributor on the optimistic side to the continuing debate about changes in the standard of life during the period of the Industrial Revolution, opined that during the war, wage rates moved up more slowly than prices.[37] Yet it is apparent that if, as the Bowley wage index suggests, a 92 per cent increase occurred between 1788–92 and 1809–15, this surpassed the upward movement in *any* of the national (whosesale) price indexes available to historians and indeed closely matched the increase in wheat prices as recorded in the *London Gazette* (96 per cent), so supporting the judgement of one eminent authority, that 'in general, agricultural wages broadly kept pace with food prices'.[38] In part, this was due to the fact that the farmworkers' incomes were buttressed by a built-in element of payment in kind.

For an extreme case of this we may look to Northumberland, where married farm servants were hired on an annual basis, and provided with a house, while the greater part of their rumuneration was made up of carefully specified quantities of wheat, oats, barley, rye, peas, potatoes and wool and the employer also usually offered keep for a cow or pig and cartage for coals. For his part the hind contracted to supply a woman labourer to work for the employer at cash wages (6d a day in 1805) when and as required for such tasks as harvesting, haymaking, weeding and hoeing. This sytem – indeed all reliance on wages in kind – was frowned upon by progressives such as William Marshall, who took particular exception to one author's advocacy of introducing such a 'relick of feudal baronage' into the south in 1813.[39] But more limited recourse to payments in kind remained general. So far as can be judged, they were not additional to the wages already discussed; it is highly probable that the multiplicity of spot references to wage levels that is the basis of the Bowley series included allowances for perquisites. Even so, it is clear that in an inflationary situation such practices favoured the worker and would have helped towards maintaining his standard of life, a point which did not go unnoticed among contemporary observers. For Devon, Charles Vancouver assumed in 1808 that the price of labour had not kept pace with the depreciation of money in the preceding twenty years, yet thought this 'in a great measure compensated by the general custom of the country, in supplying the labourers with bread-corn below the market price' and 'what is becoming still more general, of the labourer procuring potatoe ground from his employer'. In Dorset, noted Stevenson (1813), the price of labour had ostensibly undergone little variation for some years, 'yet, as it is paid partly in kind, by the allowance of wheat and barley at a low and fixed price, it has of course advanced in some measure according to the increased price of provisions'.[40]

If it would be desirable to know more about the balance of cash and kind in farmworkers' annual earnings, it would be even more valuable to be able to determine them at the family, rather than the individual level. There is reason to think that in many cases family incomes would have risen faster than those of individual argicultural wage-earners. As we have seen, war conditions were propitious for an increase in female engagement in the labour force. Beyond this, in some areas rural industries based largely on female sources of labour flourished under protection from foreign competition. This was particularly apparent in counties such as Devon, Buckinghamshire and Northamptonshire where lacemaking expanded during these years. At Hanslope (Bucks.) in 1801 no fewer than five hundred women and girls were engaged on lacemaking out of a total population of 1,275. The lace they made sold at between 6d and two guineas a yard, according to quality, and the women earned up to 25s a week.[41] Straw plaiting, chiefly found in the south midland counties of Buckinghamshire, Bedfordshire and Hertfordshire, was another domestic industry which developed extremely rapidly during the war years. In this case the war occasioned the cutting off of imports from Leghorn in Italy and home production was further protected by a tariff from 1805, while the invention of a new straw-splitting device in 1800 immensely improved productivity. The only challenge to the war-time prosperity of the plaiters came, it would seem, from the activities of French prisoners of war at Norman's Cross situated close to the modern A1 near Peterborough, where a commemorative monument stands at the roadside. Here, in 1812, it appears that up to half the 6,000 prisoners made straw plait, with the connivance of their guards, and thus earned the cash to pay for delicacies such as snakes, which in the recollection of the poet John Clare were caught on the Fens and carried to the camp strung like eels on osiers, 'which the French men would readily by as an article of very palatable food'.[42] Yet their competition counted for little, for such was the demand that there was a continuing shortage of plait available for working up into straw hats, and female labour was at something of a premium. Around Hatfield and Stevenage, by 1801 spinning had given way to plaiting, through which, according to Arthur Young, women could earn three or four times as much. At Redbourn women were earning £1. 1s a week, at St Albans 5s a day, while 'at Dunstable they begin to pick the straw at four years old; plait at five; and at six earn from 1s 6d to 2s 6d a week; at seven they use the instruments and earn 1s a day; some girls of ten years old earn 12s a week. . . . Women can earn £1. 1s a week in an average'. So lucrative was this employment that some men reputedly employed themselves primarily in getting straw for their wives, in an area where typical earnings of farmworkers stood at about 9s–12s a week. One consequence, much complained of by local farmers, was that as well as making the poor saucy, 'no servants can be procured or any field-work done'. Likewise, for Buckinghamshire it was recorded (in 1806) that on account of the prevalence of lace and straw manufacturers, dairy-maids' wages had risen greatly and 'it is with difficulty they are procured at all'.[43]

Bearing all these points in mind, it is difficult to agree with the well-entrenched view that the real reumeration of farmworkers' families tended to decline systematically during the war years. Nor does that argument find the unequivocal support that was once assumed from the history of the poor law. It is generally believed that, following the example set by the Berkshire magistrates at Speenhamland in 1795, the war years saw ever-increasing resort to scale allowances[44] and this is often taken to be a symptom of mounting distress: it is also true that recourse to the 'roundsman' system (where labourers were sent by the parish overseers to 'go the rounds' among different farmers and were employed at a wage proportioned to the rental value of each farm) was not unknown, even in wartime.[45] But modern researchers are increasingly conscious that the 'grass-roots' research necessary to establish the frequency with which such expedients were resorted to, and the extent to which it proved necessary to make up wages with outdoor relief, has yet to be done.[46] Moreover, recent work on the incidence of poor law expenditure in three south-eastern counties (Kent, Sussex and Essex) fails to support the catastrophic version of the position of the farmworker in these years, and is consistent with the view that the war years probably arrested any tendency towards a progressive decline in the standard of living of the agricultural wage-earner's family. Though all three counties certainly exhibited mounting total relief bills, with peaks in 1796, 1801 and 1813, once account is taken of population growth and changes in price levels (as measured by the annual average price of wheat) a very different picture emerges. The period from just before the outbreak of war to about 1814 can be characterized as one of 'fairly level *per capita* relief expenditure'; indeed, were one to concentrate on the years following the 1801 crisis, a slightly declining trend may be observed. These conclusions hold good when the analysis is restricted to predominantly agricultural parishes (288 in Essex, 254 in Kent, 196 in Sussex), and the author of this extremely valuable study contends, justly, that 'Because relief expenditure moved with the cost of living, the conclusion must be that farmworkers' earnings from their labour did not progressively diminish. ... For if they had, the real cost of relief should have risen by 1814'.[47]

None of this is to deny that, like other sections of society, farmworkers suffered considerable privations in certain years. As many as 14 out of 22 grain harvests in the years 1793–1814 have been characterized as deficient in varying degrees,[48] and poor men everywhere endured great hardships in the worst years. Thus the sub-standard harvest of 1794 was followed by an exceptionally severe winter, when the milk in Parson Woodforde's dairy repeatedly froze, as did the very contents of the chamber pots on the night of 25 January.[49] As is well known, another bad harvest followed in 1795 which drove up wheat and flour prices alarmingly during the following winter and spring, and these years saw, as well as the Speenhamland initiative, numerous experiments with coarser grades of bread and measures to limit or prohibit the use of wheat in distilleries or for the manufacture of starch and hair powder.[50] 1801 was another fearsome year, when expenditure on the poor at Wakes Colne (Essex), an arable parish standing on the road from Colchester to Halstead (population, 372) rose to as much as £1,181, a figure notably higher than at any subsequent point during the French wars. At nearby Terling in January 1801, no fewer than 30 per cent of the inhibitants of the village were in receipt of assistance in the form of flour, rice or herrings, notwithstanding that the men were earning up to 13s a week. Meanwhile at Catterick (North Yorkshire) 'the poor lived upon Barley Bread as long as there was any and some fed upon Oat Bread. Peas are much used and also dry'd Herrings with Potatoes, or even Turnips, as a substitute for meat'.[51] At this juncture Parson Woodforde evinced mixed feelings on the implications of such high prices. On 31 January 1801 his servant Ben returned from Norwich with the cash from the sale of his employer's wheat: '3.15.0 pr Coomb ... an enormous Price I must confess indeed and sincerely wish it might be cheaper e'er long for the benefit of the poor who are distressed on that Account – tho' much alleviated by the liberal Allowance to them of every Parish'. Charity as well as the rates responded at such times. During the Spring of 1801 the press in Yorkshire teemed with reports of the benevolence of landlords, usually taking the form of gifts of food and clothing; for not a few, like Lord Fitzwilliam, indicated a shrewd preference for allowances (in his case, of potatoes) rather than enhanced money payments since they 'woud be consider'd as given only during the scarcity, and more easily dropped than a money payment'.[52]

Modern research has indicated that, strong as the preference of consumers for refined white against wholemeal wheaten bread was, particularly in the south, their inflexibility in the face of sudden changes in price-relativities should not be exaggerated.[53] It is also clear that those most likely to riot in times of dearth were industrial workers such as colliers and weavers and the inhabitants of towns wholly reliant on outside supplies. In Yorkshire the chief disturbances occurred at Halifax, Hull, Castleford, Knottingley and Sheffield, in July and early August 1795 and again in April, May, and September 1801. Broadly the same pattern is true of Lancashire, while in the far south-west miners gave vent to their resentment in riots at St Austell, Falmouth, Redruth and Penzance in the spring of 1801. Canal or river transhipment ports (Chichester, Boston, Wisbech, Ipswich, Hitchin, Abergele, Denbigh etc.) also witnessed food riots, but it is probably correct to surmise that from the point of view of the authorities the most alarming incidents were those involving the participation of soldiers, as when men from the newly formed 67th Foot fixed prices at bayonet point in the market at Wells in Somerset. Several other noteworthy riots occurred among militiamen in March and April 1795, including the South Hampshires at Canterbury; the Herefordshires at Chichester; the Northamptonshires at Plymouth and the Oxfordshires at Seaford and Newhaven.[54]

However, none of the scrutineers of food riots have found evidence of the participation of farmworkers to any significant extent. It would be facile to argue that farmworkers were too cowed to stand up for themselves. On the contrary, there is sporadic evidence of recourse to, or threats of, strike action from the early days of the war – at Potton (Beds.) and Thaxted (Essex) in 1793 and Monkton and Minster (Kent) in 1794, all seeking either wage increases or improvements in perquisites; while in 1800 one John Little attempted to organize a strike at Steeple (Essex) to increase wages, with the threat of stopping all the farmer's horses from ploughing.[55] But the very rarity of such occurrences is equally significant, indicating that there was little 'social protest' among farmworkers and servants during the war years. This suggests that they were probably benefitting from fuller employment; also that the practice of payment in kind, coupled with timely, albeit often grudging, action in emergencies from neighbours, served to insulate the farmworker to some extent from the more desperate plight of the urban worker. Indeed, the view adopted here, that wage-paid labour in agriculture just about succeeded in holding its own during the French wars, is consistent with contemporary evidence collected by the Board of Agriculture, which suggested that the proportion of the expenses of cultivating 100 acres attributable to rent (21 per cent), tithes and rates (9 per cent), and labour (21 per cent) was virtually the same in 1813 as it had been in 1790.[56] However, what the war years did not interrupt, and in some ways hastened, was a deterioration in the farmworker's position in a number of respects which are less amenable to measurement. One of these took the form of a housing problem of increasing gravity.

Towards the close of the eighteenth century, the accommodation available to labouring men was of a decidedly makeshift description. Much was the legacy of the activities of past generations on the village waste-land, or the result of engrossing, whereby small farmhouses and farm buildings had become available to rent, usually on a tied basis; and some was the outcome of the sporadic activities of village speculators building over redundant yards and gardens, such as had produced 26 cottages upon four small farmyards at Bledington, Gloucestershire.[57] Its quality defies generalization although historians have concluded that by and large standards were highest in the south and east. Average conditions tended to worsen moving northward or westward from the Home Counties, notably towards the south-west where cob-construction (a composition of clay, gravel and straw) was common, or Wales where one reporter described the majority of mud-walled and thatched roofed cottages in the south as 'huts of the most humble plans and materials' and those of the north as 'habitations of wretchedness'.[58] As a rule men of substance found little incentive to invest in purpose-built housing for farmworkers; on the contrary, conscious of the provisions of the Acts of Settlement, some landlords and tenants had for many years evinced a desire to reduce the amount of accommodation available. Thus, in the face of rural population growth, there was a long-standing tendency for shortages of accommodation to make themselves apparent. The war was no help in this situation and indeed aggravated it to some extent, since capital invested in agricultural improvements such as drainage and enclosure necessarily diminished that available for raising the quantity and quality of housing. Inevitably the demands of the armed forces placed additional pressure upon residential construction by diverting restricted supplies of imported timber to naval construction, and by inducting into the services much of the casual labour upon which the building industry depended. There are indications of a mounting tendency towards the dual occupation of cottages. At Hawstead (Norfolk) as early as 1783 twelve out of 52 houses were double tenements and three were treble. Subsequent contributions to *Annals of Agriculture* indicated similar proportions for Ickingham, Mileham and Ketteringham in the same county, while at Wakes Colne in 1809 a local census showed a somewhat higher proportion, with no fewer than 14 among 35 cottages being double tenements.[59] It would be erroneous to conclude that no progress whatever was achieved, for here and there purpose-built rows of decent cottages were beginning to appear under pressure of necessity, as at Brothertoft on the Fens where 29 brick and slate cottages were erected in the 1790s. Even so there was a tendency for low standards of building to be perpetuated. Both on the Fens and in Lindsey, especially on the uplands where an extensive acreage of pasture was brought under the plough and something had to be done, emphasis was placed on constructing cheaper mud and stud cottages. The use of brick and tile appears to have been confined largely to farm houses and outbuildings, and only after the war was there much recourse to building cottages in these materials.[60] Absolute shortages, in particular, were apt to attract adverse comment. In his *General View of the Agriculture of Norfolk* (1804), Arthur Young remarked that cottages were 'much wanted' around Snetterton, Attleborough and Hingham, while his guide into marshland Smeeth, where no fewer than 8,000 acres had recently come into cultivation, informed him that only three cottages had been built. In Lindsey, the parochial authorities found themselves driven to involvement in the provision of housing, either acquiring cottages by purchase or building on land useless for productive purposes with funds derived from the poor rate – a practice much deplored by the population theorist Thomas Malthus, and later by the Poor Law Commissioners.[61]

Another, more subtle feature of the war years was a tendency towards the enlargement of social distance between the elements of the 'agricultural interest'. For generations landlords had been gradually detaching themselves from too close an involvement with village life, setting themselves apart in walled acres of parkland, and occasionally even withdrawing altogether. Viscount Byng, Lord Torrington was invariably distressed whenever he encountered an unoccupied hall; at Haslingfield (Cambs.) in 1790 he reflected, 'Since the increase of luxury, and turnpike roads, and that all the gentlemen have the gout, and all ladies the bile, it has been found necessary to fly to the bath, and to sea-bathing for relief ... whilst the old mansion ... is left to tumble down'. To be sure, it would be unwise to read too much into such comments, bearing in mind Byng's dubious sense of proportion, for he argued with similar conviction that singing birds would soon be extinct, 'from the certainty and wantonness of the gun, or the rage of gardeners, or the destruction and thinning of hedges'.[62] In fact most country gentlemen rarely left their estates and continued to perform their traditional duties and obligations. Even so, they were usually well insulated from contact with the lower ranks of rural society, except in social situations in which labouring men, or members of their families, were at a decided psychological disadvantage – as servants receiving instructions, as recipients of charity, or in making appearances before the judicial bench. What was more novel, more immediately occasioned by wartime circumstances, and, very probably, less easily accepted by the lower orders of rural society, was the advance in the status of their employers. Inevitably, a doubling of money incomes all round yielded a much greater reward in absolute terms to farmers, who were frequently observed to enjoy rapidly rising standards of consumption, to exhibit increasing *hauteur* and to be developing pretensions of gentility. Among many to comment on this trend was the poet George Crabbe, instancing:

> One, who is rich in his profession grown,
> Who yearly finds his ample store increase,
> From fortune's favours and a favouring lease;
> Who rides his hunter, who his house adorns;
> Who drinks his wine and his disbursement scorns;
> Who freely lives and loves to show he can –
> This is the farmer made a gentleman.

And maybe it was the children of such men that Clare had in mind when he wrote, in a sardonic spirit, of

> Young farmer Bigg of this same flimsey class
> Wise among fools and with the wise an ass
> A farming sprout with more than farmers pride
> Struts like the squire and dresses dignified . . .

and of the mincing airs of farmers' daughters who

> Deem all as rule their kindred did of yore
> And scorn to toil or foul their fingers more,
> Prim as the pasteboard figures which they cut
> At school and tasteful on the chimney put . . .
> Or paint unnatural daubs of fruit or flower.[63]

Farming families answering to this sort of description in every respect were, like absentee landlords, a good deal rarer than the literary sources imply, certainly outside the areas of large-scale arable farming. Nevertheless some came to find intimacy with their co-residing farm servants a social embarrassment; and others, if less fastidious, were moved by practical considerations to consider clearing farm servants out of their farmhouses. As Hasbach put it, many a farmer came to prefer to give board-wages as an alternative 'because he could sell the servants' victuals dear in the market, and because it did not suit him to board them'.[64] Thus Arthur Young noted that in parts of Norfolk 'a custom is coming in . . . of allowing board wages to farm servants instead of the old way of feeding in the house . . . This is one material cause of an increased neglect of the Sabbath and looseness of morals; they are free from the master's eye, sleep where and with whom they please, and are rarely seen at church'.[65] In addition farming rate-payers evinced an increasing tendency to hire servants for just under the 52 weeks that would entitle them to legal settlement, and on occasion were required to do so by their landlords, as in the case of the tenants of Sir Gregory Page Turner at Battlesden (Beds.) in 1802.[66] In Berkshire, noted Mavor, farmers kept no more servants in the house than they could possibly help, and a Cornish correspondent to the Board of Agriculture in 1808 felt he could 'positively assert, there are not one third part of the covenant servants now living in farmers' houses, to what there were thirty years since'.[67] The connection frequently postulated between the decline of indoor farm service, moral decay and demographic growth was put with graphic clarity by 'Notator', a correspondent to the *Gentleman's Magazine*, writing a few years later: the consequence of turning out farm servants and their replacement by day labourers was that 'when the day's work is done, the young labourer goes to the ale-house; or, if he is sober, he gets a room to lodge in, where he has no fire; he looks out for a wife, gets a cottage and fills it with children . . . '[68] However, as we have seen, the decline of farm service was but one among a variety of factors encouraging population growth, and its is important to emphasize that the tendency was not apparent to any significant extent in the northern counties or in Wales where indoor servants could not be readily dispensed with. All the same, in the south and east of England its decline both indicated and contributed towards a tendency for economic, social and cultural contrasts between farmers and their employees to deepen – a theme which was destined to become a favourite

For such reasons it is difficult to conclude that the position of farmworkers during the war years was in any way an enviable one. It is true that the exigencies of the war appear to have offset, for the time being, the long-term trend towards the emergence of an imbalance between the supply of and the demand for labour in the land. It is evident that despite a number of seasons of grinding hardship, the real incomes of workers undisturbed by recruiting cannot be shown to have declined absolutely and in some cases may actually have risen, especially where they were enhanced by supplementary women's work. On the other hand times were becoming more difficult in some respects, notably with regard to the important issue of housing. Moreover, the gulf between the farmworker's style and standard of life and that of his social superiors was increasing noticeably, and with the partial dissolution of farm service, the foundation of day-to-day security in farm employment was eroding away. Napoleon may have been, as Ernle remarked, 'the Triptolemus or patron saint not only of farmers, but of landlords',[69] but the benefits he conferred on the English agricultural interest were not destined to endure, least of all among its poorest and most numerous element.

THREE

Labour in agriculture, 1815–50: 'A sort of foot-cushion for the benefit of others'

'For six years after the end of the war the proverbial association between "peace and plenty" proved a ghastly mockery to all classes of the community. To agriculturalists peace brought only beggary.' So declared Lord Ernle, who went on to characterize the years down to the accession of Queen Victoria as 'one of the blackest periods of English farming'.[1] Already in 1813 a splendid harvest had administered a severe check to prices and after two more in 1814 and 1815 insolvencies and imprisonments for debt multiplied. A survey conducted by the Board of Agriculture in 1816 elicited 168 letters mentioning unoccupied farms and 241 stating that in their respective districts, 'many', 'several', or 'a few' farmers had given notice to quit.[2] Concurrently, 92 country banks failed between 1813 and 1816 and 240 suspended cash payments, while Henry Jefferies of Salisbury Square in London, with an extensive country trade extending from Dover to Penzance, found his annual sale of watches (4–5,000 'for many years past') cut back to 1,000–1,200 after the peace.[3] From 1818 a marked reduction of the number of banknotes in circulation (the prelude to the return to gold in 1821) exacerbated the situation, and although prices varied considerably from year to year the trend remained set on a downward path until the mid-1830s, the most comprehensive index averaging 211 in 1812–14, 164 (1815–20), 126 (1821–30) and 122 in 1831–5. With them fell rents as landlords were obliged to make reductions or remissions, which were widespread in 1814–15 and in 1821–3, though as a general rule they did not correspond fully to the price fall.[4] Nor were matters helped by the inadequacies of the Corn Laws. In the eighteenth century these were used to stabilize the grain trade by offering bounties on exports when prices were low or allowing imports at low rates of duty when they were high and it was not until 1815 that Parliament decided to make them an instrument of high protection. Although townsfolk were infuriated by the establishment of 80s a quarter as the figure required to be reached before foreign wheat could be sold in British markets, the measure proved to be ineffective in upholding prices, as did amendments in 1822 and 1828. This is not surprising since the crux of the problem was intensive home rather than foreign competition. Finally, these unpropitious circumstances tended to inhibit technological change, at least down to 1835. In the harvest field the displacement of the sickle by the scythe, encouraged during the war, now hesitated and there are two or three recorded cases where the newer technique was abandoned.[5] The only significant exception to this generalization was the further spread of the portable threshing machine, in the interest of achieving speed in getting grain on to the market quickly, since success in this respect might make all the difference between moderate, poor or non-existent profits. While recognizing its advantages in this respect, Marshall warned, in words that were prophetic, that if threshers were a 'positive and great good where flail men were few', they might turn out to be 'parochial evils' in counties well supplied with workmen.[6]

Such is the sombre, traditional view of the post-war state of agriculture. However, in recent years the nature of the depression has been clarified considerably. Wheat prices were hardest hit and the representations made to the 1816 enquiry and subsequent parliamentary committees in 1821, 1833 and 1836 tended to reflect the complaints of large arable farmers and landlords in the south and east of the country. Within the arable sector, a distinction needs to be drawn between those farming cold, ill-drained clays which were inflexible and expensive to work and their more fortunate brethren cultivating lighter soils, who enjoyed the benefits of lower costs: in a word, some arable farmers could still make a profit at prices below those which drove their neighbours to despair. Moreover, it is clear that the western animal-rearing districts, particularly counties such as Lancashire and Cheshire which embraced or lay close to large urban markets for dairy produce and potatoes, barely suffered at all. Significantly, rents were not reduced on the Blundell (Lancs.) or the Senhouse (Cumberland) estates, nor apparently anywhere in Cheshire.[7] Indeed, despite the adverse trend of prices, the real product of British agriculture is estimated to have increased by some 1.2 per cent per annum between 1801–11 and 1831–41, while wheat yields per acre rose by some 16 per cent between 1815–19 and 1832–6, due to the efforts of the progressive section among arable producers.[8] As Chambers and Mingay have remarked, it is not always appreciated how much agricultural development has stemmed from the stimulus of low prices and the threat of bankruptcy, when farmers are driven to seek economies through the reduction of costs.[9] Not surprisingly, farmers in their pursuit of efficiency were compelled to keep a watchful eye on the size of labour bills, and it was here that the agricultural depression, however qualified, impinged directly on the lives of farmworkers and their families.

The comparatively inflexible institution of farm service was an obvious target. By 1831, servants as a proportion of the labour force exceeded 40 per cent only in the North and West Ridings of Yorkshire, Derbyshire, Cheshire, Cumberland, Lancashire and Westmorland and by contrast were reduced below 22 per cent in eleven southern counties.[10] It is true that the decline was more patchy and attenuated than is often supposed, as a recent study of Sussex has shown:[11] also that an approximation to farm service conditions continued for many choice workers (those described, significantly, as 'constant men' and provided with a cottage, various perquisites and higher wages). Nevertheless the erosion of boarding-in had profound implications for droves of rural adolescents. In the first place, 'roving' was discouraged and local mobility reduced. Secondly, the decay of farm service threw large numbers into the ranks of the day labourers, which were further augmented, at the margin, by dispossessed small farmers with insufficient resources to ride them over the difficult years. For among the casualties of low prices were numbers of small owner-occupiers, who had over-extended themselves by wartime borrowing and whose holdings, once sold, were likely to be added to larger units.[12] There was also a tendency for small tenancies to be consolidated. On the Leveson-Gower estates in Staffordshire the proportion of holdings over 200 acres increased from 52 to 59 per cent between 1807–13 and 1829–33 at the expense of those in the range 20–100 acres, and in 1828 James Graham described how, over six years, the population of his 30,000 Cumbrian acres had been reduced as a consequence of consolidation by 10 per cent. Some tenants had become day labourers and as such were considered 'more thriving than as under-capitalized small farmers' although others had been absorbed by Graham's neighbours, following the opposite course of action in dividing their estates.[13]

Much more significant in a quantitative sense than any of these changes was the underlying rate of population increase which continued to pump labour on to the market at a rate which alarmed many contemporaries. There was considerable variation from village to village and the differences between 'open' and 'close' settlements have received particular attention. Where landownership was dispersed, it is held, the greater was the degree of population growth, due to the housing activities of petty tradesmen and village capitalists: conversely, concentration of land ownership in the hands of one or two men with an interest in strictly controlling settlement rights worked in the opposite direction. An examination of 401 'close' parishes in southern and midland England suggests that their population growth rates ranged between 5.3 and 60.5 per cent of those of all townships in their respective regions; and a detailed study of South Lindsey indicates that, in 1801–51, population growth rates in 'divided' parishes were nearly twice those recorded for a group of 'squires' parishes' which increased by only 53 per cent.[14] This is not to say that all parishes fell neatly into one or other of these categories, for the majority were not clearcut cases of either kind; nor were the links between landownership, labour supply and population growth anything like so simple as the above figures appear to suggest.[15] In any case, local variations should not cause us to overlook the significant overall increase in the rural population during the post-war years and some interesting shifts in the rural occupational structure. In general, the aggregate volume of employment in agriculture continued to rise, though only modestly: a recent reworking of census data suggests increases of 5.0 per cent (1811–21) and 2.7, 1.5 and 1.4 per cent respectively for the decades 1821–31, 1831–41 and 1841–51.[16] But this expansion was nothing like so rapid as the increase in rural population, since for every two persons residing in the primarily agricultural counties in 1815, there were three by 1851.[17] To some extent the slack was taken up by an expansion of village trades and crafts, such as carpenters, masons, blacksmiths, shopkeepers, shoemakers and tailors,[18] but a degree of mismatch between the demand for and potential supply of wage-paid employment in agriculture was virtually bound to occur.

A large catalogue of illustrations of unemployment can be compiled from sources which, by their very nature, were not inclined to understate the problem. In the 1816 report, 87 per cent of the 273 letters on which it was based gave evidence of labourers' distress. Some typical comments area: 'A third or fourth out of employ' (Snettisham, Norfolk); 'worse than ever known' (Nedging,

Suffolk; Ardleigh, Essex) and 'Four times more unemployment than ever known' (Brixworth, Northants.); while numerous respondents from all over the country echoed the sentiments of a writer from Normanton (Leics.), 'Unquestionably worse than when corn was at double the price it now is'.[19] 1816 was, indeed, one of the worst years, aggravated by discharges of troops. Yet the distress seemed all but incurable in the years that followed. In 16 Kentish parishes in 1823, 8,263 out of 21,719 inhabitants were paupers and 682 men totally umemployed.[20] According to the *Chelmsford Chronicle*, 634 labourers in 31 Essex parishes were unemployed and dependant on poor relief in 1827, while in Bedfordshire, year-by-year analysis of a record of 'surplus labourers' in the parish of Ampthill attests to the existence of a core of men regularly listed during the winter months. Of those named during the winter of 1826–7, 60 per cent were still present two years later and 40 per cent three years on.[21] In the hundred of Redbornestoke (which included Ampthill), 523 men from 13 parishes were 'almost wholly on the hands of the overseers' in 1829, while at Westoning at the latter end of 1830 only 20 able-bodied men and about as many boys were in regular employ, a situation that the vicar thought could be improved by enclosure. At Wisborough Green (Sussex), the average number unemployed in the five winters previous to 1831–2 was 80; in Suffolk in February 1830, 1,001 were out of employ in the Blything hundred, and proportions ranging from 43–80 per cent in seven parishes of the Hoxne hundred.[22]

Many of these examples are extreme instances of winter unemployment, and without exception they are drawn from the south rather than the north, the east rather than the west of England. By contrast, seasonal fluctuations were much less in evidence in pastoral areas where livestock provided year-round work, on small estates where a country house and its supporting farm or farms were run as an integrated enterprise, or where alternative occupations were readily available. For example, on the Penrhos estate in Anglesey, the winter months found the men engaged in feeding livestock, laying drains, carting coal, dung and timber, and hedging and ditching, as well as spending considerable amounts of time constructing field walls and looking after the plantations.[23] On the Blundells' Ince Hill Farm (Lancs.) the summer and winter labour forces varied little in 1817, 1826 and 1829, while at Trafford Park on the very boundaries of Manchester, the greater part of the work was performed by a core of regular attenders who worked steadily through winter as well as summer, at a daily wage of 2s–2s 4d. Likewise a surviving farm diary of 1825–6 points to the regularity of work near Barnsley, even during the winter months. Among the ten daymen covered, eight worked 120–126 days (out of a possible 126), and the others, 115–120.[24] None of this is to suggest that the position of the worker was completely secure, even in favoured districts. Attention has been drawn to the case of Burscough (Lancs.) where in 1833 up to 50 men were liable to unemployment while in Nottinghamshire, another semi-industrialized county, Smith Woolley acknowledged some unemployment in the five or six years before 1833 and estimated that, in the latter year, a man might be 'calculated to lose, on an average, a day in a week'.[25] Nevertheless, in counties such as these, labouring men were spared the hopelessness which rotted village life in the south.

Many observers, following some form of vulgarized Malthusian thinking, were inclined to invoke the spectre of surplus, or superfluous population; such was William Wilshere of Hitchin who, in giving evidence before the 1817 Select Committee on the Poor Laws, declared that 'in all cases, the population is likely to increase beyond the employment, and perhaps more in agricultural parishes than in most others ... the labourers have increased with the increase of population, and by the return of a considerable number from the army'.[26] However, from the same county in 1831, the Duke of Bedford's Woburn agent concluded that there was 'not a single efficient labourer, more than is required to manage the land properly: whether they [the tenant farmers] can afford to employ them is a different question, – but that they can be usefully and beneficially employed, cannot I think be denied, indeed all the Farmers to whom I have spoken upon this subject admit it'.[27] His views as expressed on that occasion came close to those of other authors inclined to stress the 'artificiality' of the problem, such as R. M. Bacon, who referred to 'the semblance of a redundant population'; or J. Richardson of Heydon, Norfolk, who on the assumption that the proportion of labour should be one able-bodied man to 36 acres, could not see where the superabundance of labourers was to be found.[28] This approach was not so enlightened as it might seem, for it embodied the view that the Old Poor Law, with its alleged proclivity to create and then immobilize labour, lay at the heart of the problem. So far as is known, H. B. Morris of Woodside Farm, Caddington (Beds.) did not contribute to the flood of opinionated pamphlet literature; however, in his reply to the *Rural Queries* circulated in 1833 by the Poor Enquiry Commission, he confessed to simply not knowing how many labourers were requisite for the proper cultivation of the land and added, 'there are not enough labourers in the harvest, although there is a surplus of them in winter; partly real; partly artificial'.[29] This is as honest and astute a comment on the unemployment problem of rural southern England as any made at the time, or since.

As well as contributing to unemployment, the economic circumstances of the time inevitably had a depressing effect on wages. The national (Bowley) index shows a fall from its wartime peak of 104 (average 1810–14) to a nadir of 72 (1824), thereafter recovering slightly but subsequently settling at 80 (1832–4), representing a collapse of some 23 per cent. The fall in daily rates was echoed in declining remuneration for piece-work, for example at Hilderstone Hall in Staffordshire where William Vernon paid 6d–8d a stave for threshing wheat in 1818 and 1819, reducing to 5½d by 1831.[30] Though the practice never lacked its fervent advocates, piece-work was in many districts becoming more difficult to obtain. On the Camer estate in Kent it appears to have increased rapidly during the war years, but only threshing was done on this basis by 1837. At Coltishall (Norfolk) in 1833 it was said to be unavailable to the 'plentiousness of cheap labour', and J. H. Kent, writing in 1844, thought that piece-work had declined steadily over the previous forty years.[31]

This decline in wages did not necessarily signify a diminution in real terms. Admittedly, cottage rents did not fall and remained in 1830 at about double the level obtaining at the commencement of the French wars.[32] However, the cost of food fell markedly and the abolition of duty in 1830 brought down the cost of beer. In addition, improvements in manufacturing processes were tending to reduce from the 1820s the price of articles in common use such as earthenware, household utensils, and cotton clothing.[33] Fifty years ago, Clapham set the Bowley wage index against a recently-published cost of living index constructed by Silberling, and inferred a significant increase in real wages for the post-war period.[34] Since then, further information on wage movements drawn from local estate records, rather than the parliamentary evidence upon which Bowley relied, has tended to confirm his impressions of the movement of wages, rather than to refute it.[35] Moreover it has been shown that the substitution for Silberling of any of the price indexes which have become available since Clapham's day makes virtually no difference to the conclusion that real wages rose significantly, perhaps by as much as 21 per cent if we compare the figures given for 1815 and 1835 by two recent American scholars.[36] However there is one highly significant reservation that must be made. Clapham's optimistic conclusion assumed that employment on the land was 'not perceptibly more irregular in the 'twenties than it had been in the 'nineties',[37] whereas, as we have seen, there is impressive evidence that this cannot have been the case. In practice, many labouring men did not earn weekly wages, despite the habit of quoting wages in this form, common at the time and perpetuated in Bowley's work. They were accustomed to receiving daily wages, and consequently any increase in lost time due to greater incidence of seasonal unemployment, or indeed to longer-term unemployment, is not taken into account. If, for example, a hypothetical labourer worked five days in 1830–4 against six in 1810–14, the imputed real wage gain of 21 per cent would be virtually wiped out; and certainly, if he was working only four days, the real value of his earnings would show a dramatic decline.

This rather obvious point may be applied to contrasting regions. In the north, wages were higher, the cost of living much the same, and above all, employment more regular. Students of the position of the northern labourer have repeatedly alluded to a rising standard of living in these years. In Cheshire this favourable outcome is ascribed to a tendency during the war years for wages to rise faster than prices, and thereafter, to the price fall.[38] In Nottinghamshire there are many signs that the farmworker's lot improved betweeen 1820 and 1834: weekly wages at South Collingham (less harvest earnings) were 13s in 1833 and deemed 'high in proportion to the price of food', while at Thurgarton the labourers were considered 'better-off in food and clothing than they were 25 years ago'. Likewise in Lancashire wages were tending to equate across the county at a level which implied a definite improvement in real terms; at Ince Blundell by as much as one-third between 1813 and the mid-1820s.[39] Significantly, returns of the distribution of friendly societies show that about 1820 they were far stronger in the industrialized counties, reaching figures equivalent to 63 and 52 per cent of adult males in Lancashire and Staffordshire and 43 per cent in Nottinghamshire, where there was a noticeable tendency for the movement to spread into the rural areas during these years.[40] Typical of the village societies which at this stage still accounted for by far the majority of members was that at Aslockton (Notts.), where a surviving account book for 1824–42 shows that for 1s a week a member received (initially) 8s a week in sickness pay, a £4 funeral benefit, £2 if his wife died and £1 for a child's burial, while the social aspect of the club is reflected in the accounts by references to the beer drunk on club nights, dinners (costing 1s a head), and the society's annual procession headed by a band.[41] In the counties of a more agricultural character progress was decidedly slower; the comparable returns appear to point to proportions ranging between 9 (Sussex) and 35 per cent (Herts.), and in the south the independent initiatives of villagers needed to be supported by county societies (Essex, 1818; Hampshire, 1825; Wiltshire and Kent, 1828; Rutland, 1832) or by district clubs such as the Dunmow Friendly Society or Stoke Holy Cross Benevolent, which were patronized by gentlemen or prominent clergy whose subscriptions as honorary members helped to keep down the ordinary rates. On the one hand the very existence of friendly societies in the southern rural counties suggests the presence of a class of men who remained in regular employment and could, like their northern counterparts, enjoy an improvement in the standard of living. On the other, the comparative weakness of the movement in the rural south supports the presumption that, for a majority of southern labourers, real wage increases were a theoretical rather than an attainable possibility. An exceptionally thoughtful characterization of the situation was made by J. Stallard of Red Marley (Worcs.) in answer to a question put to him by the *Select Committee on Agriculture* of 1833, as to whether the labourer was better off. He replied: 'Those that are employed ... when I say that the agricultural labourer is better off, I apply that to the regularly employed labourer; for taking the whole amount of labourers in the Kingdom, I should question whether they are better off, there are so many more out of employ than there used to be'.[42]

In any event, an examination of male real wages does not describe comprehensively the domestic economy of the cottager, and account needs to be taken of variations in the amount of employment for females. Considering the pressures on farmers in the post-war period, it may seem surprising that they did not resort increasingly to women and child workers. However, there was a sense that males had a prior claim, and anyway would otherwise have to be sustained from the rates. In case after case, replies to the *Rural Queries* of 1833 intimated that there was little or no farm employment for women. From Kelvedon (Essex) it was reported that 'the number of labourers [being] more than equal to the demand ... there is little employment for women and children', while from Great Shelford (Cambs.) the comment that 'We have no employment for women and children but haymaking and weeding' was typical of a great many more suggesting that females were limited to a narrow range of springtime tasks.[43] Moreover, the opportunities for wives and daughters to contribute to the family purse through domestic outwork were declining in many districts. Ever since the 1780s hand-spinning had been contracting, and this trend continued. In and about Lavenham (Suffolk) where once 150 woolcombers had each furnished work for 30 spinners, there were but 16 survivors by 1843. Likewise, by 1841 only 2,000 persons were employed in woollen cloth manufacture in the whole of Devon. Thornton, for one, was convinced that 'where the class of agricultural labourers is most distressed, it is usually found that each was the seat of a flourishing manufacture carried on by cottagers at their own homes, which has now decayed or moved away'.[44] There remained, however, other southern districts where domestic outwork still flourished, notably in the clothing trades. In particular, straw plaiting and lace-making continued to hold up well. According to the 1851 census returns, there were at least 10,054 plaiters in Bedfordshire and 11,675 in the adjoining counties of Buckinghamshire and Hertfordshire. These counties, together with Huntingdonshire, Oxfordshire,

Northamptonshire and Devon, also included some 35,000 lace-makers, employed by putters-out operating from centres such as Newport Pagnell, High Wycombe, and Honiton who often used village grocers as their factors or agents. Thus, at Cardington (Beds.) lace-making upheld female 'age-specific labour participation rates' comparatively well, in contrast to the position at Corfe Castle (Dorset) where a decline in spinning and knitting caused them to halve between 1790 and 1851, when only eight married women out of 296 still claimed an occupation.[45] All the counties mentioned featured low wages and considerable male under-employment during the period. For some, the situation was aggravated by deteriorating prospects of female employment; in others, notably Bedfordshire and Buckinghamshire, the problem must have been alleviated to some extent by a comparatively lively demand for female workers.

To what extent were contemporary social policies capable of meeting the problem of rural poverty? In the eyes of some, an obvious palliative was the provision of allotments. Although a few cases of their establishment are on record in the late eighteenth century, much of the impetus came after the war, the years 1816–33 seeing the publication of at least 130 pamphlets, many no doubt penned by members of The Labourers' Friend Society, set up in 1816.[46] These publications gave many instances of the effect of allotments in promoting habits of industry, such as Henry Seaman of Bexley (Kent) who eventually employed himself and his wife (they had no children) on an acre and a half, intensively manured with the dung of their increasing stock of pigs and, as well, by the contents of their privy. Again, numerous examples were given of their efficacy in saving the rates, for example a persuasive article in the *Quarterly Review* which contrasted the poor rates in four Rutland parishes (9d in the £) with those in four Sussex villages (10s 9d) where allotments did not exist.[47] Even so, many farmers remained suspicious, thinking that they might divert too much of the labourer's effort, and it is significant that little use was made of the legislation of 1819 which empowered parish authorities to procure up to 20 acres of land to be let at reasonable rents to poor and industrious men. In addition, some theorists opposed allotments on the presumption that they must inhibit labour mobility. Moreover, they were not universally popular among labouring men, for their usefulness varied with the quality of the land, its accessibility and the rent charged. In some Kent parishes the system of 'letting land at double or treble its value' had tended 'to exasperate the lower orders', while some allotment-holders found that their chances of employment or parish relief were reduced on the grounds that they were not, or ought not to be, in want.[48] Despite all these obstacles, some progress was made, mostly on the initiative of private landlords, and by 1833 allotments were known in 42 per cent of parishes (though in many cases for one or two labourers only) while adequate gardens were thought to be possessed by all or most of the poor in just over half the parishes examined. There were interesting regional variations in the pattern of provision. The south-eastern counties (e.g. Kent) appear to have been well furnished with gardens, though not with allotments to the same extent as the rest of the south and midlands (Wiltshire, Dorset, Lincolnshire), while north of the Humber-Dee line, allotments were considerably less common and, it is thought, in only a third of parishes did all or most of the poor have gardens.[49]

Whatever their merits, allotments could never have provided a complete answer to the problem of rural poverty, bearing in mind the large numbers who were so situated because they were elderly, sick or semi-infirm. This leads us to the role of the Poor Law, a topic of abiding interest to the social historian. In the first place, poor law sources, used in conjunction with evidence on population and prices, give further statistical confirmation of regional contrasts in the incidence of rural poverty. It can be shown, using information available for various years including 1803, 1813, 1821 and 1831, that *per capita* expenditure in the southern counties was 56–77 per cent higher in the low wage counties of the south than in the north, according to the year chosen. These figures include all expenditure, and despite the tenor of much contemporary discussion, able-bodied males at no time constituted a majority of the pauper host. Nevertheless, somewhat scarcer material on this aspect points to the expected distribution; in 1827–8 about 30 per cent of all paupers in 20 parishes of Wiltshire, Somerset and Buckinghamshire were adult males as opposed to 13 per cent in Shropshire, Northumberland and Westmorland.[50] Further evidence of the gravity of the problems of the south is afforded by a comparison of real *per capita* relief (taking account of price movements) in three counties, over time. In the agricultural districts of Sussex, Essex and Kent, the average cost was, respectively, 19.9, 29.5 and even 53.9 per cent higher when the years 1820–34 are compared with 1792–1814.[51]

In a few cases, parish authorities made attempts to promote long-distance migration to the industrial districts, though usually with little result. Rather more success was achieved in promoting overseas emigration. For example, the Kentish parish of Headcorn assisted emigrants annually after 1823 by borrowing money against the rates; likewise Benenden sought £1,150 from Thomas Hodges, the chairman of the Kent Quarter Sessions, to enable 145 persons to be migrated to America in 1827–8. These examples were followed by others in the county and by the early 1830s, parishes in Sussex and on the Wiltshire–Somerset border were also organizing sizeable parties. In all, Corsley in Wiltshire lost 200 persons by emigration between 1828–31, and in 1830 the parish assisted the departure of 66 of its 'least desirable' inhabitants with a view to relieving some of the pressure on agriculture caused, in this case, by the demise of the cloth-making industry.[52] Such steps remained exceptional, however, and were quite incapable of making more than a small impression on the problem of rural pauperism which had arisen, so many ratepayers thought, as a consequence of mistaken policies of relief. The nub of the matter lay in ill-advised parish allowances, which were blamed, *inter alia*, for increasing expenditure, depressing wages, lowering the efficiency of labour, hindering labour mobility and promoting population growth. Not surprisingly, they engendered a fund of tales about labourers. One, with an interesting ring of modernity, concerned the case of a labourer who about 1824 was employed at Sudbury on road-making for a Mr Goody at the handsome wage of 15s: when asked why he had given it up, he allegedly replied that he had earned only eighteenpence – 'I was entitled to 13s 6d for my scale allowance'.[53]

The 'Speenhamland system' as we may for convenience call these allowances, appears to have prevailed in 1824 in 19 counties, chiefly in the south and east, where a majority of parishes responding to the 1824 *Select Committee on Labourers' Wages* admitted to supplementing wages from the rates. If these are compared to county relief levels in 1821 and 1831, it would appear that *per capita* outlays were some 60 per cent higher than in the rest of England.[54] However, the notion of a 'system' is inherently misleading, for there was immense variation of practice, within the same county and over time, as parishes wrestled with their problems on an individual basis. There is evidence of a hardening of attitudes from the 1820s and in some cases, especially where parishes controlled relief through select vestries elected by the principal inhabitants and paid overseers were employed, a positive crusade against pauperism was mounted. They included Hatfield and Welwyn in Hertfordshire, and Swallowfield and Cookham in Berkshire (where vigorous efforts were made to 'let the labourer find that the parish is the hardest taskmaster and the worst paymaster he can find'), while at Leckhamstead in the same county, all children who might have attracted allowances were despatched to the poor-house after 1827. At Llangaddock (Brecon), all persons applying for relief were compelled to move into the poor house 'or go without'.[55] All these were extreme cases of vigorous 'dis-pauperization', but even where determined policies were not consistently practised, there was scope for countless individual acts of meanness to be perpetrated against the poor, when overseers were confronted by their 'importunate' demands. They tended to be particularly severe on single unemployed males, partly because of their lack of dependants, and partly because it was believed that 'pinching the young men' might well be the means of promoting a greater readiness to migrate.[56]

Among the related expedients to which parishes turned was the roundsman system which was particularly resorted to in the immediate aftermath of the war. Cases were known where wages were driven down as low as 4d, 3d or even 2d a day (as happened at Ludgvan, Cornwall, in 1822), or where the men were let out in 'a sort of Dutch auction' to whoever would take them. At Dolgelley (Merioneth) this occurred regularly in the post-war years, in the knowledge that their wages would be made up by the parish.[57] Such arrangements did nothing to improve the men's willingness or self-respect and from the 1820s roundsman was replaced in many southern parishes by the 'Labour Rate' system. Here a parish rate was levied to cover the cost of the able-bodied unemployed and each labourer's services had a price set on them. A farmer might employ labourers in proportion to his rates and, if he spent less, the difference was payable to the parish. Numerous agreements still exist for consultation, for example from Pebmarsh (Essex), where incidentally the population had increased by 52 per cent in thirty years. In November 1832 we find employers agreeing to take surplus labourers 'alphabetically' for a period of six weeks, which was followed in February 1833 by a more sophisticated arrangement under which they were divided into six categories with prices on their heads ranging from 1s (boys, no doubt), to 9s, each farmer agreeing to take 3s worth for every pound for which he was rated.[58] Although in some respects this marked an improvement on roundsman (in that the chosen labourers received a full wage) it still retained something of an impersonal, humiliating quality.

In the circumstances, it is not surprising that parish overseers incurred a lot of opprobrium. In Bedfordshire they were roughly handled on numerous occasions, for example at Eaton Socon (1828) and Eaton Bray (1829), while parish property comprising five wheelbarrows and five tar bags for use on the roads was wilfully destroyed at Millbrook and the culprits were yielded up by irate villagers only at the point of a pistol (unloaded).[59] The situation satisfied no-one, certainly not the 'independent' labourers whose furniture was occasionally distrained for failure to pay the rates which assisted others who kept theirs; or who, like Thomas Pearce of Gorington, Sussex, complained that 'There are a great many men in our parish who like [parish relief] better than being at work'.[60] However, it was not until the 1830s, in the aftermath of the Swing riots (see below) that an apparently conclusive solution was sought out and applied. As is well known, the fundamental principle of the 1832 Poor Law Commission and the ensuing Poor Law Amendment Act of 1834 was to eradicate outdoor relief and especially allowances for the able-bodied. To this end, the famous principle of 'less eligibility' (the notion that in no circumstances should the lot of the pauper surpass that of the lowest independent labourer) and the workhouse test of destitution were invoked, with a view to reducing the charge on the public purse and reviving the spirit of independent self-reliance.

If the history of the poor laws offers one insight into the social malaise of the countryside at this period, the social history of crime is equally revealing, despite a danger that criminal records can 'mislead the student and make him mistake the exceptional for the commonplace'.[61] There are no statistics of offences, but if commitments for trial are any guide, the incidence of crime increased very significantly. In Suffolk, it amounted to 51 in every 100,000 population in 1801, but rose rapidly to reach 93 in 1821, 136 in 1831 and 157 in 1841. In Norfolk, too, the increase of commitments outstripped population growth at least down to 1830, averaging 279 in 1800–14, followed by a precipitous increase in 1815–20 (average, 558) and (with some fluctuation) 809 in 1820–30.[62] To assist the undependable efforts of village constables, at least 500 'prosecuting societies' had come into existence by the late 1830s, aiming to deter crime, to defray the expenses of advertising and prosecuting offenders, and to offer rewards to informers. The increase in criminality undoubtedly reflected hard times in the agricultural districts; the *Select Committee on Criminal Commitments and Convictions* (1826–7) admitted as much, alluding to the 'low rate of wages and want of sufficient employment for the labourer'.[63] By far the most important category was theft, particularly of wood, corn, vegetables, fruit and cheese, while tramping men and gypsies were regarded with particular suspicion. However, what particularly caught the eye of the magistracy, and has since fascinated social historians, was the increase in poaching. Of course, poaching had long been a commercial business. Ever since 1755 when Parliament ill-advisedly banned the sale of game, poulterers, innkeepers and others had depended on poachers for their supply, and the vastly increased areas of game preserves which came into being from the second half of the eighteenth century were constantly preyed on by armed gangs, such as the large concourse of 50 men, mostly ribbon weavers and colliers, who in November 1826 systematically worked their way through D. S. Dugdale's woods before making off towards Coventry.[64] The long series of measures taken to strengthen the Game Laws, notably the Night Poaching Acts of 1773, 1800, 1816 and 1819 and the much publicized resort by some landowners to spring-guns, aimed primarily to control this class of often violent offenders. However, farmworkers and estate labourers looking either to gain an illicit half-crown or to fill their pots loomed among the small fry, and their distress appears to have been a major cause of the dramatic increase in poaching after Waterloo. In Bedfordshire the proportion of prison commitments for offences against the game laws rose from 3.7 per cent in 1802–14 to 20.5 per cent in 1814–27, while in Wiltshire the number of game offenders in prison rose from an annual average of twelve or less through 1790–1810 to 58 in the immediate post war years, reaching 92 in the 1820s. Among others, Sir Thomas Baring and Lord Malmesbury concurred in the view that 'want of employment' was a primary cause of the increase in poaching.[65] Moreover, it was a habit which persisted more or less unabated after Parliament in its wisdom had decided to ban the use of spring guns (1827) and to legalize the sale of game, controlled by a system of certificates and licenses to deal (1831).

Yet crime was endemic, whereas the riotous events of 1816, 1822, and especially 1830, had the alarming character of epidemic onslaughts. Most historians allow that, rather like successive cholera outbreaks in early Victorian towns, they reflected the underlying gravity of the situation from which they sprang, and some portray them as a cumulative series of 'rebellions'.[66] Against a background of inclement weather, widespread disturbances, unemployment and wage reductions occurred in East Anglia in 1816. Pressure for reduced prices at Haverhill, Brandon, Ely and elsewhere was in line with popular traditions and many of the protesters were townsmen, manufacturers and fenmen. However, demands for money with menaces, arson and the destruction of threshing machines as far afield as Essex also occurred as the rioters vented their ire against millers, shopkeepers, clergymen and farmers. One person died in the most serious outbreak of violence at Littleport, and the situation was serious enough to cause the Home Secretary to issue a Royal proclamation and order troop movements. Subsequently, at a special commission held at Ely, 24 from among 76 prisoners were condemned to death, the rest being either acquitted, discharged by proclamation, or put on bail for good behaviour; of these, five were actually executed and the rest had their sentences commuted to transportation or imprisonment. In addition, at the ordinary Quarter Sessions of Bury St Edmunds, Ipswich and elsewhere, well over a hundred persons were brought to trial for riot and misdemeanour, or for breaking threshing machines, most receiving prison sentences of a year or less, or being bound over to keep the peace.[67] However, deterrence was not lastingly successful, for in February 1822 East Anglia saw more disturbances, this time perpetrated chiefly by farmworkers who assailed threshing machines in the neighbourhood of Diss and Eye.[68] According to a letter written by Lt. Col. Ray of Wortham to the commander of the Suffolk Yeomanry Cavalry in March 1822, 'Threatening letters are circulated among us most liberally and the firebrand, the most formidable of weapons, is the portion of those who persist in the use of threshing machines'. A week later he headed a force of troopers and succeeded in taking 20 prisoners from an assembly at Buckenham, liberating most under promise of good conduct, but conveying the 'worst seven' to Norwich Castle where the party ran the gauntlet of a hostile mob. This was one of a series of firm steps taken to quell the revolt, notwithstanding a recognition among the authorities of its underlying causes, for in April the magistrates of Suffolk were calling upon all occupiers 'to give their utmost care and attention towards the regular employment of all labourers as much as possible on their respective farms'.[69]

These events pale into relative insignificance in comparison to the 'Swing' riots of 1830–1. They were triggered by exceptional cold, hunger and unemployment during the fearsome winter of 1829, while another modest harvest in prospect must have increased the labourers' pessimism during the summer of 1830. These dire circumstances were coupled with vaguely stirred expectations turning on events across the Channel (the July Revolution) and confusion in English politics as radical opposition to the 'old system', personified by Wellington, gathered momentum.[70] The first threshing machine was destroyed at Lower Hardres (Kent) on 25 August 1830. However, the great majority of Swing-related incidents took place during November, and by February 1831 they became comparatively infrequent. Covering a rather wider timespan (January 1830–September 1832) Hobsbawm and Rudé have uncovered 1,475 incidents falling chiefly into the following categories: arson (22 per cent of all cases), machine-breaking – notably threshers (30) – robbery and burglary (16), threatening letters (7), and riots, mostly focusing on wages and some featuring assaults (24). As will be seen from table 3.1, the geographical incidence of these disturbances was strongly skewed towards the south of England, while in Wales those which occurred were located in the corn-growing districts of the south, and even there were somewhat rare because there was no 'surplus population' and wages ran higher than the average English level. In the Welsh pastoral districts there were no disturbances of any kind.[71]

Table 3.1: Incidence of the Swing disturbances by county, 1 Jan 1830–3 Sept 1832*
(Standard propensity to disturbances for England = 100)

Counties with above standard frequency
Berkshire 558 Hampshire 422 Wiltshire 421 Sussex 278 Kent 214
Huntingdonshire 210 Dorset 150 Norfolk 118 Buckinghamshire 117

Counties with below average frequency, but reaching half the standard propensity to disturbances
Oxfordshire 97 Gloucestershire 89 Surrey 87 Bedfordshire 69 Essex 61
Suffolk 61 Middlesex 57 Cambridgeshire 54 Northamptonshire 54
Cumberland 50

Counties with well below standard frequency
Lincolnshire 47 Worcestershire 34 Leicestershire 33 Derbyshire 29
Somerset 27 Devon 26 Cornwall 22 Lancashire 22 Hertfordshire 21
Nottinghamshire 21 Shropshire 21 Herefordshire 17 Staffordshire 15
Cheshire 14 Yorkshire 13

Counties with negligible or no Swing disturbances
Warwickshire 7 Durham 0 Northumberland 0 Rutland 0

* The table utilizes the list of disturbances in E. J. Hobsbawm and G. Rudé, *Captain Swing*, Lawrence and Wishart, 1969, pp. 312–58, relating their incidence to data on the numbers of labourers in agriculture given in P.P. 1833, vols. XXXVI–XXXVIII. *1831 Census of Great Britain, Enumeration Abstract*, vols. I and II.

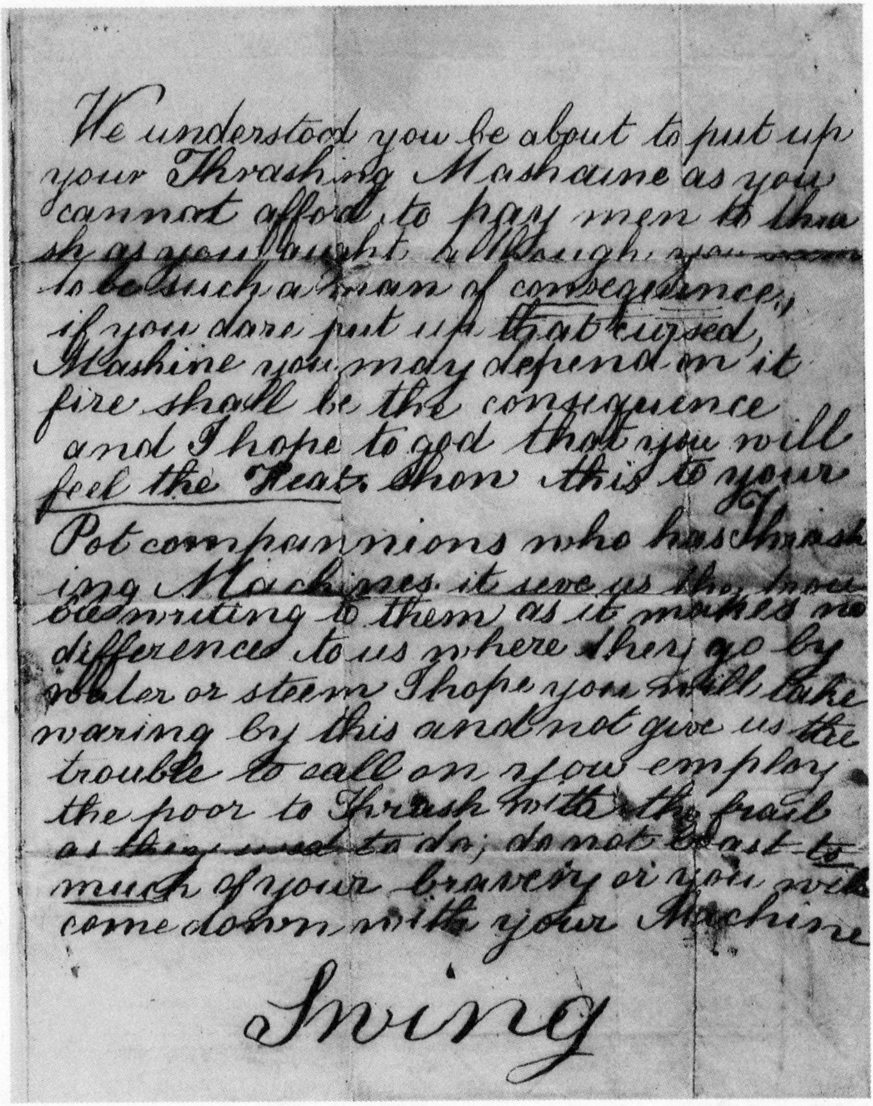
We understood you be about to put up your Thrashing Mashaine as you cannot afford to pay men to thrash as you ought although you seem to be such a man of conseqence, if you dare put up that cursed Mashine you may depend on it fire shall be the consequence and I hope to god that you will feel the Heat. Show this to your Pot companions who has Thrashing Machines it save us the trouble writing to them as it makes no difference to us where they go by water or steem I hope you will take waring by this and not give us the trouble to call on you employ the poor to Thrash with the frail as they used to do; do not boast to much of your bravery or you will come down with your Machine

Swing

A Swing letter, addressed to Mr Rumsey of Mere, Wiltshire, in the possession of Gillingham School, Dorset.

That a broad contrast between the northern and southern counties should emerge is unsurprising in the light of the economic contrasts drawn in this chapter, and although new instances of disturbances will continue to come to light as local research proceeds,[72] the overall pattern is unlikely to be disturbed. The view that the Swing riots were 'essentially a labourers' movement with essentially economic ends' and precipitated by dire economic privations derives support from answers to the *Rural Queries* subsequently circulated by the Poor

Enquiry Commissioners. The replies, contributed by clergymen, overseers of the poor and other worthies from 10 counties, pointed overwhelmingly to 'low wages' or 'unemployment' as causes of the riots.[73] Yet, as table 3.1 shows, a county-level analysis reveals some features which are far from easy to explain. It is not obvious why Swing disturbances (at least, those which came to court) should have been five times more numerous in Berkshire than in Oxfordshire, or why Cambridgeshire, Bedfordshire, Suffolk and Essex should have been so comparatively quiescent. Moreover, within counties, the pattern of variation is equally puzzling. As Snell has argued, there is some *prima facie* evidence to associate disturbances with recent (post-1800) enclosure, but this link was far from necessary or universal.[74] Students of Suffolk and Wiltshire have failed to find any close connection, while in Essex the main incidents all took place in the Tendring hundred and especially around Clacton, where there had been no enclosures for 200 years, but where population growth had been especially rapid and, in eight cases out of nine, parish expenditures on relief had risen significantly in 1829 and 1830.[75] In the further pursuit of a more disaggregated approach Hobsbawm and Rudé have produced a certain amount of evidence with which to gauge the riot-proneness of individual places. They conclude that the profile of the disturbed village is of one that would tend to be above average in size, to contain a high ratio of labourers to employing farmers, and a sizeable number of local artisans as well as showing an above average disposition to religious independence. Moreover the riot-prone village was 'more likely to be "open" or mixed than the rest . . . it was more likely to be engaged in tillage and especially grain farming, or in the production of specialized crops with a highly fluctuating demand for labour, and less likely to be engaged in pastoral farming'.[76] They allow, though, that these findings are tentative and subject to local variation. Moreover, the difficulties of identifying the determinants of riot-proneness at the parish level are compounded by the fact that persons did not necessarily take action in their villages of residence. Thus, in Kent, George Gipps, a Bekesbourne landowner and MP for Canterbury, maintained that those who broke machines there were 'supposed to have come from Elham, and I hope it will so turn out. . . . Bekesbourne where the mischief took place last night is a very well managed parish – and I believe I may say, that the labourers were never out of work. There is, as I hear, no reason to suppose *they* were concerned.'[77] The social and economic factors involved in pre-disposing one village to disturbance, and not another, are thus likely to prove difficult to isolate, and the most recent systematic study tends to revive the political dimension by drawing attention to the importance of main roads, especially the London highways, in determining the spatial pattern of the Swing disturbances. This was not because roads facilitated the travels of mysterious agitators in gigs, a view common at the time. Rather, main road villages tended to have closer associations with the outside world, particularly through such 'link men' as coachmen and carriers; moreover, the London highway 'breached rural isolation and linked the labourers through village politicians to a wider radical culture'.[78] Indeed, those brought to trial included a variable but significant number of craftsmen (14 per cent of commitments), whose wages, it was sourly commented, were 'such as to place them far above the reach of want'.[79] An element of political calculation was also in evidence among farmers, some of whom were seen to stand by placidly while their (insured) machines were destroyed. In south-east Norfolk and east Suffolk especially, the collusion of farmers was the subject of repeated comment. From Long Melford Colonel Brotherton remarked on their 'use of the labourers' movement to promote their own ends by reducing tithes', while Lord Suffield concurred in believing that farmers had encouraged the 'late outrageous proceedings' by prompting an outcry against tithes and rents.[80]

The reaction of the civil authorities was mild in the early weeks of the Swing revolt. Notwithstanding the destruction of over a hundred machines in Kent between the end of August and the third week of October 1830, the Lord Lieutenant, Sir Edward Knatchbull, was impressed by the evident distress of those involved ('without any exception they ascribe their conduct declaring they would rather do any thing than encounter such a winter as the last') and his sentences on the first machine breakers brought before him were very lenient. All seven were discharged with a caution and a three-day prison sentence.[81] This appalled Sir Robert Peel who became the Home Secretary in a new government in November, and notices were soon issued to Justices of the Peace over Prime Minister Melbourne's signature warning them against 'any remisses or inactivity in the fulfillment of functions so vitally important'. Fortified by this reminder, and given time to prepare as the movement spread westward from Kent, other magistrates tended to take a more resolute line, none more positively than James Frampton of Moreton Hall, Dorset, who proceeded on 30 November to Winfrith to quell incipient trouble. Here, according to his sister's account, 'the mob' at first advanced respectfully, hats in their hands, to demand wage increases but would not disperse even after the Riot Act was read. After an ineffectual parley the crowd was charged and three men seized and committed to Dorchester Gaol. Not surprisingly, Frampton's vigour made him especially unpopular and in early December Moreton Hall was described as 'barricaded like an Irish mansion'. Nevertheless, Christmas passed peacefully, with carol singers from Frampton's 'own' parishes, while 'the yule log blazed on the large hearth ... the peacock in full plummage (sic) was placed on the dinner table with the boar's head ... the immense candles were well covered with laurel ... and the Wassail bowl and lamb's wool were not inferior to former years'.[82] How far the pacification at Dorset was due to the 'spirited conduct' of Frampton, or even to the arrival of a troop of lancers on 12 December, it would be difficult to say. More important, probably, were the timely concessions made by landlords such as Mr Portman of Bryanston (as early as 22 November) and by farmers who in many cases laid aside or even destroyed their machines or (when assembled at the Sturminster Newton vestry on 2 December) agreed to raise wages to 1s 6d a day and embark upon a widening of the road from Newton to Bagber at parish expense.[83] Elsewhere, in situations further removed from the front, vigilance was the order of the day. In Staffordshire extra work was provided on the Trentham estate and a dance and supper given for the labourers.[84] The rich Bedford correspondence provides a particularly well-documented case of such a policy of containment. Faced with the first indications that the 'disgraceful proceedings' of the south were beginning to spread into Bedfordshire, the Duke's Woburn agent Crocker took on more estate workers in mid-November, yet, as he ruefully remarked in a letter to his London superior, W. G. Adam, 'his Grace's wish to assist ... has not been met here, I am sorry to say, as it deserved, it is reported about that the labourers are taken on because we are alarmed . . . you can scarcely ever do right'. Nor was the policy especially effective, for 'the farmers do anything but help us, and as fast as we take on, they discharge'. Nevertheless, it was persisted with. In February Crocker recommended the use of bricks from their Crawley kiln to provide work, rather than buying in cheaper ones from Fenny Stratford. We may assume, too, that he and his subordinates followed Adam's advice, that 'without any bustle' they should impress upon tenants who discharged labour that their conduct might lead to dismissal.[85]

When in due course the Swing rioters were brought to trial before the regular courts and Special Commissions held at Winchester, Reading, Salisbury, Dorchester and Aylesbury, older men and youths were conspicuously under-represented among those charged. The latter feature is puzzling, for contemporary accounts sometimes make a point of noting the youth of rioters – 'I think two thirds of the mob were under 18 years' wrote a cleric describing one Dorset incident.[86] Perhaps youths simply generated more noise than violence, or the authorities tacitly decided to concentrate attention on the ringleaders, i.e. those considered old enough to behave responsibly. At all events, those brought to the bar were overwhelmingly in their twenties and early thirties, and consequently included many married men with families. In all, 1,976 cases were heard and 800 defendants were acquitted or bound over, seven fined and one whipped; 252 were sentenced to death and 19 actually executed, the rest joining the remainder who were given gaol sentences of varying length or else transported to New South Wales or Van Diemen's Land. As Hobsbawm and Rudé justly remark, the rioters paid a bitter price, for gains that were slight indeed.[87] Although something of a check was administered to the diffusion of threshing machines until the 1850s, the Swing episode was quite incapable of improving the labourers' position in other respects, for any length of time.

Nor, it seemed, could peaceable trade unionism be made effective in the agrarian sector. The history of the luckless 'Tolpuddle Martyrs' is often taken as another mark of the oppression of the southern labourers at this, the nadir of their fortunes. Twenty months after the Special Commissioners had left Dorchester, a number of labourers led by George Loveless, a self-taught Methodist lay preacher who had made contact with the London-based Grand National Consolidated Trades Union, met in a cottage (still standing and marked with a plaque) to form a society. In itself, this action was not illegal and had not been so since 1825. Unfortunately they proceeded to hold a secret initiation ceremony intended to inculcate loyalty among members, and thereby, as it happened, sealed their fate. For when news of these events reached the ears of the implacable Frampton, he sought to insinuate into the society 'trusty persons', and was able to find two men who had taken part in the induction ceremony and were prepared to give evidence. Presented at the Dorchester Assizes under an obscure act against the swearing of 'illegal oaths' (which had been passed in 1797 to combat naval mutinies), Loveless, his brother and four others were convicted in March 1834 and sentenced to the maximum penalty of seven years' transportation. They left against the background of a public outcry which extended into Parliament and brought into being a 'Dorchester Committee' composed of respectable trade unionists and politicians. Eventually public pressure on a more sympathetic Home Secretary, Lord John Russell, succeeded in obtaining the men's pardon and free passage back to England. Only one, James Hammett, resettled at Tolpuddle, while with the assistance of the Dorchester Committee the others were set up on small farms in Essex, whence they eventually migrated to Canada and, happy to record, appear to have enjoyed modest success.[88] The men of Tolpuddle had been singularly unlucky to fall foul of so fierce a reactionary as Frampton and when in the summer of 1836 five labourers at Tendring (Essex) appeared at the assizes charged with conspiring to raise wages and assaulting a farmer, they were acquitted of the first charge and gaoled for only three weeks on the second. However, the local union they had attempted to set up, which apparently reached a membership of 1,200 in the space of a few weeks, collapsed by the end of July in the face of opposition from the local press and clergy, one describing their movement as a 'wrong and unchristian alliance'.[89] Despite the courage of these early pioneers, the obstacles to organization were at this stage too great, and the spirit of political radicalism too thinly diffused for them to succeed, as is shown by the farmworkers' reaction to Chartism. Flurries of Chartist activity occurred in the countryside, including meetings held in 1838 at Charlton Down near Blandford (upon which Frampton kept a close eye), but never with lasting success. In Suffolk much spadework was done by the townsmen of Ipswich but they never captured the firm allegiance of the farmworker.[90]

Such was the condition of rural England during the first half of the 1830s. It is not at all difficult to build up a picture of deprivation, semi-starvation, and sullen resentfulness, and the first twenty post-war years are rightly viewed as a time when the condition of the majority of farmworkers sank to a depth unparalleled in modern times. To what extent did matters improve in the later 1830s, and through the 1840s? Although there are dangers in over-emphasizing the role of the New Poor Law, it is convenient to begin by examining its implementation and actual or alleged effects. From Suffolk and from Essex came petitions objecting to the demise of the Old Poor Law (now described as 'mild, humane, generous, benevolent and noble') while at Great Bircham (Norfolk), protests took the form of a strike of labourers which, when met by the use of blacklegs, culminated in the ransacking of the houses of three prominent farmers, one of whom was an overseer and constable.[91] Around Faversham (Kent) in May 1835, the tactics of protesting mobs included assaults on guardians and relieving officers, the tearing up of papers and accounts, and the hurling of sticks and stones at buildings. Lidlington and Millbrook (Beds.) were the scenes of minor riots in the same month, while at Ampthill a crowd of some 500 persons besieged the Board of Guardians and broke the windows in the new workhouse.[92] Nevertheless, popular resistance outside the northern industrial districts was neither long-lasting nor effective, and by May 1839, 587 unions comprising 13,640 parishes had been formed, leaving only 1,849 parishes outside the system.[93]

Some attention was given under the new regime to the promotion of migration. In 1835 the new Commissioners agreed to act as intermediaries in the locally initiated transfer of several families from the parish of Bledlow (Bucks.) to cotton mills at Styal (Cheshire) and Bolton, while others were passed from Cranfield (Beds.), Woburn and Ampthill to factories at Mellor and other prominent establishments, where they impressed their new employers by the gentleness of their manners and the rapid way in which they picked up the work.[94] Subsequently the Commissioners decided to appoint two full-time agents, one in Manchester and another at Leeds; however, the official scheme lasted only until May 1837 when a depression in trade rendered the efforts of the agents nugatory, and it was never revived. A subsequent analysis of the 4,684 migrants assisted indicates that they were drawn chiefly from Bedfordshire (6.9 per cent), Bucks. (9.0), and especially Norfolk (13.5) and Suffolk (49.3) where, for a time, the scheme was eagerly supported.[95] Though represented by Richard Oastler and other Tory opponents of the New Poor Law as an attempt to force the agricultural labourers into factory slavery, assisted migration was numerically insignificant. It could scarcely be otherwise, since the manufacturing districts were quite capable of supplying the greater proportion of their labour requirements from their own natural increases.[96] The 1834 Act had included a clause enabling parishes to raise money for emigration to the colonies, and an examination of the first 6,403 cases in 1835–7 shows that Norfolk, Suffolk, Kent and Wiltshire accounted for 52, 17, 8 and 5 per cent respectively. In all, between 1835 and 1846 some 15,000 persons were assisted to emigrate, chiefly to Canada, under the auspices of the poor law. However, they did not make up more than 2 per cent of all recorded emigrants from the United Kingdom during this period[97] and we should regard both the internal and external migration schemes as no more than cautious experiments. By and large the Poor Law Commissioners pinned more faith on attacking the old evils which were thought to impede the natural working of market forces in the labour market.

Between 1834 and 1837 the national outlay on poor relief was pushed down by about 36 per cent.[98] In its early days the New Poor Law was administered with 'much severity', as Glyde later recalled, and frequent cases of harsh treatment raised in some quarters the fear that if the Old Poor Law had 'placed the ratepayers too much at the mercy of the labourers . . . the New Law places the labourers too much at the mercy of the ratepayers'.[99] In Bedfordshire, according to anti-poor law observers from the north, men unemployed during the winter of 1837–8 found it no use applying to the guardians for outdoor relief and complained of a general falling-off in their circumstances, a proposition illustrated by three householders' budgets which suggested that the rise in their aggregate earnings between 1835 and 1837 was more than offset by the cessation of their once considerable parish allowances.[100] One consequence of the squeeze thus placed on family incomes was a revival in the involvement of female and juvenile labour in agriculture. When this was looked into in 1843 the south-western investigator concluded that there were 'but few families' where the wife or children were not engaged in farm labour, although in some districts of Dorset where opportunities for lace-making or button-making presented themselves, female labour was hard to come by. From Woodbridge to Ipswich women and children probably accounted for a third to a sixth of all labour employed. In Yorkshire the position varied, but female employment was considerable at Beverley, Acaster Malbis in the Vale of York, and at Dunnington where two-thirds of the wives of the labouring class were employed in chicory cultivation. In Northumberland the bondage system was still associated with female employment on quite a large scale.[101] Yet the report attested to remarkable variations in the extent to which female and child labour was resorted to, the type of work performed, and earnings, not merely between regions but even among parishes in the same locality. The Commissioners could find no evidence that female labour had 'superseded' that of males, and by and large they concurred in thinking that field-labour was not detrimental to good health. However, one aspect attracted their forthright condemnation, namely the 'gang system', under which the farmer would contract with a 'gang-master' to have a piece of work done, for a specified sum. The gang-master would mobilize a team consisting largely of children and young persons of both sexes, directed their work, and was their paymaster. The extent of the gang system should not be exaggerated: it flourished chiefly in areas of ancient enclosures where, allegedly, cottages had been pulled down to reduce the poor rates (e.g. parts of Norfolk); or where, as in Lincolnshire and Cambridgeshire, fenland farms had been created in modern times and the number of cottages had, for the same reason, been strictly limited. It was in open townships, such as Castle Acre in Norfolk, that the gangs were usually assembled. Commissioner Dennison catalogued a number of disadvantages: members of the gangs worked hard to perform piece-work at day labourers' wages, the profit going to the gang-master; uncertainty of employment in inclement weather; long walks to work; less opportunity for education; 'imprudent' behaviour among the women; and the undue power of the gangmaster, 'who, if he be a low, hard man, illustrates the proverb that no tyranny is so grinding as that of a poor man who oppresseth the poor'. He concluded that it was 'a very pernicious system', but not one that could be remedied by abolition, on account of the number of persons who would be thrown out of work, and the increase in immorality and crime that would be fostered by 'idleness and distress'.[102]

The ramifications of the reforms of 1834 were thus, without doubt, both profound and far-reaching. However, it would be a mistake to view the position of the labourer in the later 1830s and 1840s, or even a partial revival of female employment, as being entirely determined by the operation of the New Poor Law. For the morale of agriculturalists took a decided turn for the better once the long-term fall in agricultural prices was arrested. In particular the years 1838–41 saw favourable prices for virtually all classes of farm products, against a background of reductions in local taxation, due to the declining poor rates and the commutation of tithes (1836). There was a marked increase in the use of inputs such as crushed bones and oil-seed cakes and a strong recovery in the demand for new implements. The establishment in 1838 of the Royal Agricultural Society was a further sign of returning confidence, and rents were in many cases rising from the later 1830s.[103] Corn output was expanding, and tended to increase employment, at least during the summer months. In 1838 the Chairman of Wangford Union in Suffolk wrote: 'I fancy that I perceived, at an early day, a suspicion growing up ... that the surplus population of which we have heard so much, would, in the end, prove more imaginary than real', while nine years later a leader in the *Agricultural Gazette* reflected, 'Time was when the supply of labour in the country exceeded the demand ... but this question has passed away and has ... given place to its exact opposite'.[104] Railway-building also alleviated matters to some extent. Peter Lecount, assistant engineer on the London and Birmingham railway, suggested that 15–20,000 men had been drawn from the 'surrounding rural population' during its construction (1835–8). In 1839 several counties reported the migration of labour to railway works, and in 1845, according to the *Farmer's Magazine*, the rural labour market was positively disrupted from the same cause.[105] These intimations of an improvement in the employment situation are supported to some extent by the way in which friendly societies continued to expand their social and geographical coverage. The records of the South Buckinghamshire Friendly Society (originally the Great Missenden Provident Society, founded in 1832), show that of 396 males admitted between July 1838 and May 1840, 53 per cent were labourers or worked in occupations closely related to agriculture,[106] and the affiliated orders were making significant headway. By 1845 the Manchester Unity of Oddfellows had as many as 388 lodges in 15 primarily agricultural counties, including 242 established over the preceding ten years. Other expanding groups included the Ancient Order of Foresters (with 159 courts in these counties in 1845, but mostly in Lincolnshire) and the Nottingham Ancient Imperial Order of Oddfellows, into which the above mentioned Aslockton club was absorbed in 1842.[107]

However, these favourable signs should not be exaggerated. The expansion of employment opportunities after 1837, while real, was decidedly erratic, varying from season to season, from one district to another and from one year to the next. In the first place, the number of railway construction jobs available was limited. Contractors such as Thomas Brassey required men with a background of good feeding and consequently employed many northerners. At the time when the South-Eastern Company's main line was under construction (1841–4) Assistant Poor Law Commissioner Tuffnell concluded that nine-tenths of those employed belonged to no county in particular, and that the remaining jobs signified only the addition of 'the evanescent quantity of 1/660th' to the usual demand for labour in Kent.[108] As yet, the problem of rural unemployment was far from being solved. The rector of Fairstead was not alone in claiming, in 1847, that 'as far as agricultural pursuits are concerned there is a surplus of labour in Essex', while sundry reports to the *Journal of the Royal Agricultural Society* touched on the same problem. From Devon (1848) employment was described as 'too fluctuating ... during the months of winter and early spring it is too often the case that the industrious labourer, unable to find work, is compelled to seek relief'. In Northamptonshire the problem of surplus labour was reduced rather than abolished: 'About 15 or 20 years ago there would be during the winter months, in large and populous villages, from 30 to 40 men ... maintained in comparative idleness; even now every winter we see with regret young active men seeking employment and finding none'.[109] The long-standing contrasts between north and south remained entrenched; one need only compare the budgets of two industrious labourers deriving from the same source in 1843, to show how the fortunes of similarly composed families at Lavenham, Suffolk, and Bolton Percy near York, could vary.[110] County-based figures for 1841, 1845 and 1851 agree in showing that the *per capita* incidence of relief remained highest in the south (especially the south-east) and lowest in the north (particularly the north-west) and that it continued to run some 30–40 per cent higher in the one-time Speenhamland counties, thus underlining the deep-seated nature of the problems of the south which could not, as events had proved, be solved simply by administrative changes.[111] Moreover, despite some early signs of a tendency for farmer-guardians to revert to allowances in the form of outdoor relief in regions as diverse as East Anglia and Wales,[112] the regime remained, on the whole, more severe in the south: the percentage of the non-sick able-bodied poor relieved in workhouses in the year ending Lady Day 1843 was 42.3 per cent in the rural south as against 10.3 and 21.2 per cent in the industrial and rural north respectively.[113] Behind these aggregate figures, we can sometimes turn to local sources which illustrate vividly the seasonal variations in the guardians' workload. At Ampthill during the first three weeks of the quarter ending June 1840, only 31 among 83 cases considered were labourers and many of these applicants were merely seeking medical relief for their dependants. Others reflected obvious unfitness for work such as the wretched William Sharman (aged 75), or a recently discharged trooper with chronic hepatitis; indeed only five cases involved men out of work without evidence of aggravating factors of this kind. However, by Christmas the picture was different. Among 58 cases considered in the eleventh and twelfth weeks of the December quarter, a much higher proportion was comprised of labourers (32, or 55 per cent) and of these, 24 were described as destitute or out of work. The general policy was to offer the house, a prospect which Joseph Clark and William Geddings, each with a wife and substantial numbers of children, showed great reluctance to accept ('did not come in'); though the resolution of William Gillett of Houghton lasted only until 11 January when he arrived, no doubt reluctantly, with his wife and children aged 2 and 8 months. What is particularly striking is the high proportion of young, single men aged 16 and upward who were unfailingly subjected to the workhouse test.[114]

Not much sympathy (then as now) was expended on this class, and in districts where farm service survived, perhaps none was needed. In the south, however, farmers gave preference to married men with dependants whenever employment was scarce: 'They first send off such as have no families, lest, by discharging them that have, a greater burden should fall upon the parish' commented a labourer to a *Morning Chronicle* investigator in 1849, indicating the continuance of long-established practices.[115] During the era of the Old Poor Law young single persons were given assistance on only the most grudging basis, and now, were likely to be offered it only in the form of indoor relief. Consequently it is not surprising that young males featured so prominently in the statistics of crime. In Suffolk statistics for 1844–6 indicate that the proportion in the age groups under 20 and 20–25 were 14 and 20 per cent above the average for England and Wales, while the corresponding proportion among those aged 30 and over was 27 per cent below average.[116] Youths and young men also featured prominently among the perpetrators of incendiarism, viewed by Hobsbawm and Rudé as the characteristic form of rural unrest after 1830, embodying 'a new note of embittered despair'.[117] Fire-raising was not a novelty in the 1840s and cases such as the Great Shelford fires of 1833 (which turned out to be the work of a man who sought only to occasion the working of the fire engine, for which, as one of the operators, he was paid 6s 6d a time), together with numerous attempts at insurance fraud qualify the impression tht arson was invariably the work of those seeking to articulate popular grievances.[118] For all that, the personal pique to which many cases were ascribed, such as that of 17-year-old

THE HOME OF THE RICK-BURNER.

(*Punch*, 1844, vol. VII, No. 155)

James Micklefield who fired a farmer's property following a gaol sentence for stealing his potatoes,[119] were rooted in the labourer's social situation: it would be perverse to suggest that the increased incidence of arson, after the death penalty for this offence was abolished in 1837, was devoid of social meaning. Certainly it was not viewed that way by insurance companies such as the Norwich Union, which ordered its agents to avoid known obnoxious or unpopular applicants in December 1843, and instructed surveyors to enquire into the scale of wages paid to farmworkers whenever attending a fire. At this juncture employment was scarce following a dry summer and a poor wheat crop which required little threshing, and Suffolk and Norfolk headed the list of disturbed counties with 47 and 38 commitments respectively. Such figures grossly understate the incidence of arson and recent research has shown that these two counties alone suffered at least 302 incidents in 1843–4.[120] In the majority of cases, no suspect could be identified and in others farmers no doubt thought it prudent to preserve silence rather than risk further trouble, for sometimes the labourers were observed to stand idly by the conflagrations, and even to take a grim pleasure in them. The property of farmer-guardians appears to have been particularly vulnerable: 'Such persons were in some cases known as good masters – no matter, their position as guardians neutralized, in the eyes of the poor, all their estimable qualities', and the New Poor Law, along with inadequate wages and lack of employment, was identified by Thomas Campbell Foster of *The Times* newspaper as a chief cause of East Anglian incendiarism.[121] So far as commitments offer a guide, it would appear that two-thirds of those who appeared before the Norfolk and Suffolk Assizes in 1844 were agricultural workers, mostly resident in the parish of the crime, who in many cases had worked or were working for their victims. Significantly, the *average* age of those convicted at the Norfolk and Suffolk Assizes in 1844 was only 24.3, and of those acquitted, 22.3.[122]

The persistence of incendiarism throughout the 1840s, particularly in East Anglia, suggests continued malaise and in 1849–51 there was a sudden increase in arson, judging from figures for commitments.[123] To explain this, we need to take note of the trend of prices, which after 1847 dipped alarmingly, the average for 1848–51 falling well below the levels of even 1822, and 1834–5. The collapse, which chiefly affected cereals, reflected good harvests and, as well, rising imports of wheat, flour and maize in the aftermath of Peel's controversial repeal of the Corn Laws in 1846. This move, while probably in the best interests of the nation as a whole, created among arable farmers widespread gloom and apprehension and the situation soon transmitted itself into wage reductions and rural unemployment. In fact the paradoxes of the 1820s and 1830s were, for a time, re-enacted. Caird could point out that within the space of ten years (1840–50) the price of the principal articles of the labourer's consumption had decreased by 'upwards of 30 per cent', which suggested a potential increase in the real value of farm earnings.[124] Unfortunately, there was also quite a considerable fall in earnings and a new rise in unemployment. It extended even to Yorkshire which, amazingly, saw more commitments for arson in 1849 than Norfolk and Suffolk together.[125] In January 1850 the editor of the *Yorkshire Gazette* elicited from 'an experienced argiculturalist within ten miles of the City of York' that wages had dropped from 11s–12s a week to 8s within the space of a year, even at Ferrybridge where railway construction continued to give employment to some labourers. Above all the labourers complained of want of employment: in the neighbourhood of Beverley, the greatest evil was 'the scarcity of work even at the reduced rate of rumuneration'.[126] At this time there were signs of a revival of interest in promoting emigration, the newly instituted Colonial Commissioners for Land and Emigration (1846) having provided a fresh source of passage money from the sale of crown lands in the colonies. At Banham in Norfolk the Revd Scott Surtees concluded that there was 'still more labour in this parish than there is profitable employment for' and gave instances of local men who had bettered themselves. Even James Spurling, recalled as 'a notoriously inferior workman', was reckoned four times better off than he would have been by remaining at Banham.[127] In Wiltshire, Lord Bruce took the initiative of forming an emigration association in September 1850, which in the following year despatched 258 persons, mostly agricultural workers and their dependants, to Australia while the Colonial Commissioners declined about 95 more nominees on various grounds of unsuitability. The party due to depart from Plymouth in *The Navarine* and *The Statesman* on 17 June encountered a minor problem which offers an interesting sidelight on the paradoxes of the time. They did not arrive until midnight, after lengthy delays at Exeter 'owing to the immense traffic on the line in consequence of the Great Exhibition'.[128]

Looking at the position of the agricultural worker through the period 1815–50, we find some features which are reminiscent of the situation of the industrial workforce in the inter-war years: the depressed level of prices improved the standard of living of those who remained regularly employed and there were strongly marked regional contrasts in employment prospects. Historians have shown a marked tendency to overlook the experience of farmworkers in counties where employment remained relatively secure, and it is salutary to recall that, in 1841, the West Riding employed more farmworkers than Wiltshire, while those of Lancashire approached twice the numbers in, say, Berkshire, Dorset, or Oxfordshire. On the other hand, the West Riding and Lancashire, together with ten more characterized by Caird as 'high-wage' counties, accounted for only just over a quarter of the total number of agricultural workers in England.[129] This weighting makes it difficult to avoid arriving at a pessimistic conclusion when assessing the position of farm employees in the round. John Clare's suggestion that they were 'a sort of foot-cushion for the benefit of others'[130] is justified and, as we have seen, there is ample reason to believe that social relations were put under severe and unprecedented strain during the period. There is no shortage of literary comment lamenting the rupturing of the agrarian interest and in particular expressing the view that among the labourers, 'attachment to their superiors, respect for their employers and loyalty to their rulers is fast passing away'.[131]

The charge most frequently levied against landlords by social historians is of increasing dereliction of their natural duties, or an 'abdication' of their role as governors.[132] We need not assume that this reflected the capture of their minds by a fresh set of doctrinaire, laissez-faire principles, although this was true of some individuals. Rather, their long-standing tendency to withdraw into the privacy of walled parks was reflected in increasing ignorance by successive generations of the lives of their poorer neighbours. As a frank letter from a London commercial traveller to Lord Stradbroke complained, they might be shielded from such knowledge by being 'surrounded only by toadyism and flunkeydom'.[133] For want of awareness, Sir George Crewe concluded, 'necessity was called Improvidence: Despair was deemed fecklessness; the broken-hearted and the worn-out were called Idle and Importunate'.[134] However, for their part landlords and their spokesmen tended to blame farmers for poor rural social relations. These were worsened, according to Charles Collyer of Gunthorpe in Norfolk, 'by the Farmers themselves, through ill will and opposition to their neighbours, refusing to employ their own poor'; while in Berkshire R.C. Lambert remarked, in the aftermath of the New Poor Law, that 'the illiberality of the Farmers towards the Poor by no means diminishes . . . I have endeavoured with little or no success to persuade Farmers in Parishes where I am certain that rates are decreased ... to subscribe to clothing funds, etc. but no – in many instances they the occupiers have as yet pocketed the difference . . . and gentlemen generally speaking have done the work for them'.[135] Of course farmers were a diverse set and no doubt Tennyson's distinction between 'old' and 'new style' men fell far short of exhausting the subject. The small Wealden farmers who at the time of the Swing riots showed signs of throwing in their lot with the labourers, or the Welsh farmers who dominated the Rebecca riots of 1839 and 1842–3, had little in common with large-scale entrepreneurs in the arable east of England, whose contact with their employees tended to be more remote. Such men as these were highly likely to occupy the offices of overseers or guardians, and it is significant that testimonies to the bitterness of social relationships tend to emerge chiefly from poor law-related literary sources: for example, the claim that 'All friendly relations between farmers and the poor ceases' (Burghclere, Hants., 1833), or the assertion heard in Suffolk by the *Morning Chronicle* investigator (1849), that the farmers would not speak to the labourers, 'except in terms of reproach and abuse'.[136]

These are, of course, vast generalizations. That there remained many landlords who were approachable, benevolent and well-regarded there is no doubt. Even the radical William Cobbett found space in his pages for favourable mentions of Lords Egremont and Winterton, Sir John Astley ('good to the common people'), and Mr Drummond of Albury, Surrey, 'famed for his justice and his kindnesses towards the labouring classes'.[137] Historical sources say even less about well-liked farmers, a breed one might assume to have died out, from the tenor of some writing on rural social history. Yet harvest frolics continued and were appreciated even in dismal Suffolk during the period, while the farmers of South Wiltshire were recalled as 'kindly in their disposition for the most part' by a contributor to *The Hungry Forties*, published in the Free Trade interest in 1904.[138] The difficulty is that satisfactory social relationships tend to leave no records. However, when we turn to the labourers' attitude to the established church, we have at least a vaguely quantitative basis from which to gauge the degree to which they had become detached from existing institutions.

Many clergymen of the period took their duties very lightly, and in possibly a rather extreme case, the *Kent and Essex Mercury* claimed to be able to point to 20 adjoining Essex parishes where two-thirds of the incumbents were absent and left their duties wholly to curates.[139] Others earned the resentment of farmers by their unrelenting attention to tithes. This did not touch the labourers directly and the example set by in 1832 by the Rector of Lockington (East Riding), who attempted to collect tithes on the wage of farmworkers, was happily rare if not unique.[140] The unpopularity of clergymen was likely to arise chiefly from their role on the bench. In the early Victorian period between a quarter and two-fifths of all magistrates were men of the cloth and some richly deserved the hatred of the poor, such as the Revd Vachell, Rector of Littleport, or James Cook of Whittlesea, described as 'a dam' bad un' in a threatening letter of 1816.[141] The rapid growth of village nonconformity is sometimes viewed as an index of dissatisfaction with the existing order, endorsed as it undoubtedly was by the Anglican church. Indeed religious revivalism, particularly Primitive

Methodism, has been portrayed as the passive (terrorism being the active) response to the suppression of the Swing riots.[142] Several studies have shown that nonconformity flourished more strongly in small market towns, rural craft centres, industrial villages and in parishes characterized as 'open' or 'much subdivided' in terms of landownership.[143] Moreover, the conspicuous absence of many labourers from any place of worship, pointed to in the *Morning Chronicle* survey, might appear to be an even more revealing sign of their alienation.[144] Yet the 1851 Religious Census showed that, overall, attendances were notably higher in the rural areas than in the towns, that the strongest areas of nonconformity were not generally in the south and east, and that the counties with the highest proportions of Anglican attenders were all predominantly agrarian in character.[145] Furthermore, if we take the ten agricultural registration districts most heavily dominated by labourers the index of attendance stood significantly above that of small towns and rural districts, and in all but two of them Anglican attendances easily surpassed all others combined.[146] Admittedly it can be assumed that labourers were present at church only to ingratiate themselves with their social superiors, or that they were merely a minority imbued with 'false consciousness'. All the same, such evidence queries the view that resistance to the dire pressures of the times can be readily interpreted in terms of class conflict and, as well, the suggestion that 'hatred and revenge were universally felt'.[147]

FOUR

The dawn of a new era? Farmworkers during the 'golden age' of agriculture

The symbolism of the Great Exhibition and the taking of an ambitious and accessible population census have made the year 1851 a kind of *annus mirabilis* for social historians. It cannot have been regarded as such by farmers, for as a whole agricultural prices remained lower than at any time during the first half of the century and, following a mild wet spring and hot summer, wheat averaged only 38s 6d a quarter, the lowest figure within living memory, or at least since 1780.[1] For all that, there was increasing recognition that although the battle over the Corn Laws had been lost, the situation was not irretrievable. As an Essex land agent put it, 'I fully believe that other things will in time accommodate themselves to the price of corn and that, under a new state of circumstances, the energetic and skilful farmer may prosper again', while even the ultra-Tory *Quarterly Review* was beginning to take the line that the prospects for British agriculturalists were 'not of a nature to lead to despondency'.[2] A turning point came in the Autumn of 1853 when, at the outbreak of the Crimean War, the prices of all classes of agricultural goods rose smartly. Over the years 1853–72 they would average 119 against 99 in 1848–52 and 1873–96, giving rise to what Ernle later described as the 'Golden Age' of agriculture. With hindsight, the conditions of this new-found prosperity can be discerned. Although by the early 1870s the proportion of imported wheat in total consumption had risen to nearly one-half, the general effect of free trade was to bring the world price of wheat up to the British level, rather than to severely depress the home price, which in 1853–72 averaged out at the reasonably remunerative figure of 54s 7d. However, it was less the enhancement of cereal prices which underpinned the 'Golden Age' than the buoyancy of livestock prices. Under the influence of rising living standards, the multiplication of urban consumers and improved railway facilities, prices obtained for beef were 43 per cent higher in 1871–5 than in 1851–5, while milk rose 40 per cent, mutton 35 per cent and wool prices fared at least equally well. In short, market conditions favoured a swing away from arable to livestock production. Such a shift indeed occurred, chiefly through the intensification of animal enterprises within mixed farming and by integrating wheat cultivation with the fattening of stock, although its extent was limited by a number of factors: these included a rooted prejudice in the minds of some farmers that their proper business was growing wheat, poor cost-accounting methods which made the more profitable lines of production difficult to identify and the reluctance of some landlords to consider erecting extra housing for livestock.[3]

Reflecting the new-found buoyancy of agriculture, rent increases, though variable, averaged about 25 per cent over the period. This looks like a handsome increment to landlords' incomes, though in many cases the increases were offset by expenditure on farm improvements. Between 1846 and 1876 landowners are believed to have poured some £24m. into drainage and other improvements, many of which never paid; indeed the investment sometimes produced a yield below the rate at which they borowed the necessary funds. Thus it is possible to detect behind the facade of the Golden Age a distinct weakening in the economic position of landlords.[4] This can be illustrated from the returns derived by the Duke of Bedford from his agricultural properties. In Bedfordshire and Buckinghamshire net income as a proportion of gross receipts declined from 49 per cent (1816–35) to 31 (1836–55) and 19 (1856–75) and on his Thorney estate in the Fens from 42 to 41 and 23 per cent.[5] On the whole, farmers fared better. Their aggregate income is computed as having risen from £123m. in 1851 to £155m. in 1870–3 and, within this figure, the 'incentive income' of farmers and their relatives (i.e. their return for initiative, effort, management, and risk) rose from £21m. to £44m. while the number of farmers scarcely changed.[6] Most large, well-managed estates enjoyed in these years a long waiting list of promising applicants. This is not to suggest that enhanced incomes simply fell into the farmers' laps, for, as ever, success in farming involved an ability to read the shifting conditions of prosperity correctly and 'the effort, technical skill and experience to make appropriate responses'.[7] From a social standpoint they remained an heterogeneous body. On the one hand their ranks included those who, though not considered gentlemen, could live a comparable life style – like the greater tenants on the Holkham estate, who resided in some state with a complement of domestic servants in houses with names such as Weasenham Hall, Burghwood Hall and Penworth Hall: on the other hand, no special cachet attached to being a farmer if a man were poor, even if his legal status were that of a freeholder. In Wales small owners were accounted 'probably the worst farmers in the Principality, and live from hand to mouth, a harder life than labourers'.[8]

The position of the farmworker during this period is particularly enigmatic. On the whole, students of agrarian economics infer that the workforce had a stake in the 'Golden Age'. The return to labour, says Jones, was 'expanded beyond precedent', while Thompson points to a rise of about 40 per cent in earnings, with particularly rapid increases coming in the early 1860s.[9] The impression that the position of the labourer was easing is supported by studies of the pattern of rural crime, which was mostly of a petty variety ranging from drunken and disorderly conduct through minor theft to poaching, which remained endemic. Actions embodying an element of social protest, however, declined: although in 1851 Caird could still suggest that 'A man might as well expose his life to the risk of a shot from a Tipperary assassin, as live, like a Cambridgeshire farmer, in constant apprehension of incendiarism', even in East Anglia the incidence of arson diminished. This was partly because the emotions of social protest were not running so high, and partly because of the socializing influences of education,

THE PIG AND THE PEASANT.

PEASANT. "AH! I'D LIKE TO BE CARED VOR HALF AS WELL AS THEE BE!"

(*Punch*, 19 September 1863)

religion, and a greater respect for law and order. Increasingly, fires were traced to the hand of vagrants and the labourers now invariably helped to extinguish them. All this is consonant with the view that the 1850s and 1860s saw a considerable strengthening of social cohesion, as society achieved a balance which most contemporaries regarded as satisfactory.[10] Yet social historians have taken a more sombre view. One might search in vain even a modern work such as Samuel's *Village Life and Labour* for any indication that wages were improving, while MacGregor insists that if these years were a 'Golden Age', then 'the human derelicts of an industrializing society who got subsistence by working on the land would not have recognized that description'.[11] In this tradition, any lessening of the incidence or seriousness of rural crime tends to be ascribed to the increased effectiveness of rural policing (under an act of 1856 the establishment of rural constabularies became compulsory) or to more insidious forces of social control, deployed so as to inculcate in the lower orders a meek acceptance of the status quo; discontent nevertheless rumbled just below the surface and found a new, more disciplined mode of expression in the agricultural trade unionism of the early 1870s.

The difficulties of drawing firm inferences from wages alone are considerable, for the familiar problems of their precise determination were still acute. Thus, Clifford noted that wages were in practice 'a mixed payment in coin and kind not easily estimated: varying as rents, cottage accomodation and size of garden do vary even in the same parish and upon the same occupation: and misleading not only outside critics, but the very parties to the contract, who see only dimly where they stand.'[12] Nevertheless, as a modern author has remarked, 'one should be prepared to sacrifice some of the finer points or risk losing the overall pattern in a confusion of local detail'.[13] Like his predecessors, Hunt is impressed by the differential between north and south. In 1851 Caird found weekly wages ranging from 15s a week in Lancashire to 6s in south Wiltshire. The average wage in 12 counties north of a line running approximately from the Wash to the Dee estuary (see map, p. 9) was estimated to be 37 per cent higher than in 19 counties to the south of this line, illustrating unequivocally the advantage of manufacturing enterprise to the prosperity and advancement of the farm labourer. These figures were thrown into a relationship with poor law expenditure in a most telling way[14]:

	'Northern Counties'	*'Southern Counties'*
Average wage	11s 6d	8s 5d
Average poor law rate per head of population	4s 7¾d	8s 8½d
Proportion of paupers to population	6.2	12.1

Looking at the situation again in 1867–70 a broad regional contrast in wages is still apparent, covering a range from 20s (Durham) to 11s 6d (Dorset and certain Welsh counties, i.e. Anglesey, Caernarvon, Pembrokeshire), while if attention is focused upon the counties considered by Caird, the evidence suggests a 19 per cent differential in favour of the north.[15] Either it was narrowing (a possibility acknowledged by Hunt), or Caird had exaggerated it twenty years before. However, its existence is beyond dispute and represents the firmest statement that can be made concerning wages. Unfortunately, the extent to which increases in money wages signified an advance in real terms is more difficult to decide, on the basis of the evidence available. The Bowley wage-index, already drawn on in earlier chapters, moves from 72 (1848–52) to 122 (1872), and may be set against Wood's retail price index and two independent series covering the wholesale prices of agricultural products (table 4.1). The three series agree in pointing to a noticeable advance in real earnings starting about 1869, but those generated by using indexes of agricultural prices convey a general impression that in real terms, wages stagnated during the 1850s and through most of the 1860s. However, the application of Wood's retail price series suggests a more cheery picture, especially for the early 1860s. It is unfortunate that little is known about the construction of this index, whose credibility depends chiefly on the massive reputation of its author.[16] If the case for improvement in the farm-worker's standard of life depended entirely on real wage movements some scepticism might indeed be justified. However, before any premature inferences are drawn it is necessary to review the extent and nature of farm mechanization

Table 4.1: Movement of farm workers' earnings, 1850–72*

		Real earnings		
	Earnings (Bowley)	*(using Wood's retail price index)*	*(using Rousseaux' agricultural price index)*	*(using Sauerbeck's agricultural price index)*
1850	100	100	100	100
1	100	103	104	101
2	100	103	104	100
3	115	109	100	95
4	129	106	101	96
5	133	106	102	99
6	133	106	102	101
7	126	106	95	93
8	117	107	105	100
9	118	110	103	99
1860	129	116	103	99
1	125	110	105	97
2	125	113	106	100
3	125	117	108	105
4	125	118	109	107
5	125	117	106	103
6	125	110	99	99
7	128	106	102	95
8	131	110	109	99
9	132	117	114	106
1870	133	118	117	107
1	145	128	118	111
2	157	134	119	116

* All series are taken from B. R. Mitchell and P. Deane, *Abstract of British Historical Statistics*, Cambridge, 1962, pp. 343, 349–50, 471–2, 474, recalculating the index numbers where necessary to the base 1850 = 100.

during the period; changes in the composition of the farm labour force; and evidence relating to the quality of the labourer's life in the 1850s and 1860s, as it was lived out in the subtly changing context of village life.

Agriculture remained a highly labour-intensive industry and, despite the promise of numerous exhibits at the Crystal Palace, farm mechanization made only limited progress. A number of spectacular steam cultivators were tested under actual field conditions, but it was not until after Fowler produced in 1856 a more reliable cable apparatus that an expansion of steam ploughing occurred. Even in 1867 only about 20,000 acres (about one part in a thousand of the arable acreage of Britain) was being regularly worked by steam. Among the factors which hindered its more rapid diffusion were the frequency of breakdowns and high cost of repairs, especially to cables and tines, excessively damp, uneven or strong terrain, and small field sizes. The editor of *Punch* was decidedly

A reaping machine of the kind used by progressive farmers, by Garretts of Leiston. From S. Copland, *Agriculture Ancient and Modern*, Virtue and Co., 1866.

premature when he suggested, in 1853, that the days of the ploughman were numbered:

> The stubble-headed ploughboy
> No more afield shall stride
> Smock-frocked, with whip on shoulders
> The steer or steed to guide.[17]

More rapid and extensive, though coming chiefly in the 1860s, was the spread of mechanical mowers and reapers which about 1870 might cost £30–36, as against £2,600 for a double-engine steam ploughing set, and by 1869 many of the larger arable farms cut their corn and hay with Hussey, Bell or McCormick machines. However, at all times scale of use was a major constraint on the adoption of relatively high-cost machinery and the importance of comparatively inexpensive machines such as hand-operated chaff and turnip cutters, horse-drawn hoes and simple seed drills (all costing under £10) in raising productivity without threatening to displace labour, should not be underestimated. Nor, indeed, should the final stages in the revolution of hand-harvesting techniques: there remained plenty of work for scythesmen and mowers, for between 1850 and the mid 1860s the bagging hook and the scythe appear to have gained ground even faster than the mechanical reaper.[18] From time to time, instances of labour opposition to machinery still occurred. Firings of workshops took place in Chelmsford in 1858 and East Dereham in 1860, while some expressed their opposition in more subtle ways. According to an item in the *Norfolk News*, men were known to make their horses nervous of mechanical reapers or break machines by turning too sharply. However, the knowledge that labourers were apt to chuckle over any difficulties encountered with machinery may have encouraged some employers to suspect their workpeople of undue carelessness or malice.[19] At all events, it is clear that there was no question of mechanization reducing the overall demand for labour on farms in the period, as expert observers agreed, any more than it brought down the number of horses in use for agricultural purposes. Thus, Clifford contended that the introduction of machinery 'set free some hands, but generally to employ them only in other ways' while Morton, stressing 'the more vigorous cultivation which the land now receives' concluded that more rather than less labour was needed, especially for tasks requiring skill and carefulness rather than great bodily strength.[20]

The 1851 census gives a detailed picture of the composition of the labour force at approximately its zenith.[21] From the published aggregates it appeared that there were 226,515 male and 22,916 female farmers in England and Wales, and the labour force is broken down by category in table 4.2.

Table 4.2: Distribution of farm employment, England and Wales, 1851*

	Males		*Females*	
	Number	*Percentage*	*Number*	*Percentage*
Bailiffs	10,000	0.9	—	—
Farmers' relatives (Son, daughter, brother, niece, etc.)	111,704	9.0	105,147	42.3
Farm servants (indoor)	189,116	15.3	99,156	39.9
Agricultural labourers and shepherds	921,195	74.5	44,319	17.9
Others in agriculture	3,535	0.3	18	—
	1,236,111	100.0	248,640	100.1

*Calculated from P.P. 1852–3, vol. LXXXVIII. *Census of Great Britain, Population Tables*, II, *Ages, Civil Condition, Occupations and Birth Places*, vol. I, pp. clxxii–ccxxvii. Note that a further 164,618 persons were included under the heading, 'Farmers' wives'.

In addition, farmers were required to state their acreages and numbers of employees. Unfortunately, farm sizes were not elicited for 9 per cent of all holdings. Moreover, nearly 41 per cent of farmers claimed to employ no work-people, or at least failed to mention any on their enumeration schedules, though these would have included those who were retired or for other reasons not currently occupying land, as well as men whose holdings were simply too small to require regular hired labour.[22] There is evidence to show that there was a considerable amount of variation in the way farmers responded to these questions, so that at the local level, the returns need to be treated with circumspection.[23] Nevertheless, they yield a useful if approximate picture of the national position. Viewed regionally, the distribution of workers and farm sizes fell into an intelligible pattern. As might be expected, outdoor labourers abounded where large holdings were common – in the east, south-east and south midlands where they accounted for over 80 per cent of all engaged in agriculture, and where one fifth of all holdings were above 500 acres in size. By contrast they were far scarcer in the north-west, in parts of Yorkshire, and of course in Wales, where farms were on average much smaller, leaned towards pastoral production, and relied much more upon family labour and indoor farm service.

Twenty years later, the census authorities attempted to elicit similar information, and produced a comparison of the returns made by farmers in 17 'representative counties' which suggested a small decline in the number of labourers to employing farmers, from 6.1:1 to 5.7:1.[24] This points to a reversal of the long-run tendency for such ratios to increase, and suggests the need for a closer inspection of changes in the size and composition of the farm labour force (table 4.3).

Table 4.3. Changes in the composition of the farm labour force, 1851–71*

	Percentage change 1851–61	*Percentage change 1861–71*	*Percentage change 1851–71*	*Absolute change 1851–71*
Males				
Farmers' relatives	−17	−17	−32	−35,238
Agricultural labourers and shepherds	+2	−16	−14	−133,298
Farm servants	−16	−15	−29	−54,959
Females				
Farmers' wives	−0.5	(Returns discontinued after 1861)		
Farmers' relatives	−20	+10	−12	−12,960
Farm servants	−53	−47	−75	−74,557
Agricultural labourers	−1	−24	−24	−10,806

* Data for 1851, as table 4.2; P.P. 1863, vol. LII. *Census of England and Wales, 1861*, II (Pt. I), *Ages, Civil Condition, Occupations and Birth Places*, pp. xlii–lxv; P.P. 1873, vol. LXXI. *Census of England and Wales, 1871*, III, *Ages, Civil Condition, Occupations and Birth Places*, pp. xxxvii–xlvii.

There is no doubt that female 'farmers' relatives', farm servants, and domestic servants were confused in these mid-nineteenth century census returns. For example, a farmer's niece living in and performing mixed duties around the farmhouse and farmyard, with occasional work in the fields, might well find her way into any of these categories. For this reason, the fall of 75 per cent in the number of female farm servants over just twenty years may seriously overestimate the extent of their decline, although it may be significant that female relatives on farms were also diminishing. At this time the number of domestic servants in England and Wales was rising rapidly, from 784,000 in 1851 to 1.23m. in 1871. An increase of some 30 per cent in their wages has been inferred from advertisements appearing in *The Times* newspaper, reflecting what the 1871 Census authorities described as an 'excessive demand for female servants' as the normative standards of middle-class living rapidly advanced during the 1850s and 1860s in cities, suburbs and country towns alike.[25] Moreover, table 4.3 suggests also that the number of farmers' co-residing male relatives contracted markedly. This, Wrigley has suggested, may be attributed to variations in censal procedures, which almost certainly allowed a sizeable overcount in 1851 which was subsequently corrected: but the sons of smaller farmers particularly may have envisaged better prospects in the towns or indeed abroad, like the sizeable contingents 'in the flower of life' noticed leaving Llanbrynmair for America in July 1852.[26] More can be said about the further decline in male farm servants, although here again, important regional contrasts present themselves. In the south, indoor farm service continued its secular decline, finding a reflection, according to an elderly farmer from Marston Morteyne (Beds.), in a want of that respect for and attachment among young labourers to those above them, which used to characterize their forefathers. Or, conditions of service were diluted, as in the case of Hertfordshire: here the younger boys were brought food from home while older lads were expected to find their own provisions which in some cases were cooked for them, though in others they were expected to make use of the 'messroom with fireplace' found on most farms, rather than eating with the farmer's own family.[27] This style of service would have been unrecognizable in the north, where indoor farm service continued and in some counties (e.g. the North Riding, Westmorland and Lancashire) actually accounted for an increasing proportion of hired staff in the 1851–71 period, or in Wales. However, the reasons for the survival of farm service are easier to enumerate than to weigh. It flourished where farmsteads were relatively isolated from the villages (e.g. the Yorkshire Wolds) and wherever there was a combination of small farms, pastoral activities (needing men to be on hand at any hour of day or night), rugged terrain and manufacturing activity within reasonable proximity, which increased the need for servants whose annual contracts made them more reliable.[28] Everywhere, hiring fairs in the larger towns showed greater survival powers than those in the smaller ones; at Hull, Selby and York, for example, against Hedon or Howden. This tendency was strengthened by the willingness of young men to move further afield in the age of the railway. A case in point was Thomas Irving who first attended the Penrith hirings in 1856: his subsequent movements show a range extending to reach Hexham in Northumberland, and also a tendency to intersperse his engagements with periods of living at home relying on piecework.[29]

To what extent did farmers look to women and children for field work, either to make economies or to fill the gap caused by the loss of farm servants and their departing relatives? At the time, public attention focused mainly on the gang system which, despite its condemnation in the 1843 report, continued to flourish through the 1850s and 1860s. In the main these gangs were concentrated in Lincolnshire, the Fens and East Anglia, though they were not entirely unknown elsewhere: at Penrith in about 1849, eight male and seven female gang-masters were reputed to exist who between them employed some 300 women and children 'of the lowest class'. The precise composition of these groups varied, but usually, as at Binbrook (Lincs.), March (Cambs.) and Grimston (Norfolk), 40–50 per cent were juveniles aged from 7–13.[30] It was not until after a further enquiry that the Gangs Act of 1867 laid down that no child under eight might be employed; that no woman or girl could be employed in a gang in which men worked; and that gang-masters should be licensed by Justices of the Peace after enquiries into their character. This act may have been successful in getting rid of the worst characters but it was easy to evade the spirit of the law while complying with its letter, for example by making 'public' gangs become 'private' through the simple expedient of the farmer paying members directly.

This was done promptly in a number of Lincolnshire towns in the year following the act.

It is easy to become over-preoccupied with the gang system; as in the case of the factories, public opinion was more sensitive to the hardships and moral changes to which women and children were exposed when they appeared in a concentrated form. Moreover, it would be misleading to infer from evidence of this kind that there was increased reliance on child and female field labour at the expense of the livelihood of adult male workers. Indeed, on the evidence of table 4.3 the number of female agricultural labourers was small, and declined by 10,000 over twenty years. It is true that the censuses (taken in late March or early April) are a very imperfect guide to the extent of female and juvenile employment. We might expect them to have included permanent female agricultural workers such as the bondagers of Northumberland who, in their characteristic dress of a rough straw bonnet, kerchief, short cotton dress, apron of sackcloth, woollen stockings and stout hobnailed boots, were still to be found in the 1850s and 1860s undertaking virtually all of the tasks of the farm except ploughing and ditching: also perhaps the dozen stout women and girls encountered at Brotherton near York in 1862 by a solicitor, Arthur Munby, for they were 'regular day labourers' and had 'no other occupation'. But the enumerators would not have identified as agricultural workers the gang of young women, 'ordinarily pit wenches', which he came across at Twickenham fruit-picking and who told him they came there in June, usually for about nine weeks.[31] Nor would they have picked up the legion of cottagers' wives who found employment at harvest time, or part-time child workers whose tasks included, in the spring, stone-picking, potato-setting and the lonely and monotonous task of bird-scaring, or tending grazing animals for some 3d–6d a day. Yet, despite these various qualifications regarding the coverage of the censuses, the likelihood is that these years saw a modest decline in the involvement of adult females. According to Snell this was merely the continuation of a long term tendency, at least in the south and east, which had been interrupted only briefly during the French Wars and for a few years in reaction to the pressures exerted by the introduction of the New Poor Law. His argument implies that women had little choice in the matter, and that the direction of change was unmistakeable long before Victorian moral sentiments regarding the proper role of women came into vogue.[32] Nevertheless, there were signs that they were becoming increasingly unwilling to take up field work, as if tacitly agreeing that all outdoor work had 'the most certain effect of vitiating the female character, and debasing every finer feeling'. In the late 1860s Farmer Rollinson of Igborough (Norfolk) had been unable to get a woman worker in the last three years, while at nearby Salhouse it was remarked that the women 'did not care to come out' as their husbands' wages improved. At Felthorpe in the same county able-bodied women were said to prefer to walk three miles to the paper mill at Taverham, and in Bedfordshire straw-plaiting and even the bizarre occupation of onion-peeling in the district of Sandy provided alternatives. Likewise, in the Westhampnett Union (Sussex), female labour 'once largely used' was, by the late 1860s, rarely employed outside hay and harvest time, and at Slinfold there was scarcely one-tenth of the employment of labour characteristic of twenty years before.[33]

The smaller involvement of females in field work was part of a widespread, though very gradual tendency to decasualization. The seasonal exchange of labour between town and country which Samuel has depicted so vividly[34] continued; however, the trend over time has been investigated from the farmer's angle in greater detail, with special reference to the corn harvest. In contrast to the position in Arthur Young's day, by the 1860s industrial wages were usually higher than even the peak agricultural wage obtainable by most casual workers, not least because the shift to the use of the scythe and the bagging-hook tended to confine them to the less rewarding, subordinate tasks of gathering and binding. Moreover, the flow of 'Celtic' harvest-labour was beginning to falter. The Welsh influx to the English Midlands and the Border counties of Shropshire and Herefordshire fell away from the 1850s as the population of the source areas drifted to the developing South Wales coalfield, and even the annual influx of Irish harvesters was waning. Their numbers appear to have risen sharply in the aftermath of the Famine, 1846–50, and subsequently, on account of massive emigration and improved opportunities at home, fell away to level off in the 1880s at some 20–30,000, or approximately one-third of the peak of the late 1840s. Increasingly the Irish contingent fell back on districts especially noted for high wages (the Fens and Yorkshire Wolds), and particularly those adjacent to the quays (Lancashire and Cheshire). Against the background of a probable increase of some 20–25 per cent in the demand for harvest labour over the period 1835–70, complaints of shortages became numerous and harvest earnings showed a tendency to rise faster than agricultural wage-rates in general, increasing between 1849 and 1859 by fully 30 per cent on a sample of 42 farms.[35] The drying-up of these alternatives was one of the factors encouraging the spread of the mechanical reaper; however, the situation was also favourable to young, vigorous, full-time agricultural workers. By the 1850s it had in some areas become 'almost a tradition that ambitious young men should take to the roads in the summer, selling their labour to the highest bidder' says Collins, instancing flows from North Hampshire into Sussex and Wiltshire, Stour Valley scythesmen into Foulness and the Marsh Hundreds, Vale of Taunton men to the Mendips and Dalesmen into the Yorkshire Wolds. Conversely, the flows were cometimes reversed at haytime, as is illustrated by the recollections of William Blades who in July 1862 strode forth from Nunnington in the East Riding to Conistone in the West for the hay harvest, where he was paid £4 plus lodging and washing, with abundant food: here he returned nine years in succession.[36]

There is no reason to suppose that the gains of migrant workers, whether drawn from English towns, from Ireland, or from other agricultural districts, were at the expense of local people, for normally outsiders were not taken on until all local labour was taken up, and custom decreed that the first refusal of casual work was given to the wives and dependants of permanent workers. In particular, they were unlikely to displace adult males. It is important to recall here the evidence of table 4.3, which suggests only a tiny increase in the number of agricultural labourers during the decade 1851–61 and a considerable fall of 133,298 in 1861–71, which meant that for every farm servant lost in the decade, some 2.4 labourers disappeared from view. This must have enhanced the prospects of those who remained on the land. Of course, the improvement was gradual and incomplete. It would be erroneous to conclude that the horrors of underemployment or seasonal unemployment simply melted away in the mid-Victorian period. Still, taken in the round the inference must be that male workers were more regularly employed as the demand for and supply of labour more nearly approached equilibrium, due to the townward migration and to the progress made by agriculture in raising production and creating opportunities for employment. This has rarely been traced in detail, though an excellent pioneering study has provided a useful illustration from the extensive Bodrhyddon estate in the Vale of Clwydd. Here, the modification of cultivation patterns and a considerable augmentation of herd and flock sizes tended to reduce the aggregate amount of labour required, particularly from females and casuals; but seasonal variations in employment diminished markedly and the number of days worked by individual named men rose considerably, especially among those tending livestock.[37] To sum up, the case for inferring an improvement in the farm worker's position rests less on demonstrable improvements in real wages than on better opportunities to earn those wages.

An examination of more direct evidence on material standards of living should begin, no doubt, with food consumption. To view the labourer's diet at its best, contemporary accounts agree, his cottage needed to be visited at Christmas when most employers were in the habit of presenting their workmen with a piece of beef, graded carefully according to size of family, or even on occasion a fowl. This would be enjoyed with, perhaps, a Christmas cake or pudding and apples or hazelnuts gathered in the Autumn, a bottle of elderberry wine and some sweets in the form of white and pink sugar mice or pigs. During the rest of the year the fare was of a much less exciting kind with boiled salt pork accounting for something like two-thirds of all meat consumed, the rest being offal such as bullock's or pig's liver, a sheep's head and pluck, or chitterlings, the nutritional value of which had not yet been recognized by those who kept daintier tables.[38] Nor did the families of those fortunate enough to keep pigs usually consume the choicer joints, which were often sold to raise cash to pay for flour and boots, or to settle accounts run up with local shopkeepers. However, the most systematic evidence on food consumption comes from a study of 377 English farmworkers chosen as 'representative in their industry, thrift and intelligence' in a survey conducted by Edward Smith of the Medical Department of the Privy Council in 1863. The results of this enquiry are summarized in table 4.4, where the nutritional standards reached by farmworkers' families are compared with those of workers in 'indoor occupations', mostly domestic manufacturers such as silk weavers from Spitalfields, Coventry and Macclesfield, and needlewomen, glovers, stocking and shoemakers.[39] These figures are, of course, averages. Burnett has drawn attention to the way in which regional differentials in earnings were reflected in northern and southern menus and to the rule that the lion's share of the best food went to the man, a situation accepted by the wife, in Smith's words, as 'right, and even necessary for the maintenance of the family'. Both points emerge from these specimen menus:

> WILTSHIRE (Case No. 211). *Breakfast* – water broth, bread and butter. *Dinner* – husband and children have bacon (sometimes), cabbage, bread and butter. Wife has tea. *Supper* – potatoes or rice . . .

Table 4.4: Diets of indoor and outdoor workers, 1863*

Quantities	*Indoor workers*	*Rural workers*
Bread (lbs./week)	9.1	11.6
Sugar (oz./week)	7.9	6.6
Potatoes (lbs./week)	2.4	4.4
Milk (pts./week)	0.8	1.6
Meat (oz./week)	12.3	15.3
Fats (oz./week)	4.7	5.2
Nutritional equivalents		
K. cals (per day)	2,190	2,760
Protein (gms./day)	55	70
Fat (gms./day)	53	54
Carbohydrate (gms./day)	370	460
Iron (M.gms./day)	12.5	15.9
Calcium (gms./day)	0.36	0.48

*T.C. Barker, D.J. Oddy and J. Yudkin, *The Dietary Surveys of Dr Edward Smith, 1862–3*, Department of Nutrition, Queen Elizabeth College, University of London, Occasional Paper No. 1, Staples Press, 1970, p. 43. The calculation of calories and nutrients was made by computer from tables of food composition.

> LINCOLNSHIRE (Case No. 248). *Breakfast* – milk gruel, or bread and water, or tea and bread. *Dinner* – meat for husband only: others vegetables only. *Tea and supper* – bread or potatoes.

> LANCASHIRE (Case No. 304) *Breakfast* – milk porridge, coffee, bread and butter. *Dinner* – meat and potatoes, or meat pie, rice pudding or a baked pudding; the husband takes ale, bread or cheese. *Supper* – tea, toasted cheese, and bacon instead of butter.[40]

The shortcomings of the aggregated diets, analysed in table 4.4, are obvious enough. Like those encountered in third world countries today they are strong on carbohydrates, arising from the heavy consumption of such 'filling' foods as bread and potatoes, but show inadequacies with respect to the consumption of protein, fats and calcium, reflecting modest levels of meat and milk consumption. Still, the intake of calories, protein, iron and calcium among rural workers was substantially higher than that of their 'indoor' contemporaries and in some respects as high as, or higher than those revealed in low-income diets of the 1930s or even 1965.[41] Reflecting this dietary situation and the outdoor nature of their work, health conditions among farm workers were, by contemporary standards, moderately good; Grey remembered few serious ailments among the cottagers of Harpenden and recalled both the middle-aged and the young as a 'strong, hard-working, healthy set of people'.[42] However, statistical evidence tends to suggest a more complex picture. According to the morbidity statistics of the Manchester Unity of Oddfellows for 1846–8, the record of 'aggregate sickness' among its 'rural labourers' aged 20–60 was bettered by a number of trades and was 6 per cent above that registered for rural districts as a whole; likewise in 1856–60 they ranked only seventh (out of 23 occupational groups) with respect to sickness. On the other hand, the rural labourers' longevity was the highest of all groups considered in 1856–60, and exceeded only by carpenters in 1846–8, making them a very good example of the lack of congruence between morbidity and mortality rates which is general in these mid-nineteenth-century statistics.[43]

The relatively high proportion of income which was necessarily devoted to the purchase of food limited advances in other respects. At this income level incipient consumerism expressed itself primarily through shifts towards 'smarter' dress, especially among the young. In southern England smocks were slowly going out of use, being replaced by 'slop' jackets made of strong 'canvas-looking cloth' or in the winter, short thick overcoats of navy or blue cloth known as 'reefers', worn with corduroy trousers and sometimes leggings. Instead of a clean smock, the younger men desired a ready-made cloth suit for Sunday best, especially if keeping company, and a pair of boots lighter than the stout-soled hobnailed boots, dressed with tallow and grease, that were their ordinary footwear during the rest of the week. Women's wear changed rather less in this period, and frivolous attire was distinctly discouraged by organizers of village clothing clubs to which wives and mothers were encouraged to subscribe; but young women, like their male counterparts, aspired to a lighter kind of boot, often with elastic sides, to go with the best dress made up by cottage dressmakers from materials purchased from itinerant packmen or village drapers.[44]

'Walking-out', when couples sought to look at their smartest, was the prelude to marriage and procreation, nor necessarily in that order. Pre-nuptial conceptions which duly led to the altar were commonplace, and studies based on the family reconstitution method have shown a high but variable range running in 1800–49 from 15 per cent of first live births (Gainsborough, Lincs.) to 59 per cent (Gedling, Notts.). Becoming pregnant was one way of securing a husband and in Snell's view was encouraged by the precariousness of female employment.[45] But it was not an entirely reliable strategy, and the fact that illegitimate birth rates were distinctly higher in the rural areas than in the towns was attested to again and again in data collected by the Registrar-General during the nineteenth century. It has been shown, when data is arranged according to the proportion of illegitimate births, that counties varied relatively little in their position in the rank order. In 1842 the servant-keeping county of Cumberland, where 11 per cent of all births were illegitimate, topped the list, as indeed it still did in 1870–2; yet Norfolk, a county offering many contrasts, ran a close second in 1842, came fourth in 1870–1 and actually headed the table thirty years later.[46] Despite all this evidence of rampant rural sexuality, it should not be concluded that farmworkers and their brides were impelled into exceptionally early marriage, by mid-nineteenth-century norms. The contributor to the *Cornhill Magazine* who invited his readers to picture the labourer 'some fine morning, before he is two and twenty, on his way from church, with his bride, who is only seventeen', exaggerated wildly.[47] The 1911 Census, which was the first to carry questions on fertility, makes it possible to peer back as far as the marriages of the mid-nineteenth century. We do so at some risk, because it could reckon only with survivors whose life-histories may not have been typical. From these data, the average age at marriage of farmworkers' wives married in 1861–71 was 22.2, against an average for England and Wales of 22.5, and the number of children they bore was only 4–5 per cent higher than the corresponding national figures. Nevertheless, this meant that in general, labourers' wives would produce five to six children each, and it is important to notice here the superior survival chances of children born in rural areas. When this is taken into consideration, the effective family sizes for the farmworkers' marriages of the 1850s and 1860s stood about 11 per cent higher than the national norm.[48] This factor is of no small significance in assessing the position of agricultural workers in relation to other groups, or indeed, as individuals, to one another. Moreover, the demographic profile found its reflection in patterns of saving, which for the most part was confined to single men and women and, particularly, to farm servants. The Annual Report of the Penrith branch of the Carlisle Savings Bank for 1868 showed that the average deposit of 260 male servants stood at £35, and of 240 females, £33. Outside their ranks, there can have been few systematic savers: as Grey recalled, a few were thrifty, 'but this one thing I noticed, that nearly all these thrifty ones were men with only one or two children or no family at all'.[49] For all his exaggerations, the anonymous contributor to the *Cornhill Magazine* was correct in identifying the stage at which the labourer had to maintain a number of young children as 'the most trying time of the peasant's life', and in this he showed awareness of what Rowntree was later to call the 'poverty cycle': significantly, Snell's work on settlement examinations shows that 34 was the age at which men were most likely to become chargeable to the poor rates.[50] The labourer's condition would be eased as his children went out to work or into service, but by this time he would be in his mid-forties. After the lapse of another decade he could expect to bear successive wage reductions and would in illness be driven to the union, as would his wife, and there they would end their days.

That this hypothetical cycle was actually enacted in the lives of thousands of farmworkers there is no doubt, although like all such models it threatens to obscure the diversity of individual experience. Certainly, it appears to exaggerate the role of the union workhouse, for it was only in exceptional cases, such as the Atcham Union in Shropshire under the firm control of its chairman, Sir Baldwin Leighton, that the policies of the central poor law authorities were carried through to the letter.[51] As a general rule, control over relief tended to pass increasingly into the hands of elected guardians including a preponderance of farmers. This did not always assist the seemliness of proceedings; the rector of Wortham, Suffolk, was shocked by the way in which the simple-minded Billy Rose was 'most scandalously jeered and treated in a manner very unbecoming' when he applied for relief for the first time in thirty years.[52] However, if recent studies of relief policies in Norfolk are any guide, actual practice formed less of a contrast with the regime of the Old Poor Law than is commonly supposed, for during the 1850s and 1860s well over 80 per cent of all able-bodied paupers in the county were in receipt of outdoor relief. While entailing some manipulation of the returns sent up by the guardians to their London masters, this policy suited the poor and was seen as more economical than indoor relief by the ratepayers who, it should not be forgotten, included numerous working men.[53]

The consequence in many parts of the south and east was that the new workhouses were half-empty: they became and remained the last recourse of those so incapacitated by infirmity or old age that institutional provision was the only means of keeping them alive. There remained a strong reluctance to enter them, not because material conditions were excessively bad, but because of the psychological trauma involved. However, our readiness to condemn this form of institutionalized provision for the aged should be tempered by a recognition that, in the second half of the twentieth century, satisfactory answers to the problem continue to elude us.

The other arm of mid-Victorian 'welfare' provision for the poor was charity, which took many forms. A few landlords took a doctrinaire view of potentially pauperising doles. For example, the appeal of the curate of Wing in Bedfordshire to a new landowner that 'there is not upon any, so direct a claim as on yourself, the owner of the soil', was promptly repudiated by Lord Overstone (a banker) who disclaimed any personal responsibility for the distress of the poor and added a lecture couched in Malthusian terms: 'Casual charity, administered only under the influence of kind feeling, and not directed by any principle to an effectual correction of the evil causes at work, usually does but little of even apparent, nothing of real good'.[54] However, most landlords acknowledged some responsibilities in this area. From the scrutiny of estate records it is estimated that the aristocracy devoted some 4–7 per cent of their gross income to charitable purposes in the mid-nineteenth century and gentry families perhaps 1–2 per cent, while many gave blankets, calicoes and coal to their workpeople at Christmas and during the winter.[55] Amid signs of an increasing scarcity of labour, farmers, too, tended to increase their philanthropic activities, recognizing that 'the good workman would serve that master who took the greatest care of his moral and domestic comforts'.[56] The village clergy played an especially important role. As well as being involved in the distribution of endowed charitable funds (sometimes, it is true, showing a strong bias against dissenters), it is probable that, as a body and in relation to their means, parsons and their families tended to lay out a more considerable proportion of their incomes in charitable purposes. Moreover, in the course of the pastoral visiting to which the younger generation of clerics attached great importance, they performed innumerable acts of kindness: Augustus Jessop was not the only young curate who could have claimed that his experience extended 'from writing a letter to making a will, and from setting a bone to stopping a suicide'.[57] There were, it is true, many drawbacks to charity as a means of alleviating distress. Variations in charitable provision between villages bore no necessary relationship to the extent of their needs (open parishes in particular were apt to be poorly provided for due to the absence of a major proprietor); it was capricious; and the deference and gratitude expected in return could be humiliating to recipients. At Tysoe in Warwickshire, awareness that what was managed by the vicar as a charity estate was in fact the town lands and, properly speaking, communal property, caused some village friction. Joseph Ashby's mother declined to take 8s 6d offered by the vicar's wife and another woman ostentatiously immersed her parcel of unbleached calico and scarlet flannel, to wash the charity out of it. Nevertheless, as a rule the labourer felt himself and was believed by his neighbours to be far less dishonoured by accepting private charity than by receiving public assistance,

Billie Main's Cottages at Bunkle, Berwickshire, from W. J. Gray, *A Treatise on Rural Architecture*, Lizars, Edinburgh, 1852. The illustration shows new cottages and those which they replaced, *c*.1848. Single-storey cottages were common on both sides of the border.

and even in Tysoe, years later, less independent spirits were still curtseying gratefully to the vicar's wife and her sister when they brought round the flannel.[58]

The concept of charity can be extended to cover cottage-building, which in the eyes of landlords was a philanthropic activity since it could never be made to pay, except, hopefully, by improving the character of the occupants. During the 1840s and after, sanitary reformers had no difficulty in producing numerous instances of 'shattered hovels' set in 'low, damp' situations with cess-pools or accumulations of filth close to their doors, their occupants sometimes dependent on ponds and ditches for their supplies of drinking water.[59] In addition, rural housing was in short supply. Before the passing of the Union Chargeability Act of 1865, the settlement laws continued to discourage building and occasional cases of cottage clearances still occurred, as at Charlton Marshall (Dorset), where 43 habitations were dismantled in 1851–61 while the population nevertheless grew by 90 souls.[60] At the mid-century, shortages were reflected in comparatively high rents, which Caird claimed had doubled since 1770, and in the frequency of multiple occupation. Thus on the Holkham estate 45 per cent of cottages could be regarded as overcrowded while at Milton Abbas (Dorset) the cottages flanking the main street, which are so much admired and photographed today, were, in the 1840s, grossly overfilled.[61] Of course, the period saw the publication of numerous pattern books and, to a limited extent, the construction of sound, brickbuilt cottages which are still occupied today. However, their builders often took the opportunity to pull down older tenements which disgraced their villages. On the Bedford estates in Bedfordshire and Buckinghamshire, 372 new cottages were erected between 1846 and 1861, but the

Duke had 'a wholesome fancy for the destruction of bad ones', being 'generally credited with pulling down three cottages for every one he has built'.[62] Whether or not this is literally true, the record accords with the general feeling, expressed for example in a *Norfolk News* survey of 1863, that the condition of cottages owned by aristocratic landlords tended to be better than those of the lesser gentry, while those belonging to tradesmen and village speculators were undoubtedly the worst, including some which were owner-occupied. The nub of the matter was stated by a Norwich sanitary inspector, Samuel Clarke: there was a need not only to build new cottages, but enough new cottages.[63] It cannot be said that the need was met in the period, although in two respects the comforts of the cottager stood to improve. First, the provision of gardens, allotments and potato patches made further progress. Although in the arable east of England whole villages which lacked these amenities could still be found, they were widespread in many counties by the late 1860s, notably in Hampshire, Devon, Hereford, Lancashire and in Yorkshire where cottage gardens were virtually universal. Secondly, while the collection of wood for firing continued as a general practice, the spread of railways went far towards completing a process which the canals had begun years before, of augmenting fuel supplies by bringing cheaper coal to the rural parishes of southern and eastern England, enabling subscribers to the 'coal clubs' found in numerous villages to take as much as half a ton at a time.[64]

The provision of schooling was, to some degree, another field for charity; it should certainly be considered part of the return to labour, and it takes us from the material to the mental milieu of the labourer and his dependants. Suffolk, for example, stood high among the counties characterized by widespread illiteracy in the 1840s. No fewer than 143 parishes lacked a day school, while in 26 schools Glyde found only 7 per cent of pupils aged above twelve and 50 per cent below eight, giving evidence of the shortness and perfunctory nature of attendance. To him, the fact that 42 per cent of the 2,133 persons committed to Ipswich gaol in 1847–52 could neither read nor write and only 3.6 per cent could perform well at both, signified both a danger and a need. Generally speaking, provision was better in the north, although Grey's statement that Northumbrian children were 'not unfrequently capable of extracting the square and cube root with great expedition and accuracy' may well exaggerate the contrast.[65] However, under the impetus of the voluntary school movement, hundreds of new schools came into existence in the middle decades of the nineteenth century. In Devon, for example, over 150 national, church or endowed, and 15 rival British and Foreign or nonconformist establishments appeared between 1840 and 1870, in the context of a nation-wide effort which increased the number and capacity of voluntary schools four or five-fold in the 25 years ending in 1861.[66] In them, a heavy emphasis on learning by rote and on the inculcation of the three 'R's made for monotony, from which children were anxious to escape, as hundreds of surviving school logbooks show, whenever their labour was in demand on the farms. Moreover, the tedium was aggravated in some measure after the institution for assisted schools of 'payment by results' in 1862, which made government grants dependent on a capitation fee paid in respect of each child attaining a satisfactory standard in an annual examination conducted by an inspector. Still, despite the qualitative deficiencies of this style of education when judged from a twentieth-century standpoint, the battle against illiteracy was being won, by degrees. By the time of the 1870 Education Act, it was considerably reduced. Thus, a study based on 14 Lincolnshire marriage registers shows a fall in the numbers of labourers and their brides signing with a mark, for males from 52 (1837–50) to 33 per cent (1851–75) and for females, from 62 to 29 per cent. Applying the usual convention that those able to sign could read and write, and that a further 50 per cent of those signing with a mark were nevertheless able to read, it follows that before 1850 some 30 per cent of the labourers and over 40 per cent of their wives were illiterate, but that after that date the great majority of both brides and grooms reached basic literacy.[67] This was no mean achievement in view of the chronic difficulties experienced in raising adequate funds, in Lincolnshire as elsewhere.[68] As a rule, farmers tended to be lukewarm concerning the schooling of their future labourers, and although a profession of interest was more common among landowners, even they were far from dependable. The great Lord Leicester supported only one school at Holkham, and initiated none of the others found on the estate, paying out in 1855 only £46 in school subscriptions, rising to £73 by 1865. Many did less: the report of the Newcastle Commission on Popular Education (1861) felt bound to state that 'as a class the landowners, especially those who are non-resident (though there are many honourable exceptions) do not do their duty in support of popular education'.[69] In this as in other fields of 'social work', much depended on the tenacity of the parson, and some individuals took an ongoing interest in maintaining the skills picked up in school, which were so easily lost through disuse. It was in this spirit that the Brooke Deanery Association provided facilities for reading such periodicals as *The Illustrated Times, The Churchman's Magazine* and *Sunday at Home* in 13 Norfolk parishes in the mid 1850s, and we may suspect that clerical prompting lay behind the establishment by Major Stapylton, of Myton Hall in Yorkshire, of a reading room and the Wass Mental Improvement Society, 'devoted to the intellectual advancement of its members', in the early 1860s. Wives and daughters of the clergy were frequently involved, none more deeply than Mary Simpson, daughter of the incumbent of Boynton and Carnaby (East Riding) who became celebrated for her devotion to Sunday classes for ploughboys, even going out into the fields where they worked to recruit them.[70]

Many clergymen also took an active interest in promoting the spirit of self-help, as expressed in the friendly society movement which was expanding rapidly during these years. On the other hand, clerical interest in the moral welfare of parishioners could take some decidedly negative forms. Within the church itself the targets of reformers might include bell-ringing and church music, seeking to replace male instrumentalists prone to unseemly behaviour with choirs of children and an organ played by the incumbent's wife.[71] Outside it, the clergy sometimes opposed old-established games and pastimes. Hiring and amusement fairs and long-standing customs such as the crying of largesse at the conclusion of the harvest (seen by labourers as a legitimate component of their earnings but by critics as a form of mendicity), and farmers' harvest frolics, especially if held in public houses, were frequently the target of clerical criticism. At Banham (Norfolk) the Revd S. F. Surtees was active from 1854 in promoting monster tea parties in their stead, where aristocrats and other worthies made speeches giving sound advice, and from the 1860s many parishes instituted a day of harvest thanksgiving, characterized by a special morning service and followed by a celebratory tea.[72] In the pursuit of moral improvement clerical reformers sometimes met with hostility or indifference (the Banham experiment was described in 1867 as 'by no means a complete success'), and did not escape being blamed for spreading a 'black parsonic gloom' in the villages.[73] The leaders of the nonconformist churches shared the mistrust of the reforming clergy towards the indecorous traditional culture and the ancient beliefs which went with it. Neither parson nor minister was likely to agree to say a few words over a stricken sow, or intervene in cases of witchcraft, nor could they be expected to accept alleged wizards or 'wise men' as legitimate rivals, which up to a point they still were among the rural poor. To this extent, church and chapel were at one in opposing what they called superstition and what today's historians, more cautiously describe as 'pre-scientific attitudes of mind' or 'the prior culture'.[74] In other respects they were rivals, for village nonconformity provided a haven for those suspicious of the close connection between the landed interest and the church. Wesleyan Methodism played a particularly important role in the establishment of village Sunday Schools and enjoyed some success in holding adults attracted by its relative spontaneity and informality. One aspect of its appeal was that within its organizational framework the respectable worker might become a steward, class leader, or even a local preacher. However, if the case of South Lindsey is typical, labourers were distinctly under-represented among office-holders. Primitive Methodism was more likely to be encountered in open villages with large populations and numbered proportionally more labourers and cottagers among its chief adherents, which supports the view that it was 'in an important sense a working-class sect'. On the other hand it attracted far fewer farmworkers than the parish churches and the Wesleyan chapels, which gave the Primitive Methodist Church a curiously ambivalent role as a nursery of village radicalism which never succeeded in building up a mass membership among the labourers.[75] Indeed, it has to be said that despite their involvement in so many aspects of village life, none of the churches was especially successful in gaining a firmer hold over the hearts and minds of the lower strata of village communities. Although the unique Religious Census of 1851 showed that attendance ratios in the countryside were significantly higher than in the towns, there were many signs of creeping erosion. Using a number of returns from Lincolnshire, Obelkeich has shown that few young labourers in the 1860s were regular attenders at communion services, suggesting that instead of inaugurating adult religious practice, confirmation frequently marked the end of the period of Sunday School attendance. Meanwhile on the Yorkshire Wolds, where once farmers had been in the habit of hiring lads on the understanding that they would attend church, the custom had fallen into disuse by the early 1860s, 'because the young servants so resisted it'.[76]

Our review of the various factors which impinged on the life of the mid-Victorian farmworker tends, on balance, to support the view that the period saw some amelioration of conditions. However, progress was decidedly modest and contingent in several respects on migration, which was considerable, though not on a scale so great as to promote dramatic improvements in the position of those who remained on the land. This statement requires a little elaboration. When village populations are examined in detail using the census returns, the degree of mobility seems low. In the Berkshire villages of Ardington and Lockinge in 1851, 64 per cent of residents were natives, as were 72 per cent of the inhabitants of 'Ashworthy' (Devon). At Elmdon (Essex) ten years later, the native-born accounted for 81 per cent of the male population and as many as 87 per cent of farmworkers.[77] As Snell has suggested, the long-term erosion of farm service in the south and the abolition in 1834 of service for a year as one of the 'heads' under which rights of settlement could be gained, worked together with some curtailment of non-resident relief to inhibit local mobility.[78] Moreover, many farmworkers were notoriously averse to long-distance migration. Dorset labourers were said to consider transference to the industrial north as no less terrible than migration overseas, and some Devon men were unsure whether or not the northern counties were overseas, as Canon Girdlestone of Halberton found when in 1866 he embarked upon a scheme of organizing migrations to high wage areas, to the chagrin of local farmers.[79] Against this, we know that *net* losses from the 'rural residues' of England and Wales were considerable, totalling 443,000 in 1841–51, and 743,000 and 683,000 in the following decades. Since in many districts the outflow exceeded natural inceases (births minus deaths), rural populations were already beginning to fall. Among 56 registration districts in Norfolk, Suffolk and Essex, all of which saw demographic growth down to 1841, four showed decreases in the 1841–51 inter-censal period, and 38 and 32 in the 1850s and 1860s. Concurrently, 24 among 65 districts in Dorset, Devon, Wiltshire and Somerset indicated population losses in 1841–51, and 42 and 23 in the decades beginning 1851 and 1861.[80] While there is no reason to believe that agricultural employees predominated among these who removed themselves entirely from the rural labour market, their future replacements were beginning to do so to a noticeable extent. As a correspondent to *The Times* put it, there were 'some wise men among the agricultural labourers in some districts . . . the sons of those in these districts have moved themselves off to a better market instead of stopping to eat their fathers and brothers up.' A comparison of the census returns for Elmdon illustrates the trend: 66 per cent of surviving farmworkers of 1861 were still present ten years on, but of the 34 per cent who had left, seven out of every ten were aged initially 10–19.[81]

However, the rural outflow had yet to reach its peak, and though powerful, was a slow-acting engine of social improvement among those who remained on the land. An alternative route, perhaps offering the chance of more rapid gains, was trade unionism. Its importance in buttressing the position of skilled town workers was manifest, although leaders of the existing labour movement mostly took a low view of the capabilities of the farmworker in that direction. 'In intellect' suggested one, 'he is a child, in position a helot, in condition a squalid outcast . . . his knowledge of the future is limited to the field he works in. . . . The Squire is his King, the parson his deity, the taproom his highest conception of earthly bliss.'[82] This view proved to be as erroneous as it was condescending, for towards the close of the period came signs of a new determination, seen, for example, in a strike of 28 labourers at Gawcott (Bucks.) for a two-shilling increase in the face of price increases in 1867; while around Maidstone in 1866–8, a Kent Agricultural Labourers' Protection Association afforded its few hundred members direct experience of combination and fellowship with urban trade unionists and radicals, before collapsing in face of farmer opposition.[83] Early in 1871, in somewhat more propitious circumstances, a labourers' union was started at Leintwardine in Herefordshire which soon spread over six counties and is said to have enrolled 30,000 members within less than a year. Signs of incipient unionism were also noticed on the borderlands of north Warwickshire and Staffordshire, with the formation during the winter of 1871–2 of a small Agricultural Labourers' Protection Society at Perry Bar, while in the south Warwickshire village of Harbury ('Hungry' Harbury as it was known locally) labourers met at the New Inn late in January 1872 to discuss a collective demand for an advance in wages.[84] A week later, on 7 February, came the momentous knock on the door of Joseph Arch, of Barford, a Methodist and itinerant hedger known as a plain-speaking and independent man, who was asked by two rain-drenched labourers to assist them to form a union. The meeting which took place that evening under the branches of a green chestnut tree at Wellesbourne was attended by several hundred people, and was the forerunner of many more. The story of the stirring events during the months that followed, including a successful strike of labourers at Wellesbourne; the great demonstration at Leamington on Good Friday out of which sprang the Warwickshire Agricultural Labourers' Union; the spread of the movement into adjacent counties, notably Oxfordshire and Northamptonshire; and the foundation of the National Agricultural Labourers' Union at a further conference at Leamington towards the end of May, has often been told, and told well.[85] By the close of the year membership of NALU was claimed to approach 40,000,[86] while in addition significant (though unknown) numbers were enrolled in several independent unions, including the Lincolnshire Labour League founded at the Spread Eagle Inn, Grantham in May 1872, and the Kent Labourers' Union, revived by news of the Warwickshire movement. An upward fillip was imparted to wages and, while the influence of trade unionism is always difficult to disengage (Hasbach, for example, suggests that the rise was greater in the north although no unions had been founded there), they appear to have moved some 2s–2s 6d a week by the close of 1872, representing an increase of some 16–20 per cent over the level obtaining two years earlier. The examination of surviving farm records, for instance at Blandford, Dorset, Audley End in Essex, and on Viscount Dillon's model farm at Ditchley, Oxfordshire, bears out the trend.[87] To contemporaries, the 'Revolt of the Field' seemed a long overdue reaction to oppression and conditions of wretchedness, and in a modern restatement of that view Aldcroft has suggested that a failure of living standards to improve eventually forced the labourers to take action 'as a last resort'. By contrast, Dunbabin sees the movement as originating out of a mixture of anger and hope.[88] The occasion for anger is evident from table 4.1, for in the late 1860s wages were not keeping abreast of changes in prices, whilst hope resided in a longer-run trend for circumstances to move gradually in the labourers' favour. In the light of the evidence reviewed in this chapter, there seems more to be said for Dunbabin's interpretation.

FIVE

The 'affluent' farmworker, 1873–95

The flowering of trade unionism in agriculture was facilitated by a major boom which carried the British economy to full employment and price inflation was brisk during 1871–3,[1] but there followed a period of crisis and considerable change in agriculture, often described as 'the Great Depression'. The late Victorian era was remarkable for a concentration of catastrophic seasons. Wet summers in 1877–82 affected harvest yields and promoted pleuro-pneumonia among cattle and liver-rot in sheep. The summers of 1885 and 1887 were notable for drought, while massive blizzards in the west country in March 1891 were followed by a wet harvest, more droughts in 1892 and 1893 which created shortages of hay, and severe frosts during the winter of 1893–4 when snow covered the ground for weeks on end.[2] In times past, prices had invariably risen to compensate for short-falls in production, but by the later nineteenth century they could no longer be relied upon to do so. Leaving aside year to year fluctuations, the downward drift of prices was remarkable. Wheat selling at an average of 57s a quarter in 1871–4 fetched only 25s 8d by 1892–3, a fall paralleled if not matched by other cereal prices. Lincoln wool by the late 1890s sold at only half the figure reached in the early 1870s and prices received for dairy produce declined by between one-fifth and one-quarter, chiefly in the later years of the period.[3] These trends reflected massive increases in international supply. Ever since the mid-century, railways had been penetrating the prairies of America, the hinterlands of the Russian Empire, Brazil and Argentina, the outback of Australia, and the plains and valleys of New Zealand. Moreover, the closing decades of the century saw a transformation in the efficiency of merchant fleets as more economical coal-burning ships replaced sailing vessels, so that by 1902 a quarter of wheat could be brought from Chicago to Liverpool for as little as 3s. In 1880 the first shipment of frozen mutton arrived from Australia and by 1895 imports accounted for about one-third of total meat consumption. Danish and Irish produce made inroads into cheese and bacon markets, leaving only milk and market garden produce immune from foreign competition.[4]

Rents at Holkham in Norfolk fell by 45 per cent and in 1895, for the first time, farms becoming vacant were having to be advertised. On the Bedford estates rent adjustment took place on 17 occasions after 1879 and by 1893–5 they were running at a loss, causing the Duke to complain of the rate of return on capital and the burdens of taxation. On the heavy claylands that characterized much of Essex, landlords had to go to almost any lengths to keep their tenants, and in an extreme case rents paid for two farms at Steeple, which had stood at £760 in 1873, fell to a nominal one pound in 1891.[5] By contrast, in those parts of the south which had good grassland and easy access by rail to markets, such as the Vale of Aylesbury, reductions were comparatively modest; and rents remained firm in the dairying districts of Cheshire and Lancashire, where the Fylde revenues of the Earl of Derby actually rose by 18 per cent between 1871 and 1896. However, average reductions were of the order of 25 per cent and in *The Importance of Being Earnest* (1895), Oscar Wilde's Lady Bracknell uttered an acerbic comment which must have articulated the feeling of many a proprietor: 'Land has ceased to be either a profit or a pleasure. It gives one position and prevents one from keeping it up.'[6] Farmers were vociferous in their complaints, especially the large-scale arable producers who provided much of the evidence put before the two Royal Commissions on Agriculture which sat in 1879–82 and 1894–7. True, it has been estimated that the total net income of farmers decreased by only 7.5 per cent, from which (since the prices of non-agricultural goods were also falling) it would be possible to infer an increase in their average real incomes, and it is clear that specialist livestock producers benefited from a soaring demand for meat, milk and dairy produce as well as from reductions in their costs attendant on the falling price of feed.[7] But the uncertainties with which farmers were beset should not be underestimated. The number bankrupted nearly quintupled between 1871 and 1881, and then and in the early 1890s failures were about twenty times more numerous in the most stricken than in the least affected counties.[8] Speaking generally, small-scale arable farmers were the most vulnerable category although even men of substance were often obliged to go carefully: in Warwickshire, commented Margaret Ashby, 'You could see that the farmers had suffered. They no longer paid subscriptions to the Hunt or sent their daughters to Cheltenham College or the good Leamington School where a foreign princess had spent a year, but to poor little establishments in Kineton or Banbury with cheap teaching and much foolish lisping.'[9]

In these circumstances, the prudent farmer kept a watchful eye on his outgoings in respect of labour. 'Over and over again' wrote Graham in 1892, 'have I been told by successful farmers of my acquaintance . . . that the great secret of earning a profit nowadays is to keep down the labour bill.'[10] Small farmers with little capital often had no choice in the matter and the Scotsmen who moved into Suffolk and Essex to take on cheap but sizeable holdings were noted for their parsimonious use of hired labour. On one such occasion the men advanced to seek re-engagement:

> The first said he was a horseman. 'Oh . . . then I shan't want you as my eldest son will look after the horses.' No.1 having retired crestfallen, No.2 tried his luck . . . he was a cowman . . . 'Then I shan't want you as my second son will look after the cows and my daughters will make up the butter.' Next came the shepherd and his mate. 'I shan't want you . . . as I do all the shepherding myself.' And so it went on, in the end few of the old hands finding re-employment.[11]

However, the strategy of most farmers was simply to avoid filling all the vacancies arising from death, old age or dismissals and to seek to eliminate excessively lavish applications of labour. Three or four ploughings might be good for a root field, conceded Rider Haggard, best known for his authorship of *King Solomon's Mines*, but 'in our time we can scarcely afford to put too much labour into the land'.[12] Economies of this kind nibbled at the edges of the labour bill, but there were two ways in which the aggregate demand for labour stood to be reduced more systematically. One was through the furtherance of mechanization and the other reflected shifts in the national composition of farm output and land use.

The fact that there were at least 900 firms producing agricultural equipment by the end of the century might encourage the impression that machinery carried all before it during the closing decades of the nineteenth century. On the contrary, the growth of the industry lost some of its momentum. There was a definite check to the market for tillage equipment. In the late 1880s the Dorchester Steam Plough works survived only by switching to road rollers. In the early 1890s, Ashby and King thought that less steam power was being used for ploughing than ten years earlier, an impression supported by reports stating that the market was glutted with used sets of tackle, available for as little as £600 as against the £2,000 they had cost when new.[13] Even the mechanization of the harvest was a slower process than is sometimes assumed. While reapers and, from the 1880s, the first self-binders were produced in thousands each year, as late as 1892 the vast majority of British farms managed without any such equipment, as Fussell has pointed out.[14] Accordingly, the implications of late nineteenth-century mechanization for labour were complex but muted. On the one hand, the deployment of steam engines generated a number of comparatively well-remunerated new jobs. In 1871 the Northumberland Steam Cultivation Company employed 90 men, two-thirds of whom were 'ordinary but intelligent farm men', once in receipt of 14–15s a week but now earning 20–23s,[15] and wages of this order certainly encouraged among such men a certain *hauteur* and pride in their order. By 1881 over 4,000 agricultural machinery proprietors and attendants were separately enumerated, yet the number of new jobs of this kind would certainly have risen faster had conditions of prosperity obtained. On the other hand the sedate pace of technological progress limited the scale of the threat to agricultural jobs in general and did not justify the apprehensions of one Fenland sage about 1895: 'You'll see what machinery will do. spoil all your stuf. starve all your cattle, ruin your land ... everywhere men out of work workhouses full of starving people. And England ruined ... why they ought to have a law to have all these machines collected up and droped into the sea.'[16] Most agricultural experts continued to adhere to the view that machinery was 'in the long run the friend of the labourer',[17] although this is not to say that it had no effect on the pattern of labour demand. Among others, Jefferies noticed a tendency for work to be concentrated into 'rushes', and nowhere was this more obvious than in the harvest field. Farmers were able to dispense with some of the casual labour upon which they had hitherto relied. 'Since I have availed myself of the machinery that there is' declared Farmer Horswell of Tavistock, 'I can comfortably complete my harvesting with my regular labourers alone.' In the north too, there was less recourse to 'catch' or casual men as farmers appeared to follow the maxim that extra harvest work should be 'let to the constant hands so far as possible'.[18]

Much more potent than mechanization as a factor reducing the aggregate demand for labour was the shift in land-use patterns which occurred as farmers sought to adjust to the changing price-relativities of the period. Locally, the result of such changes could be quite dramatic: on two Wiltshire farms turned over to grass during the 1880s, a single shepherd replaced all the farm workers, who had previously numbered 14.[19] Few employers were able to effect so dramatic a transformation, but some reduction in the overall farm labour requirement was implied in the shrinkage between 1875 and 1895 of the wheat acreage of England and Wales by 57 per cent, and of corn in general by 24 per cent, while with increasing importations of cattle feed the area devoted to root crops (traditionally thought to require two or three times the man-hours of wheat) fell by 17 per cent. In contrast, land under permanent grass increased by about 25 per cent.[20] There was a further decline in the size of the hired labour force, which in the two decades following 1871 contracted by 18 and 14 per cent for adult males and youths respectively.[21] However, there are difficulties in ascribing the 'flight from the land' wholly to changing agrarian circumstances. First, the reduction in the number of employees was no greater, and in fact rather smaller in 1871–81 and the ensuing decades than in 1861–71. Secondly, the scale and intensity of rural population decreases showed no obvious relationship with the quality of soil or type of farming, except in areas featuring arable land of the highest quality.[22] Thirdly, the losses bore only a tenuous relationship to agricultural wage levels: as Graham commented in 1893, 'If they have low wages, as in Wiltshire, they leave; but if they have high wages, as in Northumberland, they leave also. Where the farms are small, as in the Sleaford division of Lincolnshire, they go away; and in Norfolk, where as a rule, they are larger, the process of desertion still procedes.'[23] Moreover, 'the flight from the land' and 'the rural exodus' were by no means synonymous: those leaving the villages included significant numbers of rural craftsmen whose livelihoods were theatened by competition from factory-made products, and journeymen who in many cases found they could earn more in the towns. Such findings cast doubt on the adequacy of a much-quoted passage in which the novelist Thomas Hardy linked rural–urban migration to a 'tendency of water to run uphill when forced', and on the proposition that men were simply 'propelled out' of agriculture.[24]

The more carefully the matter is considered, the more obvious it becomes that it was the reluctance of sons to follow their fathers on to the land that was the chief feature of the reduction of the farm labour force, and the departure of their daughters into service which made the greatest single contribution to the net losses from rural areas. Older men well embarked upon a lifetime of agricultural employment were likely to remain, giving rise to an occasional comment on their immobility, as when Richard Heath instanced residents of Swaledale who had never in their lives been to Richmond.[25] With the young, habits were different. In the parish of Welborne (Norfolk) there were 56 names on the school register in 1881 and, commented the Rector in the late 1890s, of these only two remained in the village.[26] The outflow was particularly noticeable among girls, due to the insatiable demand for domestic servants. Flora Thompson recalled that at 'Lark Rise' (Juniper Hill, Oxon.) in the 1880s there were none over 12 or 13 living permanently at home, and with some excess of enthusiasm Pedder pictured the daughter's return 'with amazing shoes and headgear of the latest fashion, rings on her fingers and bangles on her wrist, a dress copied ... from a fashionable paper, perfectly cool and composed, picking and choosing her employer and trying to decide whether London, Cheltenham or Leamington would be the most agreeable place to work'.[27] For their brothers, the most hazardous path was to go soldiering, the danger lying in its lack of long-term prospects. Rider Haggard noted the existence of a hoary and frequently unjust prejudice against returning soldiers: 'The farmers say ... that they have lost touch with the land and are of little use upon it. ... The worst thing that a young fellow ... can do is enlist unless he wants to make soldiering the profession of his life.'[28] Going into the police was a better proposition: it was not so much the pay, contended Jessop, but 'the prospect, the promotion by merit, the recognition of faithful service, the appreciation of moral character, the pension for old age' that were attractive, and from the village in which he wrote (Scarning in Norfolk), 31 'sons of the soil, the pick of the parish' had been enrolled as policemen over thirty years.[29] Railway service was another source of uniformed employment as the system continued to expand, along with workshops at places such as Swindon, or Crewe where 6,800 were employed in 1891, three-quarters of whom according to the managers 'would otherwise have been available for the neighbouring land'; or Ashford (Kent) where the Chairman of the Metropolitan Railway Company remarked that their apprentice mechanics, fitters and moulders were as a rule the sons of agricultural labourers.[30] Quarrying and brickmaking were also sources of alternative employment, notably in the Peterborough district, while about Southwell (Notts.) many young men were tempted to the nearby pit-banks.[31] In South Wales the exceptionally rapid development of the coalfield created such a shortage of native-born farmworkers that there was an inflow of replacements from Wiltshire, Somerset, Devon and Herefordshire, which had to be constantly replenished as the newcomers in turn were soon drawn to the mining districts.[32] Here, men were also partially lost to agriculture through their seeking work in the mines for nine months in the year, returning only for piece work during the summer, a form of bi-employment found also among some young men of Suffolk who became 'amphibious', i.e., they took service on the Lowestoft smacks during the herring season. Whenever the search for non-agricultural work involved leaving home, young men were apt to reappear on Sundays and at holiday-times looking well-dressed and comparatively prosperous and confident even when, as in a Bedfordshire instance, further enquiries revealed that they were but scavengers.[33]

Such were the currents of internal migration, not essentially different from those of the 1850s and 1860s, which permitted some villages to grow but in general favoured the growth of towns, and of great ones most of all. In many districts the population growth characteristic of the first half of the century, and sometimes later, was put into reverse. Despite a sevenfold increase in the size of Bournemouth, the population of Dorset struggled to increase from 196,000 (1871) to 200,000 (1901): research has shown that it was losing by far the greater part of its natural increase (births minus deaths), and in villages such as

Tolpuddle the population was falling consistently, being 20 per cent smaller in 1901 than in George Loveless's time.[34]

Notwithstanding the hardships and dangers that might be involved, dramatized in the loss by fire at sea of the *Cospatrick* carrying over 400 passengers in November 1874, a significant minority ventured overseas. Recent work on the flawed statistics of emigration suggests that the proportions born in the rural counties, or who were classed as agricultural workers, rose significantly in the 1870s.[35] All the new agricultural unions sought to promote both internal and external migration, reckoning that the departure of every family made some contribution to the welfare of those who remained behind, by reducing the competition for work. Moreover, colonial governments realized that their best chances of securing immigrants lay, apart from the obvious step of providing free or assisted passages, in appointing union officials as their agents. Although Joseph Arch initially entertained some strong reservations about emigration, in 1873 he visited Canada with the approval of the union and returned very impressed. Likewise Christopher Holloway, Chairman of the Oxford branch of NALU, on a visit to New Zealand in 1874 found himself courted by the greatest in the land.[36] By then the pages of the *Labourers' Union Chronicle* had begun to feature rousing articles ('New Zealand! New Zealand!! New Zealand!!! Off we go; now's your time, my boys') and many newspapers began to publish letters from contented emigrants, of which the following is not untypical:

> New Zealand. Oct. 22nd. Dear Brothers. ... We are doing well and you need not wonder at it, for we eat half a sheep in a week. ... I have a good master ... when he sent my wife and family to me he went to Christchurch and bought two hundred of flour, half a sheep and bread and some salt and hops ... he also gave tickets for my wife and family and saw them safe in the train. I don't know how far I might have travelled in England to have found a master to have done that. ... We are fifteen miles from the Snowy Mountains and can see them quite plain ... I wish I had come ten years sooner. ... Remember us to all. We feel very thankful to those who helped us here. From your affectionate brother, George Addington, late of Cardington, Bedfordshire.[37]

In the late 1870s some of these circumstances changed. The unions, as we shall see, were now in a much weakened state, and several colonies, including New Zealand, had begun to phase out their various assistance programmes.[38] Even so, total net emigration from England and Wales accelerated sharply during the ensuing decade, reaching over 600,000 in 1881–90 against about 160,000 in 1871–80. Recent research has considerably clarified our picture of the situation. The number of emigrants born in 34 rural counties rose absolutely (by some 34–38 per cent, comparing 1881–90 with 1871–80), but fell as a proportion of all emigrants. The number of adult males embarking from British ports whose occupations were recorded specifically as agricultural workers likewise rose, suggesting that as many as one-sixth of all British emigrants during 1881–90 were agricultural workers, who were by then over-represented in relation to their numbers in the occupied population. In the 1890s the situation was different again: total emigration fell back markedly, as did the number (considerably) and proportion (slightly) of outward-bound passengers recorded as agricultural workers.[39] From these findings we may conclude that the propensity of farmworkers to emigrate was running at its height in the 1880s, which is a corrective to certain contemporary impressions on that point.[40] However, two important qualifications must be subjoined. Firstly, it is erroneous to suppose that heavy emigration from England and Wales in the 1880s can be ascribed chiefly to the depression in agriculture: over two-thirds of all emigrants were drawn from the cities (or at least, the more urbanized counties) and many of these were townsfolk born and bred.[41] Secondly, in any decade through the years 1861–1900, the overwhelming majority (68–77 per cent of males, 81–89 per cent of females) of those who left their rural birthplaces were engaged in internal rather than external migration.[42] In the main, they were destined to fill the places of townsmen, who at all times showed a greater proclivity to emigrate.

In the early 1870s, when the supply of labour seemed satisfactory and some still feared 'surplus population',[43] many landlords and farmers were inclined to think it necessary for the good of the country that there should be an outflow. Thus we find the Duke of Bedford appearing somewhat incongruously alongside the Labourers' Union in a list of subscribers to a fund assisting 19 persons to emigrate from Eversholt (Beds.) in 1874.[44] In the years that followed, countless testimonials were written to help young people on their way. A typical source was the parish clergyman, though on occasion he could prove capricious: the Rector of Laceby (Lincs.) often refused, perhaps because his parish harboured a very active shopkeeper and emigration agent, J. H. White, who was also a nonconformist. Most were more obliging, as were many landlords – including Lord Wantage, who assisted with his testimonials many Berkshire lads into the Army, Navy or police, or the railway works at Swindon.[45] Some employers, however, were less sanguine about the situation. When a Mr Bucknowle travelled by train from Swaffham to Kings Lynn in May 1873, he encountered 19 men and youths and five women and children en route to Stockton and Manchester. 'The Union song was sung in the carriage and three cheers given for the Union for sending them. Several farmers and dealers were in the same train to attend Lynn market and were much chaffed.' Alighting from the train, Bucknowle overhead a conversation on the platform to the effect that 'it was getting a serious matter for the farmers as the young blood was going out of the country'.[46] This view certainly gained ground as time passed. Counter-measures usually took the form of counselling men who had expressed a wish to emigrate against too rosy a view of conditions elsewhere, but might also take on a more coercive character. According to William Burton, a New Zealand emigration agent, chapels and schoolhouses of all denominations were regularly closed at the instigation of farmers to thwart his meetings in Lincolnshire in 1875, and he was the victim of an assault by a drunken farmer at South Ferriby in the same year.[47]

Slowly, the balance of demand and supply was turning in the men's favour, but because for the most part farmers still had ample resources upon which to draw, fears of absolute labour shortages were not yet a feature of their complaints. What they inveighed against increasingly was the quality of the labour left on the land. Migration, it was widely held, was taking 'our best bone and sinew so that soon we shall have no servants left' (W. W. Carus-Wilson) while even so august an authority as G. C. Brodrick was inclined to think that the labourer who remained was 'too often a degenerate specimen of his ancestral type'. Such views were aired regularly in evidence collected by the Royal Commission on Labour in 1893–4: from Zeal (Devon), it was reported that 'our young men have all gone, only old people and cripples left', while from Buntingford (Cambs.) the lament was that 'all the quick-witted ones go to London'.[48] Men of greater perspicacity were more cautious. Caird suggested that though the numbers had been diminished, those remaining were 'not less skilful and effective', while W. C. Little commented privately that 'if all my friends the farmers have said about the deterioration of the farm labourer is true, they must be a race of monkeys by now'.[49]

Despite the obvious element of exaggeration in farmers' lamentations about the quality of labour, two points, at least, are worth pursuing. First, a great deal of the criticism was aimed at men of the south who were often contrasted unfavourably with their northern counterparts in respect of their capacity for work. Estimating that a Scotsman would perform two or three times as much in a given period, a Suffolk farmer remarked to Clifford that it made 'one's flesh creep to see some of our men at work'.[50] According to Jefferies, labourers were decidedly reluctant to work overtime and showed 'an Oriental absence of aspiration', while Flora Thompson recalled of the men at 'Lark Rise' that the one thing they detested above all was hurry.[51] There is a distinct possibility that the leisurely pace adopted by many southern farmworkers was the legacy, as Wilson Fox put it in 1906, of 'generations of bad feeding'.[52] Taking up this argument, a modern author has likened the situation through much of the nineteenth century to that often encountered by labour economists in the third world countries of our own day. There was a vicious circle in operation: low wages gave rise to poor diets, which were duly reflected in low productivity, in turn supporting only low wages.[53] This very plausible argument has been disputed and is difficult to establish conclusively, due to the lack of hard quantitative data on both labour productivity and the relative amounts of capital in use per worker employed.[54] However, statistics of the simplest kind confirm that migration certainly had profound effects on the age-composition of the farm labour force. At the time, Little contended that a comparison of the census returns of 1871 and 1891 gave no support to the prevailing impression of an aging labour force. The Registrar-General was of the same opinion and succeeded in misleading Hasbach entirely on this point.[55] In fact, a lateral rather than an historical comparison is more revealing, since migration had been going on for many years. Even a cursory inspection of the 1891 census returns shows that elderly workers (i.e. those aged 55 and over) were about three times more numerous in the farm labour force than among railway employees or coal miners. Table 5.1 gives a more broadly-based comparison, from which it can be seen that agriculture relied heavily on older men and on youths, finding the latter difficult to retain. By contrast, men in the prime of life, when their experience was considerable and their bodily strength unimpaired (let us say, in the age group 25–44), were conspicuously under-represented. The facts are clear, but it is far from easy to gauge their economic and social significance. On the face of things, the age-composition appears to have had some potential to inhibit labour productivity, although contemporaries did not unanimously take this view. For example, Canon Bury was convinced that the need for sheer bodily strength was being reduced by machinery while the value of experience was as great as ever, and others found young men, if reluctant to learn the old-fashioned

Table 5.1: Age comparison of the male labour force, England and Wales, 1891*

	Percentage aged					
	Under 20	20–24	25–34	35–44	45–54	55 and over
A. Agricultural labourers, farm servants, shepherds	28.0	11.9	16.8	12.7	11.9	18.6
B. Remainder of occupied male population	19.8	13.9	23.6	18.1	12.9	11.7
C. % by which A exceeds B	+41.4	−14.3	−28.8	−29.8	−7.7	+58.9

* Based on P.P. 1893–4 (C.7058), vol. CVI. *1891 Census, England and Wales. Age Abstract*, Table 5, pp. x–xxv.

accomplishments, 'quicker in getting hold of machinery'.[56] Arguably, the peculiarity of the age-composition was more significant in social terms. Youths cannot have relished working alongside men who were fatalistic, set in their ways and often sour, while the situation certainly helped to reinforce among the public an image of agriculture as a stronghold of all that was unprogressive and un-modern.

The wage material gathered after 1867 was on several occasions assessed and interpreted by able contemporaries, whose work has not been superseded, notably W.C. Little, A. Wilson Fox and A.L. Bowley. However, the determination of farmworkers' renumeration proved to be, as ever, far from simple. A variety of factors could affect weekly wages, and there were still more difficulties involved in estimating average earnings (i.e. total annual renumeration, divided by 52). Any discussion of wages and earnings can be as tortuous as we choose to make it, as a brief indication of some of the chief complications will show:

1. In many parts of the country there was a difference of a shilling or more between ordinary weekly wage rates in summer and in winter, and sometimes the rates paid on estates were a shade above those offered by tenant farmers.
2. There were many variations in the course of weekly wage rates over time. Thus, the wages received by single hinds at Stocksfield Hall, Northumberland peaked at 24s (1875) and fell away to 18s by the late 1880s before recovering to 20s in the early 1890s. At Thomas Girling's farm (Frostenden, Suffolk) wage gains of the early 1870s were sustained until 1879, though by the late 80s a reduction of some 3s a week had taken place, which was partially recovered in 1891–4; and, while wages on an Essex farm followed a similar course, they showed signs of coming under pressure rather earlier, from 1875. By contrast, the ordinary labourers on certain farms at Wootten Bassett (Wilts.) were earning in the early 1890s wages as high or higher than at any time in the 1870s, and the men on a Devon farm not merely held on to their gains of the early 1870s, but actually increased their wages marginally, to reach 16s by 1890.[57]
3. Specialist skills always commanded a premium over the wages paid to ordinary labourers, although those to whom they were paid often had to work

longer hours to secure them. On the other hand, reduced rates were usually paid to semi-incapacitated or elderly workers. Sentiment and self-interest often coincided in influencing employers to provide light tasks whenever possible. 'Everywhere you find', commented Clifford, 'old servants retained sometimes as full, or three-quarter, or half men.' Other instances are met of aged men 'if strong enough' being able to earn 1s 6d a day at Morpeth (Northumberland) in the 1890s, while some, at Brampton (Cumberland) were paid 'children's wages in food only'.[58]

4. Perquisites were featuring less frequently. In Wales, they virtually disappeared between the 1860s and the 1890s. Elderly labourers in Herefordshire claimed that since about 1874 fewer 'gifts', such as the occasional meal, milk, broth, beer, cider and fuel had been made available, and Wilson Fox discerned a general tendency to substitute money for payments in kind.[59]

5. Piecework was also tending to decrease due to reductions in the arable acreage, and also because many farmers no longer felt able to hoe and weed, or keep their ditches and hedges as tidy as before. Nevertheless it continued to offer exceptional earning opportunities to the young, vigorous and mobile. Charles Slater (then aged 27) recalled earning 6s a day, or nearly three times the general level of wages, by going sheep-shearing from farm to farm between Wisbech and King's Lynn in 1895.[60]

6. Farmworkers could normally count on a considerable boost to their earnings at harvest time. Mr Flatman of Chippenham (Suffolk) emphasized to Clifford in 1874 that although their 'nominal' rate of wages was 13s a week, his men averaged 17s 6d when account was taken of harvest earnings.[61] While the complexities of surviving agreements drawn up between farmers and their assembled companies of harvesters are such as to defeat a precise assessment of the extent to which harvest earnings rose above the normal weekly wage, there is little doubt that for a few weeks the men would be receiving, in cash and in kind, at least twice their normal rate of pay. On the other hand, it was contended by some that the spread of machinery, partial though it was, sometimes caused a significant curtailment of the operations of the harvest field. Before the Royal Commission in 1882, Alfred Simmons estimated the harvest earnings of Kent labourers to have declined from £6 to £4, and in Wiltshire where they had once reached £6–8, they were considered good at £3 in the early 1890s.[62] However, it is difficult to know how general this was. While the introduction of self-binding machines had a tendency to reduce the number of people required for harvest operations, it did not necessarily reduce the extra earnings of those employed: in contrast to the opinions just cited, evidence from the wage-books of two farms in Essex and Suffolk suggests that the sums paid to men were no smaller in 1891 than in 1871, and indeed, rather higher.[63]

7. There was infinite variation in the extent to which inclement weather could affect wages. According to Clifford, no employer ever paid for time lost by piece or task workers, although where the men were on weekly wages, the larger employers would ordinarily find them something to do under the cover of their more numerous buildings and sheds.[64] With those employed by smaller farmers, or reliant on casual work for different farmers, this would rarely happen. Going through the Essex villages of Latchington and Steeple on a

wet day in the early 1890s, A.J. Spencer noticed that 'most of the male occupants of cottages seemed to be at home or in the public-house', and concluded that there were few farms where the men did not lose *some* time on account of bad weather.[65]

Despite this formidable catalogue of difficulties, there was a considerable measure of agreement among expert observers as to the course of weekly wage rates over time. Table 5.2 shows that the gains registered in the early 1870s, noticed in chapter 4, were not sustained into the late 1880s, and even the partial recovery after 1891 did not succeed in effecting their complete reinstatement in some regions, especially in the eastern counties.[66]

Table 5.2: Average weekly cash wages of ordinary labourers in England and Wales, 1867–95*

	England and Wales (67 farms)	*North (8 farms)*	*Midlands (22 farms)*	*East (13 farms)*	*South/ South west (21 farms)*
1867–71	11s 11d	14s 9d	12s 2d	11s 5d	10s 11d
1872–8	13s 5d	17s 4d	13s 11d	12s 11d	11s 9d
1879–90	13s 0d	16s 9d	13s 4d	11s 6d	12s 1d
1891–5	13s 4d	17s 4d	13s 6d	11s 5d	12s 7d

* Based on data given in A. Wilson Fox, 'Agricultural Wages in England and Wales during the last Fifty Years', *Journal of the Royal Statistical Society*, 1903, vol. LXVI, reprinted in W.E. Minchinton, ed., *Essays in Agrarian History*, David and Charles, Newton Abbot, 1968, II, pp. 181–2. The composition of groups is as follows – (North) Northumberland, Cumberland, Westmorland, Lancs., Yorks.; (Midlands) Derbys., Cheshire, Notts., Leics., Rutland, Shropshire, Worcs., Warwicks., Northants., Bucks., Beds., Herts.; (East) Hunts., Lincs., Norfolk, Suffolk, Essex; (South and South-West) Surrey, Sussex, Hants., Wilts., Dorset, Gloucs., Somerset, Hereford, Monmouth, Devon, Cornwall.

Average weekly earnings were somewhat higher than these figures indicate. In 1893 Little investigated this for 38 Poor Law Unions, taking account of such factors as extra harvest earnings on the one hand, and loss of time through bad weather and sickness on the other. There was a considerable variation in the ratio of estimated earnings to weekly wages, ranging from 147:100 (Pewsey, Wilts.) to 106:100 (Uttoxeter, Derbys., and Wetherby, Yorks.). However, the average ratio was 119:100 and justified Little's conclusion that nothing could be more fallacious than inferring the level of farm earnings from wage rates alone.[67] Unfortunately it is not possible to produce a table of weekly earnings over time, comparable to Table 5.2, and Table 5.3 is included rather for the light it throws on regional differences in farm renumeration. The time-honoured differences were still much in evidence, but were less marked with respect to total earnings, reflecting the fact that harvest payments were normally greater in counties where the nominal weekly wage was low, notably in East Anglia.

While this discussion does not exhaust the complexity of the subject, the broad inferences are reasonably clear. It is accepted that, whether wages or earnings are under consideration, the farmworker of the mid 1890s might expect to enjoy a money income that was a little higher than that of the late 1860s,

Table 5.3: Wages and earnings of ordinary labourers in 1892–3, by region*

Region	A Average earnings	B Average weekly wage	*Ratio A:B*
I Northern Counties	18s 6d	16s 5d	113
II East Midlands	16s 7d	15s 1d	110
III West Midlands	15s 5d	12s 6d	123
IV South-West	14s 9d	11s 8d	126
V South Midlands	14s 11d	12s 5d	120
VI South/South east	15s 5d	12s 10d	120
VII East Anglia	15s 2d	11s 10d	128

* The table utilizes data compiled in W. C. Little's *Report on the Agricultural Labourer*. See P.P. 1893–4 (C.6894-XXV), vol. XXXVIII–Pt II. *Royal Commission on Labour*, pp. 74–84, arranged according to the regions used in C. S. Orwin and B. I. Felton, 'A Century of Wages and Earnings in Agriculture', *Journal of the Royal Agricultural Society*, 1931, vol. XCII, pp. 233, 245 but incorporating some minor corrections to their figures. The composition of the regions is as follows: I, Cumberland, Westmorland, Northumberland, Durham, Yorks., Lancs., Cheshire; II, Derbys., Notts., Lincs., Rutland, Leics.; III, Warwicks., Worcs., Staffs., Shropshire, Herefords., Gloucs.; IV, Somerset, Cornwall, Devon, Dorset, Wilts.; V, Cambs., Beds., Hunts., Northants., Herts., Bucks., Oxon.; VI, Hants., Sussex, Kent, Surrey, Middx., Berks.; VII, Essex, Suffolk, Norfolk.

though a trifle lower, in many cases, than in the early and mid-1870s.[68] However, the purchasing power of the coins in his pocket was rising comparatively rapidly. Between 1873 and 1896 there was a fall in the cost of living of the order of 32 per cent, from which, like working-class consumers in the towns, the farmworker stood to gain. Indeed, in real terms the purchasing power of the average agricultural wage increased by some 25 per cent.[69] This laid the foundation for a considerable advance in the standard of living. By the 1880s the character of cottage diets was visibly changing. Although in many districts milk in small quantities continued to be in short supply, more tea, sugar, and meat was being consumed. From Dorset in the 1880s it was reported that the labourer '"sees", "smells" and "tastes" meat regularly, instead of once a week as formerly', and from Somerset that the ordinary supper of the labourer consisted of 'hot vegetables with meat or fish of some kind, with tea, bread and butter', while for northern farm servants, more beef and less bacon was being provided.[70] The cost of clothing and footwear was falling too, though some complained that quality also was on the decline: according to a Wiltshire observer, factory-made boots costing 8s (against 14s for a hand-made pair some years before) 'seldom resisted the wet for more than three months'.[71] Cheap lamps and paraffin, which were by now almost universally used, made the home more inviting in the evenings than in the days of rushlights and candles, and reduced the incentive for husbands to repair to the public house at 7 o'clock. Various authorities agree that less beer was imbibed, and by the 1890s, according to a farmer of Chatteris (Cambs.), nearly every labourer was taking a weekly newspaper and many patronized day trips by rail to the seaside, while a tremendous increase in the use of tobacco showed that the men had 'more money to spend on small luxuries'.[72] Every young man of 16 and over was supposed to carry a watch, and some were acquiring bicycles, if usually second-hand ones. A significant broadening of the range within which courtship took place is noticeable in the marriage registers of rural Dorset from the 1880s.[73] Cottage wives took a pride in displaying good linen rather than rags on their clothes-lines, their homes were more comfortably furnished (including, in some cases, a clock) and respectably curtained, while according to Jessop, perambulators and in some instances sewing machines were to be found in the cottages of Norfolk by the 1880s.[74] Children were visibly better dressed and cared for, and even the cottage pig had a stake in the improvements, for the price of 'toppings' had come down with that of wheat, and at Tysoe (Warwicks.), men were building new sties in red brick, sometimes studded with blue bricks shaping the year of construction, as it might be '1881' or '1891'.[75] We are, of course, listing *all* the various ways in which increased real incomes might be laid out, for no farmworker's family could avail itself of all these novel satisfactions simultaneously. Nevertheless, to an extent never before seen, there was a margin for discretionary expenditure. The impression that men's choices were frequently exercised in a very responsible way is suggested by the ubiquity of coal and clothing clubs and pig insurance societies which abounded in the villages and, as well, by the further spread of friendly society membership. By the early 1890s it was considered that the vast majority of the younger men belonged to a benefit society of some kind, usually to the affiliated orders which were carrying all before them.[76]

The general standard of cottage accommodation continued to leave much to be desired, a large proportion still falling, according to Little, 'below a proper standard of what is required for decency and comfort'.[77] The effect of the depression on landlords' willingness or ability to spend on cottages is illustrated in the best index of rural house-building activity, which shows a rise between 1841 and 1871 but a significant contraction in the following twenty years.[78] Neglect as well as age could be a factor in dilapidation, claimed J. C. Thresh in the most systematic study of this question, which covered 65 Essex villages, among which only six boasted a public water supply and six were satisfactorily sewered, the rest relying on privies and cesspits which were nearly always defective. Draughts and damp were the source of much preventable sickness, and the old problem of shortage of bedrooms, he suspected, fostered immorality.[79] Some, like Jessop, therefore regarded housing as 'the one notable and shameful exception' to the labourer's progress'.[80] Nevertheless, while there is no doubt that the worst houses of the 1830s and 1840s could be matched by examples from the 1890s, there is reason to believe that the accommodation of farmworkers improved at least marginally, due to the closer approximation of supply and demand. Thus on the Holkham estate, where once all the members of the Carr family had lived together, by the 1880s they occupied three houses and the Barnards occupied four. For the first time, in 1890, three cottages were actually vacant. A survey of the ten most rural English counties has shown that with one exception (Herefordshire), none had a higher proportion of empty houses than the national average down to and including 1871; but by 1901, all showed a high proportion of empties, ranging from 27 per cent above the national average (Lincs.) to 72 per cent (Hunts.).[81] These circumstances presumably permitted some of the most horrendous accommodation to fall out of use. They were conducive, too, to keeping the general level of cottage rents low.

Wilkinson encountered in the early 1890s a labourer who had been to the mines but considered himself better off on his return to Holbeach, due chiefly to his cottage rent being 1s 6d against 5s 6d in the 'coal country'.[82]

A balanced view of the position of the farmworker in the later nineteenth century should take some account of the experiences of his family. To an ever-increasing extent, the role of women was becoming confined to home-making. Although islands of busy domestic outwork still existed, notably gloving in the Yeovil district and around Worcester, opportunities to augment family incomes in this way were continuing to contract. Between 1871 and 1901 the number of plaiters in Bedfordshire declined from over 20,000 to fewer than 500, the industry having succumbed to cheap importations from China. Likewise, by the 1890s it was patently clear that the pillow-lace industry had lost its protracted struggle against machine-made lace, and the numbers engaged in the pursuit had sharply declined.[83] Yet as Bear noticed, in reference to Bedfordshire, 'now that the industries referred to are utterly unremunerative and nearly extinct the women still refrain from farm work'.[84] According to census statistics, the number of female farmworkers declined by 58 per cent between 1871 and 1891, and there is a considerable volume of supporting literary evidence. At 'Lark Rise' (Oxon.) in the 1880s only about half a dozen women were engaged in field work, and for the majority it was only a memory; meanwhile in Norfolk women were said to have 'almost passed out of the labour market altogether', and in Northumberland the bondage system which relied on a supply of unmarried females had virtually died out by the 1890s.[85] There is not much room for doubt about the direction of change, but there are conflicting opinions about the underlying explanations as well as about its extent. Some invoke the factor of technological change. For example, Hostettler has noticed that the diminishing role of female labour is unconsciously revealed in drawings of the harvest field made for successive editions of Henry Stephens's *Book of the Farm*, first published in 1844: the ousting of the sickle by the scythe, she believes, had already by the 1850s and 1860s reduced the role of women to subsidiary tasks such as gathering and binding, while the appearance of the self-binding reaper made even these roles redundant.[86] Yet, as we have seen, the rate at which mechanization advanced was by no means spectacular, and there is considerable evidence to suggest that single women were willing rather than obliged to turn their backs on agriculture. In Wales by the 1890s farmers were often 'at their wits end' to find servant girls for dairy work, on account of their preference for taking domestic situations at watering places and resorts.[87] In Scotland, too, recent work has suggested that it was the pull of opportunities elsewhere that was the decisive factor in reducing the number of women in agriculture,[88] and the situation is unlikely to have been different in most English districts. The position of married women was different again. Although some commentators discerned a general reluctance amongst them to go into the fields, and interpreted this as 'evidence of improvement in the labourer's situation',[89] there is reason to believe that their role in agriculture was not declining at anything like the same rate as that of their unmarried counterparts. A study using a small selection of farm wage books in Gloucestershire (where the censuses show a decline of nearly three-quarters in the female labour force, 1871–1901), suggests that the involvement of women, chiefly the wives of farmworkers, was massively under-recorded and continued throughout the late nineteenth century at a substantial level, many of them working for one-third or more of the farming year.[90] Clearly, sources of that kind will repay more attention than they have so far received.

If the decline of the female labour force was more gradual than is sometimes assumed, the withdrawal of children probably proceeded still more slowly. Although the Act of 1867 had mitigated the evils of public gangs, it did not touch those engaged privately. In the early 1870s laudanum based compounds such as Godfrey's cordial were still much used in the eastern counties, and at such gathering points as Croyland's triple-arched bridge, much 'evil talk' could still be heard.[91] Legislation aiming directly to control child labour in the years that followed turned out to be ineffective, notably the Agricultural Children's Act of 1875, which sought to prevent the employment of those aged under eight (or ten in a gang) and specified a minimum school attendance for those aged 8–12. When James Taplin of Kingswood Parsonage, Hollywood, near Birmingham prevailed on two or three respectable employers to dismiss those under 13, they were at once engaged by less scrupulous employers such as a Mr Humphreys, who received him with 'foul denounciations' and boasted that he had plenty of money to pay fines.[92] Meanwhile, the supply of school places under the voluntary system was augmented by the board schools which came into existence after the passing of Forster's Education Act of 1870, although it was not until 1880 that the law came to support the principle of compulsory education. It was then laid down that children aged up to 10 (11 from 1893 and 12 from 1899) should be full-time pupils, while older children (up to 14) had to continue their education on at least a part-time basis until they reached a specified level of attainment, usually standard IV or V. However, it was difficult to impose these regulations firmly. Part-time attendance officers found their job virtually impossible, for rural school boards and attendance committees connived at law-breaking in this area, and there was a coincidence of interest between employers and hard-pressed parents such as Mrs Spray of Hailsham, Sussex, who wrote to the Education Department in 1886 complaining of 'this cruel cruel law ... this school board nuisance'. The children themselves in some case felt ashamed not to be working: 'After I were about nine year old' recalled a man born at Lotting Fen (Hunts.) in the 1870s, 'I got ashamed o' going to school ... I used to get into the dykes and slink along out o' sight in case anybody should see me and laugh at me'.[93] Perfunctory attendance, early leaving and the sometimes exhausted state of pupils set limits to what could be achieved in village schools, which were in any case often notable for defective apparatus and plant, understaffing and a high proportion of poorly qualified teachers. Despite these deficiencies, which are so frequently reiterated in historical studies of nineteenth-century education, there are signs of progress in the later nineteenth century. The number of prosecutions for offences against the Education Acts ran at an annual average of 83,000 in the 1880s and thereafter fell significantly, reflecting both the advent of free schooling in 1891 and probably an increasing ability on the part of rural families to avoid at least the more blatant breaches of the law, which might attract penalties.[94] Graham was not alone in thinking that the school system was producing an improved kind of youth, 'one who had been allowed to grow in mind as well as in body'.[95] No doubt the achievement of one labourer's son who emerged from the village school at Ashwell (Herts.) to take a first-class degree at London University in 1899 was extraordinary, perhaps even unique, but the national statistics suggest that all save a small minority attained at least basic standards of literacy.[96]

The ability to maintain a wife from his own earnings and to educate his children were important indications of a man's social standing in Victorian England, and so also was his ability to maintain a union. By 1874, NALU claimed a membership of 86,214, making it easily the largest trade union in the country. In addition, the Lincolnshire League, the Kent and Sussex Union and some smaller associations which in November 1873 came together to form a federated grouping, claimed about 49,000 between them.[97] There were, however, marked regional and local membership variations – in particular, a strong relationship with the presence or absence of farm service, a system which militated against unionization for obvious reasons, not least because some farm servants were themselves the sons of farmers.[98] Accordingly, there were few signs of incipient trade unionism in the northern counties, or in Wales. Within the primarily arable counties of the south and east, and in the midlands, there was much variation from village to village. Much has been made of the connection between trade unionism and nonconformity, especially Primitive Methodism, not because there existed mass dual membership, but on account of the pre-eminent position of men whose spoke the language of Zion and who played a specific role in both spheres. Research on East Anglia has shown that, although only 46 per cent of Suffolk villages contained a Methodist Chapel, 78 per cent of union branches were to be found in them; and that in Lincolnshire, Norfolk and Suffolk 53, 52 and 46 per cent of branch activists were known Methodists. They included a surprisingly high proportion of Wesleyans.[99] However, as we have seen, the strength of nonconformity itself mirrored the varying social characteristics of villages, and other researchers have sought a relationship with the pattern of landownership. Work carried out on Warwickshire points to the contrast between villages such as Cubbington where, against the background of a dispersed pattern of ownership, unionism was particularly strong, and those controlled by a sole proprietor, such as Charlecote, Loxley or Liddington, which saw strikes in 1872 but were unable to sustain permanent branches.[100] Still, if the total membership figures given above are even approximately correct, they imply that about one farmworker in ten was in a union in 1874, with every prospect, it must have seemed, of a gradual strengthening of the workers' defences.

Alas, the movement was already on the point of demonstrating its fragility. When a renewed demand for a 1s rise in their weekly wages from unionists at Exning, Suffolk was rejected in March 1874, they came out on strike, and the Newmarket Farmers' Defence Association responded by locking out all union men in their employ.[101] Within five weeks over 6,000 unionists were idle in Suffolk and north Essex, two-thirds of them members of NALU, the rest mostly of the Lincolnshire Labourers' League. It has been suggested that, in all, over 10,000 were thrown out of their jobs as employers in Lincolnshire, Cambridgeshire, Norfolk and a number of southern counties followed the determined example set by farmers in Suffolk and Essex. Through the weeks that followed, those locked out received 9s a week, and Arch and his colleagues were busy collecting funds from urban trade unions and from collections taken on the labourers' behalf in such towns as Nottingham, Sheffield and Manchester, whose Anglican bishop weighed in with supporting letters to *The Times*.[102] In May, the intercession of two MPs succeeded in getting a compromise accepted by both sides within Lincolnshire. Some of the men's more objectionable rules and demands were withdrawn in return for the employers' recognition of the right to form a union, which was construed by William Banks, the Lincolnshire League's leader as a victory, but by Arch and the NALU executive as a defeat since no wage increase had been achieved. Meanwhile, the farmers of Suffolk and Essex were not disposed to compromise. Through July, the number of men attending such centres as the Cock and Pie at Woodbridge for their pay diminished: 'their banners were laid aside; their blue rosettes were no longer in use and the men ... looked harassed and disheartened ... the fact was that the cream of the men had found engagements. Some had given up their cards, others had been set to work without leaving the union, but were told that they were wanted only for the harvest'.[103] By 27 July Arch and the NALU Executive committee resolved to discontinue payments after one more week. 'This committee', they said, 'cannot feel justified in supporting the labourers in enforced idleness indefinitely', adding subsequently, and somewhat insensitively, that they were not in the business of offering permanent relief which was the province of the Poor Law Board.[104] The Federal Union followed suit in relation to its members and the episode ended in confusion. It was later claimed that, of the men locked-out in Suffolk, 870 had returned to work without surrendering union membership, 400 migrated, 450 emigrated and 350 managed to find work immediately after the lock-out ended (some being compelled to give up their membership), though about 350 were still out of work in the second week of August. Such an outcome was almost inevitable, given the enormous drain on union funds. No less than £24,000 was spent on lock-out pay by NALU alone between March and August, and although outside contributions accounted for a considerable proportion of this, the strain was too great for a union with a total subscription income which was no higher than £8,000 in 1872–3, and £21,000 in 1873–4.[105]

The great lock-out and its aftermath struck a massive blow at the prestige of NALU and its president, membership halving within a year and continuing to fall, so that by 1880 it stood at only about a quarter of its 1874 level. 'Depression, division and defeat' is an apt chapter heading used by one historian of agricultural trade unionism to describe the years that followed.[106] The failure of the Revolt of the Field had numerous causes, some being internal to the movement itself. For all his qualities Arch was vain and, says his modern biographer, his conceit tended to increase in direct proportion to the decline of the union.[107] His character contributed in some measure to the disunity, at times bordering on internecine strife, between the various unions. In particular there were constant, though probably unfounded, complaints of financial speculation against the executive of NALU, as well as against attempts to 'poach' from other unions individual members or even whole branches. Secessions took place from the ranks of NALU itself, notably in 1875 when the Honorary Treasurer, Mathew Vincent broke away to form a 'National Farm Labourers' Union', having as its primary objective the acquisition of land for distribution as allotments. After this the *Labourers' Union Chronicle*, owned by Vincent, submitted Arch to a barrage of abuse which was returned in the pages of *The English Labourer*, the journal founded to replace it.[108] A further major secession occurred in 1878, when George Rix drew away large numbers in the Dereham District to form a Norfolk Union. This event, and the disintegration of the Federal Union into its constituent parts as early as 1875, reflected suspicions of centralized leadership, and a tendency among farmworkers to perceive their problems in local rather than national terms.[109] Other wounds sustained by the movement were, to a degree, self-inflicted. The sickness benefit scheme introduced by NALU in 1877 was based upon no firm actuarial principles and proved to be another drain on union funds.[110] The public postures adopted by its leaders were often unhelpful to the cause, for example Arch's strident advocacy of the disestablishment of the Church of England. While it is true that the actions of some clerics earned them no credit, notably that of the Rector of Clopton (Suffolk) who in 1874 posted notices withdrawing from union men their allotments and access to parochial charities, gratuitous attacks on the position of the Church could only serve to alienate those who were positively sympathetic, such as Canon Girdlestone and the Vicar of Minster Lovell (Oxon.), and encouraged the majority to stand aloof.[111] Some of the smaller unions showed signs of stronger staying power than NALU itself. This appears to be true of Rix's Norfolk Union, and particularly the Kent and Sussex Union, whose leader, Alfred Simmons, was more artful. The favourable publicity which accrued from his encouragement of church parades, such as the half-mile procession of union members to afternoon service at Canterbury Cathedral on 11 July 1875, and from collections for local hospitals, helped his union to beat off a number of local challenges culminating in a concerted lock-out by Kent farmers seeking to impose a wage reduction in 1878–9.[112]

Landlords did not unanimously exhibit deep-seated hostility or even share the apprehensions of the Earl of Stradbroke that the unions were led by dangerous fanatics, and several Suffolk notables, including Lord Tollemache, Sir Charles Bunbury, Lord Henniker and Sir Edward Kerrison were against the lock-out of 1874. Likewise, there were individual farmers, such as Mr Lavender of Biddenham (Beds.), who allowed that their men had a perfect right to combine.[113] Nevertheless, the pressures capable of being brought to bear by those who thought otherwise were very considerable. Persuasive techniques included the publication of pamphlets warning against combining in the wrong way ('We are not a downtrodden race . . . singing songs wunnut make that better, naythur will strikes');[114] the frequent casting of aspersions against outside supporters (the labourer's 'pseudo-friends', notably 'interfering intellectuals', urban trade unionists and radicals);[115] and no doubt the proferring of 'advice' at the workplace, on countless occasions. It would be possible, too, to fill a book with instances of the harrying of individual union activists, such as John Piper of Sturry near Canterbury, or Arthur Mayhew of Bromham (Beds.), while at moments of general tension wholesale persecution could occur; this happened in East Kent in 1878–9, when in Chartham and Chilham alone, 13 labourers received summonses for eviction from their cottages.[116] However, the underlying weaknesses of agricultural trade unionism are not revealed most effectively

LAND AND LABOUR; OR, "HOW TO SETTLE IT."

LORD BROADACRES. "COME, FARMER, I THINK *WE* MAY MANAGE TO MEND MATTERS FOR OUR FRIEND HODGE, WITHOUT *THE HELP OF THAT PROFESSIONAL MEDDLER!*"

(*Punch*, 20 April 1872)

either by dwelling on its internal disunity, or by citing individual cases of vindictive persecution. At all times, the unions were financially frail. Attention has been drawn to the alarming inability of NALU, even when at the height of its strength, to collect the weekly twopenny subscriptions of its members.[117] Moreover, they were very vulnerable to economic downswings. Thus, wage reductions, discharges and shortages of work in 1878–9 were directly conducive to the crumbling of trade union membership of both NALU and the Lincolnshire League.[118] Finally, the policy of encouraging emigration, while alleviating the position of those who remained, served also to weaken the foothold of the unions in the villages. All too often those departing included the younger and more independent spirits (often branch secretaries), upon whom the vitality of the movement depended. By contrast, the position of the farmer was inherently powerful. As a Norfolk clergyman pointed out, 'a union of farmers to keep down wages is as old as twenty years or more ... and something of the same sort is the practice everywhere'.[119] From this informal basis it was not difficult to organize farmers' associations to resist the demands of labour, and as we have seen, by 1874 they had already learned the most effective answer to a strike, namely, generalizing the conflict by locking out all union members over a wide area. This was comparatively easy to effect simply because, unlike a factory or a mine, a farmer's business did not suffer immediately from a cessation of work. At most seasons of the year an arable cultivator could watch his land remain unattended with comparative equanimity, while on primarily livestock holdings he and his family would often account for much of the manpower used in any case.[120]

Perhaps because of the manifest weaknesses of agricultural trade unionism on the industrial front, the movement showed during the 1880s a tendency to concentrate increasingly upon political issues. Franchise reform had been a feature of NALU policy from its earliest days and with the increasing ascendancy of radical over Whig elements within the party, the advent of a Liberal government in 1880 offered the prospect of extending the vote to the agricultural worker, who had been excluded under the 1867 Reform Act. In 1883 came the first stage of what has been called the 'largest single instalment of parliamentary reform in the nineteenth century,'[121] with the Corrupt and Illegal Practices Prevention Act, and in 1884 Gladstone reached an accommodation with Salisbury resulting in the passing of the Representation of the People Act, which effectively extended the franchise to the counties on similar terms to those already existing in the boroughs. It was coupled with a measure for the redistribution of seats, which on the whole favoured the Tories, who could also rely on dominating the County Councils created in 1888 and the Rural District Councils of 1894 which emerged from existing units of poor law and sanitary organization. At the General Election of 1885, Arch became the first farmworker to sit in Parliament, winning the seat for north-west Norfolk for the Liberals. Here, many of the 8,282 electors who voted were labourers and Arch was returned by 4,461 votes against 3,821 for the Tory candidate; his victory was assisted in some measure, it is thought, by the apolitical attitudes adopted by the Earl of Leicester and on the Royal estate at Sandringham.[122]

At this election, the land question was made a more prominent political issue than ever before. Although there were in 1873 about a quarter of a million allotments, the basis on which they existed was fragile, since they came into being and could be discontinued at the whim of individual landlords. These defects of the voluntary system made allotments a concern of some (though not all) trade union activists and, after two abortive efforts in 1874 and 1875, Jesse Collings, a Birmingham ironmonger and Liberal MP for Ipswich, was instrumental in the passage of the Allotments Extension Act of 1882 which aimed to enforce upon the trustees of charitable lands the duty of offering them as allotments. Unhappily, amendments made in the Lords (notably those which exempted land used for ecclesiastical, educational or apprenticeship purposes) seriously emasculated the bill and gave scope for any amount of legal quibbling.[123] The allotments issue was mixed up with the advocacy by radicals of the establishment of proprietary small-holdings, i.e. units which would occupy a man satisfactorily on a full-time basis, together with members of his family, in imitation of the continental peasantry. This notion reflected their longstanding dislike of the monopoly of land and of those who owned it, and many observers, while favourable to garden allotments, were sceptical of smallholdings which could encumber the small man with debts he might find difficult to sustain.[124] In the event, the Liberal administration of 1885–6, distracted as it was by the problem of Irish Home Rule, failed to grapple with either issue and it was left to a Tory government headed by Lord Salisbury, who had become sensitized to the electoral appeal of land reform, to pass considerably modified versions of Collings's proposals under the Allotments Act (1887) and the Smallholdings Act (1892). The first of these measures enabled local authorities to purchase or rent land for allotments, although by 1893 only 56 out of 518 had used their powers to do so.[125] However, this does not signify that the number of allotments failed to expand. It could be shown that the number of 'voluntary' allotments increased by no less than 40 per cent between 1873 and 1886, and the rate of growth doubled between 1886 and 1890, due partly to the fall in the value of land.[126] The Smallholdings Act of 1892 likewise produced only miniscule results. It enabled the County Councils to borrow funds from the Public Works Loan Commission for the purpose of creating smallholdings, which would be sold to applicants who were then required to pay one-fifth of the purchase money and the rest by instalments over a lengthy period. But as late as 1902, only eight counties had availed themselves of these powers, with a total between them of 569 acres.[127] Opinions will always differ concerning the practicability of ideals such as those held by Collings, the extent to which they were supported by other Liberals simply because they might produce a race of independent electors free from Tory influence, and the opportunist role of the Conservatives in passing limited measures which they could rely on their sympathizers on the county and district authorities to ignore. In the event, the aspirations of some individuals were doubtless thwarted. Yet it is probable that the radicals exaggerated the extent of land hunger among farmworkers, if their attitude to allotments is any guide. According to Graham, in the northern counties they were sought most eagerly by artisans, while Jessop opined that 'the genuine agricultural labourer' was not especially interested. The conclusion of E. Wilkinson in 1893, that nothing could be more variable than the desire for allotments, seems a fair summary of the position.[128] Moreover, countrymen had a better understanding than urban-based radicals of the prospects of life as a small proprietor. Arch considered the notion of 'three acres and a cow' to be 'all moonshine', and in the Ashby household at Tysoe, Collings was more admired for his 'knight errantry' than for his policy, the feeling being that a man 'could do' on either a fair weekly wage with a good-sized garden, or on a farm of 30–40 acres: 'three acres were too much or too little'.[129] Certainly, the underlying ideological issues would have proved somewhat taxing for men who were habituated to their role as wage-earners, who were deemed for the most part to be practical rather than theoretical persons and whose ordinary conversation, in many cases, was not of politics but 'how many carts they could fill in a day [and] which master had got the best horses or cows . . . or who could drink so many pints before he was drunk and who could use his fists'.[130]

However, land reform remained a live issue for years to come and its supporters derived much encouragement from an unexpected revival of agricultural trade unionism in the aftermath of the Dock Strike of 1889. At the Trades Union Congress of 1890, the President declared that during the struggles of the dock and gas workers 'there was no more regrettable sight . . . than the police-protected processions from the agricultural districts'.[131] Assistance to farmworkers to form their own unions seemed to be the best answer to the problem of blackleg labour, and officials of the Dockers' Union were soon busy in the rural counties. Tom Mann was conducting an energetic campaign in north Lincolnshire in February 1891, and the third annual report of the Dockers' Union listed at least eleven branches formed in that county. About this time, agents of the same union were also busy 'setting men against masters and masters against men' (according to a farmworker) in Chalgrove, Great Milton and other villages on the borders of Oxfordshire and Buckinghamshire.[132] Other sources of outside assistance came from middle-class socialists, such as the Misses Skerritt, leading lights in the Reading Branch of the Social Democratic Federation or, more commonly, from Liberals of advanced radical views. Among the new organizations sparked into life at this time was the Berkshire Union (571 members at its peak); the Eastern Counties Labour Federation, based on Ipswich and claiming 17,000 members by the end of 1892; and a Warwickshire Union formed in April 1893, which boasted twenty branches and an estimated membership of 5–600 but included not a single farmworker among its leaders.[133] The revival, which was confined to the southern counties and drew in only a small minority of farmworkers, also affected the older unions such as the Kent and Sussex, which in 1889 had moved its headquarters from Maidstone to London and restyled itself as the London and Counties Labour League. Arch's NALU, with its claims to be a national body, remained mistrustful of the new county unions but it, too, showed signs of a renaissance, increasing from its 1889 nadir of 4,254 members to a total of 15,000 by the end of 1891, due largely to the energetic efforts of Zachariah Walker, a Methodist local preacher in Norfolk, which by now accounted for some four-fifths of its members.[134] Another sign of better times came at the elections of July 1892, when Arch regained by a handsome majority the Norfolk seat which he had lost by a small margin in 1886.

For a time, the spectre of effective trade unionism appeared to loom menacingly and called forth some predictable reactions. A Norwich newspaper, *The Argus*, carried in November 1890 a report on a strike on Lord Walsingham's estate following a post-harvest reduction of 1s in the men's wages, and on a meeting at Tottington schoolroom where they were harangued by his lordship. 'If you take your orders from outsiders you will have to get your pay from outsiders, and you will have to get your cottages from outsiders ... don't you make fools of yourselves because some lazy talking chap wants to wheedle your sixpences out of you, to try to make him ... a gentleman without the breeding'. On being asked whether there were any grievances, one brave spirit complained that his work in drains and ditches necessitated spending 55s on long boots, but, having ascertained that they lasted seven years, his lordship opined that the boots were 'an uncommonly good bargain'. 'Honoured Sir', wrote W. Herring, a village shopkeeper in receipt of a notice to quit a couple of months later,

> whatever it can be for we don't know ... if it is anything to do with this strike it is a great injustice ... I nor my father are in no way connected with the Union ... we only paid in for the sake of our trade ... if his lordship wish us to give it up we will with pleasure and if he don't like the men being at our shop we will make them keep away in fact we will do anything ... I can't think we are as bad as Chilvers about the strike.[135]

These passages in the life of Tottington illustrate, in an extreme form, the obstacles to successful unionization found in a tightly controlled estate village. However, it was not only the opposition of landlords of Lord Walsingham's ilk that brought about the collapse of the movement within a very short space of time. The support received from outside sympathizers was far from reliable, as the labourers of Worminghall (Bucks.) found in 1892, when the promised strike pay of 15s a week from the Dockers' Union soon ceased.[136] Even the weather seemed to conspire against the success of the unions, with membership falling away rapidly during the dire winter of 1893–4, which brought extensive unemployment. One by one they collapsed, as did the London and Counties Labour League in 1895. Even NALU was reduced to only 1,100 members by 1895, and was finally dissolved in 1896. The cause of trade unionism in agriculture appeared hopeless and in December 1895 Joseph Arch, by now broken-hearted and disappointed, gloomily advised the Norfolk trade unionist George Edwards, 'never trust our class again', while his listener subsequently admitted to having lost, at that stage, 'all faith that my class would ever be strong enough to emancipate themselves'.[137]

During the later nineteenth century, the concept of an 'agricultural interest', in which the welfare of landlords, farmers and wage-earners were closely bound together, was still frequently invoked. However, the first attempt to formalize it, in the early 1890s, significantly came to nothing. Lord Winchelsea's plan to form a union of all agriculturalists was strongly suspected of being inspired by protectionist sentiment, and in the pages of *The Labourers' Union Chronicle* farmworkers were firmly discouraged from joining.[138] The unprecedented economic circumstances of the late nineteenth century had gone far towards demonstrating that the interests of the various elements in rural society were, if not opposed, at any rate far from identical. It was almost universally held that farmers, and especially landlords, had been the greatest sufferers from the depression, though according to Jessop, village tradesmen and shopkeepers should be included among those who lost out, as well as parsons who were much poorer than in the past. By contrast he held that the farmworker was 'a great deal better off than his father was' and that no class had less reason to complain of their condition.[139] This view is supported by the fall in the cost of living which, due to migration, was not accompanied, as it had been in the 1820s and 1830s, by collapsing money wages and rising unemployment. Attempts to argue the case that the labourer lost ground in this period usually turn on the costs of the implementation of compulsory education, and the diminution or disappearance of his wife's contributions to the family purse arising from the contraction of female employment in domestic industry or in agriculture, operating to reduce family earnings.[140] There are no statistics with which to measure this and while in individual instances gross family earnings may, indeed, have contracted at a rate even greater than the price fall, this seems unlikely to have been the general experience. That the farmworker of the 1890s was decidely better-off than his counterpart in the 1840s cannot be doubted, and the only area about which some room for debate exists is whether, as is possible, there has been a tendency to underestimate his gains during the 'Golden Age' and to somewhat overrate those made during the years of the 'Great Depression'.

In an accounting sense, and also in political and constitutional terms, the farmworker's position certainly improved relative to the landlord and farmer during the closing decades of the nineteenth century. But it should be borne in mind that when the Earl of Yarborough died in 1875, his stock of cigars was sold for £850, or more than 18 years' income for a Lincolnshire agricultural worker. Moreover to suggest, as did one Norfolk farmer, that the labourers now lived 'in affluence' seemed to many, even at the time, to be a flight of fancy.[141] Margaret Ashby's verdict on the farmworker's gains, taking a broader perspective, is at least as just:

> To congratulate him and condole with landowner and farmer was to assume that he could live well on farthings while they starved on pounds, that his wife fed the family from a widow's cruse, and that he had the self-control of an Indian mystic in spending his money and his time.[142]

SIX

Marking time: 1896–1914

In 1893, the experienced agricultural reporter William Bear engaged in some counter-factual hypothesizing when he questioned received wisdom concerning the position of farmworkers: 'it is necessary to imagine what their condition would have been if agriculture had remained prosperous. Migration would have been checked ... by an advance in wages. ... Bread and meat would have been less cheap but need not have been dear ... Enterprise in farming and in estate improvements would have increased ... giving much lucrative employment to workmen ... I cannot doubt that agricultural prosperity would have rendered the condition of the labourers much better than it has been since 1879'.[1] As it happened, his views were about to be put to the test, and proved to be justified in some respects but wide of the mark in others. From 1896 the tide of prosperity turned and very gradually began to flow once more, chiefly because in world markets demand was catching up with supply, giving rise to much firmer primary product prices. In Britain, the index of agricultural prices moved upwards by some 33 per cent between 1894–6 and 1911–13 and the annual average number of farming bankruptcies fell from 453 (1892–8) to 299 (1906–12).[2] There were many signs of increasing confidence. Cropping aggregates showed a remarkable stability from the early years of the new century down to the First World War and yields per acre were increasing slowly. The input of fertilizers was increasing, notably of basic slag which was seen to possess a marked regenerative value when applied to old pastures. New and improved strains of seed were brought into use and societies were established to encourage the pure breeding of livestock, such as the British Friesian cow and the Dairy Shorthorn. True, it was not until about 1909, according to the Director of Rothampstead Research Station, that there was any general recognition of returning prosperity; but in his *Pilgrimage of British Farming* (1913), Hall insisted that the industry was now in a sound and prosperous state. This view was supported by Lord Ernle, who in the first edition of *English Farming, Past and Present* suggested that 'a tenant-farmer might possibly admit to himself in secret that his industry has not been in a sounder position for the last 35 years'.[3] Rents showed a tendency to rise a little, for example by about 10 per cent at Severnake and at Wilton between 1900 and 1914. Often though, as was the case on Lord Sidmouth's Devon estate, it took until 1914 to push them back to the level of 1882 and some ancestral owners, regarding their estates as comparatively poor investments, took the opportunity to sell. The advent of a strong Liberal government in 1906, and more especially the threat of Incremental Value and Undeveloped Land duties introduced by Lloyd George in his 1909 budget, was also an effective agency in producing a flood of land sales between 1910 and 1914. In some instances farms were sold to the tenants, as when the Duke of Bedford unburdened himself of his Thorney estates in 1909, and Walter Long, the prominent Tory politician, disposed of the greater part of his Wiltshire estates the following year.[4] In others estates were sold in their entirety to the new rich such as John Wood, a Glossop cotton-spinner who purchased Lady Gage's Hengrave Hall in Suffolk: for the mystique of holding a country seat, if not land, remained as strong as ever. Photographs of shooting parties and armies of servants survive in abundance to show that country houses retained 'enough money, prestige and finesse in the art of living to enjoy an exceedingly agreeable Indian summer',[5] and a sumptuous life-style was still the expectation of summer weekend guests met at the station by the victoria, the dog-cart, or, increasingly after 1908, by the Daracq or Wolseley.

Meanwhile, the drift from the land continued to disturb observers of the rural scene. From census material of 1901 it can be inferred that fewer than half the farmworkers aged 15–24 a decade earlier remained in the industry.[6] A few years later, information collected by the Royal Commission on the Poor Laws yielded valuable information on the destinies of at least some of these men. It appeared that in four of the largest London breweries, 23, 31, 35 and 37 per cent of employees were former farmworkers, as were a quarter of the employees of the South Metropolitan Gas Company, 18 per cent of the goods porters and 47 per cent of the stablemen at King's Cross, 20 per cent of the porters, guards and signalmen employed by the South-Eastern and Chatham railway, and 22 per cent of the Midland railwaymen at Derby: while of 12,000 workpeople employed by 17 large municipal corporations, 37 per cent were country-born and 22 per cent had been farmworkers. It was against this background that Rider Haggard turned his pithy phrase, 'The plethoric population-bogey of 1830 has been replaced by the lean-exodus skeleton of 1902', quoting at length the opinions of numerous landlords, clergymen and farmers who judged an emergent labour shortage to be 'an undoubted fact' (Revd Pickard-Cambridge, Dorset), or the supply to be 'terrible short' (a Shropshire farmer); while to these complaints lamentations about the indiscipline, lack of skills and of effort on the part of those who remained were frequently subjoined.[7] Among the agencies blamed for the desertion of agriculture by more enterprising boys was the malevolent influence of urban-bred schoolteachers, who in the words of a Honiton estate agent 'did not know a dock from a thistle' and ought to be cleared away and replaced by people of a different stamp; while in the same tradition, Major Bourne in Lincolnshire lamented the way in which boys kept at school to 13 years of age became accustomed to a warm room and dry feet, and subsequently showed no liking for 'a cold north-easter with sleet and rain, and mud over his boot-tops and carrying out turnips to sheep'.[8] Concern about the drain was widely voiced again just before the war, when there was a revival in overseas emigration, especially to Canada. Men were reported to be leaving by the hundred from around Dorchester and Canterbury, and there was a loss of 2,114

THE LABOUR MARKET.

Employer. "I SHAN'T SPEAK TO YOU AGAIN ABOUT GETTING ON WITH YOUR WORK, YOUNG MAN. THE NEXT TIME I CATCH YOU IDLING ABOUT, YOU'LL HAVE TO GO."

Boy (confidentially). "CHAPS IS SCARCE!"

(*Punch*, 10 July 1918)

emigrants from 88 Devonshire parishes in 1912–13. A Board of Agriculture report of 1913 instanced Mere (Wilts.) and Floore (Northants.) as places which had experienced significant outflows, and remarked on the decimation of a troop of the East Riding Yeomanry (11 out of 21 were now doing well in Canada), while at Snaith in the same county the church choir suffered from continued attrition, and the cricket club had lost 12 members by emigration since 1912.[9]

By this time, though, there was mounting evidence to show that the apprehensions of contemporaries were grossly exaggerated. Even in 1902, discerning readers of *Rural England* might have noticed contradictions in the comments of some of Haggard's observers. It seems implausible that youngsters at Green Hammerton near York took 'but little interest in their work' (C. B. Burton), while those in the neighbouring village of Cattal displayed 'a fair interest' (Mr Machin), especially when we bear in mind subsequent recollections of Yorkshire farmworkers which agree in describing lads on Edwardian farms as 'horse-proud' and as critical observers of individual standards of ploughing.[10] In any case, as Lennard observed, to lament the passing of obsolescent skills was 'almost as absurd as to call Moltke a degenerate warrior on account of his inability to throw a boomerang'.[11] Even the evidence on the less ambiguous question of shortages left some room for doubt. In Norfolk and Suffolk, Mr

Levett-Scrivinor and George Beck, MP, both told Haggard that the scare was exaggerated, while the Earl of Leicester and his Holkham agent appeared to hold conflicting views on the matter.[12] Moreover, it transpired subsequently, from a comparison of the 1901 and 1911 census returns (which was not possible until 1912), that the first decade of the new century had seen, not a further decline, but an unanticipated increase of 9 per cent in the recorded number of farmworkers. This trend was particularly marked in districts given over to market-gardening and was noticeable in most regions, if rather less well defined in the west midlands and north-west, smaller still in Wales (about 4 per cent) and negligible in the three northernmost counties of Northumberland, Durham and Cumberland.[13] It is true, all inter-censal comparisons for 1891–1911 are to some extent vitiated by the absence of men ordinarily occupied in agriculture during the Boer War, and by the diversion of men to the construction of large military camps at such places as Bulford (Wilts.) and Tidworth (Hants.), which had the effect of exaggerating the 1891–1901 decline and of modifying the increase in the farm labour force recorded for 1901–11. However, no reasonable allowance for the war factor is capable of overturning the conclusion that the flight from the land was arrested during the Edwardian years, a trend due in some measure to the fact that rising prices were easing the squeeze on profits, which had earlier caused farmers to seek economies so vigorously. Yet, according to critics of the industry, an increase in farm employment was by no means a wholesome development. For all the signs of progress, in 1914 many farmers were still relying on the same tools as well as the same buildings which had served earlier generations, and achieving savings in time, energy and manpower was considered by many employers to be less important than achieving economies in cash outlay. In the eyes of men such as Lennard and Hall, labour was still being used wastefully, largely because in most districts it remained plentiful and cheap – so cheap, indeed, as to bolster the view that deficient diets were an important contributory cause of lassitude at work.[14]

Evidence on the relative stickiness of wages appears to give support to this analysis. The regional contrasts so evident in Caird's day had certainly diminished, a feature reflected in some limited contemporary dietary evidence; but what was so remarkable, concludes a modern observer, was their persistence.[15] Increasingly the contrasts between, say, Norfolk and Suffolk on the one hand and Derbyshire and Northumberland on the other were censured; as the Fabian socialist Bennett contended, no conceivable law of political economy could account for the wage differences observed between Devon (17s 9d) and Oxfordshire (14s 11d).

According to such critics, too much was accountable for by 'mere usage and local precedent', with wages determined not by what the farmer could afford to pay for labour but by the lowest price at which he could obtain it.[16] Even more telling than the persistence of such disparities was the movement of wages over time. From the earlier work of Wilson Fox, based on 67 farms and collated in 1903, cash wages which had averaged 13s 6d in mid-1890s showed a definite upward shift in 1898 and after two years of the South African War reached 14s 7d, a gain of some 10 per cent. Thereafter, according to a series presented in the *Abstract of Labour* statistics of the United Kingdom, increases in cash wages were so gradual that, even by 1912, they had improved by less than 5 per cent on the levels current twelve years before.[17] All these considerations argue against any general shortage of labour and, in addition, the increases over time were insufficient to match those shown in cost of living indexes published by the Ministry of Labour, which suggest, between 1900 and 1912, a rise of 14 per cent in food prices and 16 per cent for clothing.[18] In a wide-ranging enquiry based on the analysis of replies drawn from 2,292 parishes in 1912, a group of Liberal investigators claimed that only 41 per cent indicated any wage rise whatsoever in the previous five years; that, mostly, such increases as had taken place (usually 1s or less) tended to be noticed in counties which were already highly paid; and that the real earnings of nearly 60 per cent of ordinary agricultural workers would have decreased since 1907.[19] It is possible, too, that family budgets were put under further pressure by a decline in income from seasonal labour in the harvest fields, for some authorities take the view that it was from the close of the nineteenth century, rather than earlier, that the long-run trend towards mechanization began to seriously curtail the demand for women and children, as self-binding reapers made further headway.[20]

The sharpness of the check to farmworkers' real incomes might be debated at length, with respect to its extent and range.[21] Yet there can be no doubt that it was a common experience, and one that was especially disappointing against the background of rising expectations which was a legacy of the Great Depression period. Aged men, like Bettesworth, the Surrey labourer, might take it philosophically ('Whatever you earns, you lives up to it'), but the push of new felt needs was making itself very apparent, especially among the younger generation, who had 'become imbibed with new and high ideas ... [and were] imitating more people in higher grades of life, both in deportment, speech, dress, social life etc.'[22] Moreover, though this chastening experience was one which farmworkers shared with wage-earners in various other industries, such as building, engineering and railway transport, invariably all of these met the problem from a stronger base. According to one modern authority, consistently throughout the period 1879–1914 the weekly wage rates of ordinary agricultural labourers appear to have stood no higher than 50 per cent of the average found in 14 industrial occupations.[23] This comparison may not be perfectly valid, and is likely, on balance, to somewhat exaggerate the relative disadvantage of the average farmworker. On the one hand, Bellerby was quoting weekly wages, inclusive of allowances in kind, but not, seemingly, average real earnings over the year, which in the later years of King Edward's reign would have added some 2s a week to the nominal weekly wage. Differences between wages and earnings were unlikely to be so substantial in most industrial occupations; moreover, quite a large proportion of farmworkers were paid more than the rates for ordinary labourers, on account of their specialized skills, and cottage rents were decidedly lower than in the towns. Against these considerations, it could be held that shopping was generally more expensive in the villages, and that because of the peculiarities of the agricultural labour force, numerous workers were paid less than the notional weekly wage, which referred to able-bodied adult labourers in regular employment and did not include the remaining casual workers, the young, or the aged and infirm who, as we have seen, were comparatively numerous in agriculture. These factors, together with the unresolved issue of how much time men lost on account of inclement weather, obfuscated any agreement about the precise level of wages compared to those ruling in other sectors; but since to some extent they cancel one another out, we can conclude with reasonable safety that average agricultural remuneration is unlikely to have reached much more than 60 per cent of that obtaining in Bellerby's 14 industries, in the years before 1914.

Thus, agricultural employment remained conspicuously low-paid, and was ripe for investigation by the quasi-scientific methods pioneered in B. S. Rowntree's remarkable study of York, *Poverty: a Study of Town Life*, published in 1901. The first of the three most significant enquiries was published obscurely in a new journal, the *Sociological Review*, by P. H. Mann. It focused on the Bedfordshire village of Ridgmount, and postulated 18s 4d (against 21s 8d in York) as the minimum level of income needed to support a family of two adults and three children at a level which would spare them from 'primary poverty', and ensure the maintenance of physical efficiency. His researches took account of income from allotments, pig-keeping, odd jobs, outdoor relief and some pensions paid by the Duke of Bedford, who held but by no means monopolized land and housing in the village. Even so, it appeared that 34 per cent of Ridgmount's population were locked into primary poverty, while another 7 per cent were in 'secondary poverty' (another Rowntree concept; families were deemed to fall into this category where their incomes, though theoretically sufficient, were mis-spent). It is noteworthy that, in York, the overall poverty fraction was lower (28 per cent) and that the relative roles of primary and secondary poverty were reversed at 10 and 18 per cent of total population respectively. However, the most significant conclusions emerging from Ridgmount were that 52 per cent of all those in primary poverty were aged under 16, and that any man on an average wage would fall into poverty as soon as two children appeared, unless his income were supplemented by an allotment, the fattening of pigs, or other means.[24] Corsley, in Wiltshire, where information was gathered in 1905–6 by Maude Davies, consisted of a scattered series of hamlets. It was densely populated and less purely agricultural than Ridgmount, for there was some market gardening, numerous smallholdings, and dual employment, while every cottage had a good garden. *A priori*, one would expect the proportions in poverty, defined in Rowntree's terms, to be lower and this turned out to be the case. Five-sevenths of all families appeared to stand above primary or even secondary poverty, and among the 70 households headed by labourers, 41 appeared to avoid it. Still, as the author (a student at the London School of Economics) very properly pointed out, two-fifths of all children in the parish were drawn from that minority of families (one-eighth) situated below the primary poverty line.[25] Finally, the master himself was persuaded of the value of applying the methods he had worked out in York to a selection of farmworkers' households in Oxfordshire, Berkshire, Essex, Leicestershire and Yorkshire. The first, trenchant observation made in *How the Labourer Lives* (1913) was that in only five English counties (Northumberland, Durham, Westmorland, Lancashire, Derbyshire) did the average weekly earnings of ordinary labourers, as ascertained by Wilson Fox in 1907, reach the 20s 6d deemed necessary for a rural family of two adults and three children to avoid primary poverty. The rest of Rowntree's study was made up of the analysis of budgetary data gathered by enquiries at 42 cottages, each composed of two adults 'of good reputation for sobriety, thrift and honesty' and an average of 4.6 children, which placed them, we may note, at one of the most taxing phases of the family life cycle. The dietary analysis then conducted suggested that the average protein deficiency in the food obtained was 24 per cent, and that as a whole the families investigated were receiving not much above three-quarters of the nourishment necessary for the maintenance of physical health. And although on occasion the investigators might be regaled with coffee, cakes and an excellent fig and rhubarb pie (Mrs Collingwood, North Riding), they noticed that while meat was tabled daily in most homes, it tended to be 'religiously set aside for the chief bread winner'. The budgetary details were accompanied by much poignant detail on aspects of cottage life: 'The light waned as Mrs Shaw told of her difficulties, her contrivances and their scanty fare'; Mrs Leigh often cried herself to sleep with worry over her debts; Mrs Bell 'sorely grudged' the ounce of tobacco consumed weekly by her husband; Mrs Barton could not afford postage stamps to write to her children; Mrs Atkinson was grateful for the £4 per annum sent home by her girls in service; budgets were put under strain by the purchase of furniture, notably the wringer which cost Mrs Wilson 37s under the instalment system; and most families were engaged in a continual search for expedients (including cast-offs and charity) to meet their clothing needs.[26] Rowntree's calculations were certainly open to criticism on several counts. In comparing incomes of 1907 with prices ruling in 1912, he probably exaggerated the extent of poverty slightly and, as Lennard pointed out, an adjustment of, say, 4 per cent for income increases would add Cumberland, Middlesex, the North and West Ridings of Yorkshire and three unnamed Welsh counties to the list of those in which average earnings were sufficient to clear the poverty line.[27] Furthermore, in the light of later dietary knowledge, it is generally accepted that his assumptions about the necessary intake of nutrients to maintain manual work were slightly exaggerated.[28] Finally, his work was criticized by some for failing to give full weight to piecework earnings or, in some cases, wives' incomes, for example in the activity of glove-stitching.[29] Total scientific accuracy proved to be extraordinarily difficult to obtain, but these surveys went far to strengthen the impression that, beneath its smiling face, the countryside was an abode of deep-seated poverty, or at least, that many were engaged in a constant struggle to stave it off.

However, if low wages were the central feature of rural deprivation, the shape of the problem was influenced by demographic conditions which in certain respects contrasted sharply with those found in the towns. No-one would claim that country folk enjoyed perfect health by any modern standard. Decaying teeth (toothbrushes being virtually unknown in the cottages), chilblains caused by ill-fitting footwear, and cases of defective eyesight or hearing which might easily have been corrected, were rife among village children, while close contact in the schoolroom gave rise to frequent cases of infestation with head lice ('nits'), and on occasion was conducive to more serious outbreaks of epidemic disease such as the diphtheria outbreak which produced 202 cases at Sandy (Beds.) in 1898.[30] In later life, rheumatic pains and chronic bronchial complaints were often the legacy of exposure to arduous working conditions and, as well, to the damp and draughty state of many cottages. For all that, rural longevity stood well in comparison to the towns, a feature attested to by sundry statistics of the

Table 6.1: Children born and surviving for marriages of various dates, in families headed by agricultural workers*

(a) In relation to all other occupations (= 100)

Cohort married	*Children born*	*Children surviving in 1911*
1861–71	104	111
1881–6	114	122
1901–11	114	117

(b) In relation to Social Class I (= 100)

Cohort married	*Children born*	*Children surviving in 1911*
1861–71	119	122
1881–6	150	151
1901–11	144	141

* *Census of England and Wales, 1911*, Vol. XIII. *Fertility of Marriage*, Pt. II, HMSO, 1923, pp. xcii, xciv. N.B. The fall recorded in children surviving by 1901–11 does not indicate a decline in the life-expectancy of agricultural workers' children, but reflects improvements in child mortality among the groups chosen for comparison.

Registrar-General. After standardization for age, mortality among agricultural workers aged 25–65 was but 59 per cent of the figure for the entire British male population, and that attributed to tuberculosis no more than half, in 1910–12. In 1911, when the national infant mortality rate was 125 per thousand live births, and 172, 161, 147 and 139 in families headed by dock labourers, carters and carriers, bargees and bricklayers' labourers respectively, the corresponding rate for farmworkers was well below the national average, at 97.[31] However, low levels of child mortality were linked to above average fertility among farmworkers, turning largely on their behavioural inertia in the matter of marriage and procreation. As we have seen, they were not unusually early marriers, and in late Victorian and Edwardian times their brides averaged 24 years of age when they came to the altar. Once married, however, children tended to appear regularly. Farmworkers were nowhere near the forefront in turning to artificial means of birth control and large families were accepted somewhat fatalistically: 'We've had no luck of late – the missus 'ave 'ad a kid these past four year' as one unenthusiastic *paterfamilias* confided to Holdenby.[32] On the basis of data gathered in 1911, the fertility of agricultural workers was 12 per cent higher than that of farmers, as indeed were their effective family sizes, since there was little difference in their respective experiences of child mortality. Table 6.1 makes some broader comparisons, showing, *inter alia*, that the Edwardian farmworker brought into the world 14 per cent more children than the average parent, and some 45 per cent more than those in Social Class I (consisting largely of professional persons who were the pioneers of artificial birth control), while they bred up 18 per cent more children than the average, and 41 per cent more than parents in Class I. While farmworkers' fertility was not rising absolutely (indeed it was falling, though only slightly), in a *relative* sense it was increasing. Accordingly, 'largeness of family', which Rowntree had deemed to account for nearly a quarter of the primary poverty in York, was still more significant as a factor in rural poverty.

The other distinctive demographic characteristic of the villages was a high proportion of elderly persons. Although there was a marginal 'improvement' in the age profile of farmworkers as rather fewer young men left the industry in 1901–11, the proportion aged over 55 remained 40 per cent higher than in the rest of the occupied labour force in 1911.[33] When Charles Booth addressed the implications of this in 1894, he considered that countrymen were better off than townsmen, because they kept their vigour longer and even when feeble or ailing could still obtain some agricultural work: 'in one way or another effective working life is ten years longer in the country than in the town or ... is as seventy to sixty'. Superficially, this might seem to support an image of old age that was in some ways more dignified than in the towns, but as he went on to show, from an enquiry covering 262 parishes and 9,125 old persons, the proportion likely to be supported by the parish, by charity or by their relations increased regularly from 35 per cent (at 65) to 69 per cent (at 80). Moreover, all his figures excluded those resident in workhouses, and it was noticed that in 1881–91 the decrease in pauperism had been greatest in urban unions, those representative of agriculture showing the least improvement.[34] Opinions varied concerning the readiness and ability of children to maintain their parents in old age, as they were legally supposed to. 'How often' remarked Graham, 'have I heard a weather-beaten and venerable ploughman deliver himself of the dictum that of all plans for meeting old age the most expensive and least trustworthy was that of begetting children'; and Charles Slater, for one, gave several instances from his experience in both Barley (Herts.) and Holbeach (Lincs.) of men leaving 'because if they had stopped they would have to keep their parents'.[35] Others testified to the willingness of children at no small cost to shoulder such obligations.[36] Of course, where a man had outlived his relatives, or become bedridden, there was no alternative to the workhouse. Inevitably this was the end of the line for a childless couple such as the Bettesworths in Surrey. It took three men to remove the epileptic and dirty wife when all she wanted to do was die at home, and the experience greatly upset her husband. He, in turn, entered the house in February 1905 and was almost overwhelmed by the good order, cleanliness and routine, but rather surprisingly emerged (temporarily) a few months later. In the meantime, however, he had been seen by neighbours as 'done for' and enquiries had been made about his job and his cottage.[37] The case illustrates the real terror the workhouse held for the aged. Conditions, though not above reproach, were rarely cruel or harsh and many old folk were better cared for and fed than they expected: but without exception they feared to end their days consigned into social oblivion. Some credit must be given to the Liberals for bringing to a head years of discussion, by passing the Old Age Pensions Act of 1908 which somewhat improved the prospects of the aged. Its implementation in 1909 at the rate of 5s (man) and 7s 6d (married couple) coincided with a marked diminution of outdoor relief paid to those who could earn a little, or receive support from their children. Years later, Flora Thompson recalled people coming to the Post Office at 'Candleford' (probably Buckingham) to collect them. 'God bless that Lord George' they declared, with tears in their eyes, for they 'could not believe that one so powerful and munificent could be a plain Mr', and the husband of a couple in their nineties spelled out the implications for their children: 'now we wants to go on livin' for ever, 'cus ... it pays 'em to have us along with 'em.'[38] Needless to say, pensions could not entirely solve the problems of the aged and, of necessity, the isolated or infirm continued to rely on the house. Detailed work on six Essex unions has shown that although the advent of pensions took nearly all the out-relief cases off the guardians' books, increasingly the inmates of the workhouses were infirmary cases: 'only helpless old people come now', it was observed at Chelmsford in 1913.[39]

For the purpose of developing generalizations about their condition, it has been necessary to view farmworkers as an homogeneous mass. Yet no-one who had the slightest acquaintance with the matter could fail to be aware that the agricultural labour force, which remained in 1911 the largest single occupational group in England and Wales except for coalminers, was extremely complex in its structure. Certainly, women were conspicuous by their absence from the fields of southern England by this date, although vestigial traces of immemorial tradition remained in the still quite common recourse to gleaning, a custom which had long ago been deemed to have no legal basis, but was tolerated by many farmers because it fitted in with good agricultural practice.[40] Otherwise, many features of an older agrarian world had shown pronounced capacities for survival, even if they were not intact. Farm service is a case in point; it had declined at different rates in various parts of England, passing away more slowly from the south-west than the south-east, though even here there were exceptions, notably east Kent. In Wales, by contrast, it had become increasingly the dominant form of hiring since the mid-century, and although individual farmers might make strenuous efforts to rid themselves of indoor servants, chiefly because of the burden of cooking and working imposed by it on their wives, the institution still flourished strongly in the northern counties.[41] Due presumably to the counter-attractions of other jobs, some Yorkshire farmers had to look as far afield as Stowmarket in Suffolk for lads prepared to come on reasonable terms, and one of these who made the adventure has recorded his satisfaction at the level of feeding he enjoyed there.[42] However, for the most part lads were still hired locally, and along with the survival of farm service went the institution of hiring fairs. To some extent, it is true, they had changed their character. In the long run campaigns to segregate girls at places such as Beverley, Bridlington and Kendal had proved successful, and by 1900 mixed hiring fairs had virtually died out. But for young males the pattern was not dissimilar to that known by their grandfathers. Their recollections convey the excitement of the Martlemas Fair at Doncaster, drawing in young men from a very wide geographical area indeed, 'representing the biggest babel of dialects since Noah' and featuring music and singing at every pub, with free flowing beer; or the York hirings, where they thronged Coppergate and Parliament Street, packed for the occasion with roundabouts, menageries, shooting ranges, fortune tellers, living wonders, peep shows and brandy-snap and gingerbread booths, all brilliantly lit with naphtha flares. These occasions provided, as ever, a kind of safety valve, where old scores might be settled with bouts of fisticuffs: provided that they were confined to pub yards and side-streets, these could be ignored by the police, themselves quite probably former farm-lads. In the testimony of those well-qualified to speak on the issue, few had any animosity at being hired in this way, which was reckoned to afford a true bargaining arena in which would-be employers and employees could gauge their relative strengths.[43]

Another survival was the hierarchical nature of farm employment, which covered married as well as single men, and was everywhere to be found. According to local usage, bewildering in its variety, those subsumed by social investigators under such bland headings as 'men in charge of animals' might be described as shepherds (a position of great trust often occupied by men of extremely conservative habits and autocratic demeanour), beastmen, cattlemen, cowmen, foggers, garthmen, yardsmen, stockmen, herdsmen and so on. On large farms there was typically a graded hierarchy of 'horsemen', horsekeepers, carters, wagoners (first, second and third, etc.), although as a rule small farmers relied to a greater extent on the all-round man, or 'ordinary' labourer, into whose ranks men sometimes descended from more specialized roles with advancing years.[44] Men in this category (unlike many specialists), might be on a week's notice and yet, if they were good at their work, remain on the same farm for many years, sometimes throughout their entire working lives. Moreover, despite the mention in earlier chapters of a long-run tendency towards the regularization of farm employment, casuals (catchmen, datal men, jobbers, slingers, etc.) were still encountered in significant numbers. The seasonal influx of Irishmen, though much reduced in scale from times past, remained a feature of agricultural life in northern England, much of the potato lifting in Lincolnshire and the West Riding being carried out by them in 1912. By this time, many were accomplished scythesmen and in districts where the mowing machine was still rare, such as the Yorkshire Dales, they arrived at haytime to seek engagements at places such as Skipton and Hawes unless, as was increasingly the case, prior arrangements had already been made by letter between the employer and the leader of the gang.[45] In some districts crop harvesting still drew upon urban sources of labour. The outstanding case continued to be the Kentish hop harvest; here, it was estimated in 1908 that some 45–65,000 came into the county, chiefly from the East End of London, travelling almost invariably on special trains from London Bridge. A good worker could earn as much as 4–5s a day and whole families a good deal more, by dint of hard work (7.30 a.m.–5.30 p.m., six days a week), but their evenings were enlivened by scenes of great revelry, the worst excesses of which groups such as the Church of England Mission to Hop Pickers and the Salvation Army struggled to control.[46] Here and there, examples of bi-employment characteristic of the past could still be found, among them the seasonal movement of young Suffolk farmworkers to the breweries of Burton-on-Trent, in effect following the barley they had grown. During the winter of 1896, Bass and Company alone employed 256 East Anglian workers at their maltings, exclusively young men, who, had they been at home, would still have been vulnerable to being stood off in winter. The work was physically arduous, but rewarding: while paying 12s a week for board, many earned 4–5s a day and returned to Suffolk in May resplendent in new suits and frequently bearing teapots as presents for their mothers.[47]

As diverse as the pattern of employment was the character and atmosphere of villages. In Edwardian England there still existed numerous estates where good conduct was the key to admission, where fathers strictly controlled the behaviour of their children who were taught to bob to members of the squire's family, and where adult drunkenness and immorality was, so far as possible, banished. A classic case was Helmingham (Suffolk) where the 'owd lord' presided over a village reconstructed in 1850 in 'Tollemache Tudor'. He kept an eye on the state of allotments as well as the farms and, while he did not go so far as Lord Ongley who in the 1850s had required villagers to wear red cloaks and long pointed hats to complement their picturesque accommodation, Helmingham knew an unspoken sumptuary law which regulated the dress of villagers according to their station. There were separate entrances at the village school for the offspring of farmers and tradesmen ('the upper school') and labourers ('lower school'), and all cottage tenancy agreements specified attendance at religious worship. In this ordered world, all elements of the population were reasonably secure unless they transgressed, and there was a flow of charity which included venison soup made available to the poorer families in winter: in that of 1899, 61½ stones of beef and 508 lbs of plum pudding were distributed from the Hall kitchens as well. But the Tollemaches frightened people, farmers as well as cottagers ('You dusn't say anything'), and the cost in terms of human freedom was enormous.[48] Ardington and Lockinge (Berks.) was a similar 'little rural paradise', where Lord and Lady Wantage sincerely desired to promote the well-being of 'their people'; nevertheless they were reckoned by a prominent Liberal critic to be 'radically rotten and bad', a 'political dead sea' in which, according to a labourer in a neighbouring village, 'They daren't blow their noses ... without the bailiff's leave.'[49] But more than half of all English and Welsh parishes were not directly under the influence of any single landowner. 'Orphaned' villages were to be found very generally in the grazing areas of the north and west, and even in the south, in the form of large nucleated settlements or decayed market towns. In such 'rougher' places were usually to be found more public houses and greater dependence on a 'peasant' style of life, in which men made a living by alternating bouts of farm work for various employers with other forms of employment, and raising and dealing in their own produce. Broadly speaking, these distinctions were seen as reflecting the contrast between 'close' and 'open' parishes, although as ever a vast number of places defied such tidy categorizations. In late Victorian and Edwardian England village variety probably reached its peak, much as industrialization had worked to diversify the pattern of urban settlements two or three generations before.[50] The position was complicated still further by the way in which, although some places were becoming more exclusively reliant on agriculture, others were being touched to a significant extent by the appearance of new enterprises, often in food-processing (the Chivers jam factory at Histon, Cambs., is a classic case in point), or, more frequently, by suburbanization. It was to factors such as these that the bulk of rural population growth was usually attributed: a study based on 581 parishes by the census authorities traced only one per cent of their aggregate growth in 1901–11 to agricultural development, and ascribed 46 per cent to mining or manufacture, 43 per cent to residential growth, and 8 per cent to the erection of institutions.[51]

Naturally, the extent to which individual villages might grow was closely linked with the question of cottage accommodation. Local authorities in rural areas had shown a signal lack of enthusiasm for using their powers under the Housing of the Working Classes Act (1890) which, as well as requiring them to inspect and if necessary condemn cottages, had empowered them to acquire land and build on their own account. And, although there was a rising tide of action in the wake of the Housing Act of 1909 (notices served on the owners of cottages to effect improvements rose rapidly from 18,000 in 1901–11 to 152,000 in 1913), part-time medical officers of health still thought it futile to pursue the matter with vigour, partly because they realized that the enforcement of closure orders in the absence of alternative accommodation was far from helpful.[52] At the heart of the matter, as many saw it, was a quantitative shortfall which according to the Liberal land enquiry affected half the 2,759 parishes of England and Wales which came under their purview.[53] Factors influencing the situation included a long-standing unwillingness among landowners to invest in new building and, in some districts, the encroachments of townsmen. Cases in point included Epping (Essex), and numerous villages in Surrey, while pressure on the housing stock was acute in places emerging as recreational centres. Such was the case in the New Forest, and at Wroxham on the Broads. Here enterprising speculators were beginning to convert the place to a congeries of villas, and in one instance a change in the ownership of some cottages and the evictions that followed led to the splitting up of families among neighbours, and the housing of some in an old railway carriage purchased by public subscription.[54] Still, as one expert authority observed, parishes in which housing shortages were 'a clamorous evil' were rarely primarily agricultural in character; and on behalf of landlords it could be urged that they had come to house vast numbers of non-agriculturalists (notably policemen, roadmen, railwaymen and post office employees), to say nothing of increased numbers of pensioners who in earlier times would have gone into the workhouses.[55]

In view of the variety of influences capable of shaping the character of individual villages, their 'cultural' patterns might be expected to defy easy generalization. There is a well-established tradition, based upon the work of late nineteenth- and early twentieth-century observers, that country life, at least as experienced by farmworkers, was excruciatingly dull and unrelieved by games, play or laughter.[56] Certainly there had occurred a long-run decline in feasts and fairs, participation in church music and a variety of traditional pursuits, and along with this, sometimes, in relatively modern ones. For example, the demise of the local club anniversary (considered by Williams to be 'quite the event of the year. Christmas and Easter were nothing to it') occurred in numerous villages as local societies continued to be displaced by branches of the affiliated orders. No doubt, too, there was some disenchantment with simple pastimes which had satisfied before the labourer had learned to look further afield and to 'compare Mantua with Rome'.[57] Yet, pictures of the village as a place of unbearable dullness can easily be overdrawn. Recollections of the games played by children in the Edwardian period refer to hoop-bowling, top-spinning, skipping, tiddler fishing, bird nesting, walking stilts, bonfire night celebrations and carol singing, while the sort of celebration described for Shawford (Hants.) on Boxing Day 1897, when the principal inhabitants provided a Christmas tree, crayons, crackers, toys and sweets, was far from unique. From Magdalen in the Fen Country

"THE POINT OF VIEW."

Overworked London Clerk (taking short holiday on Sussex Downs). "So you've lived here all your life?"

Countryman. "Yaas, Sir, and prashious tired of it I be. Ah, Lunnon's the place; a man can feel alive there. Why, I feels like as if I was *shut up in a box* living here."

(*Punch*, 3 April 1901)

come memories of the enlivenment provided by itinerant tradesmen, the hurdy-gurdy man, dancing bear people, German bands and a surviving horkey (harvest supper), where the broomstick dance was performed and old men were heard to praise their masters.[58] We have a rich account of the social life of Quethiock (Cornwall), where the annual flower show instituted in 1893 was a remarkably grand occasion, with a brass band from Callington, public tea and cricket match, all organized by a committee which included farmworkers as well as employers. Here, dances were held occasionally in the schoolroom where music was provided by the village postmaster ('Come on you boys, swing it! Swing it!'), and although these were forsworn by the Wesleyans, they for their part provided children's treats including regular trips by cart to the seaside at Looe.[59] No doubt it is true, as historians of leisure point out, that increasingly recreations were set within a controlled context of respectability, as church and chapel stalwarts strove to extinguish the rougher aspects of plebeian pleasures.[60] However, in citing these instances, which might be multiplied many times over, the aim is not to overturn such hard-won generalizations but to question the impression which they seem usually to convey, that the world of the farmworker and his dependants was devoid of passing pleasures which might provide a momentary diversion from their diurnal problems.

Escape in a more enduring form, taking the form of social mobility, was more difficult. The premiums usually required for craft apprenticeships had a strong tendency to exclude boys from poorer families, who mostly gravitated towards the jobs of their fathers. Within agriculture, opportunities to rise were very narrow although never completely closed. Named instances of farm servants who enjoyed social ascent without leaving their native areas are quite commonly encountered. They include William Blades of Nafferton (Yorks.), who rented his first arable land about 1872 and subsequently carried on the trade of fellmonger with considerable success and profit; Thomas Irving, who with his brother bought a butcher cart about 1866, took a shop at Armathwaite (Cumberland) in 1870 and his first tenanted farm in 1872, opened a further shop in Carlisle, and by 1909 was in a position to buy two farms in the locality, one for his son and daughter and one to rent; or Charles Slater who purchased from his employer two old cottages and $3\frac{1}{2}$ acres of land about 1895, this being the first of several transactions involving land and houses. Eventually he became a district councillor and the owner of a motor-car.[61] It will be noticed that upward mobility in all these cases was strongly associated with dealing, as if to justify the opinion of C. S. Read, the Norfolk agronomist who once declared, 'I could put my hand upon dozens of men . . . that came to Norwich Hill who have risen that way to become large farmers or great cattle dealers, but, at the same time, I could not put my hand upon half a dozen small men who had risen simply by farming a bit of land.'[62] Those successfully ascending needed to have an unusually well-developed eye for the main chance, abnormal powers of work and an iron constitution and, if married at all, their wives needed to be equally determined. Childlessness was another helpful attribute. At Corsley, Davies noted that the local farmers included several labourers who, having no children, had saved up enough capital to take on a small place.[63] Even so, the majority of those entering the agricultural labour market were fated to remain employees all their days. It could hardly be otherwise, for as Lennard pointed out, with reference to statistics collected from 64 English parishes, over 70 per cent of farmers were farmers' sons, forming to a great extent 'a close hereditary caste'.[64] The position was scarcely affected by further legislation with respect to smallholdings. The failure of the 1892 Act had not quenched interest in land reforms, a subject upon which there was a bewildering variety of views ranging from those, like Collings, who still advocated small proprietorships as a bulwark of social conservatism through to thorough-going socialists who were against any kind of private property in land and favoured its nationalization. However, the first, and as it turned out, the only practical step taken in the period came in 1908 with the passing of a new Smallholdings Act. This broke new ground by requiring County Councils to provide draft schemes for acquiring land for this purpose, and empowered them where necessary to use compulsory purchase to do so. Because the arrangements provided for the leasing of holdings (and not merely for their sale), they brought a rush of enthusiasm and a modest degree of success, some 200,000 acres having been acquired by 1914 and some 14,000 holdings provided.[65] But the overall number of small farms (under 50 acres) in England and Wales actually declined slightly during these years due to urban encroachments; and it would be misleading to exaggerate the significance of the new opportunities for the agricultural wage-earner. It appears that only about 2 per cent of farmworkers applied in the years between 1908 and 1914, and many of these were deemed unsuitable through lack of capital or displayed a reluctance to move from their native villages, so that, as sundry critics pointed out, successful applicants tended to be chiefly village artisans, publicans, carriers and higglers.[66]

The circumstances traced in this chapter suggest that, although greater agricultural prosperity was good for employment, it by no means guaranteed progress in farmworkers' living standards, or the bringing of them closer to those enjoyed by urban workers. There was even less likelihood of the achievement of greater economic equality or of the erosion of vast discrepancies of social standing within the village. By any yardstick, it seemed, the position of the farmworker was disadvantaged, and the phrase 'a want of outlook' was a neat summary of his situation.[67] Here, one might hypothesize, was fertile ground for a revival of trade unionism, virtually defunct in 1895, and a deep pool of dissatisfaction upon which the Liberal party might draw to consolidate its position, or which might be tapped even by politicians of a socialist persuasion. Yet agricultural workers, as we have seen, were finely sub-divided and had their own criteria for judging worth and standing, a point never well understood by urban radicals.[68] Moreover, they worked in many thousands of dispersed workplaces, and the communities in which they lived out their lives were infinitely varied in character, suggesting that their responsiveness to the collectivist approach of trade unionism or to the siren calls of radical politicians might be partial, at best. In both spheres this turned out to be the case.

There was a short-lived flicker of trade unionism under the auspices of the Workers' Union in 1899, but the Eastern Counties Agricultural Labourers' and Smallholders' Union, formed at North Walsham (Norfolk), repays closer attention, for this was the direct forerunner of modern agricultural trade unionism. ECALSU was steered into life against a background of a number of mean evictions by Tory landlords and farmers in the aftermath of the Liberal landslide victory at the General Election of 1906. Its leading lights included George Nicholls, a part-time smallholder who, along with Richard Winfrey, had just become a Liberal MP, and George Edwards, an indefatigable secretary who, if he lacked the fire and vigour of Arch, certainly possessed courage, devotion and shrewdness in ample measure.[69] By 1909, total membership had reached 4–5,000, due largely to Edwards who in the early years cycled thousands of miles addressing meetings and stimulating new branches into life. The most significant, though not the only, skirmish in which the infant union engaged took place at the village of St Faiths, near Norwich.[70] At the close of 1909 William Norgate, the secretary of the branch, had written to G. D. Gowing of The White House, Sprowston, condemning his lead in effecting the usual winter reduction of 1s 'at a time when farming is fairly good ... [and] the necessarys of life are dearest', couching his objection in a very traditional form: 'remember what the Grand Old Book says ... he that withhold more than is meett attendeth to Poverty.' By May 1910, a meeting of the local branch decided to demand a general rise of 1s a week on top of that given with the return to summer hours and, as well, a Saturday half-holiday. Each member should give his employer one week's notice on 28 May, failing a satisfactory settlement. This step was taken against the advice of Norgate and of Edwards, who counselled greater moderation and sought to do all he could to avoid a strike. Unhappily, the non-response of local employers to his letters led inevitably to a withdrawal of the men's labour. The dispute proved to be long and bitter, featuring the importation of non-union men and very active policing in the village. It soon attracted the attention of the Norwich Independent Labour party. Every Saturday members stood outside the gates of the main factories, such as that of J. and J. Colman, and were not disappointed with the contributions of workpeople who in many cases doubtless sprang from an agricultural background. The money so raised was used to supplement the 10s a week strike money paid out of union funds. Yet the farmers, with the aid of their blacklegs, defectors and, presumably, local non-unionists experienced no difficulty in gathering their hay and grain harvests. By November, a majority of the central executive decided to accept an offer from the St Faith's schoolmaster to act as an intermediary in negotiations with the farmers, and achieved through a ballot of the whole union membership consent to these efforts to reach an honourable conclusion. However, what was not made clear was that the executive envisaged a return to work on the old terms, 13s a week and no half-holiday, which amounted to a clear defeat. Edwards and a minority of the executive resisted these steps, and an indignant St Faith's branch demanded a second ballot, spelling out more clearly the alternatives. On the second count, the union members voted to continue the strike, but only narrowly by 1,102 to 1,053. The executive then overrode the vote, proceeding to settle with the farmers, who agreed to take back only 33 of the 76 men on strike, on the old terms. It was left to Edwards to carry this news to St Faith's, and along with George Hewitt, a socialist who had replaced Norgate as branch secretary, to utter what words of comfort they could. The aftermath of the strike is particularly interesting. Many believed that the cause had been betrayed by Liberal leaders whose interest lay merely in using the union as a vehicle to marshal votes in elections, and at a bitter special meeting at Fakenham in February 1911, the resignations of Nicholls and Winfrey, President and Treasurer respectively, were forced. The complexion of the new executive committee was not so distinctively socialist as to justify Liberal complaints that the Independent Labour party had captured the union, but it did mark a distinctive shift away from the Liberal party towards the Labour movement.[71]

Initially, disappointment at the outcome of the St Faith's strike was reflected in a check to the union, whose contribution income fell from £1,255 (1910) to £1,084 (1911).[72] But modest growth soon resumed and showed signs of spreading beyond Norfolk, in recognition of which ECALSU changed its name to the National Agricultural Labourers' and Rural Workers' Union. Not the least important factor in its growth (by the end of 1913 membership had reached nearly 12,000), was its registration as an approved society under the National Insurance Act (1911). This embraced farmworkers within the sickness benefit but not the unemployment provisions of the legislation, which was confined to a number of trades deemed especially vulnerable to cyclical unemployment. Meanwhile, the Workers' Union was making vigorous attempts to organize in the rural districts, though well away from the areas covered by NALRWU,[73] and the scene seemed set for the advancement of union aims.

Measured by the number of individual disputes or working days lost through strikes, the years 1911–13 showed exceptional militancy in British industrial relations across a broad front, as workers in many industries reacted to the erosion of their wages through price inflation. In agriculture, the most significant pre-war strike occurred at Ormskirk in Lancashire, a district of enormously fertile moss soil which produced huge crops of vegetables, hay, grain and straw, finding a steady market in the towns of south Lancashire, particularly Liverpool where 1911 had seen a massive transport strike and confrontations between police and strikers.[74] In this district, the impetus to farmworkers' organization was given by two railwaymen, George Newman and John Phipps, both committed socialists, and by the close of 1912 seven branches of NALRWU had been formed, with a membership approaching 2,000. Initially, the demands of the men were pitched at a weekly basic rise of 4s, and 6d an hour for overtime together with a Saturday half-holiday. This was more than enough to alarm even the remodelled executive ('all Norfolk men meeting in Norfolk and out of sympathy with a demand which was for nearly double Norfolk rates'), and Edwards was despatched to see what could be achieved by a more conciliatory approach. Despite his efforts, the strike of June and July 1913 was unusually bitter, featuring cycling pickets, throwing of stones at wagons, the use of non-union labour, assault and intimidation, and a heavy police presence – they were condemned as 'only hooligans in uniform' by one militant. The outcome was decided by the intervention of other unions which contributed to strike funds, picketed Liverpool boats to ensure that strike-breakers were not brought in by sea, and encouraged the Irish either to join the union or move on; finally, the Ormskirk branch of the National Union of Railwaymen refused to handle any farm produce during the strike. In the event, the action was successful in winning a general rise of 2s a week, 6d an hour for overtime and a 2 p.m. finish on Saturdays. Nothing so dramatic occurred elsewhere, though in the early months of 1914, strikes and rumours of strikes filled the air in rural England, and were in several cases successful. Among the more notable events was a strike originating in February at Helions Bumpstead (Essex), which eventually spread to involve about 3–400 workers. In March and April, increases of 1s a week were conceded by Lord Leicester's Holkham tenants, on Sir Ailwyn Fellowes' estate at Honingham (Norfolk), by Nottingham Corporation (farming 2,000 acres at Stoke Bardolph and Bulcote), and by the King's agent at Sandringham who granted a Saturday half-holiday as well, so precipitating similar demands for 'the King's pay and the King's conditions' on neighbouring farms. The NALRWU supported strike action in a number of localities including Chitterne and Broad Hinton (Wilts.), Wilmslow and Alderley Edge (Cheshire), Wallasey on the Wirral peninsula, and at Swanley in Kent, and the wage increases won in 1913–14 just about kept pace with current rises in the cost of living, which was, perhaps, no mean achievement.[75] However, the recitation of these events can give an exaggerated impression of the depth of trade union sentiment. As *The Times* pointed out in March 1914, 'As a class ... the agricultural labourers of the country are an unorganised body, incapable of concerted action in a national strike movement, for comparatively few of them are enrolled on the books of a trade union.'[76] When its history comes to be written, it will probably be found that the National Farmers' Union, which was originated in Lincolnshire in 1908 by Colin Campbell to articulate the interests of tenant farmers and owner occupiers, was a good deal more successful in consolidating its position. Moreover, as the events at St Faith's and Ormskirk reveal very clearly, there was no uniformity of outlook and philosophy among the leaders and active supporters of agricultural trade unionism. By comparison with figures such as Winfrey and Nicholls, George Edwards was a radical; but with his background as a Primitive Methodist preacher and his instinctive caution, he seemed nothing of the kind to ardent socialists, exemplified by Phipps. It is significant that the union executive attempted to displace the latter from his post as local organizer, at first unsuccessfully in December 1913. After re-arranging the basis of representation on the Annual Council of the union in 1914 in such a way as to ensure an overwhelming majority of Norfolk men, they finally achieved their objective of ridding themselves of this troublesome syndicalist and champion of local autonomy: but only at the cost of splitting the union membership in Lancashire, many men withdrawing to form a Farm and Dairy Workers' Union.[77]

Such were the advances gained, and their limitations, in the sphere of trade unionism. In that of local government and politics, new opportunities seemed to present themselves with the advent of parish councils in 1894. Initially, these met with some enthusiasm: in 1894, 91 representatives of the interests of labour (including 54 farmworkers) were elected among 140 councillors in 24 Warwickshire parishes. However, in the longer run their participation tended to fall away, not least because the powers of parish councils were found to be too insignificant to draw out real talent and make it an object of ambition to become a member.[78] It is true, individual parish councils, or rebels within them, became involved in a number of *causes célèbres*. For example, the Chairman and Vice-Chairman of Winterbourne Strickland (Dorset) PC received notices to quit after persuading the Rural District Council to examine cottages on the estate of Sir Everard Hambro, banker and plutocrat. An individual parish councillor at Potterne (Wilts.) got up a petition, in the face of opposition from his fellow-councillors and from Devizes RDC, which moved John Burns at the Local Government Board to order a local enquiry and eventually the building of a dozen new cottages.[79] At Burston (Norfolk) a new schoolteacher, Tom Higdon, turned out to evince strong reforming and pro-union tendencies, and led a take-over of the parish council in March 1913, overturning the regime of the Vicar and local farmers. However, the Vicar fought back through the school management committee which brought forward some unsatisfactory charges against Higdon and his wife, the assistant mistress. The Norfolk County Council was persuaded to dismiss the couple, but the outcome was a strike of the majority of children, and the initiation of a trade-union supported fund to build an opposition establishment, the 'Burston Strike School' which eventually opened its doors in 1917.[80] Events such as these, where 'village Hampdens' ranged themselves against powerful forces of reaction, have their place in the annals of the rural labour movement. But they were not typical. All too often the work of parish councils, even where they included farmworker representatives, was confined to less edifying causes, such as harrying gypsies (Blaxhall, Suffolk), or, at Ashwell (Herts.), opposing a bold but expensive plan of the RDC to close old wells, create a new water system and replace earth closets with a water-based sewerage system.[81]

On the wider political front, there is no doubt that, up to a point, the Liberals enjoyed some success in driving a wedge through the agrarian interest. In Lincolnshire, according to one author, there existed by the close of the nineteenth century 'a barbed wire fence ... over which Conservative farmers and Liberal labourers eyed each other with hostility'.[82] But Lincolnshire was not typical of English rural parliamentary divisions, due to the comparative strength of non-conformity; and on a broader canvas, it has been shown, decisive shifts in rural political sentiment were thwarted by the workings of a law of political compensation. Where farmers were large-scale and prosperous (and hence likely to be Conservative), they employed a large number of labourers who *on balance* were likely to be Liberal. On the other hand, on poorer quality soils, and in the uplands, where farmers were comparatively poor and employed little labour, they themselves were likely to support the Liberal interest.[83] Socialist politicians faced even greater difficulties in winning the credence of farmworkers. Although W. H. Hudson in 1910 believed that socialism was slowly permeating the villages (due to the activities of 'sedition-mongers'), Bennett (the Fabian son of the Tory rector of a Suffolk parish) would presumably have disagreed: in 1913 he concluded that socialism was not yet understood in the villages by the poor or for that matter, the rich.[84] Successive parliamentary elections, including those of 1886, 1892, 1895 and 1900, were remarkable for the extent of non-voting in rural constituencies. This feature was due partly to fears of intimidation and a suspicion that the vote was not in fact secret, partly to the fact that elections tended to take place during harvest time, and in some measure, no doubt, to the farmworkers' widespread scepticism of the disinterestedness of those members of another class who professed their willingness to improve his lot. In that spirit Bettesworth, the Surrey labourer, regularly refused to vote in elections.[85]

It is chiefly on the basis of evidence of this kind that we must seek to make some judgement about the farmworker's perception of his place in society on the eve of the Great War. It can be argued that the relative weakness of agricultural trade unionism and a failure to make the weight of their numbers count in the political sphere do not do full justice to the depth of discontent among farmworkers at this period. Beneath their habitually cagey and often timorous demeanour[86] there lurked a seething mass of resentment, or so contemporary radicals and their successors assumed. Against these impressions, it can be argued that the figures on rural criminality, so far as they are an accurate barometer for the purpose, show no evidence of high social tension in the countryside. The incidence of sheep-stealing and poaching (considered 'a poor business' compared to fifty years before) had been significantly reduced, though this was due in part, no doubt, to a 60 per cent increase in the number of gamekeepers since the 1860s.[87] Moreover, rural crime rates in general were comparatively low. The incidence of drunkenness, homicidal crimes and assaults was less than half that encountered in the great manufacturing towns, and at the turn of the century only four in every 10,000 male agriculturists were in prisons, against 14.4 among the male population as a whole. Most significantly, arson was by now virtually unheard of.[88]

Certainly, the language of class was by now freely employed to describe the texture of rural social relations, and many farmworkers were class conscious in the simple sense of being increasingly aware of their relatively disadvantaged situation. But it is important to emphasize the limitations of this usage. There was undoubtedly a minority for whom class was an operational concept, implying opposition and hostility towards employers and landlords. The recent work of Howkins on rural labour relations strengthens the impression that a spirit of antagonism was fairly widely diffused in the arable eastern counties, particularly Norfolk. But, as he very fairly concedes, his study contains 'practically nothing on those labourers, and there were many, who were not radical';[89] and at the other extreme it was noticed by contemporaries that a certain pride was evinced by the countryman concerning his local gentry, manor house and park. 'Only listen to him', remarked Holdenby in a comment that is full of significance, 'telling an *inquiring stranger* about them.'[90] No doubt the great majority adopted variable postures which lay between these extremes, and we may suspect that, as often as not, the resentment of the farmworker was reserved for urban-based cousins who might adopt an air of wordly superiority, take an almost spiritual pride in comparing their 'learning' with his 'ignorance' and in a variety of subtle ways make mockery of his speech and manners. At all events, probably the most acute commentator on rural social life at the time was convinced that, as a body, the labourers harboured no animosity against their betters and had 'no sense of oppression to poison their lives.'[91]

In an effort to mitigate the farmworkers' material disadvantages, which were conceded to a greater or lesser extent across the political spectrum, attempts were made to establish by legislation minimum rates of pay during the summer of 1913, following precedents set in a handful of sweated industries and, in 1912, in coal-mining. Some enlightened Unionists, perhaps seeking to forestall anything worse, put forward a bill which would have given a uniform wage to 'men of full age' and hence threatened to cause employers to turn increasingly to boys, while that introduced by the Labour party, proposing a uniform rate across all age groups, carried the opposite danger that lads would face dismissal.[92] There remained immense practical difficulties and nothing came of either initiative. Still, the issues which gave rise to such proposals remained very much alive. In May 1914 there came from Rowntree's pen a leaflet entitled *The Labourer and the Land*. Drawing freely on the results of the Liberal land enquiry, it restated the case for minimum wages as part of a far-reaching programme of rural reform which would embrace measures to provide security of tenure, regulation of rents, the encouragement of smallholdings, allotments and rural education facilities, together with a vigorous attack on the rural housing problem. It concluded with a moral peroration announcing that 'Class warfare threatens us today – not because we hate one another, but because we love ourselves – because groups and individuals, bent on their private ends, forget the common good'. It also carried, in the form of a preface, a promise from Lloyd George that the strong arm of the state would be used to achieve these ends.[93] Against such Liberal challenges, the forces of conservatism were rallying. *The Land Retort*, also published in 1914 by Adeane and Saville, urged agriculturists to be prepared to defend themselves against 'the onslaught of ignorance and prejudice' and, whilst falling in with any sound and practical proposals, to oppose vigorously any wild and revolutionary schemes. Meanwhile, extensive researches were being put in hand by the Land Agents' Society which eventually resulted in the appearance of a more solid, well-analysed statistical counterblast and defence of the land interest.[94] The stage was set for a trial of strength over these issues at the elections due in 1915, but by that time, men's minds had been diverted to other, more pressing problems.

SEVEN

The Great War and its aftermath, 1914–20

On the eve of the war, Britain's neglected agriculture produced but a fraction of the nation's food. Four out of every five slices of bread were made from wheat produced abroad, and three from every five spread with imported butter. The British bought in four-fifths of their lard, two-thirds of their ham and bacon and three-quarters of their cheese.[1] Yet there was an unquestioning faith in the Royal Navy's ability to keep open the channels through which these imports flowed, and every reason to suppose as *The Farmer and Stockbreeder* concluded three months after the outbreak of hostilities in August, that 'Agriculture of all industries is the least likely to be affected by the war'.[2] The only immediate difficulties arose from the requisitioning of some 9,000 draught horses, and from an incipient labour shortage. Individual reservists such as Jack Lamb of Berkshire, who had 'heard the spiteful whine of the Pathan bullet' and seen the Taj Mahal, received the fateful letter bearing the imprint OHMS; while at Sledmere in the East Riding where there is a remarkable monument depicting their contribution, the swift departure for France of a thousand men enrolled since 1912 in Sir Mark Sykes's Wagoners' Reserve was immediately felt on the local labour market.[3] Meanwhile, many landed proprietors were prompt to offer their houses and their sons for military purposes, and zealously promoted recruitment among their employees. G. L. Courthope of Rye in Sussex was one of these, not only volunteering himself but taking 15 of his estate workers with him; while Col. Borton of Cheveney, Kent, though too old to serve himself, conveyed his cowman, footman and butler to Maidstone to enlist within three weeks of the outbreak of war.[4] Many young farmworkers, like men in other walks of life, needed little encouragement: they flocked to the colours thinking 'it would be a nice change to spend a few weeks learning to march, use a rifle, and then if it wasn't all over, a trip to France and into Germany just to finish off the Kaiser'.[5]

During the early years of the war the government, firmly wedded to orthodox doctrines of free trade and individualism, intervened in the economy only at selected points. However, as awareness of the sheer magnitude of the task of fighting an all-out war increased, so the need for a more comprehensive system of economic controls became apparent. Several factors contributed to inflation, which raised the wholesale price level by about 60 per cent between the outbreak of war and 1916. They included the distorted growth of the munitions industry and a shortage of imports, while the government, as in the French Wars a century before, was spending freely without withdrawing equivalent amounts from the purchasing power of the population, thus encouraging unseemly luxury consumption and some profiteering.[6] Moreover, in 1916 the dangers of the situation were compounded by a poor harvest and by Germany's embarkation early the following year on an unrestricted submarine campaign, aiming to force Britain to sue for peace by August. That it failed, despite the sinking of 4m. tons of shipping within six months, was due largely to purposeful economic counter-measures which came about with the replacement of the Asquith government by a coalition headed by Lloyd George in December 1916. With respect to ensuring food supply, the new policies took three forms. A new ministry supervised the allocation of all shipping space and sought to confine imports, other than food, to real essentials. Secondly, an extensive system of controls was imposed on distribution, so that by the end of the war the government bought and sold 85 per cent of the food consumed in the country. During 1917 a new Ministry of Food, prompted into being by signs of unrest in the industrial districts, set out to purchase and allocate virtually all supplies of essential foodstuffs, and the price controls which were an essential aspect of this policy were eventually supplemented by rationing schemes, starting with a national scheme for sugar (1 January 1918). Other schemes followed during the summer, but it was never found necessary to ration potatoes or bread, though millers were allowed to repeatedly raise the extraction rate, rendering the wartime loaf dark and unattractive. The third aspect of government policy was the Food Production Campaign which made a less significant contribution to upholding food supplies, but was of more direct significance to agriculturalists.[7]

In the summer of 1915 a committee headed by Lord Milner urged the need to develop a policy directed towards greater concentration on arable production, and suggested a scheme of guaranteed prices to encourage farmers to change. Its recommendations came to be supported by two other bodies, the Hobhouse Committee on the settlement or employment on the land of discharged soldiers and sailors (reporting in spring 1916), and the Selborne Committee charged with considering post-war policy which sat in 1916–17, the feeling being that such a strategy would be conducive to employment on the land, and would reduce future dependence on imported cereals. However, it was not until New Year's Day 1917 that decisive steps were taken, with the appointment of a Food Production Department within the Board of Agriculture. It took as its point of departure the fact that the relative number of persons per annum capable of being fed from land used for various purposes was: from potatoes 408, from wheat 208 and oats 172, but from grassland only 45 (milk) and 9 (meat). Under Lloyd George's more receptive administration, the outcome was the 1917 Corn Production Act, the chief provisions of which were to establish guaranteed minimum prices of 60s and 38s 6d for wheat and oats respectively and to uphold them, on a descending scale, until 1922; and the transference to the agricultural departments of powers already in existence under the Defence of the Realm Acts to regulate the cropping and stocking of land and to dispossess inefficient farmers or landowners. Meanwhile, for the implementation of its policies, the Food Production Department sought the aid of county 'War Agricultural Executive Committees',[8] each backed by a network of local committees composed of prominent landlords and farmers, whose initial task was to visit all farms to see how much extra ploughing could be undertaken in the spring of 1917, and to persuade, cajole or even take over the holdings of the incorrigibly inefficient or uncooperative. The County Committees in turn spawned sub-committees dealing with specific aspects such as cropping orders, land in possession, and above all labour, and were the essential link between farmers and the planners in Whitehall. In 1919, after hostilities had ended, the question of a post-war policy for agriculture was remitted to a Royal Commission, which was split, 12 members taking the view that a positive policy of providing guaranteed prices should be continued to keep land in tillage, the other 11 maintaining that they were no longer necessary. The view of the bare majority was embodied in the Agriculture Act of December 1920, which was understood to guarantee cereal prices for at least four more years, although the County Committees were shorn of their powers to impose orders on the use of land.

Such was the changing political and administrative framework within which the agricultural industry operated during the Great War and its immediate aftermath. In many respects it was very successful. While reductions occurred in the acreage devoted to high value products such as hops, and there was a diminution in the output of animal products, increases in the amount of wheat grown (65 per cent, comparing 1918 to the average of 1904–13), potatoes (40), and oats (47 per cent) ensured that the output of the UK agriculture at the close of the war was very nearly the same as in 1914.[9] Moreover, though consumers missed their sugar and butter, and the better-off found their meat consumption curtailed, average calorific intake (taking all foods together) fell very little, perhaps 2½ per cent by the end of the war. Indeed, due partly to rationing, but more especially to the virtual disappearance of unemployment and the employment of married women, food was somewhat more equitably distributed than in peace-time. It is striking that, during the war, the national decline in infant mortality continued unabated, and there was a marked tendency, in the great cities, for the proportion of children found to be poorly nourished to decline.[10] By contrast, in Germany where agriculture had been protected and some attention given to the strategic significance of agriculture, food output fell by some 43 per cent, due to shortages of farm inputs of all kinds and a lack of effective administrative action.[11]

On the land the war years are remembered for the appearance of farm tractors, mostly made available through the operations of the tractor services organised by the County Committees from 1917. These included several hundred home-produced caterpillars, and light three-wheeled 'Ivel' models made in Bedford. However, the United States was the chief source of supply, the Food Production Department favouring Fordsons for their reliability and all-round versatility. It is estimated that between 1916 and the end of 1918, the number of tractors in use on British farms increased sixfold to reach 23,000.[12] Harry Reffold recalls that, with the arrival of a tractor on an East Riding farm, Ted the foreman 'was in his element. Nobody was allowed to drive it but him'; but he also remembers the spectacle of the tractor being towed back by a horse team when it broke down, a sight relished by the older hands who regarded it as a twenty-minute wonder.[13] This incident was not untypical, for many difficulties were experienced with servicing and repairs by blacksmiths and others unaccustomed to dealing with such machinery. With other classes of farm machinery, similar problems arose. By 1917, it was claimed, only half of the 500 or so steam ploughing sets in use before 1916 were still operational, and while the Food Production Department's orders in 1917 included 65 new sets, 6,000 ploughs, 5,500 sets of harrows, 5,000 binders and 3,365 rollers, these were miniscule additions to the total stock of farm machinery.[14] Thus, although the tractor was making a significant contribution by 1918, across the war years as a whole the achievement of British agriculture did not depend on wholesale technological advances. Moreover, there were marked shortages of nitrogenous and phosphoric fertilizers in 1915–17, and even by the end of the war inputs did not exceed pre-war levels.[15] There were some minor changes in established practices. Reffold remembers his foreman contriving to avoid the traditional thatching of stacks ('Takes too much time up') and especially the 'opening out' of the harvest field, in 1917, with the reaper rather than with the scythe ('Never mind what folks will say.... What bit of corn we waste is nothing compared to the labour we save').[16] But in the main the success of agricultural policy depended on ensuring that the number of farm horses did not fall too far (many of those used by the Army after 1914 were imported),[17] and above all on maintaining the supply of labour.

Intensely patriotic Squire (mustering remnant of farm-hands). "NOW, THEN, LADS, PULL YOURSELVES TOGETHER. KITCHENER MAY EXTEND THE AGE LIMIT YET."

(*Punch*, 2 June 1915)

By July 1915, as a consequence of the calling up of reservists, voluntary enlistments and a movement of labour out of agriculture into higher paid occupations, it was estimated that about 150,000 self-selected men (the comparatively young and fit), a figure equivalent to some 15 per cent of the pre-war labour force, had left the industry.[18] In August, the first steps to reduce random losses had been taken, a national register being made of all men aged between 15 and 65 not serving with the armed forces, with skilled men engaged in important civilian work 'starred', i.e. they would neither be accepted as volunteers for military service nor solicited for it. The agricultural departments listed various specialized occupations as skilled, although the all-rounder was not so starred. In the autumn, the War Office was persuaded to allow tribunals composed of council representatives, firms and employers to hear appeals by employers against the enlistment of men judged to be indispensable to civilian production. Then, in March 1916, by which date the agricultural sector had yielded up on a voluntary basis much the same proportion of its pre-war labour force as industry (28 per cent),[19] reliance on voluntary recruitment was abandoned. The Military Service Act of 1916 conscripted all single men of 19–30, and in April all married men in this age group, although starred individuals over 25 were to be allowed temporary exemption. The scope of such exemptions continued to be much argued over. During the Autumn of 1916 the tribunals refused them to some 60,000 men in agriculture, who were still being called up in 1917 when the district committees were visiting farms and asking for more land to be planted with crops, and at the local level much confusion reigned. Recruiting officers sometimes called up skilled men with vague promises of substitutes, and in November 1917 the War Office was taking all 18-year-old men, in spite of protests both locally and centrally. In the spring of 1918 the conflict intensified. On the one hand the biggest crops ever sown required attention; on the other, the War Office was calling desperately for men to meet the German summer offensive which pressed back the allied armies in France. April brought a Cabinet decision that agriculture must yield up another 30,000 and that these should be selected by the War Agricultural Committees, to fill quotas set by the Food Production Department. These requirements caused an inordinate amount of work (the Cumberland Committee sat on 23 occasions between 3 May and 24 June) and widespread, indignant protests which caused the Cabinet, on 27 June, to defer further call-up notices until after the harvest – although not before 75 per cent of the quota had been filled.[20] Thereafter, the military position so far improved that it proved unnecessary to take the rest. Indeed, in August came an unexpected announcement that the War Office would be releasing some men for the harvest. According to the Cumberland Committee, this gave the impression to many farmers that they could get their sons or former workmen released, and its overworked staff was inundated with applications. Moreover, the committee felt that its authority was being undermined: while many applications for the return of men serving in the Royal Engineers and Army Service Corps had been refused on military grounds, it had 'come to the Committee's knowledge that in several of these cases the applicants have written direct to the man's C.O., and in one instance to the King and have been successful in getting the men they wanted ... this also is calculated to make farmers mistrustful....'[21]

Such was the capricious machinery of military recruitment and selection. In all, it has been suggested, English and Welsh agriculture yielded up some 300,000 men, a figure equivalent to some 24 per cent of the total numbers of employers or employees in agriculture in 1911.[22] Throughout its course, farmers were wont to complain of staff shortages, and were particularly critical of the way in which civilian industry tempted their men away with higher wages. Instances quoted included the diversion of men to furniture-making in High Wycombe ('the government demand for chairs appears to be enormous'), while problems over labour were encountered in any district where camps or aerodromes were under construction, for example at Uxbridge, Feltham and Ruislip in Middlesex, Cranwell (Lincs.) and Witney, Hayford and Weston on the Green (Oxon.), or wherever munitions works exacerbated the situation. One Worcestershire farmer drew particular attention to the wages paid at the Austin works, as much as £4 a week for unskilled men ('They don't care what they pay; it only comes off the excess profits, which would otherwise go to the government').[23] It should be said, though, that the position was variable. In Norfolk there was said to be practically no shortage in some localities, and in Wales, where 70 per cent of holdings were under 50 acres in size, farmers could generally get by with family labour aided by the custom of *cymhorthen*, or mutual self-help.[24] Even in a county as industrialized as Warwickshire, a systematic survey showed the position to be very mixed. In 1916 there were numerous places, especially in the south of the county, where no overall shortage was reported, only grumbles that what was available was 'inferior'; and even in the northern districts from whence there came general complaints of loss of men to collieries, factories and munitions works in Coventry and Birmingham, difficulties were alleviated in some places (around Atherstone and Nuneaton for example) by the willingness of industrial night-shift workers to work part of the day on the land.[25]

Nevertheless, circumstances were such as to inculcate among employers a greater degree of appreciation of their men, and some claim that only in the context of the First World War was the discovery made that the agricultural worker was precious and skilled.[26] Pensioners were brought back to work and, in Northamptonshire, much commended for their skill and the pride they took in their work. Overall, it was estimated, the war lifted the proportion of men over 45 from one-third to above one-half of the agricultural labour force.[27] However, with the working hours of farmworkers already comparatively long (9–10 in summer, 8–8½ in winter), the scope for increasing the length of the working day was limited: indeed, in some areas of the midlands it was found necessary to bring them down towards industrial norms 'in order to retain the labour',[28] and established sources of casual or seasonal labour supply were short. It was during the Great War that the 'Wolds Rangers', men who led a roving life taking on odd jobs for farmers, disappeared from view; and although the Irish appeared on schedule in 1914 and 1915, supplies of labour from this quarter thereafter dried up, due in part to ill-feeling after the Easter Rising in Dublin in 1916, and also to fears among the Irish that they might be conscripted.[29] Accordingly, it was found necessary to draw upon a wide variety of auxiliaries, giving the wartime labour force a decidedly polyglot character.

Soldier labour, where it could be released by the military authorities, was one source of supply. This was less popular with farmers than might be assumed, for it was considered expensive. At Stowmarket in 1915, farmers were trying to get the official War Office rate reduced from 24s to 16s a week to allow for time lost through wet weather, in accordance with established practice, and at least in the early stages of the war farmers were heard to say that they would let their crops rot rather than pay such wages.[30] East Riding employers complained of

SERVICE ON THE LAND.

The New Recruit. "SIR, I HAVE FINISHED FEEDING THE NON-RUMINANT PACHYDERMS. HAVE YOU ANY FURTHER ORDERS?"

(*Punch*, 3 August 1910)

the quality of southerners working on their farms and others were furious when they learned that the capable men they had lost were not actually fighting Germans, but employed by farmers elsewhere.[31] Some highly unsuitable men were drafted into agriculture including, in Herefordshire, a lift attendant, a ship's painter, a brass polisher, a needle maker, a chocolate maker and a ladies' tailor, while one Shropshire farmer complained bitterly, 'One of the men I got was a piano-tuner. I could knock nothing into him.'[32] Reffold remembers some soldiers bringing with them effete garments known as pyjamas, never before seen by farm-lads on the Yorkshire Wolds, but allows that the soldier-farm-workers did a lot to 'open our dust-covered eyes to another world' – none more than a Cockney, Tommy, whose stories were 'great fun to us who had only read of London', and who got on well once the attention he paid to the foreman's nubile daughters had been cooled by their father's dextrous demonstration of his skill in castrating bull-calves ('It's just as easy to do a chap like you. . . .')[33] On the whole, gross mis-matching tended to be reduced as time passed and gradually soldier labour was used more effectively. From Spring 1917 they were paid the ruling rates of the War Agricultural Committees which were perhaps a fair reflection of their efficiency, though some employers continued to regard the Army as an expensive source of supply: in November 1918 a Nottinghamshire farmer sought permission from the War Agricultural Committee to employ prisoners of war instead, stating that they were cheaper, a request that was severely deprecated.[34]

With prisoners, much depended on their variable demeanour and previous experience, as well as that of their guards. As a rule, it was impracticable to employ them on isolated farms where employees lived in, as the Cumberland Committee pointed out in 1918, and here and elsewhere the labour of prisoners was most effectively used in gangs, on specific tasks such as potato harvesting, timber felling and drainage operations.[35] To some extent their effectiveness was limited by the rather low levels of feeding that were officially permitted and, as a camp commandant in Cumberland reminded farmers early in 1919, anyone offering extra food to prisoners was liable to prosecution. The local War Agricultural Committee's minutes suggest that this was neither sensible nor enforceable, for the rations allocated were not sufficient for the labour on which the prisoners were employed and there is evidence to show that the regulations were widely ignored.[36] By the end of the war, prisoners were making a very worthwhile contribution. The Wiltshire War Agricultural Committee was anxious, in January 1919, that no prisoners should be withdrawn from the land until demobilization was further advanced.[37] As late as September, nearly ten months after the Armistice, some 25,000 were employed in agriculture, creating some controversy. It was contended that farmers were taking advantage of a cheap, disciplined labour force to the detriment of British civilians, said to be the case for example near Brailes camp in Warwickshire; while the decision of the Nottinghamshire Committee to refuse applications from the River Idle Commissioners of Sewers and B. G. Selby of Newark for prisoners to assist with drainage work was doubtless in deference to public opinion, as well as a recognition that there were 4,500 'bona-fide unemployed civilians in the county'.[38] In the event, plans for the repatriation of aliens, though delayed until November, largely removed the problem by the end of 1919.

Patriotic and sentimental feeling may have exaggerated the role played by women, to whom rallying cries were frequently addressed. 'The call has come to *every* woman, rich or poor, gentle or peasant, strong or weak, to do something and do it now', declaimed Miss Edith Broadly of Hollingbourne (Kent), an appeal quoted with approval by Viscountess Wolseley in *Women and the Land* (1916). In true patrician style, Lady Wolseley distinguished a special role for 'educated women' (supervisory work in gardens and dairies, and lecturing), and listed a variety of light branches of farm work 'within the range of the village girl'. Echoing many before her, she inveighed against the stealthy spread of the idea that farm work was 'derogatory to women', as well as the way in which village schools had tended to weaken among rural schoolchildren their natural love of the land. She also supposed that the 'comfortable separation allowances paid to the wives of soldiers' made them disinclined to exert themselves.[39] There may have been substance to this rather surprising claim during the early years of the war, for in October 1914 the wife of a private or corporal with two children obtained an allowance of 17s 6d per week, and with three, 20s. Although these sums were not princely, they compared quite well with the average weekly earnings of 17s 10d to 22s 6d secured by ordinary labourers in 1912–13.[40] One of the first steps in mobilizing women workers was taken with the setting up in Essex of a Women's National Land Service Corps, organized by Mrs Rowland

Williams. This was the precursor of the Women's Land Army, formed in 1917, which trained volunteers at either a centre or on a farm for four to six weeks, before sending them out to employers. Meanwhile, committees were established to mobilize village women. That of Wiltshire, headed by Lady Pembroke, soon established a register of available women in every village. By July 1916, 2,665 had registered and 1,887 were currently employed, besides which 'in many villages, the Registrars reported that others had said they were willing to do so, but did not wish to register'.[41] Thus there existed classes of women workers which were distinct in an administrative and, to some extent, a social sense. The Land Army looked to single females, often better educated and from diverse backgrounds. It was selective in character, favouring girls of 'sufficiently high character to make it safe to send them out to live alone on the farms or in cottages', and between 1917 and 1919 nearly half the 43,000 applicants were rejected.[42] Burning with a desire to get on with the job, they would frequently object to requests to wash floors, cook, or mind babies as they were sometimes asked to by farmers' wives, notably in Wales, who did not fully appreciate the distinction between land girls and traditional farm servants.[43] 'Village women' were eventually drawn into the fields in increasing numbers, especially as inflation began to bite into the real value of their separation allowances, and came to outstrip by a considerable margin the number of Land Army personnel. Thus, by 1918, there were 2,533 part-time or full-time women workers against 143 land girls in Cambridgeshire; 2,827 against 217 in Cheshire; 3,801 and 127 in Devon; 2,900 and 230 in Somerset, 1,358 compared to 64 in the East Riding, etc.[44] Although according to a new periodical, *Women's Industrial News*, the initial prejudice against women was considerable, by the end of the war the number employed as 'permanent workpeople' on British farms had increased by 35,000, or 60 per cent.[45] Their earnings were subjected to no controls and were not closely monitored. However, one estimate suggests that the usual daily rate in 1918 was 4½d an hour, or 2s 10d a day, with those on weekly earnings averaging 18s; while land girls were initially paid 18s a week, rising to 22s by the end of 1918.[46] Another source of supply was juvenile labour, which was the first recourse of farmers who had long suspected that village children were in danger of being over-educated: one, at a meeting of the Yorkshire Farmers' Union in October 1914, suggested that where schools had been taken over as temporary billets, the best arrangement would be for 'all the lads to go on to the farms and for all the teachers to go to the front.'[47] Many a farmers' organization busied itself petitioning the county education committees to release boys aged 13 or even 12 from school, a request with which they frequently complied. Later, Selley called this 'the meanest agitation of modern times', and noted that, even in France, the central government had issued a directive to local education authorities stating that the school attendance laws should be strictly maintained.[48] Certainly, the surviving statistics grossly understate the extent to which child labour was employed, because they were based on formal exemptions from schooling.[49] It should also be borne in mind that their children's earnings were welcome to many parents. Schoolboy labour at Brampton (Cumberland) was paid at the rate of 4d an hour in the first week by 1918, and 6d thereafter, with a guarantee of 15s a week; and Charles Slater, a school attendance officer during the war, recalled that summonsing an employer did not go down well with the people, and that a child could earn in one day what his parents paid in a fine.[50]

Until recently, no-one had attempted to assess either the incease in the farm labour requirement or to apportion the input of these various types of labour. Although there are no direct statistics of the labour demand in agriculture, it seems that there was little change in man-hours required (2.083m. in 1914 and 2.073 in 1917) until 1918, when the drive for more cereals implied an increase of some 5 per cent to reach 2.182m.[51] In theory, shortfalls in the usual sources of labour could have been met partially by increases in labour productivity; but since hours of work were already lengthy and the deployment of new machinery was limited, comparatively little improvement could be expected under this heading. Thus, by elimination it appears that the aggregate input of labour cannot, in fact, have been much below the pre-war level. As will be seen from table 7.1:

1. The aggregate supply of labour reached its nadir in 1916, recovering by 1918 to within 3 per cent of the pre-war level.
2. While the contribution of women certainly needs to be scaled down, it was second only to that of soldiers. A rough estimate is thus established of the extent of reliance on different types of auxiliary labour.

Table 7.1: Supply of labour on farms in England and Wales during the First World War*
(000 man-units)

	1908	*1915*	*1916*	*1917*	*1918*
A.					
'Conventional' labour	1,318	1,231	1,195	1,173	1,172
B.					
Replacement labour					
comprising					
Village women		0	6	25	30
W.L.A.		0	0	3	14
Soldiers		11	14	40	45
P.O.W.		0	0	3	14
Miscellaneous		4	10	15	17
Sub-total		15	30	86	114
Total labour supply	1,318	1,246	1,225	1,259	1,286
(1908 = 100)	100	94	93	95	97

* Adapted from tables in P. Dewey, 'Agricultural Labour Supply in England and Wales during the First World War', *Economic History Review*, 2nd series, vol. XXVIII, 1975, p. 104. N.B. These calculations assume a weighting of 1 for males over 20, 0.8 for females over 20, 0.6 for males under 20; 0.5 for females under 20, and casuals (on the assumption that they worked for three months), 0.25.

Since the government either directly or indirectly was responsible through various agencies for something like half the replacement labour,[52] it can be given some credit for upholding agricultural output in very difficult circumstances. On the other hand, the widespread use of auxiliaries clearly had some important implications for the remaining full-timers on the land, which takes us to the question of wages.

Under wartime conditions, due in part to the mixed character of the labour force and the difficulties of establishing rates due to price and wage fluctuations, there was a definite, though unmeasurable decline in piecework. By the end of the war, except for certain specialist operations such as sheep-shearing or hedge-laying, what was left tended to be concentrated in the eastern and south-eastern counties (mostly Kent), or in the fruit-growing areas of Herefordshire. Likewise, the 'standing off' of men in bad weather was substantially reduced; the use of soldier labour with its strictly defined hours and rates of pay tended to encourage the establishment of more regular employment for farmworkers.[53] The early months of the war brought increases of about 2s a week, taking the national average to about 17s 10d in April 1915, which implied a widespread reluctance on the part of employers to concede increases: in February 1915 the Manager of the Worcester Labour Exchange told the Chairman of the Bromyard branch of the National Farmers' Union that he had plenty of labourers ready to work in the country, 'but not at the present rate of wages'.[54] Thereafter, by January 1917 the average rose to 22s 3d, to which should be added perhaps 1s 3d for the value of allowances, pointing to average earnings across the country of 23s 6d against 16s 10d in June 1914.[55] Individual increases must have varied enormously. On a single farm in east Kent, the total remuneration of four workers advanced between 1913 and 1916 by 29, 38, 39 and 56 per cent respectively, while the wages of ordinary labourers moved up by 61 and 62 per cent, and of wagoners by 58 and 73 per cent in Kesteven and Holland (Lincs.) respectively, between 1914 and 1917.[56] However, it was at this point that minimum wages in agriculture, much discussed before the war, took effect. As well as providing a framework of guaranteed prices for farmers, the Corn Production Act of 1917 set a minimum wage of 25s; it also created, through the Board of Agriculture, a Central Agricultural Wages Board with powers to fix the rates for able-bodied men, set the hours for which these were payable, and define and value allowances in kind. The first meeting of this board, which was comprised of representatives of employers and workers, together with seven members appointed by the Board of Agriculture, took place in December 1917, and it quickly called into being District Wages Committees, similarly balanced, 39 of which had been constituted by May 1918.[57] In practice, agricultural cash wages in January 1918 averaged 27s 10d, a figure distinctly higher than the minimum stated in the Act, and at the district level, minimum rates were soon moving upward. Thus, in Norfolk where the first order came into force in May 1918, the rate was fixed at 30s for a 54 hour week (summer) and 48 (winter), with overtime rates of 8½d an hour (weekdays) or 10d (Sundays). The minimum rose a year later to 38s 6d, and subsequently to 42s (April 1920) and 46s (August).[58] It was at this time that an Essex labourer concluded that 'all my life the farmer's bin sittin' on we, an' now its our turn an' we're sitting on the likes of him'.[59] Table 7.2 shows how the greatest increases came after the advent of statutory wage-fixing machinery. Under the new regime there was, as well, a remarkable tendency to regional levelling-up. Thus, if we compare estimated earnings in 1914 with minimum wages in 1920–1, the three counties which head the list are Oxfordshire, with a 245 per cent increase, Suffolk (229), and Norfolk

Table 7.2: Changes in agricultural wages in England and Wales, 1914–20*
(Average weekly wages including allowances)

	Amount	*Percentage*
1914 (July)	16s 10d	100
1915 (April)	18s 10d	112
1917 (Jan.)	23s 6d	140
1918 (August)	31s 9d	189
1919 (May)	38s 0d	226
1920 (May)	42s 9d	254
1920 (August)	46s 9d	277

* A. L. Bowley, *Prices and Wages in the United Kingdom, 1914–20*, Clarendon, Oxford, 1921, p. 172.

(221), while the four bringing up the rear are Lancashire (122), Durham (119) and Northumberland (116). At the second date, the average minimum wage in the first trio of counties (46s) was only 3s 6d below the level of the three northern counties.[60]

So far, we have taken no account of the cost of living. Until the last year of hostilities, farmworkers' remuneration showed a tendency to lag behind price increases. Between 1914 and January 1919, it is calculated that the index of agricultural workers' wages increased by 91 per cent, against 103 per cent for wages in general and 122 per cent for the cost of living.[61] From a report of the Central Agricultural Wages Board published in 1919, it appears that there was a marginal deterioration in the quality of diets and that less meat, bacon, cheese and butter and imported goods such as syrup, treacle, sugar, tea and coffee were being consumed, although, on the other hand, milk consumption was upheld and that of bread increased.[62] Not surprisingly, a sharp increase in the demand for allotments was noted in many counties, 'a natural result of the food difficulties during the war'.[63] However, there were wide variations of individual experience. Single men living in were to some extent protected from increases in the cost of living, and among their married counterparts much depended on the family profile. As a Kent observer pointed out, 'A man who has four or five children of school age . . . will probably lose more by the rise in prices than he will gain by the rise in wages; but a man who no longer has any young children, but two or three aged 14–18 and a wife with more leisure to work on the farm will probably gain more by the rise in wages than he will lose by the rise in prices.' A family in the latter category might well have £3–£4 a week coming into the house, against 30s or 35s for the former.[64] The impact of the war on cottage availability must likewise have been very variable. New building, never brisk, quite ceased with the commencement of the war, and the difficulties of getting work done went far to perpetuate existing qualitative deficiencies. Overall, it was said, the effect of the war was to 'render the demand for more cottages in many districts less insistent',[65] although there were numerous instances where this was not true. 'Air-raid funkers' were accused of adding to the demand for cottages in the Chilterns and along the Thames Valley, while in

Kent 'refugees' from the coastal towns, afraid of bombardment, competed for inland cottages. In districts where munitions works drew in workers, competition for cottages had a noticeable impact on rent levels, seen for example in a ring of villages encircling Norwich, including Catton, Sprowston, Hellesdon and Drayton.[66]

The war was bound to affect the trade union movement. The position taken up by R. B. Walker, General Secretary of the NALRWU was uncompromising throughout the war. He wanted to take full advantage of the exigencies of the times to improve labour's negotiating position, and to this end he led opposition to all efforts to augment supply by using women and children, and counselled direct action over wages.[67] On the other hand, George Edwards, still a powerful figure in the union, published a stirring patriotic appeal to the 'working women of Norfolk, the wives and sweethearts of our brave boys', which described in vivid detail German atrocities in Belgium and France. He was responsible for patching up 'for the sake of peace' an incipient strike in Norfolk in 1915, by-passing ordinary channels by negotiating directly with five great farmers, including the Earl of Leicester and Henry Overman of Weasenham; and in 1916 he told the TUC that the avoidance of a strike during the war was more important than securing a 25s wage.[68] In any case, the unions were in no position to pursue a militant programme. It has been estimated that NALRWU lost a quarter of its members by 1916, while the number of Workers' Union branches fell from 250 (1914) to 40 within two years as 'the war took the live [*sic*] blood from our new branches', in the rueful words of a Wiltshire organizer.[69] But, as the war progressed, circumstances bolstered the prestige of the movement just as, incidentally, they enhanced that of the National Farmers' Union, whose membership was advancing rapidly to reach 80,000 by 1918.[70] This is seen in the involvement of union leaders (Walker and Edwards for NALRWU and Beard and Dallas for the Workers' Union) on the Central Wages Board in 1918: while at the local level, the War Agricultural Committees obliged even those farmers who had been stridently anti-union in peacetime to sit round a table along with union representatives who could voice their opinions on a wide variety of questions.

It is true that effective power of decision on the Central Wages Board tended to lie with the government nominees,[71] while the perusal of local War Agricultural Committee records suggests that the representations of union men were often ineffective. Thus, in September 1918 an attempt by Brother Mackley to block supplies of labour to a Clipstone (Notts.) farmer who was in dispute over wages was unavailing, the committee preferring to believe the farmer's word that the worker in question had been paid his full wage. Mackley was no more successful with a similar case at East Bridgeford in November, and in February 1919 his charges that some farmers were evading regulations concerning the hours and minimum wages of prisoners of war were dismissed, in the absence of specific evidence.[72] For these reasons it would be unwise to suppose that trade unionists could exercise a major influence, yet their admission into decision-making processes certainly gave the impression of mounting power. Moreover, wage increases secured under the auspices of the wage-fixing machinery were conducive to increases in membership towards the end of the war and in the first year or two of peace, when the ranks of potential members were reinforced by demobilized men. By 1920 NALRWU, having recently transferred its headquarters from Fakenham to London, had increased its 1917 membership by a factor of about 12 to reach 93,000; in addition the Workers' Union, whose strength lay more in the midlands and the north, may have achieved an agricultural membership topping the 100,000 mark.[73] Even in such hitherto unpromising territory as the East Riding, union badges were being openly worn, and among others Selley was convinced that trade unionism in agriculture had at last 'come to stay'.[74] At the General Election of 1918, R. B. Walker only narrowly missed being elected as a Labour member for King's Lynn, and George Edwards, having put up a strong showing against the Coalition candidate in South Norfolk, eventually won that seat for Labour in a bye-election in 1920.[75]

In retrospect it can be seen that, despite widespread contemporary impressions that employees had gained the whip hand and that their status had certainly altered for the better, labour did not fare very well during the war, and that the advances of 1919–20 achieved little more than making up lost ground. Taking for the moment a narrowly economic view of the situation, table 7.3 presents the way in which the net return from agriculture was apportioned to its 'shareholders'. It should be noted that the figures derive from a single east midland farm, but their eminent author evidently believed that they were representative.

Table 7.3: Shares in the net return from agriculture, 1913–20*

	Landlord	*Farmer*	*Labour*
% Share in 1913–14	20	40	40
Relative changes (1913–14 = 100)			
1913–14	100	100	100
1914–15	97	104	99
1915–16	94	108	98
1916–17	91	115	95
1917–18	90	111	99
1918–19	87	115	98
1919–20	88	109	103

* C. S. Orwin, *Farming Costs*, new edition, Clarendon, Oxford, 1921, p. 111. Net return is ascertained by deducting from net output a sum representing about 7 per cent interest on the farmer's capital and one-third of the amount of the rent.

Moreover, the war imposed differential levels of sacrifice which in some respects accentuated the inequities hinted at in the table. These should be taken into account not only to assess the immediate impact of the war, but also to facilitate understanding on fundamental shifts in the character of rural society, which, if they were not entirely due to the war, were certainly hurried on by it. They are best considered by taking each of the social categories of table 7.3 in turn.

It is clear that farmers fared comparatively well. Recent work suggests that profits, assessed as a percentage return on capital employed, rose from 6.1 per cent (1909–13) to 16.3 per cent (1917) and, although under the regime of government intervention they fell back in 1918 to 12.5 per cent, this remained over twice the pre-war level. In part this was due to the fact, as Lord Ernle admitted in a moment of candour, that 'blackleg' labour had kept down wage costs, but no less significant was the wartime stasis in rents.[76] Many landlords had thought it improper or unwise to raise them in the early stages of the war, and the Corn Production Act of 1917 had effectively protected tenants against any increases attributable to the introduction of guaranteed prices. Nor were the enhanced incomes of farmers tapped to an appreciable extent by increased taxation. In pre-war days they had been assessed on the basis of rent rather than income, profits being assumed to equal one-third of the annual rental. Although in September 1915, the basis was raised to the full annual rental, not until 1918 when assessments doubled again did income tax make any significant inroads into profits.[77] As A. G. Street reflected, '... it was impossible to lose money at farming just then'.[78] Moreover, farmhouses were inevitably a haven from the dangers of active service. Farmers themselves were exempt from conscription, but they were also adept at protecting their sons. Some 'retired' in favour of their offspring, and many sons were made up to foremen who could be deemed indispensable. Others, like a Cardiganshire farmer in 1916, went to the length of buying additional holdings, with a view to installing their sons as titular landholders; while from the East Riding Reffold recalls boys from well-to-do families evincing a new interest in farm jobs, and being prepared, in some instances, to work for virtually nothing.[79] This was not soon forgotten and, during the post-war period, was liable to be brought up to the discomfiture of farmers on any occasion of village tension or inter-personal conflict.

By comparison, landowners and their families suffered many privations. As is suggested by table 7.3, they were faring least well in the wartime distribution of the product. From Burton Constable in Yorkshire came a typical complaint: 'You can see the profits oozing out of the farmers ... but the unfortunate landlord doesn't get any look in ... the tenants ought to be weighing in with 10, 15 or 20 per cent added to their rents to make it anything like square.'[80] Some were bound by promises made to pay half the weekly wages of those who had enlisted voluntarily to their dependants, or had allowed these to live rent free for the duration of the war. More seriously, all landlords were harassed by increased taxation. Thus, at Wilton and Severnake the burden of all direct taxation (including rates and the land tax) rose from 9 to 30 per cent. The 1919 budget was also hostile, raising death duties to 40 per cent on estates worth £2m. or more.[81] Worse than this, their sons died in disproportionate numbers on the field of battle. Although staff officers were rarely exposed to danger, junior officers and subalterns perished at a rate even faster than their men. One in 6 of the aircrew in the Royal Flying Corps, one in 7 army officers, one in 5 of the alumni of public schools and of members of the universities of Oxford and Cambridge who served during the war failed to survive it. Not since the Wars of the Roses, declared one observer, had the aristocracy suffered such losses.[82] In these circumstances, the resolve of many owners to carry on weakened. 1919 saw the beginning of a positive avalanche of sales and by 1921 the *Estates Gazette* estimated that within four years, as much as one-quarter of the land of England had changed hands. Among the purchasers were County Councils acting under the Land Settlement (Facilities) Act of 1919, which was intended to provide smallholdings for ex-servicemen, causing friction in some cases.[83] At Plymouth in 1919, when the Corytons' Quethiock estate was sold by auction, there was an outcry from small tenants, outbid by pale-faced 'indoor men, official-looking fellows' sent by the Cornwall County Council ('You'm biddin' with tax-payers' money. We'm biddin' with our own').[84] However, while by 1927 the proportion of English and Welsh land held by owner occupiers had reached 36 per cent (against 11 per cent in 1914) there was no increase in the number of smallholdings. On the contrary, those in the ranges 1–5 and 5–50 acres fell, respectively, by 18 and 5 per cent between these dates.[85]

As we have seen, farmworkers on average experienced declining real wages during the war years, and although the increases won between January 1919 and December 1920 were rather greater than the upward movement of wages in general,[86] their low starting-point needs to be kept constantly in mind. Thus, during the years of hostilities, the increases secured by miners ran well ahead of those working on the land: in 1917–18 there were bitter complaints from South Wales about the lowering of the income tax exemption limit from £160 to £120,[87] which was not a problem likely to exercise the agricultural worker. Yet the situation of those who remained at home might well have been envied by those serving with the colours. If it was the case, as suggested above, that 300,000 men were drawn from agriculture, and it is assumed (arbitrarily) that four out of five of these were farmworkers who were subject to average chances of being wounded (1 in 4) or killed (1 in 8), this would imply that some 36,000 made the ultimate sacrifice, their names eventually being inscribed on countless village war memorials, and another 70,000 were wounded with varying degrees of severity.[88] Many others who had originally joined up under class A1 of the military health code returned as B2s, like Henry Ellis of Standon (Essex) and William Langston of the same parish who in 1922 was still under treatment for shattered nerves, deafness and an injury to his right leg.[89] Some of the survivors, it is true, came to look back on their war experiences in an almost nostalgic spirit. James Seeley, a horseman from Loddon, rose to the rank of sergeant in the Eighth Norfolks and gained the Military Medal; he lived to reflect that 'the happiest time I ever had was in the Army – when we'd be overtopped with mud and water in the trench there'd allus be someone to say something to make you laugh . . . we were all Norfolk chaps in my platoon . . . we all clicked in one lot'. But others remember a profound sense of relief at the cessation of hostilities. 'Generally speaking, we were thankful that it was all over' said one septuagenarian, interviewed in the 1960s, and another recalls 'We were fed up you know. And we had seen terrible things.'[90] There is a refrain to such oral evidence, that the survivors saw themselves and were to some extent perceived by other villagers as changed men, having experienced extremes of misery and danger which the civilian population could comprehend only dimly. The rural world which awaited them was one in which the underlying conditions of 'spiritual bondage' had been eroded, where increasingly the airs assumed by the older generation of landlord proprietors and their families were seen to be more laughable and grotesque than intolerable, and where, on the farms, the 'power of the boot' was fast fading.[91] In some districts, nevertheless, a reluctance on the part of the returning soldiery to return was apparent. Among 1,400 discharged men communicated with by the Secretary of the Naval and Military

War Pensions Committee at Christmas 1918, only 25 were prepared to take work on the land. In Nottinghamshire there were complaints to the War Agricultural Committee that some, whose early discharges had been secured by contracts of employment with farmers, had subsequently refused to take up their jobs; while in April and May 1919, the Cumberland Committee, remarking on the difficulty farmers were having in obtaining labour, sought to have the names of those refusing to accept employment at the ruling minimum wages struck from the lists of those eligible for unemployment pay.[92] Yet for many former farmworkers no obvious alternative presented itself, and they might return, in 1919 and 1920, in the knowledge that the rate of remuneration had improved latterly and with the expectation that the new-found strength of the unions would enhance their prospects further. Like those of so many others, their hopes for a brighter future were soon to prove unfounded.

EIGHT

Poverty and progress between the wars

The youthful A. G. Street was rejected for military service on account of flat feet, and succeeded his father as the tenant of a substantial 700 acre holding in Wiltshire in March 1917. He subsequently described the feverish orgy of pleasure that followed the Armistice, at his level of rural society.

> Hunting, shooting, fishing and the like, suddenly reappeared ... we all had money to burn. I find this hard to write ... I was ... as daft as anyone. I kept two hunters ... went shooting at least two days a week during the winter. We went to tennis parties nearly every fine afternoon in the summer ... [and] journeyed far afield in search of excitement ... In short, farmers swanked ... [they] now went far away from home for frequent holidays ... [and] discarded the breeches and gaiters of their ancestors for plus-fours of immaculate cut, incredible design and magnificence, in which garb they were to be found on every golf course.[1]

Alas, the conditions which underpinned the prosperity of agriculture were soon to change, and in a dramatic manner. No sooner was the Agriculture Act of 1920 on the statute book then world prices began to descend rapidly, reflecting a swift recovery of agricultural output in Europe, and the continuing expansion of overseas production in the face of relatively stagnant consumption levels. The index of agricultural prices for England and Wales fell from 292 (1920) to 157 in 1923; by 1933 it had slipped further to 107, and even the slightly relieved conditions of 1937 and 1938 did not lift it higher than 133.[2] Reverting to the trends of the 'Great Depression' years, the period saw a definite swing towards dairy and livestock production at the expense of arable, though even here farmers were not allowed to enjoy their home markets unchallenged. In fact, the only unequivocally bright spot was the cultivation of fresh vegetables which, on account of their perishability, could not yet be profitably imported. Districts such as Biggleswade (Beds.), the Vale of Evesham, and Holland (Lincs.) enjoyed a comparatively high level of prosperity, but it should be borne in mind that horticultural products made up only about 12 per cent of total agricultural output in 1938. In the United Kingdom as a whole, the contribution of agriculture to the national income fell from 5.9 per cent in 1920–2 to 3.2 per cent in 1935–9,[3] and it may, for these reasons, be classed with coal mining, ship-building and cotton textiles among the beleaguered staple industries of the time.

Public policy in relation to agriculture mirrored that of economic strategy as a whole in returning, at first, to a laissez-faire stance. Alarmed at the enormous cost of the price guarantees entered into in 1920 the government revoked them in 1921, an 'act of betrayal' which would rankle in the minds of corn producers for a generation. Through the 1920s the only significant measure of financial assistance given to farmers, apart from the de-rating of agricultural land and buildings in 1928, was a subsidy on sugar introduced in 1924: at considerable cost, the area under beet was pushed up to 350,000 acres by the mid-1930s, thereby providing, perhaps, employment for some 32,000 men in agriculture, besides others in local processing factories.[4] It was not until the economic blizzard of 1931 that the National government took the momentous step of moving decisively away from free trade. Once this was done, primarily to protect manufactured goods, there were no longer any grounds for opposing the protection of agriculture. In 1932 came the Wheat Act, assuring producers of a standard guaranteed price (45s a quarter), while horticultural products (and later, oats and barley) received a measure of protection under the Import Duties Act of 1932. By 1938, compared with 1927–9, total food imports from foreign countries had fallen by some 17 per cent in volume, although under imperial preference arrangements imports from the Empire had offset this, so that, overall, imports were six per cent higher.[5] Another interventionist step taken by the National government, under the Agricultural Marketing Act of 1931, enabled two-thirds of the producers of any agricultural commodity to prepare a scheme which, once approved, became compulsory upon all. From 1933 producers received authority to control output as well as prices, while the government could add protection to any scheme deemed to require it. By 1934, Marketing Boards had appeared for Hops, Potatoes, Milk and Bacon, some schemes being more effective than others. Taken overall, the annual cost of agricultural subsidies in the 1930s has been estimated at between £32m. and £41m. Pollard has suggested that, with the additional costs of raising food at home which could have been bought more cheaply abroad, they were nearer £100m. per annum, and points out that even with this level of assistance, prices scarcely rose to levels at which the British farmer could make a profit. Even in 1937–9, they remained some 10 per cent below those of 1927–9.[6] No-one would claim that these expediencies embodied a coherent strategy or a clear philosophy concerning the role of agriculture in the industry state, for which, in the opinion of many independent observers, the need was ever more apparent as time passed.[7] At the same time, they did betoken the final dethronement of laissez-faire in the sphere of agricultural economics. From the 1930s onward the future of the agricultural industry would be increasingly determined by public policy, and so also, inevitably, would the economic position of the farmworker.

Further reductions in the size of the farm labour force were an obvious feature of the inter-war years. Notwithstanding the ravages of war, the entire occupied labour force of England and Wales was actually a shade higher in 1921 than in 1911, but in agriculture it was lower. Although the 1921 census recorded some 24,000 more female workers, the number of youths had shrunk by 16,000 (11.4 per cent) and adult males by 66,000 (12.5 per cent) reflecting, no doubt, a reluctance on the part of some returning soldiers to return to the plough. Altogether, the reduction of farm staffs was of the order of 8.8 per cent.[8] As it happens, from 1921 we are no longer reliant on the decennial census returns,

Table 8.1: Composition of the labour force in agriculture, England and Wales, 1921–39* (000)

	Regular male workers		*Regular female workers*	*Casuals*	
	21 years and over	*Under 21*		*Male*	*Female*
1921	457	155	73	131	53
1922	—	—	—	—	—
1923	427	139	60	104	43
1924	441	141	62	115	47
1925	442	137	60	115	49
1926	455	136	63	99	42
1927	453	134	63	85	40
1928	454	129	67	87	35
1929	452	125	67	91	35
1930	446	119	65	80	32
1931	435	117	64	72	29
1932	420	116	62	74	26
1933	423	114	60	89	30
1934	415	107	53	82	30
1935	413	105	50	77	28
1936	402	101	45	66	28
1937	395	95	46	65	30
1938	382	90	42	54	25
1939	375	96	40	63	33

* All figures relate to holdings above one acre in extent and exclude the occupier, wife and domestic servants. Data from Ministry of Agriculture and Fisheries, *Agricultural Statistics for 1921–30* (HMSO, 1922–31) and *1939* (HMSO, n.d.) for the years 1931–9. N.B. No comparable statistics are available for 1922.

and the series published in the annual agricultural returns permits the further decline of the labour force to be monitored more closely. Table 8.1 shows, first, that peacetime conditions encouraged the pre-war trend towards reduced reliance on female and casual labour gradually to reassert itself. Secondly, it indicates that the regular male labour force did not contract rapidly during the 1920s: it was during the 1930s that it began to plummet, falling by 17 per cent overall in nine years. In Wales, the contrast between the two decades was especially marked. Regular adult male workers were actually more numerous in 1931 (30,027) than in 1921 (29,003), but by 1939 had been reduced by no less than 29.5 per cent.[9]

Although there are no systematic statistics of farm mechanization for this period, it is obvious that this cannot have been the chief factor in the decline of the labour force. Of course, some spectacular instances of reductions in farm staffs are on record, in part facilitated by greater recourse to machinery. A. G. Ruston instanced the case of a large arable farm on the Yorkshire Wolds which, during the 1920s, employed 18 men and 40 horses on a four-course rotation with folded sheep, but was being run in the 1930s with five men on a rotation of wheat, barley, fallow and leys, using tractors and combine harvesters but no horses.[10] Yet in 1936 the ratio of horses to tractors on the farms of England and Wales remained of the order of 14:1 and in 1937–8 the proportion of dairy herds equipped with milking machines was still only just over one-third.[11] In Denmark, where more machinery was in use than in Britain, twice as many cultivators per thousand acres were employed in the late 1920s.[12] Moreover, decreases in the number of agricultural workers tended to be least marked where the scope for mechanization appeared greatest (i.e. in the wheat-growing counties) and were higher, by and large, in smallholding and grassland areas. Thus, in Wales, the number of tractors available for field work was only 1,640 as late as 1937, and in the opinion of one well-informed contemporary, recent mechanization was due largely to the movement out of agriculture.[13] More significant in explaining variations in the rate of loss was the comparative health of different sectors of the agricultural industry, and the extent to which farmers were successful in adapting the composition of their output to changes in price relativities. In the exceptional case of the Holland division of Lincolnshire, the number of workers decreased by only a single percentage point between 1921 and 1938, a situation contrasting very markedly with areas in which the amount of tilled land was greatly diminished.[14] Only rarely have the implications of shifts in the composition of farm output been traced in detail, but one valuable study of Buckinghamshire suggests that the index of the labour requirement for crops fell from 144 to 100 between 1921 and 1939; although the corresponding index for livestock production rose from 82 to 100, the net effect was to reduce farm labour requirements by one worker in twenty.[15]

While farmers were drawn to economize on labour where ever possible during the inter-war years, there are many indications that supply was dwindling much more rapidly. Twelve counties in England and Wales lost over 40 per cent of their farm staffs between 1921 and 1938, among them Buckinghamshire where, still more significantly, the index of casual workers employed moved down to 39 and that of regular male workers under 21 to 37 (1921 = 100) by 1939.[16] As ever, the existence of alternatives to farm employment remained critical, although the contrasting fortunes of different sectors of the industrial economy were by now ringing some variations on an old theme. In regions of heavy industry where competition for labour had been strong ever since the later eighteenth century, the drain from the land had greatly diminished. Thus, in 1931, the tendency of country-bred lads in Durham to leave the land on reaching manhood was no longer marked, 'due in part to depression in industrial undertakings in the county'. Similar comments came from Northumberland and the West Riding: 'Owing to the lack of opportunities in the towns at the present time the drift does not appear to be very marked.'[17] Indeed, the depression in industry was sufficiently acute to encourage, at times, a backflow of older workers. This tendency was noticed in Wales, where in 1929–34 the plight of the coal, iron and steel industries drew back men who still looked upon farming as a haven of refuge to which they could return in times of industrial depression and unemployment.[18] On the other hand, in districts characterized by an admixture of new and old activities, industry was still capable of exercising a very definite effect in tempting men away from the land. Thus, in north Warwickshire

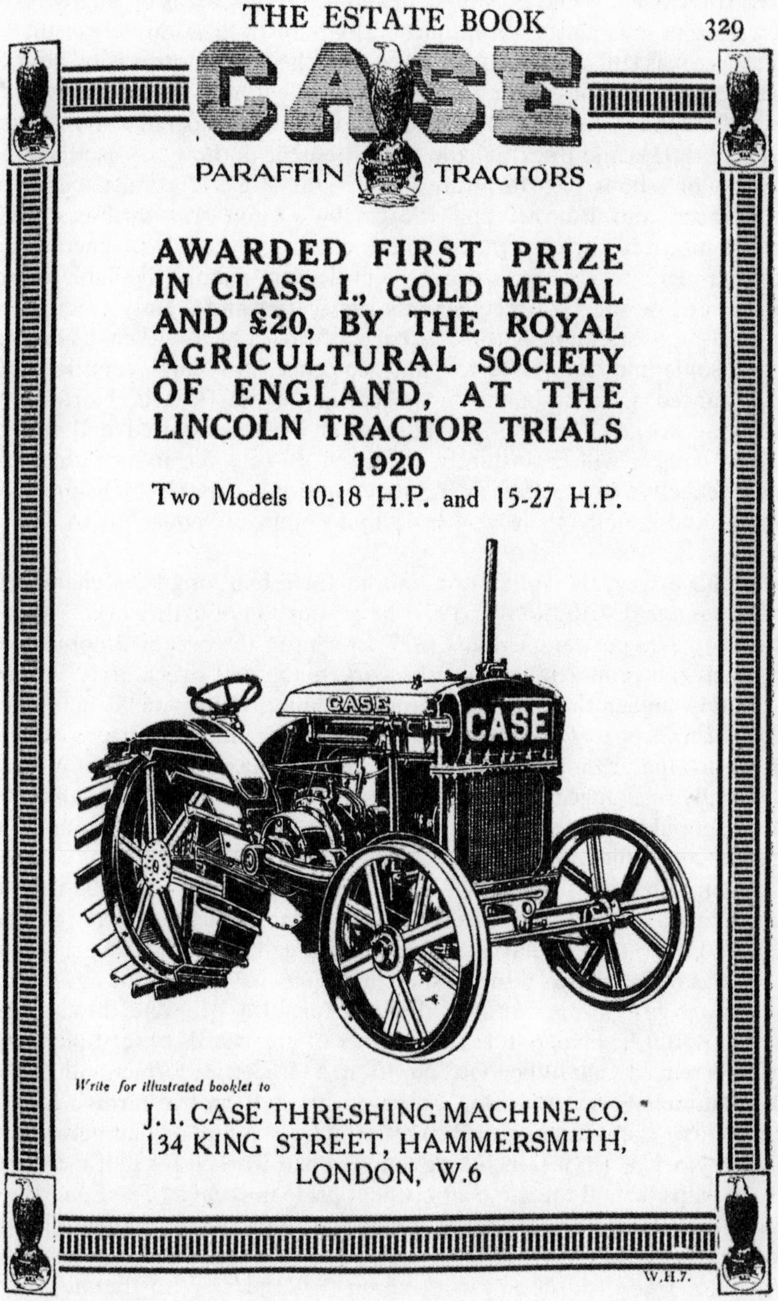

The tractor, here advertised in *The Country Gentlemen's Estate Book, 1921*, seemed to symbolize modernity in farming but horses remained much more numerous throughout the inter-war years.

in 1930 it was remarked that the rural labour market was much under the influence of 'Coventry and Birmingham and the mining areas of Rugby'. Above all it was from areas hitherto untouched by industrialization, where the farm labour force was still comparatively large, that the rate of loss was by now most sigificant. Such counties included Oxfordshire, featuring the Morris works at Cowley; Berkshire (the Abingdon MG factory was considered a special attraction here, in 1931) and Buckinghamshire, where the outflow was ascribed to the movement of labour into furniture factories at High Wycombe, paper mills near Woburn and Bourne, and the brickworks in the north-east of the county.[19] In cases such as these, where employers had long cherished the belief that agriculture was naturally entitled to readily available supplies of labour at low rates, farmers serving on district and county councils were given to arguing strenuously that their men should not be 'taken' as roadmen, etc., and sometimes they tried to influence other rural employers. Robertson Scott instanced a notice in the sugar-beet factory at Felsted (Norfolk): 'No agricultural worker applying will be started. Anyone started and found to be a land worker will be instantly dismissed.'[20] Yet even if such steps could be made effective in isolated areas, they were not capable of being applied generally, and usually there was little that employers could do to stem the outflow.

As we have seen, the agricultural labour force had long been characterized by a curious age-distribution. In 1921 the proportion of male workers aged 20–54 was only 57.5 per cent, against 69.6 per cent in the occupied population at large, while the proportion of elderly workers (55 and over), at 19.7 per cent was notably higher than in, for example, mining (10.7), metal manufacture (11.3), and transport (11.5). Due presumably to the limited horizons of village-bred youths, the proportion of workers under 20 was 22.8 per cent in 1921; it was virtually unchanged since before the war and definitely higher than in the occupied population at large (15.1).[21] Yet it was found that the younger men were especially difficult to retain. If census data for 1921 and 1931 is compared, it may be inferred that of 276,000 males aged 15 to 24 only 209,000 remained, on a net basis, ten years on. Of this loss, no more than 10,000 can reasonably be ascribed to deaths so that, assuming accurate and compatible occupational descriptions in the census returns, something like one-fifth of the age-cohort in question was lost to agriculture.[22] Figures for 1931–41, were they available, would no doubt be higher still. The number of greybeards observable in agriculture was remarkable. When Guy Stratton, a large-scale farmer and President of the National Farmers' Union, surveyed his staff on five farms near Alton Priors (Wilts.) just after the war, he noticed that 17 out of 42 had between them given 830 years of service, including ten who had worked for half a century or more. Perhaps he had the same ambivalent pride in them as *The Land Worker*, with its illustration of 'Ye Ancients', published about the same time: 'The above photo, taken by Bro. T. Mackley, shows six of our members aged respectively 81, 73, 72, 73 and 68, all still working on the land.'[23] With the middle years significantly under-represented (that is, by comparison with other industries) it is not surprising to find sharp contrasts between the generations being drawn. One contemporary author distinguished between 'the pre-war age group' characterized by immobility and dead weight of resistance to change, and the newer generation, infatuated by the mobility offered by the pedal cycle, the motor bike, and the pillion seat.[24]

During the 1920s, the familiar debates about labour productivity received an occasional airing. Robertson Scott quoted a series of opinions which closely matched those voiced sixty or more years before: 'The Essex labourer, though he is a good fellow, is not ambitious'; 'There is not the slightest doubt, in my opinion, that labour in the North of England . . . produces a far greater output at less cost than it does in the South', etc. Yet two Scotsmen farming in Essex and in Surrey preferred their present workers and another contrasted the civility and helpfulness of the men of Suffolk with the attitude of Scottish workers.[25] At all events, there is no doubt that over the inter-war period labour productivity as a whole increased markedly, since the employed labour force fell by much more than did farm output. This increase has been put at 40 per cent between 1924 and the outbreak of the Second World War, whilst a detailed study of 'performance per man' in Buckinghamshire suggests an increase of some 44 per cent between 1921 and 1939.[26] Improvements in labour productivity were no doubt facilitated by technical improvements such as land drainage, the advent of cheap and reliable weed-killers and moderate extensions in the use of power-driven machinery, but they were also assisted by better work organization and greater flexibility in the use of labour. One unusually perspicacious correspondent of Robertson Scott linked the question of labour productivity very firmly with this factor. Before 1914, he claimed, the differences between Yorkshire and East Anglia had been based on the greater 'general efficiency' of the northerners. By contrast, in the south-east there was 'much more sub-division of labour and therefore far fewer good all-round men', although, he implied, such specialization was now passing away. No doubt the 1930s accelerated this process, and the time was not now far distant when oral historians would begin to record the vanishing customs, usages and craft vocabularies associated with the peculiar tasks of horsemen, ploughmen, shepherds and so on. Another correspondent made an unusual point in contrasting English and Scottish workers, that English farms were characterized by a 'larger proportion of older and more experienced men' which accords with our earlier suggestion that the especial demographic age-profile was more noteworthy in its social aspect than for any economic implications.[27]

None of this is to suggest that still higher levels of labour productivity could not have been sought and achieved. Some were disposed to argue that if labour were dearer, more strenuous efforts to use it efficiently would be stimulated. Certainly, the unions had no time for unprogressive farmers. Reviewing a study of a hundred Yorkshire farms in December 1931, *The Land Worker* contrasted employers who were up to date and 'employed science and forethought' with the other sort, who dragged down the average and made profits look bad: 'We want to know what the best farms are doing and getting, because the future depends on them.' Yet, in any international comparison, the industry had little to be ashamed of. For 1937–8, the number of people supported by each agriculturalist (these figures include employers) was estimated at 17 for Britain which, if by no means as impressive as New Zealand (33) or Australia (29) was comparable with the Netherlands (16), slightly above the USA (13), Canada and Denmark (12), and decidedly higher than in countries where a peasant system of agriculture prevailed (e.g. Germany 7, Eire 6, France 5). The value of output per worker was calculated to be £205, and was also such as to put it behind only New Zealand and Australia among the countries surveyed.[28]

All the factors so far discussed bore more or less directly upon farmworkers' wages during the period. By 1920, cash wages had reached levels previously unheard of, buoyed up, of course, by high prices for agricultural products. However, falling prices began to make an impact during 1921 and in September the Central Wages Board reduced the minimum to 42s in 34 counties, with others remaining slightly higher.[29] This was its last act prior to abolitition, along with the District Committees, and the subsequent history of wage movements cannot be understood without brief reference to the wage-fixing machinery which followed. The Corn Production (Repeal) Act of 1921 provided for the establishment of voluntary County Conciliation Committees composed of representatives of masters and men, an arrangement in keeping with the general retreat from wartime restrictions. Having hammered out an agreement on wages and hours, these committees could transmit their findings to the Ministry of Agriculture which might make them legally binding and enforceable in courts of law. In practice, the vast majority of committees preferred to look upon their work as advisory, and in any case their ability to reach any sort of agreement was hampered by the suspicions of work-people and by the fact that employers could ignore their recommendations with impunity. Towards the end of 1923, agreements were in force in only one-sixth of 62 designated districts; only three committees had succeeded in maintaining continuous agreements, and in seven cases, no agreement was ever arrived at. The record of the Conciliation Committees as an effective wage negotiating machinery was thus disastrous, and wages fell precipitously. According to estimates prepared by the Ministry of Agriculture, the cash wages of ordinary workers fell to an average of 37s (December 1921) then to 28s by the close of 1922, and remained at that level through 1923 and 1924.[30] They remained highest at about 35s a week, in the northern counties, and lowest, at 25s, in East Anglia, where in Norfolk an extreme proposal for cutting wages to 22s 6d for a 54 hour week produced, as we shall see, a momentous strike. In effect, the question of wages had been returned to market determination, and in the climate of depression there was little that the committees could do to stem the tide of wage reductions. However, it may be claimed that these arrangements at least preserved the principle that employees had a right to participate in discussions affecting their working conditions.

In the meantime, the critical situation facing all involved in the agricultural industry was the subject of an enquiry appointed by Bonar Law's government in 1922. This tribunal suggested, in its first interim report of 1923, that with its 'absence of effective organization and the prevalence of low wages', agricultural employment fulfilled the conditions required to justify state regulation of wages as laid down in the Trade Boards Act (of 1909); and it was against the background of this enquiry, the Norfolk strike, and repeated demands from farmworkers' organizations, that the first Labour government brought forward a bill, in April 1924, to restore statutory wage legislation in agriculture. It was originally intended that a new Central Wages Board should have powers to ratify and even amend agreements made by County Wages Committees, but in the face of combined opposition from Conservative and Liberal members, a compromise was reached. The Agricultural Wages (Regulation) Act which came into operation in 1924 gave only a limited advisory role to the Central Board, which was to consist of five independent members, and equal numbers of representatives from employers and employees. In contrast to the old system, made defunct in 1921, the new arrangements placed particular responsibility on the County Committees (also consisting of equal numbers of representatives nominated by farmworkers' organizations and the NFU), which were given full power to fix, cancel or vary rates of pay, hours and conditions, and also to issue permits of exemption from the fixed minimum rates in respect of non-able-bodied workers. Only if a County Committee failed to agree, or passed a resolution calling upon it to intervene, could the Central Board step in. Another major difference between the 1924 Act and the old arrangements was the isolation of wages from the price guarantees and controls of agricultural production with which they had been inseparably linked under the Corn Production Act of 1917.

The operations of the County Wages Committees during the rest of the period reveal many aspects of the farmworker's condition. For example, allowances in kind were becoming decidedly rarer. Already, in 1925 a Liberal Land Committee Report concluded that they had become exceptional in many districts.[31] Yet it was still possible to find in Northumberland, in 1936, isolated cases of individuals still paid almost wholly in kind, such as a shepherd who received no cash whatever but was remunerated in the form of a cottage, allocations of potatoes and corn, keep of a cow, 25–30 lambs and six wether hogs. Moreover, it appeared from a study of East Anglian workers in 1931–3 that here also there remained a tendency for men of higher status to receive a greater proportion of their income in kind.[32] Thus, although there is no doubt of a powerful tendency for cash payments to become the norm, what remained of payments in kind required to be carefully reckoned by the County Committees. By way of illustration, in the counties of Flint and Denbigh in the late 1930s, milk was valued at 1½d per pint in summer and 2d in winter, and farmers were allowed to charge 4s per cwt for potatoes supplied to workers. Board and lodging allowances, as determined in 1925, varied between 12s 6d and 17s, with 22 committees settling on 15s. Much the most common form of payment in kind related, of course, to the occupation of cottages. In 1925, 39 committees defined their value as 3s weekly whilst the others ranged between 2s and 4s; this level remained typical through the rest of the period.[33] It was also the duty of the committees to guard against the exploitation of the aged or those suffering from physical or mental disabilities, permits being required by farmers proposing to pay men less than the minimum wage. Such workers accounted for 1.4 per cent of those regularly employed in 1925 and 1.6 per cent in 1937, when over 8,000 permits were in force including 1,900 for mental deficiency, 1,400 for physical injury, 2,600 for old age and 2,800 for sundry other infirmities.[34]

However, the chief responsibility of the committees was to determine minimum cash wages, and to set down terms of hours and other conditions for able-bodied farm workers. No doubt it is true that they lacked the means to control closely what went on at the level of the individual farm: writing only a few years later, George Henderson recalled that the best cowman he had ever known, who never missed a milking in 43 years, was paid 10s a week less than others on the farm, simply because his employer knew that the old man was afraid of being unemployed. By contrast, another farmer of his acquaintance paid to a labourer's widow the wages her late husband would have earned for seven years, to enable her to keep the family together, whilst (so claimed this sturdy individualist) 'the trade union to which he had paid in for years did not refund a penny'.[35] While the behaviour of individual farmers doubtless ranged from brutal callousness to extreme generosity, it has to be acknowledged that a great many, either deliberately or through ignorance, were given to paying rates below the specified minimum. This is evident from the work of the 15 inspectors appointed in 1926 to investigate complaints and carry out test inspections. That the number of complaints climbed steadily from 876 in 1925 to 3,733 in 1937 was probably due chiefly to increasing awareness among workers of their rights. However, in 1926 a sample investigation revealed that 22 per cent of 951 workers on 250 farms were incorrectly paid, and in 1935–6, by which date nearly a thousand prosecutions had been mounted, the proportion underpaid was still reckoned to be as high as 21 per cent in England and 36 per cent in Wales. More detailed investigations show that such contraventions were more frequently in respect of overtime rates than non-observance of the weekly minimum rates.[36]

No doubt the obduracy of problems such as this contributed to the luke-warmness shown by labour leaders towards the system. Another just criticism was that, by their very nature, the arrangements perpetuated anomalies in the renumeration paid in different parts of the country for work of a broadly similar nature. George Dallas, the chief agricultural organizer of the Transport and General Workers' Union, was especially critical of the power given to counties to fix their own rates, and the consequent inanition of the Central Board: 'I have known occasions when some of the members turned up five minutes late to find all the work transacted. The functions of the Board have been so limited that one might almost say a rubber stamp could do the work.' With no national minimum, he felt that there was no pressure to force farmers to a higher level of efficiency.[37] For all that, it is significant that J. F. Duncan, leader of the Scottish Farm Servants' Union, was trying to have similar machinery established there, by 1936. He had been driven, reluctantly, to the conclusion that in difficult times such arrangements would at least serve to prevent the worst happening. A comparison of the course of wage rates in England and Wales with Scotland confirms beyond any doubt that the ratio of unregulated Scottish to regulated English and Welsh wages moved adversely to the Scots in the decade following 1924.[38] Moreover, the English system of regulation succeeded in keeping agri-cultural wages steady during the singularly depressed years of 1931–4. This was in marked contrast to the experience of the early 1920s, and illustrated the truth of a comment made by the Agricultural Tribunal of Investigation in 1924: 'The greatest value of a Wages Board is in a period of depression.'[39] There can be little doubt that, had wage regulation not been in force, farmers would have sought energetically to reduce wages during the early 1930s, and that extremely tense industrial relations would have been the order of the day.

Average minimum wage levels for ordinary farmworkers, which by 1924 had sunk to 28s a week, were lifted to 31s 5d the following year reflecting the first steps taken by the County Wages Committees, and thereafter remained remarkably steady. Even 1931–2 did not see the loss of more than a shilling and after 1934 wages began a regular, though very gentle ascent, reaching 34s 9d in 1939. The tendency for long-established regional contrasts to diminish continued. Despite the impact of the original Agricultural Wages Board, in 1920 wages remained somewhat better in the regions traditionally exhibiting higher rates, notably in Northumberland, Durham, Yorkshire, Cumberland, Lancashire, Cheshire, and in South Wales, to the tune of 2-4s a week above the 44s that had become general elsewhere. When wages fell generally, in the period of the Conciliation Committees, it was a sign of the times that in these counties they fell by much the same proportion as elsewhere; a reduction of the order of 35 per cent occurred by 1924. Nor did the traditional high wage areas fare particularly well in the post-1924, regulated era. In September 1937, minimum wage levels in Durham (32s 6d) and Northumberland (32s 6d) were no higher than that in Herefordshire and Wiltshire (32s 6d), a shade lower than in Dorset (33s) or Norfolk (33s 6d), and certainly below those of Holland, Lincs. (36s 0d). Within Yorkshire the difference between the West and the North Riding rates was only 1s 6d, and by now the extremes were 36s 5½d (Middlesex – summer level), and 30s (Merioneth and Montgomery).[40] What is to be emphasized particularly is the close bunching of the minimum rates, despite the lack of a national minimum wages, thus indicating the end of once massive regional discrepancies.

It should be stressed that, in practice, many farmworkers earned rather more than the foregoing minimum rates suggest. Slightly fewer than half of the 47 committees attempted to fix higher wages for special classes of workmen, and in the remaining areas these were paid the ordinary minimum wage plus overtime rates, for extra hours necessitated by the character of their employment. Either way, the more skilled tended to find themselves working between 52 and 60 hours a week compared to the 48 (winter) and 50 (summer) required to secure the minimum wage in the majority of the districts in the arable counties. Consequently, when calculated on an hourly basis, their rates were scarcely higher than those of ordinary workers.[41] Factors other than overtime affecting total remuneration included special harvest rates adopted by a minority of County Committees. Table 8.2 compares the earnings of ordinary and certain special classes of workers between 1928 and 1937, and it seems that, taking all these factors together, the average earnings of all agricultural workers were nationally about 4s above the average county minimum wage of 34s 7d which obtained in November 1938.[42] The wages of female workers were usually set by the hour, and adult females (usually those aged 18 and over) earned in most districts from 5d–6d an hour in 1925 and the same in 1933, with the rate tending to creep up slightly to 6½d or 7d just before the Second World War. Males under 21 received payments graduated according to age and the length of the working week. Regional differences in the wages offered to youths of a given age remained striking throughout the period, especially for beginners; for example, in 1937 those aged 16 but under 17 received 13s 6d in Denbigh and Flint but 23s 0d in Cumberland and Westmorland.[43] In the most favourable circumstances, where the husband was a specialist worker putting in long hours, his wife was able to

Table 8.2: Average weekly earnings of ordinary and special workers in agriculture, 1928–37*

	Ordinary workers	*Stockmen*	*Horsemen*
1928	33s 4d	38s 6d	36s 9d
1929–30	33s 8d	39s 1d	37s 5d
1930–1	33s 11d	39s 5d	37s 4d
1931–2	33s 4d	38s 11d	37s 3d
1932–3	32s 8d	38s 6d	36s 6d
1933–4	32s 7d	38s 9d	36s 7d
1934–5	33s 2d	38s 10d	36s 10d
1935–6	34s 7d	39s 8d	37s 4d
1936–7	35s 3d	40s 10d	38s 4d

* W. H. Pedley, *Labour on the Land*, King and Staples, 1942, p. 38. The figures are derived from the Annual Reports of the Agricultural Wages Board.

perform some field-work, and where there were a couple of adolescent sons at home, gross family income could, for a time, be considerable, running to several pounds a week. By contrast, the outlook for a family dependent on only the husband's minimum wage was certain to be comparatively bleak. Such disparities, which had always been apparent, need always to be kept in mind when we turn to deal with budgetary evidence below.

A striking feature of the period is the very minor impact of agricultural trade unions. Among social historians, to confess to any scepticism about their value may seem rather like questioning the role of the army at a regimental dinner, but it does seem to be borne out by the facts with respect to wages. Year by year fluctuations in membership density were indeed related to wages, but were *dependent* upon them, for it was farm prices that determined wages. When the decisions of the first Wages Board raised pay, membership rose in consequence; but after wages began to decline from 1921, so did membership, and their stabilization in 1923 did not succeed in arresting the collapse. When the second Wages Board increased pay in 1924 unionist numbers initially rose by 12 per cent, but subsequently, when over nine years they neither gained nor lost, membership scarcely changed.[44] Another indication of union impotence was that the wage levels obtaining in different parts of the country manifestly had little to do with relative density of membership. Thus, when wage negotiations were resumed in March 1925, the men of Norfolk were unable to gain any improvement over the next twelve months through four sets of negotiations, despite a union membership estimated at 10,000. By contrast, in Glamorgan where there were only ten members and where other trade unionists such as Morgan Phillips from the coal industry had to be invited to make up the workers' side on the Wages Committee, increases were achieved which at that juncture represented an hourly rate some 25 per cent higher than that ruling in Norfolk.[45]

Table 8.3 gives the best available estimates of the membership of the National Union of Agricultural Workers, as NALRWU had restyled itself in 1920. The figures are not impressive and, during the 1920s, the record of the Workers' Union in this field was even more disastrous. By 1924 its agricultural membership reached no more than one-fifth of the peak level and was a mere 5,000 in 1929, at which point it amalgamated with the Transport and General Workers' Union.[46] In 1926 it was considered doubtful whether the two unions between them represented more than six per cent of all farm workers, and even the moderate recovery of the later 1930s, coupled with a declining labour force, can scarcely have raised the proportion to more than about one in twelve.[47]

Table 8.3: Estimated membership of the NUAW, 1918–1939* (000)

1918	41	1929	23
1919	73	1930	24
1920	93	1931	24
1921	79	1932	23
1922	36	1933	23
1923	29	1934	23
1924	22	1935	25
1925	24	1936	27
1926	25	1937	31
1927	24	1938	35
1928	24	1939	37

*H. Newby, *The Deferential Worker*, Allen Lane, 1977, p. 228. Note that there is no direct information as to numbers, and average annual membership has to be inferred from subscription income. The method was originally set out by M. Madden, 'The National Union of Agricultural Workers 1906–56', B.Lit. thesis, University of Oxford, 1957, Appendix D, and was used also by F. D. Mills, 'The National Union of Agricultural Workers', Ph.D. thesis, University of Reading, 1965. The figures given here are likely to be much more accurate than those compiled by a union official, Mr F. Bond, which are quoted in R. Groves, *Sharpen the Sickle*, Porcupine Press, 1949, p. 245.

The low density of union membership cannot be satisfactorily explained by the glib argument that 'Radicalism has left the countryside because the radicals have migrated'.[48] Nor was it rooted, as some urban trade unionists still supposed, in the innate stupidity of farmworkers. William Blades, a stalwart Yorkshireman whose recollections and opinions were recorded during the 1920s, considered trade unions 'a perfect nuisance to the world', but his life history showed every sign of intelligence and versatility.[49] Nor will fear of the consequences suffice as an explanation, for although a farmer might show his displeasure in a variety of small ways on learning that his employee was a trade unionist, overt cases of victimization were rare, at least by the 1930s, and considered deplorable by the better sort of employers. As ever, the key to the low level of union density lay in the fragmented nature of farm employment and the comparatively close contact between employer and employee, for quiet persuasion was likely to have more effect than threats. The cost of organizing scattered workers was great, and the modest subscription rates of the NUAW (about one half of what was usual in other industries) yielded a low annual income which was bound to detract from its ability to acquire and retain members.

Having recorded these weaknesses, which are admitted on all sides, an historian of labour merely as a factor of production might conclude that little more needs to be said about agricultural trade unionism. Yet the unions impinged at one time or another on the lives of a great many more farmworkers than average annual membership figures would indicate. In November 1930, *The Land Worker* pointed out that nearly 180,000 had paid entrance fees to the NUAW at one time or another; 'this means that forty-three per cent of the adult workers of this country are or have been under union protection ...' Suspect though the artithmetic may be the point is valid in principle, and in any case, for the social historian, special interest attaches to the Norfolk Strike of 1923 (both for its immediate impact and its longer-run implications); the routine work of the NUAW; and the range of views articulated in *The Land Worker*, which serves also as a basis for tracing some important shifts in union policies.

The Norfolk strike of 1923 occupies a position in the historiography of agricultural trade unionism rivalled only by the Tolpuddle Martyrs and Joseph Arch's campaigns of the 1870s. With its notoriously low wages, relatively strong union membership, and earlier history of labour disputes the county virtually suggested itself as the likely arena of conflict during the era of the Conciliation Committees.[50] As early as 1921 trouble began to brew when the local leadership, headed by Sam Peel, accepted terms of 36s a week laid down by the Norfolk Conciliation Committee, against advice from the General Secretary, R. B. Walker at headquarters. Even then, not all farmers would cooperate and in late September, when wheat stood at 30s a sack, farmer Womack Ringer of Rougham, with others, gave notice that henceforth the wages offered would use this yardstick, on what were claimed to be time-honoured principles. The 'sack of wheat strike', at one point involving 200 men in and about Docking, was not settled until March 1922, when Ringer agreed to abide by the decisions of the Conciliation Committee. Meanwhile, in the pages of *The Land Worker* and on public platforms, Walker insisted that farmworkers everywhere should stand firm and disregard the example being set by the Norfolk negotiators. Peel, however, was apparently more conscious of the local threat of unemployment. At the close of 1921 a union enquiry had shown that as many as 7,000 out of some 17,000 Norfolk members were out of employ, admittedly at the 'dead' season of the year, and evidently he regarded the national leadership as out of touch with realities. Walker next attempted, in February 1922, to reaffirm central control and to outflank Peel's conciliatory tactics by setting in hand a ballot among Norfolk members concerning the 28s which the employers were by now offering, and secured its rejection by a seven to one majority. This failed to deter Peel, who sat on the Norfolk County Committee as a lay member and could not, therefore, be dismissed by the union, from agreeing to a 30s wage (for 50½ hours) at the spring meeting of the committee. His action was roundly condemned by the NUAW executive, for the tactic being pursued by Walker was to seek to subvert local Conciliation Committee machinery with a view to regaining the wage negotiating arrangements which had obtained before the repeal of the Corn Production Act. Resignations were called for, and in July 1922 Peel departed from the post of Norfolk organizer, accepting the presidency

HARVEST HOME

"All is safely gathered in . . . Come ye thankful people, come."

(*The Land Worker*, March 1925)

of the newly-formed National Union of Landworkers. This organization was closely associated with the 'New Agricultural Party', a body recently formed by a group of landowners and farmers with the object of returning MPs pledged to the protection of British agriculture. For a time there was a real possibility that he might carry with him a significant number of Norfolk members, which was only just averted, it would appear, by an impassioned appeal from the veteran, George Edwards, to 'stick to the Union' at the county meeting in August later that year.

For the student of trade unionism, these tensions between the forces of centralization and regionalism, and the contrasting strategies adopted by Peel and by Walker are intensely interesting in their own right. Yet still more dramatic struggles were about to be precipitated. When, in October 1922, the Norfolk farmers decided to offer 25s for fifty hours to operate over the winter months the NUAW representatives, now led by Edwards, walked out, but could not prevent this wage from becoming widely operative by the end of the year. The employers' next move, in February 1923, was to propose yet another wage cut, in the first instance to 5d an hour for 54 hours, which signified either a reduction of 2s 6d a week or an additional four hours labour. On 3 March this was amended to $5\frac{1}{2}$d, which would have yielded a wage of 24s 9d on the assumption of a full working week which, however, the farmers were not prepared to guarantee. By comparison, sundry roadmen in the county were currently earning

10d an hour for a shorter working week and easier work. The position adopted by the employers was not, it seems, simply one of incredibly short-sighted parsimony, for at that juncture they were anxious to influence the new Conservative government to adopt a positive strategy towards agriculture, by either tariff protection or subsidies. Be that as it may, a confrontation was now virtually inevitable, and the NUAW executive moved quickly to set up a strike committee presided over in Norwich by Sim Lunnon, of the National Organizing Committee. Attempts to patch up an agreement between the two sides, including a well-meaning conference sponsored by the Bishop in the great drawing-room of his palace, proved unavailing and on Saturday, 24 March the strike began in earnest. It may be noted that most of east and south-east Norfolk remained outside the struggle, for the NUAW Executive sought to concentrate its efforts in the north and west of the county, where membership was strongest. The sense that the Norfolk struggle was a trial of strength, the outcome of which would have ramifications far beyond the immediate locality, was felt strongly by all concerned and the rhetoric was accordingly powerful. 'Will the labourer win?' demanded Edwin Gooch, in *The Land Worker* in April; 'He must and he will. The mantle of Kett and Arch has descended upon him ... God is on his side.' Cycling pickets deployed by the union were countered by the drafting of some 600 extra policemen from as far afield as Yorkshire, while according to the *Daily Herald*, West Norfolk farmers were busy turning hedges into dug-outs and haystacks into fortresses, and 'ex-officer blacklegs well armed with revolvers' were following the drills and harrows. Incidents featuring the intimidation of non-strikers were common and the activities of some of the younger men, like their rick-burning ancestors, were not easily controlled from Norwich: the role of embittered ex-sericemen made distinguishable by their khaki greatcoats was particularly noticeable. Among the more serious incidents was the 'Battle of Holly Heath Farm', where one farmer fired upon strike pickets (using blank cartridges), while some well-remembered scenes of violence took place at Weasenham. Having failed, in face of preventive action by the police, to stop Gilbert Overman's men from working, a gang of strikers proceeded to his brother's farm where they forced the withdrawal of ten young farm pupils. Four were beaten with cudgels, and horses were turned loose at the farm of the old enemy Ringer, at nearby Rougham. No doubt it is true that reports of a veritable social war in the Norfolk countryside were exaggerated, but large numbers of cases of intimidation were brought to the courts at Aylsham and Docking, and on 16 April a curious incident occurred at the Walsingham Court House when several local NUAW leaders, including George Edwards, arrived seeking to exercise their rights to sit as 'stranger magistrates'. Fifteen cases were heard and leniently dealt with, and when the court dispersed, there was a hostile demonstration against Sam Peel, who was also a magistrate. In the prevailing bitterness of the situation this was altogether predictable; he had recently spoken of the 'appalling lack of leadership' exercised by the NUAW and had not called out his Landworkers' Union, which in the eyes of Gooch was simply a dummy organization.

As it happened the wages issue was settled with surprising suddenness. With an election pending, the Labour Party leader Ramsay MacDonald was anxious to appear in the favourable role of peacemaker, and brought together the two sides for discussions at the House of Commons. On 18 April they agreed upon a 25s weekly wage for a guaranteed working week of 50 hours. This sixpenny hourly rate would also be payable for a further four hours which an employer might require, while above 54 hours, special overtime rates would come into operation. Unfortunately, the agreement between the NUAW and the NFU failed to restore harmony, for it included a clause specifying that 'there shall be no victimization'. Already, by 25 April, the *Eastern Daily Press* noticed that the interpretation of this clause was proving controversial. From the standpoint of the men and their representatives, its wording seemed to imply that all strikers should have their jobs back, whereas the NFU view was that it meant that no-one's place should be taken by an outsider. At Swanton Morley on 28 April only nine among 53 men were currently working, while two days later the *Eastern Daily Press* estimated that about 40 per cent of all strikers were still out, in many cases because the men refused to return if one of their number was excluded. Taking the employers' point of view, the *Lynn Advertiser* of 18 May criticized the 'stupidity' of the 'all or none' posture of union officials and could not bring itself to believe that farmers would so treat their old employees. However, there is no doubt that victimization did take place. Some according to George Edwards, were taken back, then given a week's notice and discharged and, whilst exonerating Gorman and Wright of the NFU ('who to do them justice have done their best to secure the honouring of the agreement'), the radical newspaper *Reynold's News* was critical of 'the little tyrants of the Norfolk farmers', referring darkly to secret conclaves of employers and 'much driving about in motor-cars and traps on a certain Sunday in April'. According to a union report of mid-June, 1,200 men were still away from work and this figure did not begin to dip significantly until, from the beginning of July, the exigencies of the hay harvest and root cropping obliged farmers to take on more men.

Putting the most favourable construction on these events, the union could claim to have conducted a successful defensive struggle, at least in that a guaranteed working week had been achieved. It is also highly probable, through its impact on public opinion, that the Norfolk strike helped to pave the way for restoration of statutory machinery the following year. On the other hand, the struggle had revealed once again the underlying weaknesses of agricultural trade unionism. Twenty thousand strike notices despatched at the beginning of March had produced no more than 5,000 willing to obey the call by the end of the month, and this in the most strongly unionized district of the whole country.[51] Efforts made to call out men from farms on which the 50 hour week had been conceded were regularly criticized in the *Eastern Daily Press*, and it is noteworthy that all the 31 men said to be on strike at St Faith's on 22 March were from large farms, the smaller employers having decided not to proceed with the wage cut. According to NUAW Executive Committee minutes, the number of members on strike fell significantly below its peak (4,946 on 31 March) to 4,517 (7 April) and 3,501 (14 April), even before the MacDonald settlement was reached, though during these same weeks benefits paid out rose from £3,145 to £4,049, presumably reflecting payment in arrears.[52] In all, over five weeks almost two years of total membership subscriptions had been exhausted in strike pay and, due to its depleted financial resources, there was little that the union could do beyond fulminate against the untrustworthiness of farmers during the ensuing period of victimization. As we shall see, thoughtful men were bound to draw lessons which would have a lasting impact on the philosophy of labour relations within agriculture.

If the events of 1923 loom large in the annals of the NUAW, it is no less important to acknowledge the value of its routine activities. As individuals, members were entitled to a range of benefits, and frequently had good reason to be grateful to branch officials for tenaciously pursuing legal claims on their behalf. The record of activity for 1931 serves as an illustration. In that year, accident benefits were paid to 737 members along with 267 funeral benefits (from a fund started in 1929); 88 members received benevolent grants and 15 victimization pay, while over 500 enjoyed (as members of an 'approved society') sickness, dental, optical or surgical insurance benefits. Although the union continued to experience occasional difficulties in persuading solicitors to undertake its cases, in 1931, 181 claims for wage-arrears were so settled; 180 workers received weekly compensation in accident claims, and 91 lump sum settlements were made for over £18,000. Fifty-nine members were defended in court proceedings for eviction from their cottages and another 236 were assisted in this matter without their cases going to court. Meanwhile, the union was represented at 500 meetings of the Labour party or at other public bodies or official events, and 196 of its members were currently sitting on agricultural wages committees.[53]

Many of the concerns of active trade-unionists and their leaders are, naturally, reflected in the pages of *The Land Worker*. A recurrent theme was the need to gain and retain members. Not a few of its extremely well-executed cartoons were directed against the non-union man, in league with employers to hold back the advance of the NUAW. From time to time the journal was made available for free distribution, and in May 1933, a fountain pen and pencil set was on offer to those introducing six new members. Much faith was pinned on the influence that spouses might bring to bear on their flagging husbands. In February 1924, 'Kitchen Talk' featured a homily on these lines:

> 'Who would be a wretched branch secretary like me?' grumbled Joe ... 'I tell you its exasperatin' to 'ave these 'ere fellows dropping out one after another ... It 'ud break year 'eart'. 'Not mine it wouldn't', took up Mrs. Joe firmly ... 'I've got sense enough to see that them as keeps a union together is the fellows that aren't took by every wind that blows, but sticks to their guns through thick and thin'.

Other noteworthy features include the lack of sympathy evinced by the NUAW for the smallholdings movement; rather, union leaders favoured land nationalization and the Labour slogan, 'A living wage for every man on the land' (October 1927). The union attitude to women's work was ambivalent; the reported return of some former land girls to Norfolk farms during the 1923 strike was predictably denounced as 'an act of treachery' in June, and the 1934 Biennial Conference, not for the first time, was the scene of disagreement between those who wished to protest against the employment of women while so many men were out of work, and those who thought this inconsistent with socialism, the proper course being to press for equal wages (August 1934). Workers' wives were warned against Women's Institutes where ladies gave instruction on how to make hats from the sleeves of jackets, and trimmings for bonnets from the edges of old shirts – 'all part of a splendid preparation for less

PROOF POSITIVE

CHAIRMAN OF WAGES COMMITTEE (to Farmer): Why do you want a Permit for this man?
FARMER: Because he is soft in his head.
CHAIRMAN: But how do you prove that?
FARMER: Well sir, for one thing, he's not a member of his Union, so he must be!

(*The Land Worker*, October 1924)

and less wages for the menfolk', in May 1922. In the same radical vein, the publication of Parson Woodforde's Diary was held to go far to explain 'a tradition of indifference to the church' (April 1926), while in June 1931 some well-meaning compliments from the Archdeacon of Norwich ('I take my hat off to the labourer ... he is a really good Christian man') met the indignant riposte, 'The Archdeacon takes off his hat, but watches out that he doesn't take off his coat ... we know the value of a farm labourer, but what is the use of an archdeacon?'. At all times the native male worker was defended against 'outside' competition. In August 1932 Gooch (by then President) sent letters to the Norfolk papers protesting against the employment of 1,100 Irishmen in the county: 'Why do farmers stick to the Irishmen? They cost less and are not trade unionists.' Likewise, the union set its face against the importation of unemployed Durham miners to work on sugar beet in Norfolk – 'THIS MUST STOP!' (June 1934). As well as featuring official policies, the pages of *The Land Worker* also afforded space for some lively correspondence. Machinery, contended Bro. Brumby of Boughton (Lincs.) should be a friend to the worker but under capitalist ownership of the means of production was merely a means of safeguarding and increasing profit, and of displacing labour (January 1933). The appearance of an article on 'How to become a Policeman' by Jack Hayes (former police-officer, General Secretary of the National Union of Police and Prison Officers and a Labour MP), in *The Land Worker* of February 1926, was denounced by Bro. Huxstep in the next issue, his theme being that it was improper to encourage workers to engage themselves to defend the interests of the present ruling class. From 1925 *The Land Worker* followed the practice of publishing the wills of farmers leaving £8,000 or more. By 1932 these numbered 1,815 leaving in all £39.4m. or an average £21,650 each. Venturing some bold arithmetic, the conclusion drawn was that, assuming there were 86,600 farms in Britain with over one hundred acres, about half those who died left fortunes of more than £5,000 (April 1933). Among those signalled out for specific criticism was W. A. Glynn, DL, JP, one of the founding fathers of the Royal Isle of Wight Agricultural Society, who was laid to rest in 1926 at the age of 84. Glynn was remembered as having expressed deep regrets at being unable to achieve his stated amibition to build a set of cottages for the aged and poor, due to his limited means and very heavy levels of taxation; nevertheless, *The Land Worker* pointed out (in September 1926) that he had left £46,428. In the next issue attention was focused on a £45 fine imposed on Charles Hendy of Sutterton (Lincs.) who had given much trouble over half-holidays: 'Yet it seems he can afford whisky in larger quantities than he can carry and also can afford to buy a new car and smash it up almost immediately after.'

However, it is important to stand back from the routine work of the union, and from the frequently querulous though never dull pages of its mouthpiece, to emphasize an underlying swing in the postures of the union executive. As we have seen, with Walker at the helm, the NUAW emerged from the Great War with a decidedly radical complexion. Thus, the January 1921 issue of *The Land Worker* contained (among recipes for Lincolnshire spiced peas, pork pie, and Norfolk dumplings, gardening notes and so on) the clear message that current schemes advocating a triple alliance between landowners, farmers and agricultural workers were illusory, for they ignored the real struggle, which was between capitalism and the working class. It was in keeping with such views that Peel's Landworkers' Union should be ridiculed as 'a comic opera organization' (September 1924) and in May 1925 'Tit-Willow' echoed the refrain: having reviewed inequalities of wealth and income he demanded to know 'What is the use of denying the class struggle, in view of the above facts?' On the industrial front the union policy was for years one of undeviating support for free trade, which may be considered the true test of whether the executive saw the future of members as bound more closely to that of farmers, or to the working-class as a whole.

How generally these views were accepted among farmworkers as a whole can never be known; but it is certain that many would have held contrary opinions. A letter to the *Eastern Daily Press* at the height of the Norfolk Struggle in 1923 articulated some very different sentiments. 'Furrow-maker' maintained that the NUAW would 'never do any good so long as its leaders keep on hob-nobbing with the leaders of other Trade Unions ... the agricultural labourer is being sweated by his friends (?) the labourers in the towns, not by the farmer'.[54] In the opinion of Madden, the postures of the union during the 1920s are explicable only in terms of an inability to appreciate the close interdependence of farm revenue and wages, among leaders who certainly held strong political convictions but lacked any agricultural background.[55] However, change was in the wind. Although reference to individual personalities courts the danger of over-simplifying the issues, shifts in policy are closely linked with the demise of Walker (who resigned and left for Australia in 1928) and the rising star of Edwin Gooch, who became President in 1928. Gooch, whose name was to become as inseparably associated with the cause of agricultural trade unionism as were those of Joseph Arch and George Edwards, was by origin the son of a Wymondham blacksmith and a former printer and journalist, and was in 1923 merely a prominent member of the Norfolk committee of the union. Without doubt he drew important conclusions from the events of 1923, and from the fact that, in its aftermath, Norfolk wages remained among the lowest in the country. Clearly, a change in union policies was not capable of being accomplished overnight, and throughout the remainder of the 1920s the NUAW continued to support established Labour Party policies, for example by opposing demands for a duty on imports of malting barley and, in 1928, the principle of agricultural de-rating. Yet under Gooch's leadership a gradual shift of position, eventually to culminate in a complete reversal of policies, may be discerned. In the July 1931 issue of *The Land Worker* he was ruminating on the possibilities of rapprochement with employers in an article entitled 'A Common Meeting Ground' and during some heated debates over sugar beet in 1934, gave a further indication of what was to come. In 1924 the union had opposed the sugar beet subsidies, which were by now consuming large sums of public money which in the eyes of the Labour Party faithful could have been spent more wisely on industrial investment. Yet in 1934–5 Norfolk grew 24 per cent (and East Anglia as a whole 62 per cent) of the national output of sugar beet, causing Gooch, with others, to fear that any withdrawal of subsidies could only serve to bring extended periods of unemployment to hundreds of men. He thus advocated their retention. May 1935 saw the union executive giving evidence in support of home cereals to the Standard Price (Wheat) Committee, when they adopted the line that farmers should 'not be completely at the mercy of foreign wheat producers'. For a time the NUAW Executive Committee was out of harmony with its own journal (as well as the bulk of Labour MPs) and remained so until the outbreak of war when the editor resigned in favour of Arthur Holmes. Yet in Madden's view, to all intents and purposes Gooch had already completed the reversal of union policy by August 1938, when he advocated in *The Land Worker*,

> 'a policy of an abundance of cheap food, not at the expense of the farmer or worker but with the sympathetic practical cooperation of the state. I want the agricultural industry of this country to be going at high pressure, every acre of suitable land cultivated, prices assured, and with the farm workers enjoying an economic status akin to the skilled workers in the towns. If the food cannot be produced sufficiently cheap I still want it to be produced here'.[56]

Existing arrangements fell far short of what Gooch was advocating in 1938, but the war would soon subordinate questions of principle to practical exigencies, and carry this policy into effect, virtually line by line.

Such issues of high policy were doubtless remote from the everyday concerns of most farmworkers. When we turn to assessing changes in the standard of living, the voluminous information available for this period may be interpreted from a variety of standpoints, depending chiefly on the yardstick of comparison being used. To begin with, there is no difficulty in showing that farmworkers enjoyed real wage increases, taking the period as a whole. Admittedly, the interval between the two agricultural Wages Boards (1921–4) saw a precipitous fall in cash wages, while the cost of living, though also falling, did not do so to quite the same extent, so that there was a temporary decline in real wages, accompanied by considerable distress. Thereafter, the post-1924 regulations had the effect of setting a floor to cash wages at a time when the cost of living sank, year by year, through 1925 to 1933. Subsequently, prices began to rise gently in 1933–9, but this was accompanied by more or less equivalent wage increases in the face of an increasing shortage of labour. Overall, the cost of living stood at 175 in 1925 and 156 in 1938 (1914 = 100). A comparable change in agricultural wages would have reduced them from the 31s 5d average of 1925 to 26s; instead, they were 32s 2d, suggesting an increase of the order of 20 per cent on the real wages of 1925.[57] To some employers, indeed, the level of farmworkers' wages seemed continually to threaten to be more than the market would bear: farmers of the early 1930s, whose recollections went back before the war, were given to pointing out that wages were some 75 per cent higher than in 1914, whilst prices, on balance, were only ten per cent higher.[58]

Moreover, these higher real wages were reflected in a wider range of consumption. Robertson Scott opened his book *The Dying Peasant* (1926) by contending that it was becoming increasingly difficult to distinguish the farmworker from the town worker, either by his clothes or his mind: 'His world would amaze Joseph Arch ... In the remotest village the *Sunday Scum* reaches him. Often he takes a daily paper. In his cottage there may be wireless or a motor cycle.'[59] The Raleigh Cycle Company found it worthwhile, in the mid 1920s, regularly to advertise in *The Land Worker* machines complete with Dunlop tyres and Sturmey-Archer three-speed gears, for £8 10s – or 12s a month; and A. W. Ashby's younger sister, who was a village schoolteacher and profoundly sympathetic to the farmworkers' case, allowed that their homes were becoming 'all well-equipped with cooking utensils whereas in pre-war years frying pan and saucepan were all that were available. Improved soaps, the mantle lamp, the oil stove – all products of a mechanical age – are not despicable as contributions to the decent life.'[60]

Yet there were some important limitations on the extent to which higher consumption standards came within the farmworkers' grasp. The full advantage of falling food prices and competitive prices for household requisites of all kinds, from chamber pots to brushes and boots, could be secured only by taking a moderately expensive bus journey to the nearest town. Shortfalls in basic amenities were another disincentive to the acquisition of a wider range of consumer goods. As yet, very few cottages boasted electricity, and this was far from being their most conspicuous deficiency, for in 1939 some 25 per cent of all rural parishes, (to say nothing of isolated hamlets and cottages) still lacked a piped water supply; while the ubiquitous earth midden or cesspool, accounting, for example, for over half the closet accommodation in the Ringmer district of Sussex in 1934, was a source of increasing embarrassment to the younger generation.[61] Yet another factor affecting farmworkers' purchasing power was their still relatively high rate of procreation. Mrs Maggy Fryett had nine children in all, and at the age of 84 in 1975 could recall 'No way of stopping them. If there had been I would have done'; and Mrs Aida Heyhoe (then 82, herself one of 14 children and the wife of a farm blacksmith) remembered,

> 'I'd sit up at night, after my husband had gone to bed, mending the clothes. He'd say, "Aren't you coming to bed yet?" I say, "I've got to mend these clothes before I go to bed. They'll want them in the morning." ... So if I stayed up mending, my husband would be asleep when I came to bed. That were simple, weren't it?'[62]

At least Mrs Heyhoe succeeded in restricting her offspring to three, and by one means or another, so did many other rural wage-earners, for between 1921 and 1931 the birth rate among agricultural workers fell by 21 per cent. Yet this fall was under half that recorded for semi-skilled textile workers (43 per cent) or miners (50 per cent),[63] and consequently the families of farmworkers tended to remain of above average size.

However, the most obvious barrier to a rapid advance of consumption standards remained the relatively low pay of the farmworker. Wages stayed at levels manifestly below those received even for unskilled work in the towns. In 1930 wages for milk roundsmen in Lancashire were fixed at a pound a week above those prescribed by the County Wages Committee for the cowmen who produced the milk on the farms,[64] and on a broader basis, Table 8.4 compares the wage levels of workers in a range of industries with those of ordinary agricultural workers towards the close of the period.

Table 8.4: Relative levels of weekly wages in selected occupations, 1937*

Railway engine drivers	72s–90s
Printing and bookbinding	73s 7d
Engineering – pattern makers	72s 2d
Bricklayers	71s 1d
Masons	71s 1d
Carpenters	71s 0d
Shipwrights	66s 0d
Local Authority labourers	54s 4d
Building labourers	53s 3d
Engineering labourers	49s 10d
Railway goods porters	47s 0d
Permanent way labourers	47s 0d
Shipyard labourers	47s 0d
Agriculture: average for ordinary male workers	33s 7½

* *Statistical Abstract* (Cmd. 5903), 1939, quoted in W. H. Pedley, *Labour on the Land*, King and Staples, 1942, p. 13.

All these features are reflected in contemporary household expenditure studies. One, based on 83 budgets of 1924, showed that where the families concerned had more than three children, 70 per cent of expenditure went on food and over 20 per cent on rent, light and heating, leaving rather under ten per cent for all other expenditure.[65] Food still loomed large, accounting for no less than 63 per cent of all disbursements in 169 budgets collected by the NUAW in Lincolnshire during the spring of 1937. This was actually higher than a comparable figure calculated for the unemployed in the Rhondda Valley (49 per cent); moreover, when arranged into categories of weekly income per family member it appeared that poorer households were unable to spend as much on food as households in the higher ranges, even though their proportionate outlays were greater, thus supporting the view that such households tended to be poor on account of the number of persons they contained.[66] A much more extensive enquiry conducted in 1937–8 under the auspices of the Ministry of Labour sought to compare the pattern of expenditure of industrial and 'rural working class' families under similar headings, with the results given in table 8.5.

Table 8.5: Comparison of the budgets of rural workers' households with those of industrial households in the United Kingdom, 1937*

	Rural workers' families (average size 3.79)		*Industrial workers' families* (average size 3.77)	
	Absolute amount	% of all outlays	Absolute amount	% of all outlays
Rent	4s 9d	8.3	10s 10d	12.7
Food	27s 9d	48.4	34s 1d	40.1
Clothes, footwear	5s 3d	9.1	8s 1d	9.5
Fuel and light	4s 11d	8.6	6s 5d	7.6
Other items	14s 8d	25.6	27s 7d	30.1
All items	57s 4d	100.0	85s 0d	100.0

* 'Weekly Expenditure of Working Class Households in the United Kingdom in 1937–8', *Ministry of Labour Gazette*, January 1941, pp. 7–11. The 'rural workers' included some engaged in forestry and market gardening, and the number of wage-earners per household averaged 1.6.

A point of significance emerging from the table, and the more detailed source from which it is drawn, is that the rural worker's outlay on food was higher as a proportion, but lower absolutely than that of his industrial counterpart. He spent more on bread and flour (4s 2d against 3s 6½d), cheese and margarine, but less on meat, bacon, ham, fish, butter, eggs, vegetables, fruit and, unsurprisingly, milk and potatoes, these being items which were still quite commonly received from employers as allowances. His lower outlay (both absolutely and as a proportion) on clothing and footwear offers a significant comment on the rural worker's status as a consumer, as does the pattern of expenditure on 'other items'. Under every sub-category included here, the rural wage earner spent less than the industrial worker, notably on travelling (10½d against 2s 3d) and entertainment (4¼d against 1s 4½). In conformity with our evidence on his relative health (see below) he also spent less on the doctor, dentist, nursing attention and medicine, (1s 2½d against 1s 8d), but at least as much as a proportion of his limited income (2.1 against 2.0 per cent). This was also true with respect to cleaning materials, smoking, newspapers, and insurance contributions.

While the modest consumption standards of the farmworker need no further illustration, it might be argued that one advantage he did enjoy was relative security of employment, at any rate after 1924. By and large this appears to have been true, since the first usable unemployment rates calculated for farmworkers (for 1937 and 1938), though indicating the persistent influence of seasonality, averaged 4.1 and 5.5 per cent respectively, and were decidedly lower than among the working population at large.[67] However, a number of important qualifications need to be made. In the first place the impact of loss of work on the individual, prior to the extension of unemployment insurance to farmworkers in 1936, could be exceptionally severe, for those who lost their situations were instantly vulnerable to all the humiliations capable of being imposed under the Poor Law. A Norfolk man described his experiences during the winter of 1930–1:

> I have worked on this farm fourteen years . . . we were discharged a fortnight before Christmas. All Christmas with no pay. Only remedy to go to the Relieving Officer which was three miles off. . . . He gave me a card and I had to go round to six farmers and get it signed . . . [then] go back to the Relieving Officer and hand in our cards. Then we had to go back here and wait for orders. After another week had passed we were told to report to the roadman and started work – forty hours for £1-3s. My first pay was 13s 10d on December 31 then three more weeks at £1-1-8d which have now finished. We now have to see the Relieving Officer again for a card, and get the six bulldogs to sign again. Is this fair? I have fought all these years for freedom and now, with others, have to suffer like this.[68]

Secondly, unemployment insurance was not only long-delayed but when it came, discriminatory. In 1921 farmworkers had been excluded from the general extension of the state scheme because their wages were deemed insufficient to enable them to bear regular contributions on the same scale as other workers. An inter-departmental committee headed by Sir Henry Rew produced, in 1926, divided reports on the feasibility and value of a special, low-contribution scheme for agriculture; it took ten more years of discussion, with apparently two out of every three NFU branches still against the idea in 1935,[69] before special arrangements based on three equal contributions of 4½d from the employer, employee and the state were finally established. Benefits were correspondingly low, at 14s for an adult male and a ceiling of 30s for the family initially, rising to 35s in 1939.

Thirdly, an unstated condition of security in employment was often acceptance of long hours and extremely rare holidays. This was another area where state intervention was tardy, and relatively ineffective. The Act of 1924 had encouraged Wages Committees to specify a weekly half-holiday, 'so far as is practicable'. However, the only means available to enforce one was to apply overtime rates to Saturday work. In practice, many farmers preferred to pay overtime rates and keep their men at work, a feature especially common in livestock areas. From 1936 the NUAW was pressing for a week's paid holiday and farmworkers, with others, benefited from the Holidays With Pay Act of 1938. Once again, though, they were singled out for special treatment; where Wages Committees chose so to direct, employees could not take more than three days consecutively. There is no doubt that these drawbacks were keenly felt: 'It ain't more work we want; its more comfort an' leisure an' 'appiness' contended 'Mrs Joe', conversing with 'Parson's Wife' in *The Land Worker*'s feature 'Kitchen Talk' – 'With that she gave a sniff an' walked off with 'er nose in the air'.[70]

A much cited advantage of the farmworker was his relative health and extended lifespan. It could be argued that longevity is not an end in itself, and it is not surprising to find *The Land Worker* contending (in July 1924) that 'We want quality as well as quantity ... we want to enjoy life; not merely drag our way through it from year's end to year's end'. Nevertheless, the farmworkers' well-being seems to have defied the advent of canned food, mass-produced bread and chocolate just as effectively as, long ago, it had survived the introduction of tea-drinking, so vigorously condemned by William Cobbett. By any contemporary standards the health record was favourable. Indicatively, the Dorset Rural Insurance Society in its annual report for 1930 commented favourably on 'the general health of the members being of such a satisfactory standard ... the last valuation of the society disclosed a considerable surplus.... The strong financial position of the Society demonstrates the fact that, if rural workers wish to secure the full advantages of National Health Insurance, they should join a society which caters especially for such workers.'[71] Turning to mortality levels, the experience of farmworkers remained more favourable not only than that of townsmen, but even that of rural mortality in general, by 12 per cent at 25–34, 19 per cent at 35–44, 14 per cent at 45–54 and 9 per cent at 55–64, according to data of the Registrar-General for 1921–3.[72] Another study based on the mortality ruling ten years later suggests that the record of farmworkers was superior even to that of their employers, who, it would seem, showed a significantly greater proclivity to committing suicide.[73]

Table 8.6: Comparative occupational standardized mortality rates, 1930–2*

All males in England and Wales	100
Some extremes	
Bank and insurance officials	66
Anglican clergymen	69
Stevedores	220
Tin and coppermine workers	342
Within the agricultural industry	
Farm foremen	47
Agricultural and gardeners' labourers	71
Farmers	78
Farm bailiffs	82

* B. S. Bosanquet, 'The Quality of the Rural Population', *Eugenics Review*, 1950, Vol. XLII, p. 80.

Although these facts are impressive, once again they do not tell the whole story. Rheumatism in its various forms remained common and was related, beyond any doubt, to repeated exposure in cold and wet conditions, and to the damp and draughty nature of farm cottages. Farmworkers were also vulnerable, perhaps to a greater extent than is generally realized, to occupational health hazards arising from their work, some of which are touched upon in chapter 10 below.[74] Nor does table 8.5 show all the salient facts concerning farmworkers' mortality. Suicide apart, farmers were prone to succumb to diseases associated with good living, including diabetes and cirrhosis of the liver, while their work people showed greater vulnerability to those linked with poor nutrition or living conditions, such as tuberculosis and brochitis. Moreover, the average figures of mortality given in Table 8.5 conceal differences related to status and income within the farm labour force: estate labourers yielded a standardized mortality ratio of 65, shepherds 58, and men in charge of horses 51; whilst the figure for labourers employed tending cattle, dairying, etc. was, at 45, only half that of labourers 'not otherwise distinguished' (90).[75] A final qualification is that, although rural and agricultural health and mortality levels remained relatively favourable, long-standing contrasts with the towns were beginning to diminish appreciably, reflecting much improved standards of urban sanitation and a tendency for modern facilities such as clinics and improved hospital facilities to be located primarily in urban areas. The excess of mortality in county boroughs over rural mortality had been 46 per cent as recently as 1911–14, but by 1936 was only 24 per cent, and deaths of women in childbirth were actually higher in rural areas than in London, or the county boroughs, in both 1921 and 1936. The rural–urban physical differences so widely discussed at the time of the Boer War were also disappearing. When the first wave of recruits was examined in 1939 it was found possible to place 80 per cent of those from the boroughs in Class I, compared with 84 per cent of those from rural areas.[76]

When viewed in an international context, the situation of farmworkers in England and Wales could in some important respects be construed favourably.[77] However, farmworkers were not disposed to compare their standards with those ruling in foreign parts; neither were they concerned with historical comparisons – or, even, whether they were faring relatively better than their employers, as some argued was the case. What did impress them was their situation compared to other British workers, and perhaps also to the minimum standards set for those out of work. When the Liberal Land Committee compared the wage rates of 1924 with the sums payable to an unemployed man, wife and three children under 14, it concluded that in the Christchurch Union (Hants.) a farmworker earning the county minimum wage (30s) would be only a shilling a week better off than a man drawing unemployment benefit (29s), and actually 3s a week worse off than one in receipt of outdoor relief from the Board of Guardians. This was an extreme case; in another 18 rural unions he would be better off at work, but in some cases only by a perilously small amount, for example by 1s 6d a week (Shifnal, Salop) or 1s 3d (Reigate, Surrey).[78] Much the same held true in the mid-1930s. Under current arrangements, an unemployed worker with a wife and three children (none working) would have received some 33–37s a week on 'the dole'.[79] This figure scarcely differs from the minimum wage for an agricultural worker given in table 8.4. Thus, despite twenty years of wage regulation, and the fact that wages had undoubtedly moved forward in real terms, the relative disadvantages of the farmworker in terms of income remained as great as ever and were a prime factor in the rural exodus. In a small-scale enquiry undertaken by Pedley in 1939 covering 73 current land workers, 58 per cent put wages first among their complaints and 25 per cent second; whilst among 49 former land workers they were placed first as a cause of leaving by 62 per cent, and second by 28 per cent.[80]

This emphasis on wages as the main source of discontent was natural enough.

It reflected a recognition on the part of the majority of workers that opportunities to climb to a higher status within the industry were, by now, narrower than ever. Only one per cent in Pedley's survey said that lack of opportunity to become a farmer was the most unsatisfactory thing in a worker's life, and one per cent put it second.[81] Little or no enthusiasm was evinced towards smallholdings, and farming on a larger scale was effectively closed, according to C. S. Orwin, to those without money to invest. This view would soon be contested in George Henderson's *The Farming Ladder* (1944, running to 13 impressions by 1948), who maintained, in language close to that of Samuel Smiles, that 'Given the will there is hardly anything which cannot be achieved'. As evidence Henderson offered his own case history and that of his brother, as well as the careers of some of his farm pupils. Significantly, ambitious lads who sought to follow in their footsteps were advised never to accept 'a situation entailing lodging with a labourer', lest they should begin to think like one.[82] In fact, the bulk of the evidence strongly supports Orwin's view. Even in Wales, which contained many small and unspecialized farms, 75 per cent of a sample of 834 farmers investigated by Ashby turned out to be farmers' sons, and only 11 per cent were sons of farmworkers (another $7\frac{1}{2}$ per cent were sons of other manual workers).[83] In most English districts, opportunities to rise in this way were still more circumscribed. Although the proportion of English farmers who were themselves farmers' sons was no higher than in Wales, and sometimes lower, this did not signify that recruits were drawn to any great extent from the ranks of agricultural wage-earners. A study of the eastern counties revealed that only 9 per cent of the occupiers of holdings over 20 acres were former farmworkers and 16 per cent were originally members of another trade or profession; while among 190 farmers in south Devon in 1935, only six per cent were sons of farm labourers, smallholders or gardeners.[84] In Northumberland, which had the largest average size of farm in the country, there was a high degree of inheritance of agricultural occupations, often traceable through three or four generations, but 'promotion' into the ranks of farmers was extremely rare if not entirely unknown among shepherds.[85] It was considered more feasible for a boy to seek to be a teacher than a farmer, if he were without means.[86] By and large, successive generations of farmers had reared their own replacements. The vast majority of agricultural workers could aspire to become farmers only insofar as farmers' sons transferred to other occupations; even then, entry was much easier for men coming into agriculture from other walks of life, where capital could be acquired at a rate far faster than it could possibly have been scraped together by the farmworker from his modest wage.[87]

All this is relevant to understanding contemporary perceptions of the farmworker's situation and prospects. Undoubtedly many men, especially those of the older generation, evinced moderate contentment. Acknowledging their gains, they would have concurred with Fred Kitchen that the farmworker's life was 'not now the down-trodden, all bed-and-work existence of popular imagination'; or with Charles Slater that labouring life was (by 1933), 'like being in heaven compared to what it was forty years ago'.[88] Yet other working men, those with whom farmworkers were likely to come into contact, took a poor view of farm employment and were frequently imbued with the notion that it was the last refuge of the inefficient and, probably, the mentally defective. Moreover, if the skills of the farmworker tended to be regularly underestimated, so also were the richness and variety, even the poetic qualities of his powers of expression, since an appreciation of this point presupposes rather a high degree of education on the part of the listener and a feel for language. Almost universally, the farmworker's ways were thought quaint and old-fashioned, not least among those who, having left the villages and acquired a veneer of urban smartness, were prone to gauge their own social progress by the extent to which they distanced themselves from his style and standard of life. The young were especially vulnerable when faced with teasing and condescension. Henderson lost one lad not because he disliked the work or (allegedly) could better the wage, but simply because other youths laughed at him for working on a farm. Something of the same sense of mortification is implicit in the recollection of a Suffolk farmworker that 'the girls would look at a boy in Ipswich on a Saturday night, find out that he was a farm labourer, and then stop looking sharp'.[89] If anything, women were more conscious of deprivation than their menfolk, and showed considerable sensitivity to the practical inconveniences of cottage life: this was only to be expected, given that rather a high proportion had at one time or another been engaged in domestic service. For all that the inter-war period had brought definite improvements, by any objective criteria the position of the farmworker and his family remained disadvantaged. What is more, they were increasingly conscious of the fact: the rate of decline of the agricultural labour force in the 1930s appears to have been faster than in any previous decade.[90]

NINE

Digging for Victory, 1939–45

The experience of World War I had borne in upon the nation the dangers of excessive dependence on food imports, and thereafter the strategic case for achieving a high level of self-sufficiency never lacked its advocates, particularly in the House of Lords. Yet their pleas fell on deaf ears in the 1920s and, even after the adoption of a more interventionist stance on the part of government, defence considerations remained far in the background. The chief provisions of the Agriculture Act of 1937 were to establish a Land Fertility Committee to advise the government, to make subsidies available to farmers for the improvement of grassland by applying lime and basic slag, and to adjust slightly in the producers' favour the guaranteed wheat prices which had been introduced in 1932. Yet the act was but a gesture. Any hopes that the government would proceed to prepare a comprehensive policy were scotched when Neville Chamberlain declared to an audience of farmers at Kettering in July 1938 his belief that Britain would not be starved in time of war; and that any attempt to encourage greater output of food at home would sap the purchasing power of overseas suppliers, reduce British exports, create further unemployment and thus weaken existing markets for British farmers. In that year, the United Kingdom remained dependent on overseas sources for no less than 70 per cent of its food supplies by value, and some 23m. tons of food, animal foodstuffs and fertilizers were imported to sustain the needs of its inhabitants. Moreover, in England and Wales the total acreage of agricultural land under crops and grass was still diminishing, and lower by 8 per cent than in 1920.[1] However, the following year saw a new initiative from the Ministry of Agriculture which, against the background of Hitler's invasion of Czechoslavakia in March, met with government approval. The Agricultural Development Act of May 1939 was a distinctly war-orientated measure. It offered a grant of £2 an acre to enable grassland of long-standing to be ploughed up and either reseeded or cropped, and a deficiency payment scheme for sheep, so as to encourage the output of animals largely independent of imported feed. It also gave the minister authority to purchase and store fertilizers, as well as several thousand farm tractors and related implements which would form a national reserve. It is true that these steps to bring agriculture to a state of war-preparedness were belated and in many respects inadequate; as one foreign observer was later to conclude, 'no-one would suggest that British agriculture had been intentionally prepared for the war it was to face.'[2] Yet the blame for this should not be laid at the door of the agricultural departments, and what turned out to be perhaps the most far-sighted preparatory step had been undertaken as long ago as 1936 when the Ministry of Agriculture quietly set up an embryonic scheme of War Agricultural Committees. By the close of that year, chairmen, executives and secretaries had all been selected (unknown to the persons concerned), and during 1938, the year of the Munich agreement, standby notices were issued to chairmen and key committee members. It was intended that each County Committee would consist chiefly of a small number of local men, approached by the minister and therefore representative of no special interest. They would be expected to deal with the implementation of orders relating to labour, machinery and cultivation, acting through District Committees organized on a petty sessional basis, each composed of several residents with an intimate knowledge of local farming conditions. Their executive officers were to be drawn in the main from the agricultural staffs of County Councils. Through these arrangements, it was hoped, Whitehall and the individual farm could be effectively linked and, in the event, names were publicly announced in May 1939. No doubt, as Whetham has surmised, many of those who were called upon to serve walked the lines of the implement and machinery exhibits of the Royal Show at Windsor two months later, 'mindful of what would be required of them, and ready to start work on the third of September.'[3]

Though the practical difficulties of policy implementation should never be underestimated, in principle the farming task was clearly defined by wartime governments, which sought to integrate shipping, consumption and agricultural policies in the interest of achieving a coherent food programme. It was obvious that shipping space needed to be strictly controlled, and indeed, during World War II Britain was to lose 11.4m. tons, equivalent to 54 per cent of her merchant tonnage just before the war.[4] Accordingly, the space allocated to food imports needed to be minimized, and consumption patterns were likewise closely controlled. A small Food (Defence Plans) Department had been set up as early as 1936 and this became the nucleus of the new Ministry of Food. Already, in 1939, the operational machinery for rationing had been set in hand and ration books printed. Advice from nutritionists helped to shape the schemes of World War II, which were chiefly confined to meat, bacon, cheese, fats, sugar and milk in fixed quantities per head, with extra allowances for those engaged in heavy work, including the farmworker who could purchase an extra cheese ration. Scarce foodstuffs of a 'luxury' character, mostly imported and therefore very limited and erratic in supply, were distributed according to a 'points' system from late 1941, which had the merit of leaving a modicum of choice to the consumer.[5] Moreover, special regard was paid to the requirements of children and nursing and pregnant mothers through the allocation of orange juice and milk; in the eyes of one historian of the welfare state, the decision to proceed with the distribution of school milk, taken within a week of the Dunkirk evacuation, was symbolic of 'Britain's proud assurance in the face of a danger without parallel'.[6] Fish (when available), fresh vegetables and fruit, and bread and potatoes remained unrationed.

The contribution expected from home agriculture was, naturally, that it should concentrate upon the production of basic commodities such as grainstuffs, milk and potatoes. Targets were regularly set and revised and, with increasing expertise, the government deployed a variety of monetary incentives and direct subsidies to achieve its goals. Land use fell directly under the control of the War Agricultural Committees which could, when necessary, oblige farmers to accept credit to buy essential fertilizers or equipment to put into effect cropping plans dictated to them, and were empowered to supervise or even remove occupiers graded as 'B' or 'C' in terms of their efficiency. Under such arrangements, the face of the landscape soon began to change, in some places quite dramatically. Lush and level pastures of the highest class, for example around Langston in Leicestershire and on Romney Marsh, were regretfully given over to the plough, and in 1940 the Somerset levels and the Cambridgeshire fens resounded to the thunder of explosions, as submerged oak trees hampering cultivation were dug out and blown up by the Royal Engineers. Some deplorable cases of neglect were attacked with great vigour. Thus, Hundon farm near Clare in Suffolk, disused since a tithe distraint sale twenty years before, was taken over by the War Agricultural Committee and placed under an energetic farmer. Nearly 300 acres of weeds were burned off, eight miles of ditches cleared and another 30 acres freed for cultivation merely by cutting back hedges to their proper size. Likewise, the McCreegh estate in Hampshire, long derelict for similar reasons and now overrun by game and massive hedges, was assaulted by tractors whose radiators choked and were brought to the boil by the seeds of, reputedly, 'the greatest jungle of ragwort in England'.[7] By dint of such efforts, the tilled acreage in England and Wales was increased by no less than 62 per cent between 1939 and 1945 and the proportion under temporary grass by approximately the same; while by contrast, the proportion under permanent grass was reduced by about 38 per cent. In 1943, as much as 3.28m. acres was devoted to growing wheat which, according to Ministry of Agriculture records, was the highest figure since 1875: the peak war-time acreage devoted to barley (just under 2m. acres in 1945) was, likewise, the highest since 1886, and the acreage devoted to potatoes in 1945 (0.98m.) was the largest ever recorded. Dairy cattle rose slightly in number, but sheep were reduced by 30 per cent, while the number of pigs and fowls kept on farms about halved between 1939 and 1945.[8] An increasing proportion of the surviving fowls was maintained in householders' chicken runs in country villages and suburban gardens, and strictly regulated pig clubs were set up by groups of employees of workpeople, sometimes in the most incongruous situations, for example by London firemen in the swimming pool of the bombed-out Ladies' Carlton Club in Pall Mall.[9] In town and country alike, gardens and allotments as well as railway embankments and bomb sites were vigorously exploited as householders responded to the call to 'Dig for Victory', and the efforts of amateur gardeners made a small but useful contribution to the nation's food supply, as did the food preservation centres organized by the Women's Institutes.

The implications of agricultural strategy, particularly the extension of the cultivated acreage, were obvious from past experience. More labour would be needed, and the government moved swiftly and much more effectively than in the Great War to impose restrictions which would maintain as far as possible the size of the male labour force. Farmworkers could scarcely be prevented from voluntarily joining the armed forces, which were conducting lively recruiting campaigns during the spring of 1939, but those aged 25 and over were exempted from call-up under the Military Training Act of that year and, towards its close, this was reduced to 21. The farming interest would have preferred 18, but instead the government instituted arrangements for considering the postponement of call-up in cases where the worker could be shown to be vital to food production. In fact, during the early months of the war labour supply had yet to reveal itself as a significant problem. W. H. Long, an agricultural economist at Leeds University, noted the loss from 153 Yorkshire farms of 39 youths to the Territorial Army by the end of 1939 (with 43 more due to go during the following year), and suspected that they would never return to farming even if their period of training did not exceed six months. Another feature was the loss of Irish workers since the outbreak of hostilities. Yet, during the first four months of war no general shortage of labour had been experienced in Yorkshire, and such as there was had been met by men released from road works or supplied by labour exchanges, village women, gipsies and soldiers. Writing at about the same time, another economist, J. H. Smith, remarked that despite the anticipated additional labour required as a consequence of the ploughing-up campaign, in June 1940 the demand of Welsh farmers for additional labour was not urgent. Some localized offers of the free services of members of the armed forces had met with little response, and so far there had been little request for those of pupils and students, or the Women's Land Army. Moreover, labour exchanges in Wales continued to experience difficulties in placing agricultural workers registered as unemployed. There was, Smith pointed out, still some slack to be taken up. He anticipated that as much as one-half of the forthcoming harvest could be gathered by the occupiers of small farms without need of extra labour, while on the larger holdings, organized teamwork would enable tasks to be carried out with a minimum of increased labour.[10]

Even so, by March 1940 the Ministry of Agriculture estimated that agriculture had lost some 50,000 workers overall; some 25–30,000 to the Territorial Army, 5,000 to National Service and the rest to other occupations, many being drawn into the hectic construction of camps and aerodromes in rural areas.[11] There was also the factor of quality to be weighed. When Sturrock examined labour turnover on a group of East Anglian farms, he found that at least one-quarter of the replacements for 96 workers who left during the first year of war had little or no previous agricultural experience, while the 27 or so known to have entered the armed forces included some of the very best men.[12] Finally, the government also had to consider not merely the present, but the prospective labour needs of agriculture as the demands placed on the industry grew. Accordingly, spring 1940 saw the adoption of a strategy to retain regular farmworkers. This involved setting a minimum wage of 48s a week which was intended to reduce the gap between farm and other wages, and to unify those operating in the different counties.[13] Next, on 5 June 1940 the Undertakings (Restriction on Engagement) Order came into operation. This prohibited employers in other industries from taking on men normally working on the farm, unless authorized by the Ministry of Labour, and proved to be an effective step in stabilizing the supply of labour in agriculture. There remained, however, a few loopholes: for example, a man might move from farm into self-employment. Thus, by the following year an Essential Work (General Provisions) Order took effect, which meant that every agricultural male worker over 18 years of age who left his employment came automatically into the direct service of the County War Agricultural Committee, unless he found an alternative farm situation within fourteen days. By 1944 some 9,700 male workers, mostly lacking in experience, were directly employed by the committees and usually deployed in gangs.[14] For their part, officials of the NFU were not slow to call attention to such restrictions. In March 1941, Kent farmers were urged to report immediately to local labour exchanges any cases of workers leaving for other jobs when alternative agricultural employment was available and, further, where a worker was suspected to be leaving farming, employers were recommended to refuse to hand over his insurance cards, and to send them instead to the local labour exchange. So far, restrictions on employment were confined to males, yet the problem of female workers was also, in its way, worrying farmers. In April 1941 the *Kent Farmers' Journal* remarked on large numbers of women in the Rochester area who were leaving farming for work in war factories.[15] Another administrative solution was eventually arrived at. Under the Employment of Women (Control of Engagement) Order of 1942 the Ministry of Labour took powers to direct women into forms of war work, such as the women's services or industrial employment which might be far distant from their homes. Such measures may have encouraged women to prefer local employment; they were in due course buttressed by the introduction for the first time of minimum wages for full-time female workers in agriculture, which became operative in 1943, at a level corresponding to 75 per cent of that of males.

As the war proceeded, a significant proportion of the work of the County Committees, or at least their labour sub-committees, was concerned with deciding cases of liability to military service. By October 1941 the Shropshire Committee had already adjudicated on 2,072 applications, granting certificates of exemption or postponement of call-up in 88 per cent of cases reviewed. Some gave rise to perplexing problems, for instance an application put forward by the Electric Hatchery of Church Stretton, asking for postponement in the case of J. Gadsby, a chicken sexer. Advice was sought from the Harper Adams Agricultural College at Newport as to whether his work was capable of being performed by a woman; however, once it was learned that Gadsby carried out similar work on poultry farms across a wide area, his postponement was confirmed. The committee would use information received: among a number of similar cases, in November 1940 it noted that W. Bailey of Tibberton had left his work as a tractor driver and taken up taxi-driving along with part-time rabbit-catching. The Ministry of Labour was informed accordingly. Letters acted upon early in 1942 (including some anonymous ones) included a missive from A. A. Trow 'stating that as his son is of little use in agriculture he should be sent to do war work or placed in the army'. They obligingly reclassified the lad as a general labourer in order to facilitate his call-up, and took the same step with J. Childs who complained that he could not attempt to keep four children and a crippled father on agricultural rates of pay, the Shifnal district officer having ascertained that Childs had no interest in farm work and was a very unsatisfactory employee. By contrast, two or three letters were received from men asking for reclassification in order to facilitate their call-up.[16]

Auxiliary supplies of labour in wartime agriculture were varied, and included the Women's Land Army, rushed into existence three months before the outbreak of hostilities. This had little to do with mobilizing country girls and women, for the essential objective was to attract on to the land girls from factories, offices and shops. The honorary director of the Land Army, Lady Denman, lent her home, Balcombe Place in Sussex, as a headquarters. Against a background of red velvet curtains and oak panelling, office desks and trestle tables piled with indexes, stationery, typewriters and telephones rapidly accumulated, while outside, livestock grazed on the forlorn tennis courts. From here, the efforts of county representatives, characteristically belonging to 'a different class of birth and upbringing and also ... to a different generation' were coordinated.[17] In the early days, land girls faced a distinct reluctance on the part of farmers to take them. Finding accomodation for single girls could pose a problem; farmers' wives were apt to harbour the same suspicions that a later generation would attach to *au pair* girls, and to many potential employers their services seemed expensive. Thus, in 1940 the minimum wage stood at 28s a week for those aged 18 and over, and although employers were able to deduct up to 14s a week for board and lodgings, in the eyes of many farmers adolescent youths were both cheaper and preferable. By the end of 1939 no more than 2,800 girls had been placed, but during that hard winter, it was said, while breaking through the ice that sealed watering ponds and drinking troughs the girls also 'broke down the ice-crust of prejudice that was proving to be a real obstacle to the initial placing of women on farms'.[18] As the war continued, their numbers increased rapidly. During 1941 over a thousand girls a month were being recruited, and by August the strength of the Land Army stood at 19,000. A year later it had reached 52,000, the rate of recruitment having been speeded up by the government's decision to direct women into essential industries or the women's services which seemed to some to offer a less attractive prospect than farm work. By August 1943 the Land Army had reached a strength of 87,000 before recruitment had to be suspended temporarily owing to the needs of the aircraft construction industry; though in late 1944 it was again allowed to rise slightly, with the permission of the Ministerial Committee on Manpower.[19]

On joining the Land Army, the girls were equipped with a purposeful outfit, consisting chiefly of two green jerseys, two pairs of breeches, two overall coats, two pairs of dungarees, an overcoat, oilskin, one pair of ankle boots and gumboots, a green armlet and a metal badge. Unfamiliar accents were heard in the lanes, fields and hedgerows; 'it was like having three Gracie Fields in the back of the car', recalls a WLA officer charged with driving a group of northern girls, who had come to help with the Kentish harvest, through the lanes from the station to their billets. Naturally, there were some misfits. Victoria Sackville-West instanced the case of one girl saying she would rather go through another London blitz than occupy a milking stool again.[20] Living, as well as working, conditions could breed disenchantment with rural life. About one-third of all WLA personnel lived in billets of the most spartan description and others found that their farm accommodation left much to be desired. Possibly the most unsettling conditions were to be found in rural Wales; although the girls were warned that 'the Welsh farmer is usually more thrifty than the English and ... his standard of living is consequently less high', they were likely to meet conditions which, in their urban eyes, were particularly bleak. One 23-year-old

"Now, Miss Fforbes-Wattson, have you had any experience of agricultural work?"

(*Punch*, 18 June 1941)

wrote a letter to WLA headquarters from Tregaron stating that the only water available was from a spring, while the family had been without news for a week since the wireless battery had expired; the only entertainment was a weekly sermon at the local chapel, given by a hell-fire preacher who arrived on a pony to denounce, in Welsh, the evils of theatre-going and whist drives. It has been pointed out that in many respects, land girls were worse off than their counterparts in the services, with less leave, fewer free travel warrants and relatively slender chances of promotion, while they were also relegated to the end of the queue for supplies: 'We patched our boots with cycle puncture outfits but they always leaked'.[21] Although no adequate figures are available, the rate of turnover in the Land Army is known to have been high.

Despite such problems, there is no doubt that many farmers came to find the contribution of the land girls increasingly valuable, and in time, economical. Even in 1944 their basic wage was only 48s (the same as for female workers in agriculture in general), from which up to 25s 6d was now deductible for board and lodging. Many employers evinced surprise at the vigour which the girls brought to bear and the rate at which they absorbed new skills in turning their hands to a wide variety of farm tasks, not to mention such relatively heavy work as land reclamation at Wragmire Moss in Cumberland, Nazeing Common in Essex and the Frodsham Marshes in Cheshire, and timber-felling. They also displayed an unexpected ability to manage machinery. For example, in Kent where a number of archaic steam ploughing sets unused since the First World War were brought back into service, at least one was entirely operated by land girls:

> 'Led by twenty-six years old Mrs. Olive Bass, who was a dressmaker before the war, the team has operated the set on every farm in the area.... The work has necessitated forty-eight journeys to farms and the sight of Mrs. Bass skilfully steering the high-powered tractor, with its threshing machine, caravan, elevator and trusser, along the country lanes and high roads – up and down hills – and to see her manoevre the outfit into the most difficult stack yards, setting it up to the stacks and adjusting it to a dead horizontal position – excites the admiration of both farmer and the general public'.[22]

Another source of year-round labour which inevitably grew in significance as time passed was prisoners of war. By July 1941 the first had arrived in this country and, with the agreement of the War Cabinet, 2,400 were set to work in agricultural gangs by the following month. The successful campaign conducted by General Wavell in Libya early in 1942 resulted in the capture of Italians in droves. Some 20,000 of these were allocated to agricultural work in time for the harvest, and were thereafter engaged on drainage and other heavy work. Most were based in camps and hostels, although a few (about 800) were permitted to work on individual farms, living in and employed on general farm work. By July 1943 37,000 prisoners were at work, and in June 1944 over 50,000.[23] It was widely considered that the demeanour of the Italians and Germans conformed to expectations. In general, the Italians were popular, evincing a cheeriness of disposition, a tendency to banter and sing at work, and an affectionate attitude towards children who soon responded to their overtures. The dour and unsmiling Germans, by contrast, never seem to have achieved the same level of popularity although they often gave a good account of themselves at work; a Suffolk farmer's wife recalls them performing so well (in contrast to a detachment from the 8th Army which had worked on the farm) that she gave them extra food at mid-day.[24] It is probably true, as a generalization, that all prisoners were more highly esteemed and regarded by farmers than were 'conchies' (British conscientious objectors), and many gave vent to grumbles about paying these the labourer's full wage.

At harvest time these sources of labour needed to be supplemented by temporary workers. They included adult volunteers drawn from all walks of life who were prepared to spend part of their holidays on farm work. Their contribution was variable in quality, and at times brought in some highly unsuitable people. A Buckinghamshire farmer's wife recalls the arrival and swift departure of a score of 'thin and pale' girls from the lace and cigarette factories of Nottingham, who came to help with the potato picking; on the second morning she found herself with twenty mugs of cocoa to dispose of as the girls had decided that enough was enough. Organized camps for older schoolchildren and university students on vacation appear to have been moderately successful. In 1940, some 249 were established and attended by about 8,000 children and adolescents, and by 1943 there were over a thousand, bringing in 63,000 par-

"Stockman, tractor-driver, hedge-layer—h'm—how's your Italian?"

(*Punch*, 13 September 1944)

ticipants. Local education authorities also sought to arrange school holidays in such a way as to assist the involvement of children. Thus, in Leicestershire from 1942 arrangements to help with the potato harvest were coordinated between the War Agricultural Executive Committee and 'district' headmasters acting for a number of schools. In this instance, the education authority decided to curtail holidays in August, thereby facilitating a three-week closure in October; the Director of Education reported that, although potato-picking was no novelty to rural children, those from the town of Leicester, drawn into farming activity for the first time, had enjoyed the ride, the work, and the sense of participating in work of national importance at a critical time.[25] Not all voluntary offers from the towns, it would seem, were equally acceptable, for when the Shropshire War Agricultural Committee met in August 1942, no action was taken on a letter from the Midland District Committee of the Young Communist League of Great Britain proffering help with the harvest. Doubtless the prospect of 'a very large number of young people' decanted from Birmingham for a single day, Sunday 30 August, threatened to cause more trouble than it was worth.[26] All things considered, it seems probable that children from village schools made the most effective contribution so far as juvenile labour was concerned. Countless numbers helped with all kinds of harvesting, not only of farm crops but also of the products of the wild, which took on a new value in wartime. From the earliest days of the war country children sallied forth in groups under the supervision of their teachers to collect plants of medicinal value, often previously imported, such as coltsfoot leaves, foxglove seeds and leaves, poppy petals, dandelion roots, centaury and yarrow; while particular attention was given to the collection of rose-hips, reckoned twenty times as rich in Vitamin C as oranges.

The effect of the war on the size of the agricultural labour force was to increase it after years of decline. The number of recorded part-time, seasonal and casual employees rose from a low point of 80,000 in 1938 to 153,000 in 1945. That of regular whole-time employees sank to its nadir in 1940 (502,000) under the impact of military recruitment and competing industries, but thereafter rose to reach 613,000 by 1945. A small contribution to this increase came from aged, mentally deficient or infirm employees who might not otherwise have been employed at all and, significantly, the number of permits of exemption in force rose by some 1,300 (16 per cent) in 1942 and 1943. Of far greater importance were the Land Army and prisoners of war who between them constituted nearly one-sixth of the whole-time labour force in 1945. Overall, the number of workers increased by 177,000, or 30 per cent, between 1938 and 1945.[27] However, what economists term the quantum of labour did not rise to anything like the same extent as the numbers employed. One such calculation, performed a few years after the war by H. T. Williams, assigns a series of weights to the efficiency of different classes of labour, and so estimates the index of agricultural employment to have moved to only 109 in 1944–5 (1937–9 = 100).[28] This reflects the dilution of 'quality' implicit in the changing composition of the farm labour force.

Increases in the gross output of the agricultural sector were, it follows, largely due to inputs other than labour. These included the application of fertilizers, the distribution of which was very strictly controlled, on a scale lavish by pre-war standards. Between 1938–9 and 1945–6 the quantities applied on farms in the United Kingdom rose rapidly, in the cases of nitrogen by 175, phosphate 111, lime 54 and potash by 35 per cent.[29] More significant from the standpoint of the social historian, in view of its capacity to change the nature of farm work, was the extension of mechanization. It was estimated that the sustained muscular effort of the average man was of the order of $\frac{1}{8}$ h.p., but could rise as high as 80 h.p. when he was equipped with suitable machinery. Hence, concluded one observer, 'Making the most of labour therefore consists in making the most of available machinery'.[30] During the first fifteen months of the war the Ministry of Agriculture, using its powers under the act of 1939, purchased and distributed through County Committees 3,500 tractors, 14,000 cultivating implements and 3,000 harvesting machines. Private purchases boomed also. On a sample of Yorkshire farms, the proportion with tractors rose from 51 to 69 per cent between 1937 and 1940, while by 1941 the output of Fordson tractors for the home market had reached 2,000 a month and there was a three-month backlog of orders. Imports of agricultural machinery, chiefly from the USA, had tripled by weight, though on account of competing priorities it was anticipated that there would be an increasing reliance on home production, coupled with close controls on allocation. Indeed, from July 1943 all manufacturers of or dealers in farm machinery were obliged to work under licence from the Ministry, which took the power to regulate prices, production and distribution schemes. The County Committees themselves were operating over 10,000 tractors and much other equipment by 1944, and along with the Rural Industries Bureau, organising demonstrations and courses in their use and repair.[31] While no official censuses of farm machinery were undertaken until 1942, successive figures (limited here to categories which appear to be comparable) illustrate a relatively rapid increase in the extent of mechanization on the farms of England and Wales. The spread of the versatile tractor was especially significant, and by 1946 there were approximately 10 to every 16 farms.[32]

Table 9.1: Statistics of farm machinery in England and Wales, 1942–6*

	1942	*1946*	*Increase %*
Tractors	101,500	179,846	77
Corn binders	101,970	119,388	17
Combine harvesters	940	3,253	246
Potato spinners	28,590	46,982	64
Milking machines	23,860	40,359	69

* Drawn from Ministry of Agriculture, Fisheries and Food, *A Century of Agricultural Statistics*, HMSO, 1968, Table 30, p. 71.

Changes in labour productivity during the war years are extremely difficult to assess. On the one hand, by 1943–4 the *calorific* value of the net output of British farms is estimated to have risen by no less than 91 per cent over the pre-war level. When set against the modest increase in the quantum of labour employed, this points to a signal leap in productivity. However, as we have seen, there were considerable changes in the composition of farm products and the achievement was in any case facilitated by considerably increased non-farm inputs. After all these are allowed for, the increase in the net output of agriculture by *value*, using index numbers and constant prices, moved up much more modestly: from 100 (1936–9) to a peak of 115 (1943–4), subsiding to 108 in 1944–5.[33] When these figures are set against the quantum of labour it follows, as a matter of arithmetic, that increases in productivity capable of being ascribed directly to changes in the 'performance' of labour were but slight. One such calculation, performed by Ashby and Smith in 1947, suggested a very modest improvement from 100 (1939) to 105 (1942), a figure sustained until 1944, after which there was a decline to 98 (1946). Another, that of H. T. Williams prepared in 1954, likewise indicated a small increase, to only 106 in 1943–4 (1937–9 = 100), then a fall to 99 in the last year of war, when harvest yields were badly affected by the weather.[34]

That only a small residual element in the increase of agricultural net output can be ascribed to the *additional* efforts of workers is scarcely surprising, for as we have seen, the working regime of farm employees (and in many cases their masters), even in peacetime, was comparatively arduous. As the economists who make such calculations would be the first to admit, machines did not operate themselves and farmworkers were called upon to adapt themselves to a varied range of new techniques and systems. In general they tended to put in marginally longer hours, especially during the summer months, and many continued to work (for the extra wages) through the period of their holiday entitlements, which by 1944 had been settled almost uniformly by the agricultural Wages Committees at ten days per annum, comprising four public holidays and six days with pay.[35] Upon the regular employees fell much of the burden of offering practical advice and instruction to the legions of enthusiastic, though often far from expert, auxiliary workers. As we have seen, regular workers continued to make up by far the greater proportion of the farm labour force and it is generally agreed, with due respect to the Land Army and other auxiliaries, that they shouldered the brunt of the task. We may now turn to the question of their reward, in terms of pay and conditions.

These were determined within a modified political and administrative framework. Discussions between the NFU and workers' representatives during 1939 eventually settled on maintaining the existing wage-regulating process of the District Committees, but empowering the Central Wages Board to fix a national minimum wage. This was acceptable to the farmers only on the assumption that prices for agricultural products would be guaranteed, in which they were assured of the support of workers' representatives. Yet when the Agricultural Wages (Regulation) Amendment Bill was first introduced into Parliament, early the following year, it was found not to contain any such guarantees: only after the Minister of Agriculture and the Prime Minister had given assurances to farmers that wages would in fact be related to the prices of agricultural products did farmers withdraw their opposition to the bill, which received the Royal Assent in April 1940. The first duty of the Agricultural Wages Board, composed of representatives of employers, workers and 'impartial' members appointed by the government, was to fix a national minimum wage, and the first figure agreed on in May 1940 was 42s. As we have seen, before being given effect this was raised to 48s with the acquiescence of the employers' representatives. This development was not so amazing as might at first appear. At this point the Undertakings (Restriction on Engagement) Order came into operation, and some attempt to bring farm wages more closely into line was clearly needful; while at the same time, farmers were fully compensated by an addition of £15m. to authorized prices. Through the rest of the war, changes in the fixed minimum wage were set in such a way as to correspond with farm prices. This was done with great finesse. According to one calculation, the wage established in 1945 represented a 91.78 per cent increase on 1939 average levels, whilst farm product prices had climbed by 91.26 per cent.[36] As a consequence of the operations of the Central Wages Board, the autonomy of the District Committees was much reduced. In November 1942, under a defence regulation, they lost their right to make representations to the Central Board concerning variations in the minimum, to define overtime employment and to make directions as to holidays with pay. In effect this confined their role to a consultative capacity, and to minor matters such as the issue of permits of exemption and defining the local value of perquisites.

Looking at the progress of the minimum wage as a whole, it can be seen to have moved upward somewhat faster than the cost of living, and the war years are notable for the fact that, in contrast to the late nineteenth century and the inter-war years, real wage gains were made at a time of rising prices.

Table 9.2: Indexes of changes in minimum wages and the cost of living, 1937–46*

	Average minimum wage for basic hours		*Cost of living index*
	Per week	*Index* (1937–8 = 100)	(1938 = 100)
1937–8	34s 2d	100	100
1938–9	34s 8d	101	103
1939–40	39s 5½d	115	116
1940–1	48s 5d	142	129
1941–2	57s 10d	169	137
1942–3	60s 0d	176	142
1943–4	63s 1½d	187	145
1944–5	67s 10½d	199	148
1945–6	72s 2d	211	154

* Ministry of Agriculture, Fisheries and Food, *A Century of Agricultural Statistics*, HMSO, 1968, p. 65. Note that up to 1939–40 these wages are averages of county minimum rates and from 1940–1 of national minima.

To men who had already spent half a lifetime or more in the industry the benefits must have been very noticeable, as for instance to Len Swaffield, from Stoke Abbott in Dorset, who had started in 1919 as a boy, when his first wages were 7s a week. His usual wage had risen to 24s. by December 1920, and was thereafter slightly reduced; only after the establishment of the County Wages Committee in 1924 did it rise somewhat, only to settle at just over 30s a week through the remaining years of peace. This apparently very steady worker (who remained with the same employer throughout and whose absences from work through illness were exceedingly rare) first saw his usual wage rise above £2 in 1940, and thereafter it moved in conformity with the minimum wage table, reaching 65s early in 1944.[37] Of course, wages higher than this were paid to special classes of farm employees, many of whom worked lengthy hours and were earning more than the minima given in table 9.2. Thus, a study of 95 workers on 22 southern farms showed that in December 1941 the majority of workers were receiving more than the minimum wage; all four foremen, 54 out of 58 stockmen and 9 among 10 tractor drivers, though only 11 out of 23 'general labourers'.[38] Much the same pattern can be discerned from a study of 96 employees (one-third of them 'daymen') on fifteen East Anglian farms (table 9.3). The total earnings given in table 9.3 are in all cases higher than the minimum wage because they include additions for overtime, bonuses where applicable, and the cash values of perquisites, which more than offset deductions for time lost, of which account was also taken. Small-scale enquiries of this nature confirm that it is necessary to go beyond the minimum wage statistics in any attempt to calculate the true remuneration of farm workers, although no

Table 9.3: Comparison of total earnings of various classes of workers in East Anglia, 1940–5*

	1940	*1941*	*1942*	*1943*	*1944*	*1945*
Minimum wage rates (Cambs.)	39s 3d	48s 0d	58s 9d	60s 0d	64s 0d	67s 4d
Total earnings						
Daymen	42s 7½d	52s 5d	62s 4d	64s 9d	68s 1d	70s 2d
Tractormen	46s 5½d	55s 8d	68s 8d	70s 4d	70s 5d	77s 6d
Cowmen	53s 0½d	66s 1d	80s 11d	80s 7½d	88s 9d	93s 10d
Horsemen	49s 8½d	58s 8½d	71s 11d	74s 6d	79s 4d	84s 2d
Stockmen	49s 2½d	60s 0d	71s 3½d	75s 2d	79s 8½d	87s 8d

* Drawn from J. Wrigley, 'The Rising Costs of Labour on Fifteen Farms in the Eastern Counties, 1940–5', *Farm Economist*, 1946, vol. V, pp. 75–9.

systematic official attempt appears to have been made to do so until 1945, with the inception of the Wages and Employment Enquiry, an annual survey based on a stratified sample of some 4–5,000 holdings. This adopted the concept, already current in the writings of the agricultural economists, of the 'contract wage' intended to encompass, in addition to the minimum wage, any additional sums paid for basic hours and any payments made for contractual overtime. 'Total earnings' covered all this, along with bonuses, non-contractual overtime or piecework payments and income in kind, and may be considered the most inclusive definition of the income of the farmworker. When the exercise was first performed, in 1945–6, the weekly minimum stood at 72s 2d, the contract wage at 82s 9d and total earnings at 88s 9d, though it should be borne in mind that average hours worked to attain this level of remuneration were 53.1 and not the basic minimum of 48.4.[39]

Opportunities to raise total earnings were unequally distributed and not apparent in, say, Wales to anything like the same extent. In January 1940, just prior to the establishment of the national minimum, the county rates established for Merioneth. Montgomery, Denbigh and Flint had been as low as 32s, while even the Glamorgan rate of 36s was surpassed in 28 out of 41 English Wages Committee areas, Welsh overtime rates were correspondingly low. Late in 1940, they stood at 11½d an hour uniformly, when in the Holland Division of Lincolnshire they reached 1s 3½d per hour (week-days) and 1s 6½d (Sundays).[40] Accordingly, Welsh workers stood to gain rather more from the establishment of national minimum wages, the 60s basic rate of 1943 being some 68 per cent above the average Welsh county rate in 1939. On the other hand, as was pointed out by an Aberystwyth economist, Welsh contract wages advanced rather less (by 52 per cent), and in 1942–3 there was only a two shilling difference, on the average, between weekly contract wages and actual earnings. That the relative excess of contract wages and total earnings over the minimum should have declined, if only in relative terms, is an interesting reflection on the nature of employment patterns in Wales both before and during the war. Welsh farms had always relied to an appreciable extent on family labour, and very little casual labour had been necessary to accomplish seasonal tasks. In the face of wartime increases in the tilled acreage they now began to use casual labour more freely, notably that provided by mobile teams organized by the War Agricultural Committees, and through the increased use of tractors and appliances made more efficient use of both regular and casual labour.[41] Thus, there was relatively little need to have recourse to any appreciable amount of overtime employment and the result was reflected in lower total earnings. Making exact comparisons is difficult, but it would seem that in 1943 Welsh farmworkers earned about 68s 11d on the average, whereas a (roughly) corresponding figure for the East Anglian employees given in table 10.3 was 73s 1d.

As in previous wars, any prospects of improvement in rural social amenities affecting the agricultural worker were postponed as a matter of course. Predictably, housing was the most obvious victim, which was all the more regrettable in that, just before the outbreak of war, promising signs of progress had been discernible. In 1937 the Rural Housing Sub-Committee of the Central Housing Advisory Committee had concluded that existing Acts were capable of producing a marked improvement in the availability and standard of accommodation. However, it had remarked on the contrast between the position of those working in towns or factories and that of the agricultural worker (then on a 32s wage), who could not be expected to pay more than about 3s (exclusive of rates) or somewhat under half the economic rent of new houses erected by the Rural District Councils, and had accordingly recommended a higher level of subsidies in agricultural areas.[42] This recommendation was adopted under the Kingsley Wood Act of 1938, and when the Rural Housing Sub-Committee produced its next report (in 1944), it was noted that the Act had been well received by Rural District Councils. Already, in September 1939, proposals for some 3,000 dwellings had received ministry approval and more were in the pipeline, while a 'concerted drive' was in progress to improve existing property. Alas, as a consequence of the war, building was suspended and slum clearance came to a standstill. The disrepair and deterioration of existing property increased, while as a consequence of rent restrictions introduced in 1939, the operation of the Agricultural Wages Acts, and the differences in grading between different local councils, rents in the countryside varied remarkably, without much relation to the quality of accommodation. In general, conditions were seen at their worst in Wales, where there was more leeway to be made up.[43] The only noteworthy diversion of resources towards rural housing occurred in 1943 when the government, impressed by representations from the agricultural departments concerning manpower problems, gave permission for 3,000 houses to be erected by local authorities in selected rural areas; yet this step, though welcome, made but a minor contribution towards meeting the rural housing problem, further action on which was to all intents and purposes deferred for the duration. The 1944 report foresaw that 'the low standard of accommodation represented by the old cottages, even when not in a state of disrepair, will appear more marked to young people who have become accustomed during their service with the Forces or in industry to a more hygienic and convenient way of life.' However, while recognizing that one striking change for the better was the enhanced rent-paying capacity of farmworkers, it noted also that, compared with manufacturing industry, a wage shortfall continued to exist so that after the war subsidies for farmworkers' accommodation would have to continue to be preferential.[44]

Housing was not the only area in which the war put paid to any prospect of improvement. Village schools had long trailed behind, in terms of amenities, staff qualifications and the opportunities offered to their pupils. In 1933–4, over 71 per cent of all uncertificated and 87 per cent of all 'supplementary' teachers in British elementary schools had been employed in rural areas; and in 1936, the proportion of children educated in 'all-age' elementary schools was still 74 per cent, against 35 per cent in towns where the sequence of 'junior' and 'senior' education recommended in the Hadow Report of 1926 had come much closer to realization.[45] During the war many village schools (like their urban counterparts) lost their male teachers, unless aged or unfit, and these were replaced, if at all, by retired teachers or maried women. In numerous cases children aged five to eleven, or even fourteen, were to be found huddled in a single classroom, under the care of an overworked or aging woman grappling with difficulties such as persistent shortages of paper and pencils, and increasingly tattered textbooks. School facilities and the accommodation problems of cottage-dwellers were often exacerbated by the advent of children evacuated from the towns under both private and public arrangements, who experienced – and generated for their hosts – various problems of adjustment.

The shock of the first wave of evacuees in the Autumn of 1939 has often been described, and its effect in convincing many rural foster-parents that life in the back streets of the great towns had scarcely changed since Dickensian times. A woman doctor wrote to *The Lancet* about first reactions in the Northallerton area: the children, chiefly in this case from Gateshead and Leeds, were 'nearly all verminous.... Tooth combs and Derbac soap were sold out in Northallerton by the end of the week; the only subject of conversation on market day was the best methods of de-lousing'. When the painter Sir Alfred Munnings attempted to buy a comb in Colchester to groom his cat, he was informed that toothcombs were 'All sold out for use on evacuated children'.[46] For their part, the evacuees (who included some adults such as pregnant women) found much that struck them as primitive in the country, notably its unnatural quiet, its reliance on oil lamps and well-water, and the earth-closet at the end of the garden; the prospect of visiting the latter at night-time was doubtless a factor in the numerous and much discussed cases of bed-wetting. As early as January 1940 it appeared that a very large proportion of the 1½m. evacuated at the outset of the war had returned home; but evacuations continued throughout the remainder of the war and although these provided fewer revelations and have therefore been less discussed, the later schemes affected more people overall. The problems they posed did not, of course, impinge exclusively on cottage householders. Yet it seems likely that, as the war proceeded, they shouldered an increasing proportion of the burden involved. In the earliest days of the war, evacuees found themselves in exotic surroundings such as the Duke of Connaught's estate at Bagshot Park, Lady Astor's establishment at Cliveden and Lord Beaverbrook's country home where they were photographed being waited upon by the butler and footmen. However, once the first flush of patriotic duty wore off, billeting officers found that volunteers were increasingly scarce, particularly in areas affected by suburbanization; placements were more likely to be found under cottage roofs where the billeting allowances, though modest, were a worthwhile consideration.

Less remarked on by historians has been the way in which the coming of the evacuees broadened the range of experience of the village children with whom they came into contact. In the recollections of a ten-year-old Northamptonshire girl, those who arrived from Clapton 'knew about film stars, shops and clothes.... They taught us rhymes ... and to yodel in a peculiar way that the adults called cat-calling and annoyed them intensely'.[47] The advent of the land girls also 'brightened the lives of the farmers and their workers', in the words of a Hampshire employer, not least when in hot weather they readily discarded items of their cumbersome habit. The infusion of new faces also breathed new life into patterns of village recreation, especially in the vicinity of camps and aerodromes, and the device of 'double summer time' served to extend the scope for leisure, as well as work.[48] A Suffolk girl recalls cycling to dances as often as four times a week around Ipswich: 'All the villages ran at least one a week and frequently more'. On such occasions the girls had eyes chiefly for men in uniform, as young farmers from as far apart as Lincolnshire and Hampshire complained.[49] If that was so, then doubtless the young single farmworker was even less equipped to compete, while his married counterpart probably spent a large proportion of his winter evenings at home, especially if paraffin and a wireless battery were to hand, or at the public house. All the same, no villager could have remained entirely immune from the enlivening of social life, and the war years are by no means remembered as a time of joyless unremitting toil.

Notwithstanding the absolute halt imposed by the war on any advance in rural amenities it is clear that, on balance, there was an improvement in the circumstances of farmworkers and their families. Although farm wages did not approach the average levels earned in industry, they were creeping up upon those earned by unskilled men, for example in building and on the railways.[50] Indicatively, the Beveridge Report of 1942 argued that the reasons for the special arrangements for agricultural unemployment insurance in 1936 (entailing lower contributions and benefits) no longer applied, and it seemed 'right to base social security for the future on the assumption that agriculture will have a status equal to that of other industries in respect of terms and conditions of service'.[51] Moreover, it can be argued that farm men and their dependants were much better circumstanced than the families of army privates and their equivalents in the navy and air force. Initially, the wife of a private with two small children received 32s a week, including 7s deducted from her husband's pay, leaving him with 1s a day for risking life and limb. Only in 1944 did these sums reach 60s and 2s a day respectively. On the other hand, it is just as valid to compare farmworkers' progress with that of their employers, and here we have a very different yard-stick to consider.

Generous praise has been bestowed, no doubt justly, upon the 6,000 or so leading farmers and landowners who served on the county and district War Agricultural Committees, as well as on numerous parish representatives who gave freely of their time without remuneration and brought to bear a crusading zeal and progressive influences that had lain dormant in the inter-war years. An official history finds it impossible adequately to describe their devotion, on top of the labour of running their own businesses, and concludes that 'The reward to these men, who persisted in their work over so many years, was often only the sense of having fulfilled their duty'.[52] Yet, as the historian who wrote these words well appreciated, they and the general body of farmers were rewarded for their exertions in a much more tangible way. While between 1937–9 and 1944–5 the outlay of farmers on labour is estimated to have increased from £66m. to £168m. (i.e. 155 per cent), their expenses under other headings rose much more modestly, and rents scarcely at all. Accordingly, farmers' *net* income after deduction of expenses rose by no less than 303 per cent by 1943–4, though it fell back somewhat as a consequence of poor yields in 1944–5 to a figure 229 per cent above the 1937–9 level.[53] There is doubtless much scope for querying the assumptions involved in making such calculations and for tracing variations experienced on different types of farms, and farmers could properly claim that their position before the war had been unduly depressed. Still, the fact remains that their net incomes rose more rapidly and further than wages in general (including agricultural workers' wages), salaries, professional earnings and company profits, and the farmers' share of the national income is computed by Murray as having doubled (from 1.2 to 2.4 per cent), between 1938–9 and 1944–5. As in the Napoleonic Wars and the Great War of 1914–18, this advance in the prosperity of farmers was much remarked upon; a Norfolk woman was later to recall, 'Farmers were as poor as church mice but before the war was half over they had not one but two cars to their garage. It made most of them'.[54] Nor did farmers, as a rule, share fully in the privations of the rest of society. True, they were harassed by a variety of orders and restrictions which, for example, prescribed severe penalties for misuse of petrol allocations or the killing and disposal or consumption of animals without due authorization; but these were not too difficult to evade, and a variety of pleas of mitigation ('the animal was looking dizzy'; 'it had broken its forefoot') were available should a farmer finish up in court. A visitor to an East Riding farm remembers helping to consume, after grace, two large legs of roast mutton from an illicitly killed sheep reported as having been drowned in an irrigation ditch, and a St Leonard's woman who spent her holidays in Devon and Cornwall recollects, 'None of the one slice of bacon a week or two ounces of butter of them'. An unusually candid Welsh farmer recalls never being short of petrol, even after the basic private ration was abolished in 1941. It was available for tractors and lorries, and he kept a permanent piece of work in his car for the blacksmith, whose shop happened to be adjacent to the local public house.[55]

We may be sure that these disparities did not pass unnoticed, either by the generality of workers or indeed within the National Union of Agricultural Workers. Predictably, the union was gathering strength. Although it has been suggested that the NUAW felt poorly treated in respect of its position on the War Agricultural Committees,[56] the part it played in negotiating wages at the national level (where the centralization of wage-fixing was seen to enhance labour's bargaining position), together with the actual wage rises, were highly conducive to increasing the density of union membership. By 1945 the NUAW was just about 100,000 strong, having nearly tripled in size since 1939, and membership was set on a rising trend.[57] Yet even though union leaders can scarcely fail to have noticed the way in which farmers' incomes were galloping ahead, as realists they were well aware that the prospects of improvement for their members (and hence the growth of the union), were contingent upon the prosperity of the industry as a whole. Accordingly, the rapprochement with employers, already in evidence some years before the war, was cautiously pursued. Indicative of the mood were two meetings of the Farmers' Club, at which Edwin Gooch expounded his views to a broadly sympathetic audience of members. That of 8 December 1941 was the first occasion upon which a workers' representative had addressed the Club, and Gooch took the opportunity to survey the past, present and future position of the farm employee. A noteworthy feature of his analysis of the grimmest years (identified – correctly – as the period 1815–40) was his disinclination to blame the farmers, whose attitude to their workers 'did not arise from any special dose of original sin'; rather, the degraded position of the labourer had been due, if not to the callousness and brutality of the ruling classes, then in a large measure to their stupidity. Looking at the present situation and to the future, he noted the increased value which the community was inclined to set upon the farmworker, and acknowledged a change of heart over the smallholdings issue: 'There will necessarily be the development of more large farms in order that machine production can be carried on with the maximum efficiency', whilst a more scientific approch to farming in the future would require an alert, well-educated and fairly-remunerated labour force. Anticipating that public interest in agriculture might wane after hostilities ceased, and that the industry might then have to fight a defensive battle ('politicians have short memories'), he concluded by airing the idea of creating a triple alliance of 'landowners, farmers and workers standing together in defence of their industry and their livelihood'. This suggestion was endorsed by J. F. Wright (leader of the farmers' side on the Norfolk County Wages Committee and a co-member, with Gooch, of the County War Agriculture Committee) to a chorus of 'Hear Hears'; while D. McGuffie of Alcester, having outlined his own improvements in wages and facilities, protested 'we are really fond of our workers – fond of them all'.[58] In March 1944 Gooch returned to the Farmers' Club with a talk on the theme of partnership, mooting the idea of farming as a 'social service, organised to give all those engaged in it a satisfactory return'. Farmworkers – 'the most despised of all our craftsmen' – would, he allowed, be the first to admit that the war period had marked a distinct turn for the better, although equality with other vital employees had not yet been achieved. Apart from equitable remuneration, advances in the quantity and quality of accommodation were required, and Gooch developed a powerful case for improvements in water supplies, sanitation and electrification, rural schooling (without imparting a narrowly vocational bias) and village halls: 'All the reforms to which I have referred . . . could be brought into operation by a government with the will and determination'. There was, remarked J. K. Knowles (President of the NFU), a tremendous amount in Gooch's paper with which everyone there could agree; he thought it most encouraging to learn that the Trades Union Congress had endorsed the idea of an equal standard of living for agricultural and urban workers, although he added, significantly, 'I sincerely hope that they will do a little more than give lip service to that idea. They will have to realise the full implications of support of such a policy'. In case the point had been lost on Gooch, it was driven home by other speakers, for example, by Earl de la Warre, who was glad to learn that he recognized that wages and conditions could not be discussed separately from the prosperity of the industry; and by C. H. Brown from Kent who looked to 'our friends like Mr Gooch and Mr Holmes' to do some 'missionary work' in the TUC, for 'one of the fundamental causes why things have not been better has been this question of cheap food. Those most active in voting for cheap food have been the trade union representatives in the urban districts'. Other speakers expressed politely worded, but nevertheless decided, reservations about Gooch's references to tied cottages ('a tied house is no danger to a good man'; 'as a tenant I am in the same position myself'; 'twenty years ago one of my men went blind and since then he has had the cottage free'; 'the man comes into the tied cottage willingly . . . it is his own fault when he has to leave it') and a sharp difference of interest on this point, which could scarcely be the subject of compromise, stood as clearly revealed as ever. Yet the prevailing spirit of the discussion was one of accord on the broader issues, in a climate of uncertainty about what the future would bring, and there was a genuine sense that some concerted strategy would be necessary. 'There are two wheels to a farm cart' insisted Captain Morris of, Sawbridgeworth (Herts.); 'Mr Gooch represents one of these wheels; we agriculturalists represent the other. Those two wheels have to turn round together if that farm cart is to run sensibly and to be of any use whatever to the community as a whole'.[59] Clearly, sentiments had changed significantly since 1872, or even 1923.

TEN

In pursuit of 'A place in the sun'

For those seeking a clear recognition of labour's role as a partner in the industry, and material advances which would place the farmworker on a par with other wage-earners, the triumph of the Labour Party in the General Election of July 1945 was seen as auspicious. Its plans for agriculture were announced in November and eventually embodied in the Agriculture Act of 1947, which sought to promote and maintain 'a stable and efficient agricultural industry capable of producing such part of the nation's food and other agricultural produce as it is desirable to produce in the United Kingdom, and of producing it at minimum prices consistently with proper remuneration and living conditions for farmers and workers in agriculture and an adequate return on capital invested in the industry'.[1] Eschewing straightforward protection in the form of tariffs, the central feature of the act was a system of guaranteed prices covering the principal agricultural commodities, the levels of which would henceforth be determined annually through a review to be conducted by the Minister of Agriculture. The objectives were to protect agriculture from price instability and thereby encourage farmers to plan ahead on a rational basis; to uphold the incomes of agriculturalists, which had shown an historic tendency to fall under free market conditions; and, not least important in the context of post-war problems arising from adverse terms of trade and a shortage of hard currency with which to pay for imports, to increase the proportion of food consumption supplied from home resources.

From this commitment, farmworkers as well as employers and landowners could take heart, and in the immediate post-war years their prospects seemed bright. Despite the repatriation of prisoners of war at a rapid rate from 1947 and dwindling numbers of Land Army personnel (the movement was disbanded in November 1950), the number of full-time workers reached a peak in 1949 of 748,000, a figure higher than at any date since 1929[2] and wages continued their wartime advance. Successive notices appearing in the rural post offices proclaimed new minima of 80s (July 1946), 90s (August 1947) and 94s (March 1949), when wages were approximately comparable with those of labourers employed on the railways (92s 6d), or by local authorities (98s 6d). Farm wages, thus defined, could be shown to have increased by 170 per cent since 1938 against 81 per cent for the average of all industries, and there were even signs that a few industrial workers were beginning to be recruited to, or regained by agriculture.[3] The farmworker also gained from new welfare measures, including the establishment of family allowances in 1946 and the National Health Service and National Insurance arrangements which took effect in 1948, under which their contributions and benefits were no longer set at specially low levels. Meanwhile, 1947 saw the demise of the invidious restriction which had limited them to one week's holiday and not more than three consecutive days. At work, one might surmise that agriculture had achieved a pleasing balance. In 1949 about a quarter of a million tractors were used, giving ample scope to young men fascinated by machinery; but there were more horses, 335,000 in fact, providing a comfortable continuity of working practices for the older employee.[4] Moreover, the setting in which life was conducted seemed comparatively unchanging; George Orwell was able to dwell on 'railway cuttings smothered in flowers, the deep meadows where the great shining horses browse . . . the slow-moving streams bordered by willows, the green bosoms of the elms, all sleeping the deep, deep sleep of England'.[5]

Standards of consumption were visibly advancing. In the late 1940s, a government inquiry into the household diets of heavy manual workers showed that their energy value and nutrient content were scarcely any different among farmworkers than in comparable occupational groups, although for a mixture of reasons, of habit and more limited access to shops, they continued to take more bread, cheese, milk and flour, and a little less fresh fruit and fish.[6] Further interesting details of rural consumption patterns emerged from a private survey of 1948. Very few rural housewives at any social level now baked their own bread, and only a minority made their own clothes. Greater mobility was reflected in the high proportion of consumer goods such as saucepans and bed linen now brought in the market town or nearest large city, as were electric irons and fires, the likely first purchases of those newly linked to the national grid. Country girls were following their urban cousins in adopting lipstick, nail varnish and permanent waves, any rural-urban differences being due largely to 'the resistance to change of the over-45 age group in rural areas'. Among males, ownership of bicycles, cinema attendances and football pool 'investment' all ran highest in social categories D and E (which included the farmworkers), who, however, were 26 times more likely to read the *News of the World* than the *Daily Telegraph*, and much less likely to spend their holiday entitlement away from home.[7] Family outings were more likely to take the form of the day trip, like that organized by the Wingham (Kent) branch of the NUAW in October 1949 to Southend, where members sampled the delights of the Kursaal, and 'replete with winkles and whelks and whacking great sandwiches' commenced their lengthy journey home at nightfall, 'all tired out and happy and everyone agreeing that this pleasant social venture ought to be repeated next year'.[8]

At this time Mejer concluded that farmworkers were in a fair way towards enjoying that 'place in the sun' for which Gooch had called in *The Land Worker* of January 1944.[9] But such euphoria, as it turned out, was misplaced for a variety of complex and interdependent reasons, and the drift from the land soon resumed. Although this might have been anticipated, given that the skills of the land worker were taking on an ever more readily 'transferable' character, few could have forseen that the labour force would shrink within thirty years to no more than one-third of its 1949 level. Of course, the rate of loss varied from year to year. As Cowling and Metcalf showed in a study of the outflow in 1960–4, even minor variations in regional levels of unemployment significantly affected the ability of the farmworker to choose whether or not to leave agriculture, and subsequently there was a notable diminution in the rate of outflow during the 1970s, when recorded rates of unemployment in both industry and agriculture rose very sharply.[10] Table 10.1 depicts the long-run trend, and although shifts of definition make exact comparisons across the years impossible to achieve, the main characteristics of the decline in the hired labour force stand out reasonably clearly. Most noteworthy was an increase in the tendency to rely on part-time or casual labour and a massive absolute reduction in the number of male workers. Note, though, that the shortcomings of the statistical material upon which the table is based obscure another socially significant change, namely an increase in the proportion of 'family' labour. According to an analysis of the 'regular full-time' labour category attempted in 1965, no fewer than 22 per cent were relatives of their employers. There is reason to think that this proportion may have risen during the ensuing years and that their contribution, along with that of farmers and their wives, accounted for over half the labour input on British farms by the 1970s.[11]

Table 10.1: Hired workers in agriculture, England and Wales, 1949–80*

I	*1949–65*	*No. in 1949* (000)	*No. in 1965* (000)	*% change*
	Regular whole-time males	385.4	201.1	−48
	Youths	68.4	34.0	−50
	Females in regular employment	37.1	13.3	−64
	Part-time and seasonal workers	157.3	137.5	−13
	All hired workers	648.2	385.9	−40
II	*1965–80*	*No. in 1965* (000)	*No. in 1980* (000)	*% change*
	Regular whole-time males	199.0	115.2	−42
	Regular part-time males	27.3	16.4	−40
	Regular whole-time females	16.8	10.9	−35
	Regular part-time females	31.7	22.9	−28
	All seasonal and casual workers	82.8	89.6	+8
	All employees	357.6	255.1	−29

* Ministry of Agriculture, Fisheries and Food, *The Changing Structure of the Agricultural Labour Force in England and Wales*, HMSO, 1967, pp. 5–7 (for 1949–65) and P. J. Lund, T. G. Morris, J. D. Temple and J. M. Watson, *Wages and Employment in Agriculture: England and Wales, 1960–80*, Government Economic Service Working Paper No. 52, Ministry of Agriculture, Fisheries and Food, 1982, p. 41, for 1965–80. They sought to accommodate some important shifts in definition and coverage introduced in 1970, notably the extension of the concept of farm work to include managerial and secretarial tasks, the redefinition of 'regular whole-time workers' as those engaged for 40 hours or more per week, and 'part-timers' as those who worked fewer hours.

Along with an even more dramatic reduction in the number of working farm horses (the few survivors were cast into statistical oblivion after 1958), these are virtually the only indications of decline for the agricultural industry in the post-war era. Since the war, writes one recent author, an area the size of Yorkshire, Lancashire, Durham and Northumberland combined has been brought into arable cultivation, while between 1954 and 1981, the yield of wheat to the acre increased by 98 per cent, barley by 62 per cent, and sugar by 23 per cent. The average dairy cow produced 48 per cent more milk and the hen 52 per cent more eggs.[12] Productivity (net output per agriculturalist) appears to have increased by no less than 5.8 per cent per annum through the later 1950s and early 1960s, a rate comparing very favourably with that of other industries (2.5 per cent per annum), and it continued to rise so that by 1981 each British agriculturalist produced enough food for 42 people.[13] Tractors in use rose to nearly half a million before stabilizing in numbers if not in size about 1965, and combine harvesters multiplied from about 5,000 in 1948 to nearly 60,000 in the mid 1960s as the industry rapidly became more capital intensive.[14] Average farm size rose and the sale value of farm land moved unevenly, but in a decidedly upward direction. By 1965 it had increased about ninefold since the late 1930s, and in 1980 had been known to reach a figure as high as £4,000 an acre on particularly fertile Fenland soils.[15] Not surprisingly, land attracted investors such as insurance companies, pension funds and city institutions looking for a hedge against inflation, especially from the 1970s. Meanwhile, the traditional distinction between farmer and landlord became blurred on account of the advance of owner-occupation, while in many cases estates were reduced in size and increasingly farmed in hand.[16] Both were rewarded for their ever more business-like approach by incomes which, though variable from year to year and subject to a very wide dispersion around the mean, tended on the whole to be buoyant.[17] Behind agrarian prosperity, of course, lay the state, which was the midwife to what amounted to a second agricultural revolution that in every respect dwarfed the first. From the Agriculture Act of 1947, through to 1964, price guarantees were usually set a little below farmers' cost increases, with a view to encouraging efficiency; but to the same end, direct grants and subsidies on new buildings, machinery and fertilizer inputs tended to increase as a proportion of total agricultural support. From then on there was a noticeable shift of approach, with increasing reliance on import controls of various kinds, which had the effect of transferring the burden of support to some extent from the taxpayer to the consumer.[18] Under the Common Agricultural Policy of the European Economic Community, which Britain joined in 1973, target and support prices came to be set annually by the agricultural ministers in Brussels, and where the market price fell below the support level, the Community would intervene to purchase the relevant commodity and take it off the market. Since the whole system was protected by a high tariff wall, European prices were maintained at a level sufficient to encourage overproduction. Under these cosy arrangements, asserts one recent writer, the average British farmer of 1980 could expect to be supported to the tune of £13,000, if account is taken of direct Exchequer asssitance, 'price support' arising from EEC operations, and sundry tax privileges, notably the offsetting of the cost of buying machinery against tax, and rate relief on farm buildings.[19]

Although in the 1950s and early 1960s the true extent of state support for agriculture was largely unappreciated by the general public, criticisms have been

"We've gone back to the Three-Field System—one belongs to an Arab, one to a Dutchman and one to a pension fund."

(*Punch*, 18 March 1981)

voiced more frequently in recent years. It is argued that, despite the much-vaunted increases in output per man, much of the gain represented merely a catching-up.[20] In any case, the achievements of the industry are far less impressive when considered in relation to inputs of capital, chemicals and energy. Indeed one critic suggests that modern British farming, far from being a net producer of energy by converting the sun's energy into the calorific value of food, is actually a net consumer because of its heavy dependence on fossil fuels and agro-chemicals derived chiefly from oil.[21] This is a contentious matter and much depends on the accounting assumptions used in such calculations, as Holderness has pointed out in a more balanced discussion of the issue.[22] What cannot be gainsaid is that the use of persistent petrochemical insecticides wrought havoc with the wildlife of the countryside, particularly in the 1950s and 1960s, while the excessive use of nitrates was linked with the entrophication of water-courses. Meanwhile, the requirements of modern machinery (with help from subsidies) led to a removal of one-quarter of all English hedgerows between 1946 and 1974, while over the same period one-third of ancient woodland was destroyed, giving rise in many eastern districts to a featureless prairie landscape. Almost two-thirds of scheduled field monuments in Wiltshire were damaged or destroyed by ploughing in the 1950s and 60s, and everywhere downland, moorland and wetlands were subject to attrition.[23] All this, critics suggest, is the more regrettable because it is not needful. The environmentalist, the consumer, the taxpayer, and the poor populations of third world countries who are effectively excluded from competing in our markets, would all benefit from a cessation of what has been called the 'wearying dash for growth in agricultural production'.[24] It need scarcely be said that these developments have virtually ended any prospect of upward mobility into the ranks of farmers for agricultural workers and their sons. By the early 1970s, Newby could conclude that farmworkers in the south and east had about as much chance of farming on their own account as winning the football pools, and even in upland north Staffordshire, where farms were comparatively small and the land far cheaper, only four farmers out of a total of 172 discussed by Nalson in the late 1960s were sons of farmworkers.[25] Consequently, we need concern ourselves only with their welfare as wage-earners.

Certainly, the nature of farm work underwent rapid change as a consequence of mechanization. Most dramatic, perhaps, was the compression of harvesting, which in most fields with the aid of the combine became unlikely to take more than a day, the grain being emptied direct into lorries and carried away in bulk, and the straw and stubble baled and removed promptly, or even burned. Tasks such as hedging and ditching were rendered less necessary or were let to contractors, spraying cut down on singling and weeding, and on the dairy farm cows could be milked mechanically using assembly-line methods which, in the case of the most advanced 'parlours', might allow one man to manage as many as 120 beasts.[26] One of the costs of all this has been the withering of the 'oral tradition'. The works of George Ewart Evans trace with imagination and sensitivity the way in which, in East Anglia, ancient superstitions, old words and sayings, in particular the specialized vocabulary associated with horses, became by the 1960s increasingly incomprehensible to the younger generation growing up with a new range of techniques.[27] But he recognizes that machinery has also taken much of the back-breaking and debasing toil out of farming, and many workers take a pride in their machinery, seeing it as a badge of their modernity.[28] Further, although it is frequently argued that mechanization and the reduction of farm staffs have obliterated the 'social' nature of many farm tasks, rendering much of the work 'lonely', or 'isolated',[29] a great deal is left to the initiative and skill of the individual operator in guiding and controlling farm machinery, in contrast to the situation in assembly-line factories. Moreover, the decline of specialization, or the increasingly blurred division of labour, has its positive side in that it affords a good deal of variety. Even so, great as modifications to the pace and nature of work on the land have been, of necessity the various farming tasks are sequential, and the seaonal rhythms of the agricultural year remain meaningful. These two aspects of the farmworker's experience, namely, variety and the satisfaction derived from seeing crops and animals grow, loomed large in explaining Newby's findings, among a group of Suffolk workers in 1972, that 93 per cent found their jobs to be either interesting all the time, or mostly interesting.[30] And yet, as we have seen, they left in droves.

In accounting for this, we may begin with wages. Under the terms of the Agricultural Wages (Regulations) Act of 1947 and a measure of consolidation and clarification passed the following year, the Central Wages Board retained its war-time power to determine minimum wages, leaving minor matters, such as the authorization of individual exemptions, to County Committees. Of course, the very existence of such a board symbolized the weak market situation of the farmworker, but that is not to deny its value, of which NUAW leaders whose memories extended back into the 1920s were very conscious, in setting a floor to agricultural wages. It should be emphasized, however, that comparatively few workers earned only the specified minimum, which tended to fall over the years as a proportion of total earnings from 81.3 per cent (1945–6) to 74.5 per cent (1964–5), while the difference rose absolutely from 5s 9d to 22s 1d over the same period.[31] This 'earnings gap' was determined informally by the premiums and overtime offered by employers and, while it reflected the value set on individual workers, took little or no account of formal qualifications which were rare among farmworkers and increased only imperceptibly during the post-war period. Thus, an apprenticeship scheme started in 1953 and revised ten years later made a poor start, the average number enrolled in England and Wales being 200 a year. In the County Farm Institutes fewer than 4 per cent of the 2,359 students registered for one-year courses in the mid-1950s were from farmworkers' families, while the proportion of under-18 year olds released to take part-time courses was as low as 11 per cent in 1962, compared to 84 per cent in the gas, electricity, and water industries. One reason why young farmworkers failed to avail themselves of such opportunities was that they were aware of the low value set on paper qualifications by employers. While it was frequently proclaimed from agricultural platforms that brains rather than brawn were requisite in the new agriculture, the behaviour of farmers as individuals belied this. Significantly, a study of advertisements appearing in the *Farmers' Weekly* in 1952 and 1962 showed only a tiny increase in those requiring qualifications, except for managers.[32] This is not altogether surprising: with the exception of some large-scale agricultural entrepreneurs and trained managers, farmers as a body were not conspicuously well-educated, the majority leaving school at fifteen, succeeding to their roles by accident of birth, and having no formal training themselves.[33] Among 55 Yorkshire farmers surveyed about 1966, Black found a widespread suspicion that trained men would challenge or argue. Not one was willing to pay more for formal qualifications, and all emphasized that what differentiated one worker from another was character.[34]

These beliefs also worked against the adoption of a progressive wages structure, which would give a recognized and dependable reward for increases in skill, experience or proficiency. As early as 1945, the appointed members of the Agricultural Wages Board had suggested some such arrangement, but in the event, changes in this direction took many years to accomplish, for several reasons. First, it was thought that any scheme involving a promotion ladder would be difficult to implement on many farms, where only one or two workers were employed.[35] Secondly, for reasons which will be touched on below, the NUAW did not agree to endorse the principle until 1958, and by this time opinion in the National Farmers' Union had tended to harden against the idea, fearing that it would result in a general upward push to wages. Through the 1960s discussions proceeded in a somewhat desultory fashion, the NUAW arguing that the job and not the man should be graded and the NFU taking the opposite view, but eventually agreement was reached in 1971. The scheme then adopted featured four adult gradings – I, II (these were supervisory categories), craftsman and ordinary worker – the first three carrying, respectively, 30, 20 and 10 per cent premiums prescribed by the Agricultural Wages

Board.[36] Existing staff were to be graded according to their employer's declaration of competence (which was capable of being challenged by taking an independent proficiency test), and to this extent it was clear that the man rather than the job was being graded. On the other hand, some of the discretion which farmers had been used to exercising was lost back to the Wages Board, whose discussions were henceforth more vigorous and acrimonious. It is difficult to say how far the introduction of a wages structure has benefited farmworkers, on balance. Certainly, farmers were put under considerable pressure to assimilate their men to the craftsman grade when the scheme was introduced in spring, 1972, and there is evidence that the proportion of all workers in the higher grades was increasing between 1974 and 1980, although at that date 59 per cent (against 64 per cent in 1974) still fell into the 'ordinary' category.[37]

Leaving aside any further discussion of the technicalities of wage determination, we may ask how the average farmworker's remuneration has moved in the long term. In 1948–9 he could expect to receive in total earnings £5 9s, and thirty years later, in 1979, £72.04 with a quarter earning less than £58.34 and a quarter over £82.53.[38] Such figures mean little unless they are recast in real terms. As it happened, the early 1950s saw a cumulative worsening of the farmworker's position, since for four or five years in succession, increases in minimum wages and even estimated total average earnings failed to keep abreast of changes in the retail cost of living index. This reflected a decline in the world price of primary products which improved Britain's terms of trade, but also, for a time, limited the growth of income in agriculture. Nevertheless, taking a longer view, between 1948–9 and 1960–1 minimum wages for the standard working week rose by 80 per cent and average total earnings by 97 per cent, against an increase in the cost of living of roughly 50–60 per cent.[39] As is shown in table 10.2 overleaf, advances in real earnings continued through the 1960s and 1970s, which showed gains of the order of 25 and 26 per cent respectively. As might be inferred from these figures, standards of consumption rose from the mid-1950s, in such a manner as to make a profound impression on older workers with long memories. Sometimes increased disposable incomes found an echo in more elaborate and expensive fraternal excursions than the Wingham trip of 1949. By 1960 the Wetherby (Yorks.) branch of the NUAW was offering its members an inclusive weekend trip to North Wales, spending one night in the coach and the next at Llandudno, and for £2 12s 6d participants had the opportunity to visit, as well, Chester, Llangollen, Bettws-y-Coed and Puffin Island.[40] On the whole though, rising private consumption was more significant. Among 131 estate workers at Lockinge (Berks.) 80 per cent had acquired television sets by 1961, and their near ubiquity had already been seen by the Kent Area Organizer of NUAW as a cause of members neglecting to attend important branch discussions, preferring to watch the 'high-kicking activities of Flossie and her Frightful Floosies'.[41] Thirty-seven per cent of the Lockinge workers also had cars, which had been exceptional only ten years before, though many of them, like farmworkers' conveyances observed in Wiltshire, were no doubt elderly.[42] It was a sign of the times when, in 1966, the Wetherby branch drew attention to the ample parking facilities available at the venue for its Annual Dinner and Dance; while in 1972 Kent members were offered stickers

Table 10.2: Changes in the money and real value of farm workers' earnings, 1960–80*

	(A) *Earnings index* (1960 = 100)	(B) *Cost of living index* (1960 = 100)	(C) *Real earnings* (A/B) (1960 = 100)
1961	106	103	103
2	111	107	104
3	119	109	109
4	123	113	109
5	133	118	113
6	142	122	116
7	148	126	118
8	157	132	119
9	171	139	123
1970	184	147	125
1	208	161	129
2	234	173	135
3	273	189	144
4	340	219	155
5	424	272	156
6	490	317	155
7	571	367	156
8	601	397	151
9	700	450	156
1980	841	532	158

* Based on P. J. Lund, T. G. Morris, J. D. Temple and J. M. Watson, *Wages and Employment in Agriculture: England and Wales, 1960–80*, Government Economic Service Working Paper No. 52, MAFF, 1982, p. 48. The earnings series includes adjustments for payments in kind at 'market' values, the most noteworthy being houses occupied as payment in kind which have been revalued at the average council house rent applicable in rural areas.

for their cars which were to pass in cavalcade through Maidstone, Canterbury and Ashford in support of a current wage-claim.[43]

However, such advances were not achieved without strain. A report of the Low Pay Unit in 1975 pointed out that motor cars had become a practical necessity, and that farmworkers, though using them sparingly, often found difficulty in meeting the running costs involved.[44] A quarter of families with dependent children drew Family Income Supplements, while fewer than half had enjoyed a holiday away from home during the previous year and many relied on second-hand sources of supply, such as jumble sales, for clothing. In part, the difficulties experienced by farmworkers and their families were due to high rural retail prices for basic essentials such as foodstuffs, and to the fact that, owing to lack of opportunities or poor public transport, less than a quarter of wives in the Low Pay Unit's survey were able to work to supplement the family income.[45] But at the heart of the farmworker's relatively disadvantageous situation lay the problem of comparatively low pay. Farmworkers were obliged to put in unusually long hours, compared to workers in other industries. True, the hours of the standardized working week in relation to which the minimum wage was set were reduced over the years, from 48 (1946) to 45 in 1963 and, eventually, 40 in 1974; but between 1945–6 and 1964–5 actual hours, inclusive of seasonal or contracted overtime, fell only to 50, and at the latter date dairy and stockmen still worked 53 hours a week in the majority of cases. Among Newby's sample of Suffolk farmworkers in 1972, only 12.9 per cent earned the minimum rate for their age, but the average working week was 51.6 hours and some claimed to work as many as 60 hours a week.[46] Even so, the aggregate level of farmworkers' earnings soon showed a renewed tendency to fall behind. According to one study, between 1947–8 and 1955–6 workers in 'all industries' saw a gain in the real value of their earnings which was twice as great as that of farmworkers, i.e. 18 per cent against 9.5; while a longer-run calculation suggested that through the period 1949–72, average weekly earnings increased by 291 per cent in agriculture and 376 per cent in other industries: this contrast is exacerbated of course, if account is taken of hours, so that, relative to industrial wages, the hourly earnings ratio slipped back from 69 per cent in 1949 to 60 in 1964, where it still hovered in 1972.[47] Subsequently, perhaps partly in consequence of the implementation of the new gradings, the relative earnings of farmworkers were jacked up slightly but not spectacularly. The ratio of gross weekly earnings in agriculture relative to all industries and services rose from 75 (average, 1970–3) to 82 (average of 1974–80).[48]

Low pay has loomed large in discussions of the causes of the renewed drift from the land through much of the post-war period, and emerged strongly as a source of dissatisfaction in an elaborate enquiry conducted by Cowie and Giles covering over 500 Gloucestershire workers in the mid-1950s. Among men who had left agriculture, pay levels were the most important single reason advanced in all age groups up to 56; and among 170 current workers who had seriously considered leaving, 116 gave low wages as the reason, or one of the reasons. Likewise, 'money' and 'advancement' were prominent among the explanations given by workers leaving some 300 survey farms in the districts of Haverhill, Stevenage and Cambridge in the early 1970s.[49] However, it would be a mistake to conclude that the causes of the drift from the land were reducible to this single factor. Cowie and Giles noticed that the frequency with which reasons other than pay were mentioned varied according to the age of their respondents. Thus, although pay and long hours were overwhelmingly important to young men aged 16–25, those aged 25–45 also attached importance to issues such as the uncertainty of hours (as distinct from their length), accommodation, and promotion propects, perhaps because of their family responsibilities. For those older again, anxiety over accommodation remained common, and ill-health or redundancy were increasingly likely to be given by ex-farmworkers as the causes of their withdrawal from the industry.[50] It seems justified, and it is certainly convenient, to pursue these issues by following a path through the experiences and attitudes of successive age-groups.

The number of youths (i.e. males aged 15–19) engaged on farms in England and Wales peaked in 1950 but within fifteen years had shrunk to 45,000, while the proportion of all school-leavers entering agriculture approximately halved, to 4.6 per cent, over the twenty years 1950–70.[51] Nevertheless, in many districts few alternatives existed for boys whose school achievements were undistinguished and who were too young to drive or own a vehicle, or to join the armed forces. Thus, in a 1967 study of village boys leaving secondary modern schools in rural Norfolk, more than half those who found local jobs worked on farms, and Newby's study shows that although three-quarters of the agricultural workers surveyed did not encourage their sons to follow them on to the land, some 38 per cent did so, showing that 'ascription' was by no means a thing of the past.[52] It should be borne in mind that the earnings of youths at this age were reasonably tempting. Just after the war they were actually higher than those of their counterparts in industry (because many of the latter were serving apprenticeships) and, even in 1969, stood at 90 per cent of those available in manufacturing industry.[53] Moreover, the degree of satisfaction with farmwork among youngsters was high. Many told an official enquiry of 1970 that they were 'always interested in farming', and only one per cent actively disliked the work. Nevertheless, among farmworkers aged under 25, 17 per cent expected to leave the industry within five years, the most commonly cited intention being to seek jobs in motor transport. This showed, according to Bessell, that young farmworkers were mindful of their future prospects, for at the time he wrote the average earnings of adult workers were as much as 56 per cent below those in road haulage and 40 per cent less than those of employees in the construction industries.[54] In the 1960s a young Suffolk farmworker, recently engaged to be married, expressed to Ronald Blythe the nature of his dilemma:

> 'I like it well enough but I'm thinking of the future you see. . . . A farm of my own is out. . . . There are so many trying to get the few really good jobs and so many bad jobs. . . . You work for a farmer and one day he will make you his farm foreman, but what is that. . . . I must think about what I shall be doing when I am thirty or even forty. . . . You wouldn't think that working – and *wanting* to work – on a farm would be so worrying, would you?'[55]

The rate of attrition among youths employed on farms was particularly great as they passed into their twenties, but as table 10.3 shows, relative to other industries it tended to decline as farmworkers moved up the age-range. In other words, if a man remained in agriculture to, say, the age of 30, he was increasingly likely to stay. This does not necessarily imply lack of mobility, for surveys conducted at various points of time and in different locations concur in the conclusion that some 40–50 per cent of all farmworkers' shifts of employment were within agriculture.[56] Men in their prime, say 25–44, might change employers in order to better their prospects in terms of overtime wages, promotion possibilities, or a better standard of accommodation. A conjuncture of such favourable factors could well present itself on the larger farms, or on those adjacent to growing towns. Thus, Gasson provides evidence that farmers near to Stevenage (Herts.), Haverhill (Suffolk) and Cambridge were ready to pay a pound or two a week more in premiums than those in more distant parishes. Proximity to towns had other attractions, too. It has been suggested that the development of Scunthorpe, with its associated shopping and extertainment facilities, stabilized the farming element in accessible villages during the immediate post-war period, while recruitment was no problem for farmers on the outskirts of Birmingham in the late 1960s.[57] Moreover, one of the greatest advantages of easy access to a town was the wider opportunities available to members of farmworkers' families. Thus, among those working on farms near Haverhill, only eight among

Table 10.3: Retention of male employees in British agriculture compared to 'all other industries', 1950–5, by 'birth-groups'*

Age in 1950 (May)	Under 20	20–	25–	30–	35–	40–	45–	50–	55–
No. of employees retained in May 1955 compared to May 1950									
(a) 'All other industries'	122	111	101	98	99	98	96	93	87
(b) Agriculture	85	75	73	78	77	79	82	81	82
Employees retained in agriculture as a proportion of 'all other industries' retention, in 1950–5	70	68	72	80	78	81	85	87	94

*J. D. Hughes, 'A Note on the Decline in Numbers of Farmworkers in Great Britain', *Farm Economist*, 1957, vol. VIII, p. 38.

66 sons and daughters living at home in 1970 took up farming, while 32 were employed in factories and another 22 in building, garages, shops and offices.[58] Still, it should not be concluded that, overall, labour turnover within agriculture was especially brisk. In England and Wales in 1972, 62 per cent of employees, undifferentiated by age, had served for five years or more on the same farm, and 30 per cent for 15 years or longer. The average length of service among the Suffolk workers interviewed by Newby in the early 1970s was 16.7 years, which is lengthy by comparison with other industries, such as engineering in Birmingham.[59]

Finally, some mention should be made of the situation of the older worker. While poor health, unemployment and redundancy, and problems arising from the tied cottage system were by no means confined to men in their fifties and sixties, they were increasingly likely to be encountered with the passage of years. On the question of health, it is clear that the agricultural worker has never been subject to any highly predictable health risk, such as the pneumoconiosis notoriously present in coal-mining. On the other hand, as Keatinge and Littlewood pointed out in 1948, conditions on the farm gave rise to a formidable list of hazards, admittedly often shared by employers. These included an above-average propensity to non-respiratory tuberculosis, associated with the ingestion of infected raw milk; sundry diseases communicable from animals to man, such as abortus fever, anthrax, and ringworm; and arthritic changes in the joints of the middle and index fingers, associated with milking. Moreover, toxicological risks were linked to the increasing application of scientific products to farm work. These included mercurial compounds used in treating seeds, arsenical compounds used as sheep-dip, sundry dangerous insecticides and exposure to oils capable of causing dermatitis.[60] Nor should the accident rate be overlooked. Writing about the same time, Mollett estimated, from the incidence of farmers' claims on workmen's compensation policies covering 1,300 men in Buckinghamshire, that in 1947 workers stood a one in 20 chance of sustaining injuries that would keep them away for seven days or more. The most common injuries

A

B

Punch's reaction to the latest official statistics on farm accidents, 10 June 1981.

were sprains and fractures, and the main causes were falling or slipping from unsafe ladders, or on ice-bound roads, with vicious animals playing a subordinate but still noteworthy role.[61] Since the early post-war period it is clear that some risks have been reduced as a consequence of increased hygiene (especially the mechanization of dairies), and a greater degree of safety consciousness is reflected, for instance, in the tractor cab regulations of 1967 and 1974. Between 1967 and 1975, fatal accidents fell from 115 to 82 and the number of non-fatal accidents from 27 to 17 per thousand hired workers: even so, in 1980 there were 4,248 reported accidents to agricultural employees, 24 of them fatal.[62] Moreover, despite restrictions imposed on the use of the most toxic compounds from the late 1960s and the institution of a standing advisory committee to authorize the use of new products, organized labour has remained suspicious of the side-effects of chemification. A campaign against the use of the dioxin-based weedkiller 245-T was mounted in 1979, and in 1981 the NUAW was calling, in a pamphlet entitled *Pray before you Spray*, for a complete overhaul of the system of pesticide control in Britain.[63] These points are not made in order to show that farm work is outstandingly dangerous or deleterious to health, as manual occupations go, for we know that the age-standardized death rates of workers are some 10 per cent lower than those expected from males of similar social class.[64] However, they do show that farm work can be more hazardous than is popularly imagined, and that in individual cases, eventual incapacity arising from working conditions may be the direct cause of premature retirement from the labour force.

Nor is it generally appreciated that adult unemployment has tended to run at consistently above-average rates in agriculture, since it is not a very 'visible' phenomenon, the absolute numbers being comparatively small and less likely to attract the attention given to larger concentrations of urban unemployment.[65] The dreaded word 'redundancy' was rarely heard in the 1950s, and only a small minority of the ex-farm workers investigated by Cowie and Giles were displaced by it. However, it has since played a more significant role. In 1968, having analysed the cases of 92 men who left his Yorkshire farms, Black concluded that redundancy had played a larger part than Cowie and Giles allowed for in their work. In the early 1970s, Gasson found that farmer-initiated quits (including dismissal) ran at 23 per cent in her three districts, and in one study in Norfolk, redundancy was said to have accounted for 42 per cent of all departures. Moreover, a number of farmers freely conceded that, had not some of their men left voluntarily, the number of redundancies would definitely have been greater.[66] Even so, a number of points should be made to qualify the impression that from the 1960s farmers were engaged in 'driving' men off the land at a rate which their forbears had failed to achieve in the days of enclosures, or even during the depression following the Napoleonic Wars. Firstly, all the studies cited suggest that around two-thirds of all moves were *not* initiated by the men's employers. Secondly, redundancy in agriculture did not necessarily signify the end of a man's active working days. While it is certain that the older the individual concerned, the more difficult it would be for him to get another engagement, Gasson discovered that 44 per cent of those leaving her survey farms found other farm employment, and the job histories of Newby's sample of Suffolk workers currently employed on farms, in 1972, showed that no fewer than 32 per cent had left their previous employment due to redundancy or dismissal.[67] Thirdly, it is clear that the greater part of the overall reduction of the agricultural labour force was achieved by natural wastage: that is, farmers who lost workers either because they quit, or simply retired, were frequently disinclined to replace them. This was due chiefly to the effects of continuing mechanization and other labour-saving techniques which steadily reduced the quantum of labour required; but it also reflected rapid increases in the cost of employing a man, of which farmers became increasingly conscious as time passed. The index of UK farm product prices, inclusive of subsidies, increased by 392 per cent between 1960 and 1980, and farm wages by 532 per cent; but the average cost of employing a man rose by 818 per cent when such factors as rapidly rising employers' national insurance and liability insurance contributions, along with the real (rather than the notional Wages Board) valuations of payments in kind – notably housing provided with the job – were allowed for.[68]

Lastly, the issue of accommodation was of no small importance to the security of the family man and especially of the older worker. The problem did not lie primarily with quality, for post-war improvements came at a rate which was brisk by historical standards. Thus, on the Lockinge estate in Berkshire, electricity was by 1961 universally found in cottages occupied by the manual workers, while 56 per cent enjoyed bathrooms and the – formerly ubiquitous – earth closet had been replaced in 92 per cent of the cottages.[69] This trend was very general, gradually bringing the average standard of amenities in tied cottages to a level only a shade below that of local authority housing. Still, there remained wide disparities, and one study of the Tiverton district of Devon has drawn attention to the way in which employers and landlords put more effort into improving conditions for their younger workers, while older men and those living in distant locations remained more likely to have to endure lower standards.[70] However, conditions are not at the heart of the controversy over accommodation. More important in the eyes of its critics, both inside and outside farming, has been the basis on which housing is occupied, often described as 'feudal'. To see this problem in perspective, it should first be emphasized that, on account of his comparatively low earnings, the farmworker has never been in a position to obtain the mortgage which would enable him to join in the rush to owner-occupation that has been such a marked feature since the war. In all but a small minority of exceptional cases, he was and is housed either in private rented accommodation (a shrinking sector as cottages are sold off); by local authorities whose record of council house building in rural areas has been by no means impressive;[71] or, most frequently, in tied accommodation going with the job.

Although the actual number of farmworkers living in tied cottages has declined slowly, it is very striking that the proportion has tended to increase, from about 34 per cent in 1947 to just over 60 per cent in the early 1970s, when fewer than 10 per cent owned their own homes, 11 per cent lived in other rented accommodation, and the rest resided chiefly in council houses.[72] From the employer's angle, the institution of the tied cottage is still frequently seen as essential. To the traditional case that stockmen, especially, need to be close at hand farmers have subjoined the argument that in remote areas alternatives are simply not available, or that workers insist on a house being provided. They prefer to describe tied cottages as 'service' accommodation, because this is the correct legal term and because they see themselves as offering a valuable service to the employee, pointing out that they are foregoing the opportunity to sell or rent their houses on the open market at a massively enhanced rent. Among any cross-section of farmworkers, it seems, opinions are divided. In the late 1950s, among the Gloucestershire workers interviewed by Cowie and Giles, 22 per cent thought that the system had 'no disadvantages', 31 per cent 'no advantages' and 36 per cent, both advantages and disadvantages; while among the 233 Suffolk workers whose opinions were elicited by Newby in 1972, half wanted no change and only 29 per cent favoured a complete abolition of the system. However, their support for it tended to be of a negative kind, stemming from a recognition that there was no viable alternative, to an acknowledgement that it was essential to farmers, or that it offered the advantage of being 'rent-free'.[73] To some extent this acquiescence reflects a reduction in the power and perhaps the inclination of farmers to use tied cottages as an instrument of labour discipline. By the 1950s, the threat of eviction as a means of preventing workers from joining a union was no longer a serious one, and in 1964 the farmer's ability to order immediate eviction was sharply curtailed under the Protection from Eviction Act. This meant that he had to obtain an order from the Court which could be suspended at its discretion for up to twelve months, and in 1970 the security of the employee was strengthened a little further.[74] Accordingly, while in the mid-1970s resort to legal proceedings was most common in the south and east, and near towns, over the country as a whole only 1,268 possession orders were granted to farmers and the harrowing scenes of actual evictions occurred in only about 20 cases a year.[75] Despite these improvements, the NUAW remained implacably opposed to the system in principle, as it had been ever since 1909, and there is much evidence to show that it has been a strongly felt source of dissatisfaction and worry among at least a substantial minority of the labour force. In his Devonshire study Fletcher discovered that although only one in ten of workers wishing to leave the industry gave the tied cottage as their reason, nine-tenths said they had been prevented from going because of a lack of alternative accommodation, thus giving support to the contention that agriculture enjoyed a captive labour force.[76] Moreover, older men facing gradually increasing chances of ill-health or redundancy, and eventually the certainty of retirement, might easily be unsettled by hearing about even the isolated case of hardship, and with good reason envy neighbours or relations who enjoyed the security of owner-occupation, or even a lifelong council tenancy. Newby instances a poignant case where a Suffolk widow was informed on the day following her husband's death that there was 'no hurry' to move out of the house. This was no doubt intended as a kindly gesture, but the widow (and the other workers on the farm) believed the employer was callous to remind her of her insecurity at such a moment. In the last analysis, as Newby points out, the tied cottage problem remains peculiarly intractable because it represents a straightforward conflict of interest in which the arguments of both farmers on the one hand and their opponents on the other are equally impossible to refute, since they start from different premises.[77] From the farmer's viewpoint he does require service accommodation and, while rural housing remains in short supply, no alternative to the tied cottage is available; but from the worker's point of view the system tends to tie him to the land (if not to any particular employer) and in this way undermines his independence, as well as storing up problems for him in later life.

The social situation and the psychology of the farmworker cannot be fully understood by referring exclusively to conditions within the farming industry. Some account must also be taken of the avalanche of changes which has occurred in village life since the war, moving from some obvious and measurable features to their subtle consequences for the farmworker. Ringmer in Sussex offers an excellent example of village transformation and colonization by immigrants. In 1861, its population stood at 1,522 souls, and even a hundred years later reached only 2,208. However, between 1961 and 1971 the population was swollen by no fewer than 1,500 persons. By this date, 53 per cent of the population fell into the Registrar General's social classes I and II, and seven out of ten occupied persons made their living outside the village, chiefly at Lewes and Brighton. Thus, the few surviving farmworkers, who in 1971 accounted for only 32 out of a total of 422 jobs in the village itself, must have felt swamped.[78] Ringmer is perhaps an extreme case of its kind, but elsewhere an outstanding feature was the very high proportion of people coming to villages to retire. Thus, at Cerne Abbas in Dorset, one in seven householders fell into that category and one in six at Tolpuddle, disturbed only by increasing traffic along the A35 and by annual union gatherings celebrating the heroism of the martyrs of long ago.[79] At the other end of the age-range, the cumulative effects of migration and the spread of birth control might be reflected in dwindling school rolls, which offer another interesting insight into changing social composition. For example, at Seaton Ross and Huggate in Yorkshire, new admissions averaged over 20 in the 1880s but only seven by the 1950s, while in Dorset, no fewer than 44 village schools were closed down between 1945 and 1972.[80] The nature and pace of change undoubtedly varied from village to village, and was as uneven as that in agriculture itself: but few if any rural settlements were unaffected in one way or another by the trends of the times. Even where villages developed neither as dormitories nor as havens of retirement, a greater diversification of employment patterns might erode the communality of work experience on which the coherence of the village community ultimately rested. As Cowie and Giles noticed in the late 1950s, 62 per cent of those leaving agriculture for other jobs in Gloucestershire were able to continue to reside in their houses and, while 36 per cent had to move because they occupied tied cottages, a mere 16 per cent were forced to move out of their respective villages and districts.[81] More potent in the longer run were changes in educational provision. With the reduction in the number of 'all-age' schools to a mere 775 by 1962 (from 13,000 in 1938),[82] children from the age of eleven were bussed out of countless villages to secondary schools in the towns. Perhaps they did not, as the poet Betjeman supposed, learn much about 'Civics, eurhythymics, economics';[83] but they were certainly likely to make new friends outside the village and to become used to the routine of commuting from an early age.

It is not necessary to discuss here all aspects of change in the village, but one facet is particularly significant, namely, the suggestion that as the village community became diversified and in some ways weakened, so a sense of occupational community within farming was strengthened. Village newcomers often brought with them a range of views and values likely to irritate farmers, particularly when they attempted to seize the initiative and enliven the villages through the provision of better social amenities. 'People who have just arrived in a village always want to do something in it, or to it' complained a youngish (31) farmer at 'Akenfield', adding that they were 'often just kidding themselves that they are real village people'.[84] In fact, his complaint that 'when their work is done they want to play in the village and when our work is done we want to play outside it' reflected with accuracy the tendency of newcomers to regard the village and its countryside in primarily aesthetic and recreational terms, and to be frequently in the forefront of conservation societies complaining about uprooted hedgerows, blocked paths, stubble-burning and so on. For their part, farmworkers were likely to share these suspicions of newcomers as potential, if often transient, trouble-makers having often in a real sense been disadvantaged by their appearance. It was not that the newcomers posed any threat to farm-workers' jobs, but they could be accused of appropriating rural housing which could otherwise have been let, and then compounding this by opposing, in their role as guardians of the environment, the building of council houses or light industrial enterprises that might offer a wider range of employment prospects.

'Few with any first-hand knowledge of working conditions on farms . . . would suggest that employer-worker relationships are anything but good' claimed Cowie and Giles in 1957[85] and, given the changes in village life since then, it seems that farmers and their employees have drawn more closely together, much in the way that common Welshness is said to be a factor unifying locals against newcomers to the Principality.[86] With the aid of Newby's very illuminating sociological study, it is not difficult to see why this should be so. The status of the individual farmworker had always been based on his skill, appraised within his own occupational community according to criteria which society at large, and townsmen in particular, did not comprehend. Now, within the village itself, his qualities could be gauged only by a minority, which included other farmworkers but also, very significantly, the farmers. Moreover, the closeness of the ties between men and their employers was often cemented by a range of gifts and considerations which might take the form, for example, of presents at Christmas or family birthdays, days out at shows, occasional use of the farm telephone or Land Rover, while even overtime might be regarded as a kind of gift by many workers. Tied cottages, where they were sited on the farm rather than in villages, further encouraged 'farm-centredness' on the part of the worker.[87] In these ways, though with great variations according to the style in which farms were run, employers and workers tended to move closer together without disturbing to any great extent established authority structures, and many villages showed evidence of an agricultural minority tending to retreat in on itself to form an 'encapsulated' community within a community.[88]

From this observation it is but a short step, in sociological analysis, to arguing that farmworkers are understandably confused about where their loyalties ought to lie. In the 1960s, Blythe noticed among Suffolk farmworkers that signs of the farmers' prosperity (deep-freezers, oil-fired central heating, Rovers and Jaguars) seemed more to be wondered at than resented by their workers. The latter, as Newby later pointed out, were for the most part ignorant about the wealth and income of their employers, and unable to make any informed judgement about farming profitability either in general or in any particular case.[89] Thus, only 38 per cent of workers in his sample from rural Suffolk assented to the proposition that farmers were getting 'more than their fair share of farm income' and, although most saw themselves as occupying a lowly position in terms of 'social class', only a minority perceived of relationships with their employers in conflictual terms. On the contrary, 60 per cent agreed that 'most farmers have the welfare of their workers at heart', and in the main their animosities were directed more towards either village newcomers (particularly if they flaunted their 'class' by assuming airs and graces), or, more significantly, against workers in other industries. No fewer than 92 per cent felt they had more in common with farmers, while 86 per cent reckoned that industrial workers were getting more than their fair share of wages, some adding their recollections of ancient slights:

> 'Workers at Garrett's at Leiston used to spit on farmworkers if they saw them in leggings and a smock. It was a real class distinction. They wouldn't sit with us in a pub. They always classed the farmworker as a nobody.'[90]

These sociological findings from East Anglia are surely of great interest to all observers of the modern rural scene, and they certainly assist us to comprehend the post-war history of the NUAW. Even at the peak of its strength in 1948, when membership stood at 137,000 or three times the 1938 level, a majority of farmworkers remained outside the union. In the event, membership soon began to dwindle, perhaps reflecting lack of success on the wages front in the early 1950s. Recruiting drives were frequent, including in 1959 the introduction of area branches into previously unorganized districts, serviced by members supplied with a moped, or motor-assisted bicycle. Moreover, the union could not afford to be exclusive in character. In the early 1960s the proportion of NUAW members in other occupations (notably forestry workers, roadmen, gardeners and drainage workers), was of the order of 30–35 per cent.[91] Particular attention was paid to attracting workers in rural food-processing plants where, in time, some of the union's fiercest local battles would be fought, notably with 'bootiful' Bernard Mathews, the Norfolk turkey baron, in the early 1980s.[92] From 1968 this policy was reflected in the incorporation of the word 'Allied' into the union's title, henceforth abbreviated as NUAAW. Although it proved impossible to reverse the long-term decline in membership, which was inevitable given the contracting size of the farm labour force, it is likely that the density of union membership increased gradually. Thus, in Kent, according to rough figures published by one district organizer, the number of full-time agricultural workers fell from 21,000 in 1955 to 10,000 in 1968 of whom a quarter were 'family' labour. This left 7,500 'organizable' workers in the county of whom 5,000 were in fact members. Likewise, in Staffordshire local officials estimated that by the mid-1970s, 60–65 per cent of farmworkers in the county were members, a figure no doubt higher than at any earlier period. However, these figures may exaggerate the strength of the union. Over the country as a whole Newby estimated, after allowing for those members who were not farmworkers, that about 40 per cent of regular full-time employees were members of the NUAAW, and noted that three counties (Lincolnshire, Norfolk, Yorkshire) accounted between them for about two-fifths of all members.[93]

In any case, increased density of membership was not associated with vitality at the branch level. Thus, at the Tuttington (Norfolk) branch in 1948 the Chairman and Secretary who had held office for 13 and 21 years respectively both expressed a wish to stand down, suggesting that it was 'time that some of the younger men should get into harness', but no nominations could be wrung from the meeting. Over one-third of Berkshire branches in the 1960s never met and attendances were 'notoriously poor', while Newby found that one of the largest branches in Suffolk was run by a retired carpenter and part-time caretaker who was not even a union member: 68 per cent of members had not attended a branch meeting in the year before their interviews, while 24 per cent could not state accurately which branch they belonged to.[94] In Kent a district organizer could express sympathy with one branch secretary, who complained that members had 'found it too easy in latter years and what was needed was for the employers to clamp down on them to bring them to their senses'.[95]

However, 'apathy' among trade union members is far from unknown in other fields, and may be understood in terms of the reasons given by members for joining in the first place. A clear majority in Suffolk had joined mainly to obtain the union's friendly society benefits (accident cover, cheap car insurance, etc.), while 26 per cent had succumbed to 'pressure from workmates' (this was particularly strong on the larger farms), or kin, and 13 per cent from a vague sense of generalized collectivism ('You need someone behind you', etc.). Among his interviewees as a whole, Newby uncovered a considerable ambivalence towards trade unionism. While 71 per cent agreed that farmworkers needed a stronger organization to fight their corner, 84 per cent considered that unions in general had too much power in this country, an apparent contradiction explicable only in terms of the farmworkers' strong sense of dissociation from an urban-industrial world in which most unions played their role in a suspected conspiracy against the interests of farmer and worker alike.[96] Also, the level of militancy was low. A majority of all Newby's respondents (55 per cent) said that they would be unwilling to come out were the union to call a strike (ideological reasons and an unwillingness to see livestock suffer were the predominant reasons advanced), while nearly half of those prepared to strike would do so only because of anticipated pressure from workmates. When, in 1972, the Biennial Conference resolved by a single vote to take direct action if need be in support of the current wage claim, one delegate complained that 'Among all these hollerin' for strike action there were none of them farmworkers.' In the event, the 20 per cent increase achieved that year (at least £5 below the union demand) was frozen under the Conservative government's Counter-Inflation Act but (at least in Suffolk), many farmers who had enjoyed a good year found ways and means of paying it. Soundings taken at this time by a reluctant union executive also revealed little disposition at grass-roots level to support direct action, much to the disgust of left-wing elements in the union.[97]

Many of the day-to-day difficulties of running the NUAW, as well as its internal tensions, are intelligible against this background. Due to the great proliferation of local branches (over 3,000 in the 1950s) the union had always adopted a highly centralized character which, said Self and Storing in 1962, was needed to compensate for its lack of solid foundations.[98] The national leadership, headed by a President and General Secretary with an elected twelve-member executive and a team of officials, represented the moderate wing of the union: often their relationships with district organizers, frequently more militant but allowed little say in the determination of union policy, lacked harmony. While there might be little scope for disagreement about such minor issues as the removal of foreign labour (1948) or, later, over the threat to farmworkers arising from 'moonlighting' by other workers,[99] major issues of strategy undoubtedly became more contentious as time passed. As we have seen, Edwin Gooch as President had long played a dominating role. He was prompt to come to the defence of the farming interest when Stanley Evans, the Parliamentary Secretary to the Ministry of Food, made a speech asserting that farmers were 'featherbedded' in 1951. For him, the issue of land nationalization (rejected at the Biennial Conference of 1950 but adopted in 1954) was academic since, as he said, the measure could not in itself produce one more ounce of food; and he continued, in his speeches and articles, to emphasize the community of interest between farmworkers and their employers and the need for 'the greatest possible degree of unity in agriculture'.[100] Only in one important respect did Gooch and the moderate leadership move very significantly. In view of the frustrations of wage-bargaining in the early 1950s, the executive gradually became convinced of the value of a wages structure and sought the endorsement of the Biennial Conference in 1956. Due to a curious alliance between extreme conservatives and a handful of Marxists, who thought such distinctions would set man against man and weaken class consciousness, the proposal was turned down, and although the executive succeeded in getting the decision reversed two years later, as we have seen many years of protracted negotiations with the NFU ensued before a scheme was finally implemented.[101] To many observers, outside as well as within the union, it seemed that one reason why the NUAW's voice was feeble was that it had never been able to decide firmly whether the true interests of farmworkers lay alongside those of their industrial comrades, or in an intimate relationship with their employers. After the death of Gooch in 1964 there was an unusually rapid turnover in the leading positions of the union, and some embittering of personal relations as long-established moderate policies came into question from more radical elements. This is not to suggest that the fundamental dilemma of where the farmworkers' loyalties should lie was resolved, merely to say that the issues tended to be argued over more heatedly.

Meanwhile, the practical problems of running the union were becoming ever more acute, raising the issue of a possible merger with a stronger partner. The obvious candidate was the Transport and General Workers' Union, which had been in the field since before the First World War and was thought to have about 20,000 farmworker members in 1962.[102] However, relations with the TGWU had been cool over the years, especially at the grass-roots level. This was due chiefly to local rivalries over recruitment. Even after the signing of an agreement to respect each other's membership in 1946, sporadic difficulties continued, seen, for example, in 1948 when the Kent county organizer complained that the TGWU's agricultural officer had devoted the greater part of an address to running him and the NUAW down, even though the activities of the 'silly fellow' were thought in this instance to have boomeranged.[103] Against the legacy of such suspicions, and strong fears on the part of the farmworker of losing his identity in an organization run predominantly by and for urban or industrial workers, an overture from the TGWU for a merger was given short shrift as late as 1971. Nevertheless, the view that such a step was probably inevitable gained ground. At the Biennial Conference of 1980, a resolution to remain independent was carried by only a small majority, and later that year a special conference voted (by 47 against 39) to seek a merger with either the TGWU or one of two other unions, facing reality, as General Secretary Jack Boddy declared, but walking in 'with our heads high'.[104] By June 1981 it became clear that the Executive favoured the TGWU and, as negotiations proceeded, a vigorous debate flourished in the articles and correspondence columns of *The Land Worker*. It was a case of 'merge or submerge' claimed the Totnes branch secretary, though a Staffordshire member argued against selling the union's birthright and others suggested that there were 'too many old men on the Executive Committee', or that too much was spent on 'flashy halls, and the big buildings and paper work'.[105] In November *The Land Worker*, which had very fairly allowed all shades of opinion to be aired, set out details of the financial position of the union, whose deficits (notwithstanding regular increases in subscriptions and the implementation of various economies) had mounted to reach £134,458 in 1980, while the value of its investments had tumbled from £485,000 (1962) to £99,000 in 1980. If the NUAAW were to 'go it alone', it appeared that either large increases in the existing contribution rates of 47p per week or massive cuts in services would be required; and Boddy recommended the terms of the merger with the TGWU, stressing particularly that members need have no fears of being called out on a strike to which they were not a party. Finally, in December, *The Land Worker* came out in unequivocal support of the merger, and a few weeks later members at large expressed their views in a ballot which gave a very decisive result: 29,787 members voted for and 4,709 against. It was noticeable, however, that approximately 50 per cent of members did not vote at all.[106] In May 1982 the merger was finalized, with farmworkers retaining some degree of separate identity, including their own district organizers, central office facilities and newspaper. Whether this step will be successful in advancing the cause of farmworkers only time will tell, but the demise of a separate union is certainly highly symbolic. While the powerful NFU is unlikely to be driven into this position, it can nevertheless be argued that agriculture is itself increasingly being merged into the engineering, chemical and food-processing industries, and that its reliance on state support has increased its vulnerability and removed much of the farmer's practical independence.

ELEVEN

Retrospect

Ever since England and Wales became a predominantly urban society, sentimental and Arcadian images of rural life have flourished. Continuity, order and harmony are seen as characteristics of the countryside, while quintessential English values, if they are to be found anywhere, linger on in farms and in our villages. Academic historians and sociologists may show that village society has never been noteworthy for its stability,[1] and a skilful literary critic such as Raymond Williams can trace back to the Middle Ages the belief that it was *yesterday's* countryside, ever-receding, that embodied rural virtue to the full.[2] It makes no difference, for the tenacity of idealizing myths is remarkable. There is an enormous fund of nostalgia for our rural past, which is currently reflected in brisk sales of periodicals such as *Country Life* and in the phenomenal publishing success of ephemera such as *The Country Diary of an Edwardian Lady*: it is tapped regularly in the advertising of such factory-made products as brown bread, preserves, floral prints, beefburgers and latterly even bathroom fittings, a singularly incongruous example. In this romanticized vision, the farmworker, if he features at all, is likely to be seen as someone like Walter Gabriel in the long-running radio serial *The Archers*, whose cantankerous demeanour is tempered with folk wisdom and common sense: he is a 'character' of the kind enjoyed by townsfolk and those who, especially since the Second World War, have taken up residence in villages. In marked contrast to these conservative images is the radical viewpoint, first propounded by advanced Liberals and developed by socialist writers. Rural England was marked by exploitation in feudal times, while the onward march of rural capitalism, epitomized by enclosures, gave rise to new forms of oppression for an ever increasing army of wage-earners, otherwise known as the dispossessed. In line with this approach, it is suggested that eighteenth-century painters such as Gainsborough and Constable failed to reflect adequately 'The Dark Side of the Landscape',[3] and the more recent history of the farmworker is frequently represented as one of persistent poverty and submission to authority, punctuated by occasional, heroic efforts on the part of ordinary villagers to throw off their shackles. But this opposed interpretation also embodies a good deal of myth and ideology and, although it is impossible to pursue all these complex issues here, some light may be thrown on them by reflecting on two hundred years of the farmworker's experience, focusing on the nature of, in turn, his employment, comparative standard of living, alleged psychological attributes and perception of his place in society.

In a country moving rapidly along the path of industrialization and urbanization, it might be expected that incomprehension of the nature of farm work would increase. 'Well, take the navvy and put him on the farm, and I contend that any man who has ordinary gumption and strength could do the work' declared a Workers' Union leader in a speech to the TUC in 1918; and the jeering remark of one lorry-driver to another who had run his vehicle off the road – 'Why, you ought to be at the plough' – was not untypical of inter-war attitudes.[4] For their part farmers, if not the general public, might be depended upon to recognize special skills and qualities, and up to a point were obliged to reward their 'choice men' accordingly. But even they were to some extent prisoners of a myth of their own creation, namely that the abilities, attitudes and commitment of exemplary men had been typical of the agricultural labour force as a whole, in bygone days. Yet, remarking on the charge that men's 'pride in their work' had been lost during the Great War, Venn observed that 'exactly the same complaints have been made by farmer witnesses before all the commissions that have sat since 1833, and if in every instance they were true, the standard of labour today would be farcically low'.[5]

Of course, many sympathetic observers have presented the skills of farm-workers in a much more favourable light. Writing in 1913, Bennett asserted that the work called for infinitely greater ability and experience than carrying mortar up a ladder or wheeling boxes along a quay, and a few years later Mackenzie summarised the skills involved in various farm operations. For example, a man with two or more horses and a 'somewhat complicated instrument' would, in the course of ploughing a ten acre field, cut '880 strips of soil ... of equal depth and width [in] ... parallel lines [and] ... in such a way that the greatest possible area of surface is exposed'; and the operator of a reaper actuated three levers and watched five distinct pieces of machinery in motion, whilst guiding two or three horses.[6] In the same vein, Bellerby was later to conclude after a systematic enquiry that 'in any comprehensive point-rating of industrial and agricultural occupations ... agriculture is likely to receive points about equal to the average of the rest, any appreciable divergence ... being more probably in an upward than a downward direction.'[7]

By the time he wrote these words (in 1952) farm mechanization had advanced enormously, though with curiously mixed effects. Obviously modern agricultural techniques have to a large extent put an end to team-work, reduced the dominance of the seasons and mitigated the influence of weather conditions. But for all that, the farming calendar retains a perennial character. Likewise, although mechanization has caused various ancient skills to fall into desuetude and calls forth new ones in their stead, the disruptive effects of such changes can easily be exaggerated. This is due partly to the fact that the old and new skills tend to be the perquisites of different generations and partly to the fact that, being moveable, the effect of machinery on the farm does not have the same deadening impact as it often can in a factory context.[8] But farmworkers are certainly conscious of living through changing times, and during the present century have shown an increasing aversion to the expression 'agricultural labourer': the title of this book and the use wherever possible of the alternative, 'farmworker', is an acknowledgement of the justice of their case. The view taken here is that although its nature has changed over time, farm work is and always has been skilled.

The fact that it has often failed to be accepted as such no doubt derives in part from a subconscious association of farm work with small wages. For, despite the adaptability shown by successive generations to the changing demands of the job, the return to labour in agriculture has always been comparatively niggardly, causing some to contend that the farmworker was always the last to benefit from and usually the first to suffer from vicissitudes in the prosperity of farming.[9] Prior to the Great War there were considerable regional variations in real wages and most observers based their impressions on the state of farm workers in the south of England, where, as Robertson Scott once remarked, 'most of the artists and writing people seem to live'.[10] Regularity of employment was always a critical factor, as was recognized by observers ranging from Adam Smith in the 1770s to Lady Howard in the 1930s, and individual family circumstances was another. It would be no exaggeration to state that the condition of a single male farm servant in Cumberland in the 1790s was altogether more comfortable than that of a married worker in Dorset or Devon a century later, or even, one is tempted to suggest, than that of the head of a sizeable family in Norfolk by the 1920s. Nevertheless, a summary judgement needs to be essayed. To recapitulate briefly the contents of successive chapters: there were signs of a definite deterioration in the later eighteenth century, probably arrested during the French wars; in the ensuing period, conditions reached their nadir, but there were indications of improvement in the 1850s and 1860s which became more striking during the era of the Great Depression, but were followed by something of a check in the Edwardian era; subject only to a noticeable deterioration in the early 1920s when public policy, as in other areas, was attempting a reversion to 1914, the twentieth century has undoubtedly seen a considerable advance in farmworkers' material living standards.

Moreover, at least until very recently, the position of the English or Welsh farmworker compared favourably with that of his European counterpart, and even with that of many peasants. The Agricultural Tribunal suggested that, before 1914, the real value of agricultural wages was higher than in any other western European country and concluded that this was still broadly true in 1924.[11] This accords with modern interpretations of the condition of the continental peasantry. Weber has shown that the consumption of meat and white bread rose much more rapidly in French towns than in the countryside and (in contrast to England) that the physical condition of rural recruits was poorer than that of their urban counterparts.[12] In the 1930s, Lady Howard's able and sympathetic international review showed that the remaining deprivations of English and Welsh farmworkers were to be found everywhere overseas. Thus, long hours and periodic bouts of overwork were general, as were housing problems (the tied cottage system was by no means peculiar to England and in Eastern Europe many unmarried servants still slept with animals); rural elementary schooling was universally deficient, and vocatonal training for farmworkers virtually non-existent; while agricultural trade unionism was weak all over the world. Indeed, in some respects the English farmworker emerged from this report as relatively favoured, not only by a comparatively high wage but also by the degree to which he was covered by protective legislation, backed by government inspection (only Poland had anything comparable); and he did not, of course, suffer from restrictions on his mobility of the kind found in Nazi Germany.[13]

Naturally, the agricultural workers of England and Wales were in no position to make either historical or cross-cultural comparisons of this kind, and even if they had been, might well have regarded them as irrelevant. Their eyes were fixed on the earnings and other advantages enjoyed by their urban kinsfolk and, increasingly in the twentieth century as villages became more suburbanized, by neighbours working in other jobs. At no stage, except for a brief interlude in the immediate aftermath of the Second World War, did their earnings approach the average attainable in manual occupations outside agriculture. However, as in the rest of society, modest gains tended to fuel disproportionate increases in expectations and aspirations among farmworkers, a tendency noticed in Scotland as well as England and Wales.[14] It is in these terms that Martin's slightly perplexed comment that 'the gradual rise in the standard of living has made workers somehow more conscious of their comparative poverty' may be interpreted.[15] This is not, of course, a novel suggestion. Ernle, writing in 1912, noted that in relation to the employing classes farm employees had 'stood comparatively still', and that this bred in them a 'sense of social inferiority.'[16]

Did farm work engender a distinctive personality type? There is no shortage of comment to that effect, usually stressing mental torpor, wariness of manner and servility. The more mindless remarks usually emanated from townsmen, convinced of their own superiority. In 1912 Baverstock wrote critically of the race of reporters who might visit 'Slocum-in-the-Marsh', a place amusing only for its very dullness, and leave 'an impression of "Hodge" as a gaping booby with little object for his existence save to be laughed at'.[17] The attitudes of some urban trade unionists and socialist thinkers, perhaps mindful of the comments of Engels on the 'idiocy of rural life', were often condescending to a degree. They were linked to the conviction that due to the selective nature of migration the best had left, and that feeble-mindedness was increasingly a characteristic of those who remained in the villages. To some, such suggestions were given backing by quasi-scientific investigations such as the Wood report of 1929, which suggested that the incidence of mental deficiency was nearly twice as high in the country as in the town; or by the results of educational 'intelligence tests' which, while allowing that a wide range of ability was found in both types of community, suggested that country children usually trailed by about four points, or were 'a year behind' their urban counterparts. These ideas should be treated with considerable scepticism. Charles Booth, D.J. Davies and A.W. Ashby were unconvinced that migration had been sufficiently selective, in a genetic sense, to lower the mental qualities of the rural population compared to that of the past or to the urban population; and the difficulties of concocting 'intelligence' tests which are free from culture bias and the effects of applying differential teaching resources are notorious.[18]

Nevertheless, various authorities, including those whose sympathy for farmworkers cannot be called into question and who had no truck with genetic theories, claimed to discern among them the widespread existence of stolid and submissive personality characteristics. Thus, for Bennett, the southern agriculturalist seemed somehow to lack the independent character of the urban artisan, for 'habits engendered by the feudal system were more deeply ingrained in his mind', while Springall remarked on the 'instinctive fatalism' of working men in Norfolk.[19] More recently, in adopting for his book the title 'The Deferential Worker', the sociologist Howard Newby might appear to be perpetuating the popular image of the farmworker as a complaisant, forelock-tugging figure. But a close reading of the text reveals that he is not seeking to describe the personal demeanour of individual workers, few of whom, probably at any period, displayed such characteristics. Rather, Newby is examining, in a more disembodied way, a pattern of human relationships. The deference of farmworkers arises, he suggests, out of the situation in which they find themselves: they are obliged to accept material and social subordination because, so long as they remain within the industry, there are no realizable alternatives to doing so.[20] In other words, Newby is shifting the terms of the discussion away from unsatisfactory and unverifiable generalizations about the 'character' of farmworkers towards the realities, as he sees it, of their class situation. This leads us to an issue which has been deferred up till now, in order to be able to take advantage of a long-term perspective.

As we have seen, even in the 1770s the proportion of English cultivators who were pure wage-earners was high by continental standards, and by the 1930s over 60 per cent of English and Welsh agriculturalists were employees, a situation matched only in Scotland and the Netherlands.[21] Given the quite limited extent to which there existed a 'farming ladder', the language of class, itself a product of the Industrial Revolution,[22] might appear to be properly applicable to English and Welsh rural society, but it needs to be used with considerable care and discrimination. As an example, we may take the critical period following the cessation of the Napoleonic Wars. Rising rural criminality in the form of poaching, arson, and disturbances culminating in the Swing riots were clearly influenced by severe material privations, which were not merely relative (the usual trigger for outbursts of popular protest in the eighteenth century[23]), but also absolute in view of the quite exceptional incidence of unemployment in the rural south. We may go further than this, and acknowledge that tensions were rooted in what Hobsbawm and Rudé have described as a 'fundamental contradiction' at the heart of English agrarian society: 'Its rulers wanted it to be both capitalist and stable, traditionalist and hierarchical ... they advocated an economy which implied mutually antagonistic classes but did not want it to disrupt a society of ordered ranks.'[24] But, although a number of writers have done so,[25] it seems unhelpful to view the unrest of this period as a manifestation of the class struggle. As Hobsbawm and Rudé show, the demands of the rioters in 1830 were confined to higher wages, better employment and improvements in the system of social security, i.e. the Poor Law. They are surely correct to see in Swing an improvised , spontaneous and decidedly archaic form of resistance, the work of men whose horizons were for the most part still bounded by their individual villages.[26]

More convincing is the argument that class consciousness came late to farmworkers. Obelkevich has suggested that classes were forged not only by men acting on the basis of economic interest, but also as a result of their withdrawal, by stages, from the life of the village community over a very long period. The first class to do so was the gentry who characteristically emparked themselves at some distance from the villages, whose destinies they nevertheless continued to control. Next went the farmers, or at least the 'new-style progressives' in Tennyson's words who from the first half of the nineteenth century tended to retreat into isolated farm houses surrounded by ring fences, expel their servants, and remove their children from village schools. This isolated the labourers, who were objectively a class but subjectively unsure of their position vis-à-vis other classes, whose behaviour frequently disappointed and sometimes infuriated them. By degrees, as they became more literate, disciplined and self-reliant, farmworkers in their turn developed 'something of a class consciousness' and unionization in the 1870s marked their consummation as a class.[27] An advantage of this argument is that, by relating the evolution of class to the long-run emergence of capitalism in agriculture, it avoids complications arising from controversies about the precise effects of the Georgian enclosures; at the same time its comprehensiveness is appealing and it happens to accord rather well with the phased emergence of class recounted by Perkin in a more general study of English society.[28]

It must be accepted that the language of class was used more freely by the late nineteenth century. However, it is not clear what this signified, for everyday English fails to recognize the Weberian distinction between 'class' and 'status', and uses these expressions more or less interchangeably.[29] Moreover, even if it is allowed that class (or labour?) consciousness became a more pervasive feature of rural life, farmworkers evinced a marked reluctance to engage in any clearly recognizable form of class conflict, whether institutionalized or otherwise. The agricultural trade unions were not noted for their militancy and could never achieve more than a minority membership: in the 1930s there were, almost certainly, more farmworkers' wives in the Women's Institutes than husbands in the trade unions.[30] This alone was apt to confirm to urban socialists that the farmworker at best was suffering from false consciousness, and at worst was a helot with no mind of his own. No doubt it is true, as Howkins has suggested, that the extent of trade union membership is but a poor barometer of the extent of class consciousness and militancy, and that centralized bureaucracies can easily lose touch with local sentiment. However, his attempts to find evidence of the existence of endemic structural conflict in the spontaneous summertime disputes in the harvest fields of Norfolk are not entirely convincing. In a county with some 5,000 farm holdings it is not surprising that the local press mentioned 'at least one strike every year from 1870 to 1895', and it is less than obvious what this signified.[31] Moreover, there are few signs of the presence of genuine class hostility in the literary sources. True, Flora Thompson's portrayal of rural society in Oxfordshire during the 1880s and 1890s gives many indications of the importance of distinctions of social status, but concludes that 'every member of the community knew his or her place and few wished to change it . . . the social order was so generally accepted that there was no sense of injustice'.[32] Subsequently, in the Edwardian period, Green could not bring himself to believe that 'those who tie their trousers with string are filled with hatred for the booted and spurred', while another sympathetic and knowledgeable observer, George Sturt, claimed that Surrey labourers showed 'no animosity towards the rich' and evinced little hostility to their employers.[33] It is true that all these observers, and others who could be quoted, might be suspected of wishful thinking or of bias arising from their own class affiliations.[34] But even those actively seeking to translate class awareness into class antipathy encountered an uphill task. At Tysoe, Joseph Ashby, who was a doughty advocate of the farmworkers' cause, found it difficult to maintain a host's courtesy when confronted with the 'politics of class and hate' preached by students (mostly young urban trade unionists), brought home by his son Arthur from Ruskin College.[35] Charles Swingfield, a Workers' Union organizer in Suffolk during the First World War and one-time footman, gardener, London dairyman and possessor of Polytechnic diplomas, was obliged to acknowledge that although the labourers' class-consciousness was there, it was difficult to find and to mobilize; while a Labour party organizer in inter-war Sussex spoke ruefully of the existence of class differentiation but no 'class feeling'.[36] This is virtually the same conclusion as that arrived at by Winstanley, based on oral evidence from Kent. 'Social superiors' might be criticized for their personal flaws but not usually as typical specimens of the employing class and, although 'perpetually conscious of their class', few labourers evinced open hostility. Acceptance by their own kind was of supreme importance for most families, says Winstanley, 'and their quest for it detracted from any serious questioning of the structure of rural society'.[37] The autobiography of Fred Kitchen, based on his experiences in the north of England, gives another good illustration of these ambivalent attitudes: he shows a keen awareness of the nuances of social status (as the son of a cowman he was perpetually aware of the distance between himself and his sweetheart's father, a coachman), but recalls lords and ladies dancing with workpeople at the estate Christmas parties, and 'neither side knew the meaning of class distinction'.[38] Nor, in more recent times, has the farmworker's perception of his class-situation become any clearer. In a BBC broadcast based on interviews with several elderly men, one, after describing the hierarchy of farm servants on the Yorkshire Wolds, remarked 'If you were t'hossman that was your class', to which another added 'Aye, that was your job'.[39] In the late 1960s, when Newby investigated systematically the images of society held among farmworkers in Suffolk, he found that the number of classes distinguished by his informants ranged from nil to five, with 24 distinguishable types of nomenclature, though with some heaping on a 'dichotomous ascriptive model' (59 per cent). Nearly all those interviewed regarded class differences as inevitable, and most reserved their criticism for snobbery, i.e. the flaunting of social distinctions or inconsiderate behaviour, especially if exhibited by the new village middle class.[40]

The failure of working people to formulate a clear view of their class situation and prosecute the class war is, of course, fairly general and a sore point for theoreticians of a Marxist persuasion. Everywhere, workers are confronted by arguments which stress the natural harmony of interest of the parties involved in a particular economic endeavour, and nowhere is this more obvious than in agriculture where the counter-model is particularly strong and of great antiquity.

Eighteenth-century social theorists, while usually employing the language of ranks, orders and degrees to denote differences of social standing, were also wont to use the expression 'the agricultural interest' to cover all those whose incomes, whether in the form of rent, farming profits or wages, were drawn from the soil. In the nineteenth century, it is arguable that the social ties and mutual interdependence implied by this were somewhat shaken, and many bemoaned a 'loss of community' in the villages. This may be particularly true of labour-glutted East Anglia, the focus of disproportionate attention from historians and sociologists. All too often, Slater observed, farmers in these districts would speak to their men 'like an officer ordering a regiment into action it was Brown do this Smith do that ... and if a man ancer back it would be ... say that again and you will go'.[41] The return to such behaviour was, at least from the 1870s, a well-marked tradition of rural radicalism expressing itself in support for unionism, the election of Labour MPs and, of course, the 1923 strike.[42] But East Anglia was not the whole nation, and in the north, according to Wilson Fox writing in the 1890s, 'relations between employers and employees were of a more cordial character': the reasons lay, he believed, in higher wages and the fact of there being, especially in Lancashire and Cumberland, 'but little social distinction in many cases between the classes.'[43] Much the same was true of Wales where, although farmers considered themselves superior, according to Howell the social differences were decidedly those of rank and status rather than class.[44]

In regions such as these, and perhaps elsewhere in English rural society, the concept of an agricultural interest showed strong survival powers. Thus, we find Jefferies in the 1880s using the expression when discussing agricultural shows at which gentry, farmers, clergymen and farmworkers could all be expected to be present,[45] and such events, however ambiguous, were much more common than rural riots. It is true that the revival of agricultural trade unionism after 1906, and the emergence of the National Farmers' Union, appeared for a time to suggest that the interests of employers and employees were set on a collision course. But in the event, as we have seen, especially under Gooch's presidency, the NUAW came to identify its interests very closely with those of employers, in a situation where the returns to agriculture became increasingly a matter of politics. This is considered regrettable by some authorities, notably Howkins who writes that 'There is an uneasy sense about the period of Gooch's power that the policies of Peel triumphed through the back door'.[46] Nevertheless, this closer collaboration came to be matched, as Newby has shown, by a distinct rapprochement in respect of social relations between employers and employees at the level of the individual farm. In many cases, farmworkers regard themselves as having more in common with farmers than with other elements in the village. Any suspicion or resentment they evince is likely to be directed against fellow-proletarians – namely urban workers, who are commonly thought to be overpaid and whose unions are active participants in an 'urban conspiracy' intended as far as possible to limit the return to agriculture and, through this, farmworkers' wages.[47]

As will be obvious by now, this book assumes that broad interpretations of rural social change and the position of the farmworker may be anchored more safely in agrarian conditions, the impact of industrialization, and associated demographic changes. There are obvious dangers in using the concept and vocabulary of 'class' as a substitute for, rather than an aid to, social analysis: it brings to mind Thomas Hardy's warning that the happiness of a class can 'rarely be estimated aright by philosophers who look down ... from the Olympian heights of society.'[48] But, in going on to say that farm workers were 'really dissimilar, men of many moods and individualities', Hardy's words might be taken to imply that the forging of any generalization is an impossibility. Between these extremes, social historians should surely try to steer a middle course. At one level, they have an important role to play simply by seeking to correct the often wildly erroneous beliefs that social scientists with a weak background in history are prone to entertain.[49] But the role of the historian can and should aspire to more than this, as the issue of class reveals particularly clearly. Today, many historians would probably incline to a provisional view of nineteenth-century society which likens it to a piece of shot silk. Perkin, who makes this analogy, points out that it is composed of a warp of one colour (which corresponds to class), with a weft of another (status), while the fabric will appear to change its hue according to the flexing to which it is subjected, and the angle of vision of the observer.[50] In the present state of our knowledge, it is a very apt analogy, but this is not to say that more cannot be done by historians who are prepared to tackle large issues through the examination of more limited groups, in specific contexts. More effort is required to study in detail the situational factors which typically confronted people and inevitably affected the nature of the relationships in which they were engaged. Newby's able work on twentieth-century Suffolk has pointed the way, but its success is limited precisely because research of this kind on the eighteenth and nineteenth centuries is still in its infancy. The analysis of local labour markets, patterns of residential persistence and migration, marriage horizons (in both a geographical and a social sense), family composition and kinship networks should, in time, throw considerable light on social change and enable peoples' perceptions to be read more clearly. Within a couple of generations, the social history of farmworkers may come to be written in quite a different way.

Notes

Chapter 1, pp. 19–43

1. This description is from J. G. Gazley, *The Life of Arthur Young*, Memoirs of the American Philosophical Society, vol. XCVI, Philadelphia, 1973, whose work is relied on for biographical details along with G. E. Mingay, *Arthur Young and his Times*, Macmillan, 1975.
2. A. Young, *A Six Months' Tour through the North of England*, Strahan, 1770, IV, p. 347.
3. If attention is confined to the farms of Yorkshire, Durham, Northumberland, Cumberland, Westmorland, Lancashire and Cheshire, the average acreage rises slightly to 310, and the mean number of employees falls to 4.7 (175 farms).
4. A. Kussmaul, *Servants in Husbandry in Early Modern England*, Cambridge, 1981, pp. 120–1.
5. Essex R.O. T/P 87. Lists of the Labouring Persons in Terling with their Families (5 May 1775 and 7 July 1778).
6. R. S. Schofield, 'Age-Specific Mobility in an Eighteenth Century English Parish', *Annales de Démographie Historique*, 1970, vol. VII, pp. 265, 273. N.B. In this parish there was a marked tendency for the girls to remain at home, owing to the prevalence of lace-making and textile spinning.
7. W. Marshall, *Review and Abstract of the County Reports to the Board of Agriculture*, 1818, reprinted David and Charles, Newton Abbot, 1969, IV (*Midlands*), p. 352; V (*Southern*), pp. 131, 335.
8. W. Marshall, *The Rural Economy of the Southern Counties*, Nicol, 1798, II, p. 233.
9. Kussmaul, op. cit., pp. 51–2, 57.
10. Schofield, op. cit., p. 264; B. A. Holderness, 'Personal Mobility in some Rural Parishes of Yorkshire, 1777–1812', *Yorkshire Archaeological Journal*, 1971, vol. XLII, p. 454.
11. A.Z., 'On the Comparative Advantages of Keeping Married and Unmarried Servants upon Farms', *Farmer's Magazine*, 1802, vol. III, p. 4.
12. F. M. L. Thompson, *English Landed Society in the Nineteenth Century*, Routledge and Kegan Paul, 1963, p. 96.
13. E. Gilboy, 'Labour at Thornborough: an Eighteenth Century Estate', *Economic History Review*, 1st series, 1932, vol. III, pp. 395–8.
14. A. Young, *A Six Weeks' Tour through the Southern Counties of England and Wales*, Strahan, 1768, p. 336; *Annals of Agriculture*, 1796, vol. XXVI, pp. 139, 252.
15. J. Howlett, 'The Different Quantity, and Expense of Labour in Different Years', *Annals of Agriculture*, 1792, vol. XVIII, pp. 568–9.
16. J. Marchand, ed., *A Frenchman in England in 1784: Being the 'Mélanges sur l'Angleterre' of François de la Rochefoucauld*, Cambridge, 1933, pp. 217, 228–9, 233–5.
17. C. R. Dobson, *Masters and Journeymen: a Pre-History of Industrial Relations, 1717–1800*, Croom Helm, 1980, p. 23.
18. Marchand, op. cit., p. 234; Marshall, *Review and Abstract*, II (*Western*), p. 279; M. I. Williams,

'Seasonal Migrations of Cardiganshire Harvest Gangs to the Vale of Glamorgan in the Nineteenth Century', *Ceredigion*, 1959, vol. III, pp. 156–9.

19. Cited in E. J. T. Collins, 'Migrant Labour in British Agriculture in the Nineteenth Century', *Economic History Review*, 2nd series, 1976, vol. XXIX, p. 40.
20. T. S. Ashton, *Economic Fluctuations in England, 1700–1800*, Oxford, 1959, p. 7.
21. Young, *Southern Tour*, p. 76; Collins, op. cit., p. 42.
22. Collins, op. cit., pp. 58–9 citing Young, *Northern Tour*, I, pp. 151–3, 156, IV, pp. 442–5, 447–9 and the *Farmer's Tour through the East of England*, IV, pp. 312–13, 317.
23. See, e.g., p. 144 below.
24. W. Marshall, *The Rural Economy of Yorkshire*, Nicol, 1788, I, pp. 387–9.
25. J. Williams-Davies, 'Merched y Gerddi. A Seasonal Migration of Labour from Rural Wales', *Folk Life*, 1977, vol. XV, pp. 12–20.
26. W. Bailey and G. Culley, *General View of the Agriculture of Northumberland, Cumberland and Westmorland*, 3rd edition, 1805, reprinted F. Graham, Newcastle, 1972, pp. 92–3.
27. K. D. M. Snell, *Annals of the Labouring Poor. Social Change and Agrarian England, 1660–1900*, Cambridge, 1985, pp. 18, 21–22.
28. F. M. Eden, *State of the Poor*, 1797, reprinted Cass, 1966, II, pp. 84, 404, 528; III, p. 796.
29. Marchand, op. cit., pp. 77–8.
30. Young, *Southern Tour*, p. 157; idem, *Rural Oeconomy. Essays on the Practical Arts of Husbandry*, Becket, 1770, pp. 227, 233–4.
31. Wiltshire R.O. Avebury Parish Records. 1569/31.
32. E. P. Thompson, 'Time, Work-Discipline and Industrial Capitalism', *Past and Present*, 1967, No. 38, pp. 56–97.
33. For evidence on nutritional standards see pp. 42 and 100 below.
34. A. Smith, *The Wealth of Nations*, Everyman edition, 1910, I, pp. 72–3.
35. A. H. John, *The Industrial Development of South Wales*, University of Wales Press, Cardiff, 1950, p. 16.
36. A. L. Bowley, *Wages in the United Kingdom*, Cambridge, 1900. See section IV and end-table facing p. 144.
37. Young, *Southern Tour*, p. 335; idem, *Northern Tour*, IV, pp. 442–6, 460.
38. Note that Defoe (*Giving Alms no Charity*, 1704, p. 11) thought that a 'poor man' would earn 7 to 10s in Kent and 4s in the north, whilst E. Laurence (*The Duty of a Steward to his Lord*, 1727, p. 156) assumed that northern wages were lower than those in the south and recommended that task-work rates should be adjusted accordingly. I owe these references to Dr Holderness.
39. Bowley, op. cit., table facing p. 144. The counties taken as 'northern' for the purpose of this calculation are those situated north of the line later drawn by James Caird. See p. 91 below, and map, p. 9.
40. J. Holt, *General View of the Agriculture of Lancashire*, 1795, reprinted David and Charles, Newton Abbot, 1969, pp. 179–80.
41. Young, *Southern Tour*, pp. 168–9; John, op. cit., p. 67.
42. Bowley, op. cit., table facing p. 144.
43. Estimate based on a consideration of the budgets discussed on pp. 41–2 below.
44. S. Van Bath, *The Agriculture of Western Europe, A.D. 500–1850*, Edward Arnold, 1963, pp. 221–37, esp. p. 228.
45. N. Kent, *Agricultural Survey of Norfolk*, 1796, quoted in N. Riches, *The Agricultural Revolution in Norfolk*, 2nd edition, Cass, 1967, p. 138; J. Howlett, *Annals of Agriculture*, 1796, vol. XXV, p. 609; D. Davies, *The Case of the Labourers in Husbandry Stated and Considered*, C. G. and J. Robinson, 1795, pp. 24–5.
46. *Annals of Agriculture*, 1792, vol. XVII, p. 434; 1793, vol. XIX, p. 528; Eden, op. cit., I, pp. 560–1.
47. Smith, op. cit., I, pp. 66, 69–70.
48. Justices of the Peace had been given the responsibility for fixing wages under Tudor labour legislation. However, by the later eighteenth century their powers had fallen into disuse. For example, there is no record of any attempt to determine them in Kent after the 1770s, while a writer of 1795 who discovered a seventy-year-old Lancashire assessment was 'much surprised

to hear that any magistrates in the present century would venture on so bold a measure'. *Annals of Agriculture*, 1795, vol. XXV, p. 305.

49. According to the details given in P.P. 1833, vols. XXXVI–XXXVII. *1831 Census of Great Britain, Enumeration Abstract*, vols. I and II, which is the earliest source of information bearing on this point, approximately one-quarter of male labourers in agriculture in England resided in the thirteen counties situated to the north of the wage line traced by Caird in 1851.
50. Allowing for differences in the sources of wage-data and price indexes used, these conclusions are broadly in line with the findings of two recent studies which touch on real wage changes in agriculture in the late eighteenth century. P. H. Lindert and J. G. Williamson, 'English Workers' Living Standards during the Industrial Revolution', *Economic History Review*, 2nd series, 1983, vol. XXXVI, p. 13, suggest that real wages fell by some 7 per cent between their benchmark years, 1755 and 1781, while G. N. von Tunzelman, 'Trends in Real Wages, 1750–1850, Revisited', *Economic History Review*, 2nd series, 1979, vol. XXXII, pp. 45, 47, draws attention to the likelihood of divergent experiences in the north and the south, on the basis of existing series.
51. Karl Marx, *Capital*, 13th edition, Glaisher, 1909, p. 769; W. Hasbach, *A History of the English Agricultural Labourer*, P. and S. King, 1908, pp. 29, 38, 41–2, 57–61, ch. III, passim.
52. E. P. Thompson, *The Making of the English Working Class*, Gollancz, 1963, p. 218.
53. J. R. Wordie, 'The Chronology of English Enclosure, 1500–1914', *Economic History Review*, 2nd series, 1983, vol. XXXVI, p. 486.
54. J. A. Yelling, *Common Field and Enclosure in England, 1450–1850*, Macmillan, 1977, pp. 124, 125–6.
55. G. E. Mingay, *Enclosure and the Small Farmer in the Age of the Industrial Revolution*, Macmillan, 1968, pp. 29, 31–2.
56. J. Saville, 'Primitive Accumulation and Early Industrialization in Britain', *The Socialist Register*, 1969, No. 6, p. 250; M. Turner, *Enclosures in Britain 1750–1830*, Macmillan, 1984, p. 76, quoting K. Tribe, *Genealogies of Capitalism*, 1981.
57. Turner, op. cit., pp. 17, 19, 20, 23, summarizing his longer work, *English Parliamentary Enclosure*, Dawson, Folkestone, 1980.
58. Notable studies include E. Davies, 'The Small Landowner, 1780–1832, in the Light of the Land Tax Assessments', *Economic History Review*, 1st series, 1927, vol. I; J. D. Chambers, 'Enclosure and the Small Landowner', *Economic History Review*, 1st series, 1940, vol. X; D. B. Grigg, *The Agricultural Revolution in South Lincolnshire*, Cambridge, 1966, pp. 85–94.
59. See, e.g., J. M. Martin, 'The Cost of Parliamentary Enclosure in Warwickshire' in E. L. Jones, ed., *Agriculture and Economic Growth in England, 1650–1815*, Methuen, 1967; M. E. Turner, 'Cost, Finance, and Parliamentary Enclosure', *Economic History Review*, 2nd series, 1981, vol. XXXIV; B. A. Holderness, 'Capital Formation in Agriculture, 1750–1850', in J. P. P. Higgins and S. Pollard, eds., *Aspects of Capital Formation in Great Britain, 1750–1850*, Methuen, 1971, esp. p. 167.
60. G. E. Mingay, 'The Land Tax Assessments and the Small Landowner', *Economic History Review*, 2nd series, 1964, vol. XVII; and see the comments on the subject by D. E. Ginter and G. J. Wilson in *Economic History Review*, 2nd series, 1982, vol. XXXV, pp. 416–26.
61. M. E. Turner, 'Parliamentary Enclosure and Landownership Change in Buckinghamshire', *Economic History Review*, 2nd series, 1975, vol. XXVIII, p. 568.
62. G. E. Mingay, 'The Size of Farms in the Eighteenth Century', *Economic History Review*, 2nd series, 1962, vol. XIV, p. 469.
63. Yelling, op. cit., p. 225 and see P.P. 1822, vol. XV. *Census of Great Britain, Abstract of Answers and Returns, Enumeration Abstract*, p. 162. Drayton was a small township with only 104 souls in 1821.
64. Yelling, op. cit., p. 214.
65. E. C. K. Gonner, *The Common Land and Inclosure*, Macmillan, 1912, p. 443; J. D. Chambers, 'Enclosure and Labour Supply in the Industrial Revolution', *Economic History Review*, 2nd series, 1953, vol. V, p. 332.
66. See B. D. Baack and R. P. Thomas, 'The Enclosure Movement and the Supply of Labour during the Industrial Revolution', *Journal of European Economic History*, 1974, vol. III,

pp. 401–23; N. F. R. Crafts, 'Enclosure and Labour Supply Revisited', *Explorations in Entrepreneurial History*, 1978, vol. XV, pp. 172–83; idem, *British Economic Growth during the Industrial Revolution*, Oxford, 1985, pp. 115–24.

67. Crafts, 'Enclosure and Labour Supply Revisited', pp. 180–2. Note that he is speaking of gross, not net migratory movements.
68. Snell, op. cit., pp. 147–66, 180–3, 210. He remarks (p. 210) that Chambers relied heavily on evidence from enclosures of wasteland, which were more likely to increase employment. On the other hand Snell concentrates on counties where open-field arable made up a high proportion of all land enclosed (see p. 147). The critical point is that the proportion of enclosed land made up of wastes is not yet settled. While Turner, *English Parliamentary Enclosure*, p. 71, follows Tate in concluding that 'the enclosure of *mainly* open field arable was at all times the more important', others, notably J. Chapman, are sceptical. See, e.g., his article, 'The Parliamentary Enclosures of West Sussex', *Southern History*, 1980, vol. II, pp. 73–4 and a forthcoming paper read at the Agricultural History Society's conference at Ripon, 1985.
69. G. D. H. Cole, *A Short History of the British Working Class Movement, 1789–1947*, new edition, Allen and Unwin, 1948, p. 22.
70. J. L. and B. Hammond, *The Village Labourer*, new edition, Longman, 1978, p. 58.
71. Yelling, op. cit., p. 230.
72. Eden, op. cit., III, p. 749; J. Billingsley, 'The Uselessness of the Commons to the Poor', *Annals of Agriculture*, 1798, vol. XXXI, pp. 27–32.
73. Carlisle Public Library, Jackson Collection, John Heysham Correspondence. M839, Letter dated 12 June 1786; (Arthur Young), *General Report on Enclosures, drawn up by Order of the Board of Agriculture*, 1808, reprinted Kelley, New York, 1971, pp. 12–14, 158. Note that Young did not mention these injuries 'to show that such enclosures should not have taken place; nor to assert that an increase in regular employment by the cultivation of the farmers might not more than make amends for them, which is another question'.
74. Dr Neeson's researches are summarized in R. W. Malcolmson, *Life and Labour in England 1700–1780*, Hutchinson, 1981, pp. 32–3, and in her article, 'The Opponents of Enclosure in Eighteenth Century Northamptonshire', *Past and Present*, 1984, No. 105, pp. 118–22, 127–8, 132–4.
75. Snell, op. cit., pp. 194–209.
76. Malcolmson, op. cit., pp. 34–5.
77. J. M. Martin, 'Village Traders and the Emergence of a Proletariat in South Warwickshire, 1750–1851', *Agricultural History Review*, 1984, vol. XXXII, p. 185.
78. These figures use the 1750 population totals given by R. S. Schofield in R. Floud and D. McCloskey, eds., *The Economic History of Britain since 1700*, I, *1700–1860*, Cambridge, 1981, p. 21, and B. R. Mitchell and P. Deane, *Abstract of British Historical Statistics*, Cambridge, 1962, p. 6. At the county level the figures cited are from P. Deane and W. A. Cole, *British Economic Growth, 1688–1950*, Cambridge, 1962, p. 103. The sixteen counties classed as 'agricultural' on the basis of the 1811 census are Beds., Berks., Bucks., Cambs., Essex, Herefs., Herts., Hunts., Lincs., Norfolk, Oxon., Rutland, Suffolk, Sussex, Wilts. and Wales treated as one county.
79. These death rates are simple averages of the figures in E. A. Wrigley and R. S. Schofield, *The Population History of England, 1541–1871*, Edward Arnold, 1981, pp. 333–5.
80. R. E. Jones, 'Infant Mortality in Rural North Shropshire, 1561–1810', *Population Studies*, 1976, vol. XXX, p. 313; D. C. Levine, *Family Formation in an Age of Nascent Capitalism*, Academic Press, 1977, pp. 91, 99, 100.
81. G. Philpot, 'Enclosure and Population Growth in Eighteenth Century England', *Explorations in Economic History*, 1975, vol. XII, pp. 29–45; M. Turner, 'Parliamentary Enclosure and Population Change in England, 1750–1830', ibid., 1976, vol. XIII, pp. 463–8.
82. See letter cited in footnote 73; and E. Chadwick, *Report on the Sanitary Condition of the Labouring Population, 1842*, ed. M. W. Flinn, Edinburgh University Press, 1965, pp. 150–2.
83. M. Dobson, '"Marsh Fever" – the Geography of Malaria in England', *Journal of Historical Geography*, 1980, vol. VI, pp. 384–6.
84. W. R. Lee, *European Demography and Economic Growth*, Croom Helm, 1979, p. 14; T. Bengts-

son, G. Fridlizius and R. Ohlsson, eds., *Pre-Industrial Population Change. The Mortality Decline and Short-Term Population Movements*, Almquist and Wiksell, Stockholm, 1984, pp. 8–12.
85. M. Anderson, 'Marriage Patterns in Victorian Britain: an Analysis based on Registration District data for England and Wales, 1861', *Journal of Family History*, 1976, vol. I, pp. 65, 76.
86. Wrigley and Schofield, op. cit., pp. 244, 255, 260; and see E. A. Wrigley, 'The Growth of Population in Eighteenth Century England. A Conundrum Resolved', *Past and Present*, 1983, No. 98, pp. 130–1.
87. N. L. Tranter, *Population and Society, 1750–1940*, Longman, 1985, pp. 50–1.
88. Levine, op. cit., pp. 5, 11, 62–3, 95, 97, 116, 119, 123, 147.
89. Snell, op. cit., pp. 210–11.
90. ibid., p. 215.
91. G. Utterstrom, 'Population and Agriculture in Sweden, *c.*1700–1830', *Scandinavian Economic History Review*, 1962, vol. IX, p. 188.
92. R. E. Jones, 'Population and Agrarian Change in an Eighteenth Century Shropshire Parish', *Local Population Studies*, 1968, No. 1, pp. 9–10; A. E. Newman, 'The Old Poor Law in East Kent, 1606–1834. A Social and Demographic Analysis', Ph.D. thesis, University of Kent, 1980, pp. 228–31, 376–7.
93. Chambers, 'Enclosure and Labour Supply', pp. 338–9.
94. The budgets are set out in Eden, op. cit., III, Appendix XI, pp. cccxxxix–cccl and Davies, op. cit., pp. 131–91. The example given is from Davies, pp. 164–5.
95. J. L. and B. Hammond, op. cit., pp. 69–70.
96. Davies, op. cit., pp. 131, 132; Eden, op. cit., I, p. xxvi.
97. These relationships are more fully discussed in my contribution to G. E. Mingay, ed., *The Agrarian History of England and Wales*, VI, *1750–1850*, Cambridge, forthcoming.
98. The mean number of co-residing children in the budgets is 4.05 (Davies) and 3.62 (Eden). From studies based on mid-nineteenth- century censuses it would seem that the average number present in agricultural labourers' families was just over two. In one group of Lincolnshire parishes in 1851 it stood at 2.08. See P. Tillott and G. S. Stevenson, *North-West Lindsey in 1851*, University of Sheffield, Department of Extra-Mural Studies, 1970, p. 16.
99. D. J. Oddy, unpublished paper which he has kindly allowed me to quote. For the methods of analysis involved see his article 'Food in Nineteenth Century England: Nutrition in the First Urban Society', *Proceedings of the Nutrition Society*, 1970, vol. XXIX, pp. 155–6, and T. C. Barker, D. J. Oddy and J. Yudkin, eds., *The Dietary Surveys of Dr Edward Smith*, Occasional Paper No. 1, Department of Nutrition, Queen Elizabeth College, University of London, Staples Press, 1970, ch. III.
100. Eden, op. cit., I, p. 496.
101. Oddy, unpublished researches. See footnote 99.
102. Davies, op. cit., p. 24.
103. See J. B. Huzel, 'The Labourer and the Poor Law' in G. E. Mingay, ed., *The Agrarian History of England*, VI, *1750–1850*, forthcoming.
104. J. D. Chambers, *The Vale of Trent, 1670–1800*. Supplement No. 3 to the *Economic History Review*, 1957, p. 58.
105. A. Digby, *Pauper Palaces*, Routledge and Kegan Paul, 1978, pp. 34–5.
106. B. Kerr, *Bound to the Soil. A Social History of Dorset, 1750–1918*, John Baker, 1968, p. 93.

Chapter 2, pp. 44–60

1. J. Beresford, ed., *The Diary of A Country Parson*, Clarendon, Oxford, 1924–31, IV, p. 4.
2. There are numerous technical problems of comparing like with like, without affecting the main point at issue. The 1786–90 figures for gross public expenditure (GB) given here are from P. Deane, 'War and Industrialization' in J. M. Winter, ed., *War and Economic Development*, Cambridge, 1975, p. 94; while the 1815 peak in gross public expenditure (UK) is identified from B. R. Mitchell and P. Deane, *Abstract of British Historical Statistics*, Cambridge, 1962,

p. 396. The estimate of the proportion of gross national product devoted to military purposes is that of J. E. Williams in 'The British Standard of Living, 1750–1850', *Economic History Review*, 2nd series, 1966, vol. XIX, p. 587.

3. Estimates of the size of the armed forces are from C. Emsley, *British Society and the French Wars, 1793–1815*, Macmillan, 1979, p. 133.
4. That is, using the Gayer Rostow and Schwartz index reprinted in Mitchell and Deane, op. cit., p. 470, and comparing 1790–2 with 1813–15.
5. See, e.g. W. H. B. Court, *Concise Economic History of Britain, from 1750 to Recent Times*, Cambridge, 1958, pp. 146–9.
6. A. H. John, 'Farming in Wartime, 1793–1815' in E. L. Jones and G. E. Mingay, eds., *Land, Labour and Population in the Industrial Revolution*, Edward Arnold, 1967, p. 28.
7. J. D. Chambers and G. E. Mingay, *The Agricultural Revolution, 1750–1880*, Batsford, 1966, p. 115; M. Olson, *The Economics of the Wartime Shortage*, Duke University Press, Durham, North Carolina, 1963, pp. 65–6, 71.
8. M. Turner, *Enclosures in Britain, 1750–1830*, Macmillan, 1984, pp. 20–1; A. Redford, *Labour Migration in England, 1800–1850*, 2nd edition, Manchester University Press, 1964, pp. 72–3. Note that the General Enclosure Act of 1801 aimed to simplify the procedures and reduce the expense involved, but without much success. See Chambers and Mingay, op. cit., p. 121.
9. D. Thomas, *Agriculture in Wales during the Napoleonic Wars*, University of Wales Press, Cardiff, 1963, pp. 31–2, 130–4.
10. A. Young, *General View of the Agriculture of Lincolnshire*, 2nd edition, 1813, reprinted David and Charles, Newton Abbot, 1970, p. 281; A. Harris, *The Rural Landscape of the East Riding of Yorkshire, 1700–1850*, Oxford, 1961, p. 83; M. Williams, *The Draining of the Somerset Levels*, Cambridge, 1970, pp. 123, 128.
11. Thomas, op. cit., pp. 140–1; D. B. Grigg, *The Agricultural Revolution in South Lincolnshire*, Cambridge, 1966, pp. 28, 31; Williams, op. cit., ch. V passim.
12. G. Hueckel, 'Relative Prices and Supply Response in English Agriculture during the Napoleonic Wars', *Economic History Review*, 2nd series, 1976, vol. XXIX, pp. 401, 405–14; S. MacDonald, 'Agricultural Response to a Changing Market during the Napoleonic Wars', *Economic History Review*, 2nd Series, 1980, vol. XXXIII, pp. 59–60, 63, 67.
13. MacDonald, op. cit., p. 64; Beresford, op. cit., IV, p. 298.
14. G. Hueckel, 'English Farming Profits during the Napoleonic Wars', *Explorations in Economic History*, 1976, vol. XIII, pp. 342–3.
15. Grigg, op. cit., p. 37.
16. H. G. Hunt, 'Agricultural Rent in South-East England, 1788–1825', *Agricultural History Review*, 1959, vol. VII, pp. 102–3.
17. F. M. L. Thompson, *English Landed Society in the Nineteenth Century*, Routledge and Kegan Paul, 1963, pp. 218–19.
18. J. L. and B. Hammond, *The Village Labourer*, new edition, Longman, 1978, pp. 116–17; P. Horn, *The Rural World, 1780–1850. Social Change in the English Countryside*, Hutchinson, 1980, p. 57.
19. *Annals of Agriculture*, 1796, vol. XXVI, p. 126; *The Times*, 14 August 1797; *Farmer's Magazine*, 1803, vol. IV, pp. 116–17; 1806, vol. VII, p. 401; 1808, vol. IX, p. 410; J. Duncombe, *General View of the Agriculture of Herefordshire*, Phillips, 1805, pp. 148–9.
20. Nottinghamshire R.O. DD4P 67/27; E. L. Jones, 'The Agricultural Labour Market in England, 1793–1872', *Economic History Review*, 2nd series, 1964, vol. XVII, p. 323.
21. H. F. B. Wheeler and A. M. Broadley, *Napoleon and the Invasion of England*, Bodley Head, 1907, II, pp. 301–2.
22. Emsley, op. cit., p. 102; Horn, op. cit., pp. 64, 281; P. Lindert, 'English Occupations 1670–1811', *Journal of Economic History*, 1980, vol. XL, p. 710.
23. *Evans and Ruffy's Farmers Journal*, quoted in E. J. T. Collins, 'Harvest Technology and Labour Supply in Britain, 1790–1870', Ph.D. thesis, University of Nottingham, 1970, p. 156.
24. Jones, op. cit., p. 325.
25. C. G. Spence, *God Speed the Plow*, University of Illinois Pess, Urbana, Illinois, 1960, pp. 8, 14.

26. J. Holt, *General View of the Agriculture of Lancashire*, 1795, reprinted David and Charles, Newton Abbot, 1969, p. 34; S. MacDonald, 'The Progress of the Early Threshing Machine', *Agricultural History Review*, 1975, vol. XXIII, p. 67 et seq.
27. E. J. T. Collins, 'Harvest Technology and Labour Supply in Britain, 1790–1870', *Economic History Review*, 2nd series, 1969, vol. XXII, pp. 456–7. However, his view that the diffusion of the scythe was closely related to emergent shortages of harvest labour has not gone uncontested. See J. A. Perkins, 'Harvest Technology and Labour Supply in Lincolnshire and the East Riding of Yorkshire, 1750–1850', *Tools and Tillage*, 1976, vol. III, pp. 47–58, and 125–35.
28. Jones, op. cit., p. 324; Emsley, op. cit., p. 111.
29. R. J. Olney, *Rural Society and County Government in Nineteenth Century Lincolnshire*, History of Lincolnshire Committee, Lincoln, 1979, p. 81; Collins, thesis, p. 122.
30. ibid., p. 79; J. G. Cornish, *Reminiscences of Country Life*, Country Life, 1939, p. 121.
31. K. D. M. Snell, *Annals of the Labouring Poor. Social Change and Agrarian England, 1660–1900*, Cambridge, 1985, p. 22.
32. *Annals of Agriculture*, 1799, vol. XXXII, pp. 85–6; 1802, vol. XXXVIII, p. 21.
33. A. L. Bowley, *Wages in the United Kingdom in the Nineteenth Century*, Cambridge, 1900, p. 40.
34. The index is reprinted in Mitchell and Deane, op. cit., pp. 348–51.
35. B. Eccleston, 'A Survey of Wage Rates in Five Midland Counties, 1750–1834', Ph.D. thesis, University of Leicester, 1977.
36. A. Kussmaul, *Servants in Husbandry in Early Modern England*, Cambridge, 1981, p. 122 notes that according to Board of Agriculture reports, the weekly wages of day labourers rose by 3 per cent per annum from 1794–7 to 1804–13, whereas the yearly wages of farm servants increased at a rate of only 1.1 per cent. This casts considerable doubt on the value of the array of graphs produced by Snell,op. cit., pp. 23–47, at least for the war years, since they are based exclusively on farm servants' yearly wages.
37. W. Hasbach, *A History of the English Agricultural Labourer*, P. and S. King, 1908, p. 183; Lord Ernle, *English Farming Past and Present*, 5th edition, Longmans, Green, 1936, pp. 314–15; T. L. Richardson, 'The Agricultural Labourer's Standard of Living in Kent, 1790–1840' in D. J. Oddy and D. Miller, eds., *The Making of the Modern British Diet*, Croom Helm, 1976, p. 110; T. S. Ashton, 'The Standard of Life of the Workers in England, 1790–1830' in F. A. Hayek, ed., *Capitalism and the Historians*, Routledge and Kegan Paul, 1954, p. 134.
38. M. W. Flinn, 'Trends in Real Wages, 1750–1850', *Economic History Review*, 2nd series, 1974, vol. XXVII, pp. 404, 407; John, op. cit., p. 34. See also P. H. Lindert and J. G. Williamson, 'English Workers' Living Standards during the Industrial Revolution', *Economic History Review*, 2nd series, 1983, vol. XXXVI, p. 13, whose statistics for the benchmark years 1797, 1805, 1810, 1815, do not appear to negate this point.
39. J. Bailey and G. Culley, *General View of the Agriculture of Northumberland*, 3rd edition, 1805, reprinted F. Graham, Newcastle, 1972, pp. 164–5; W. Marshall, *Review and Abstract of the County Reports to the Board of Agriculture*, 1818, reprinted David and Charles, Newton Abbot, 1969, V (*Southern*), p. 384.
40. C. Vancouver, *General View of the Agriculture of Devon*, Sherwood, Nealy and Jones, 1808, p. 362; W. Stevenson, *General View of the Agriculture of Dorset*, Sherwood Nealy and Jones, 1812, p. 428.
41. Horn, op. cit., p. 59.
42. ibid., p. 60; E. Robinson and G. Summerfield, eds., *Clare: Selected Poems and Prose*, Oxford, 1966, p. 114.
43. A. Young, *General View of the Agriculture of Hertfordshire*, 1804, reprinted David and Charles, Newton Abbot, 1971, pp. 222–3; Marshall, *Review and Abstract*, IV (*Midlands*), p. 529.
44. S. and B. Webb, *English Poor Law History*, I, *The Old Poor Law*, Longmans, Green, 1927, p. 182; M. Blaug, 'The Myth of the Old Poor Law and the Making of the New', *Journal of Economic History*, 1963, vol. XXIII, pp. 151, 160.
45. E.g. in Bedfordshire at certain seasons, according to T. Batchelor, *General View of the Agriculture of the County of Bedford*, Phillips, 1808, p. 608.
46. E.g. J. D. Marshall, *The Old Poor Law, 1795–1834*, Macmillan, 1968, p. 33; J. B. Huzel, 'The

Labourer and the Poor Law' in G. E. Mingay, ed., *The Agrarian History of England and Wales*, VI, *1750–1850*, Cambridge, forthcoming.

47. D. A. Baugh, 'The Cost of Poor Relief in South-East England, 1790–1834', *Economic History Review*, 2nd series, 1975, vol. XXVIII, pp. 54–6, 60–1. A graph of real relief per capita for Ardleigh and St Osyth (Essex) in Snell, op. cit., p. 89 suggests that the year-to-year fluctuations in the war years were more significant than any discernible trend.
48. Ernle, op. cit., p. 269.
49. Beresford, op. cit., IV, pp. 160–84, esp. 169.
50. W. Stern, 'The Bread Crisis in Britain, 1795–6', *Economica*, new series, 1964, vol. XXXI, pp. 181, 184, 185.
51. Essex R.O. D/P 88/18/10. Return of the Cost of the Poor Rate in Wakes Colne, 1801–17, and D/P 299/12/3. Return of Poor Inhabitants of Terling, January 1801; R. A. E. Wells, *Dearth and Distress in Yorkshire 1793–1802*, Borthwick Papers, No. 52, York, 1977, p. 16.
52. Beresford, op. cit., V, p. 297; Wells, op. cit., p. 16.
53. E. J. T. Collins, 'Dietary Change and Cereal Consumption in the Nineteenth Century', *Agricultural History Review*, 1975, vol. XXIII, p. 104.
54. Horn, op. cit., pp. 44–5; Wells, op. cit., pp. 25–6; idem, 'The Revolt of the South-West, 1800–1: a Study in Social Protest', *Social History*, 1977, vol. II, pp. 722, 732; A. Booth, 'Food Riots in the North-West of England, 1790–1801', *Past and Present*, 1977, No. 77, p. 89; R. Quinault and J. Stevenson, *Popular Protest and Public Order*, Allen and Unwin 1974, pp. 43–5; Emsley, op. cit., p. 42.
55. C. R. Dobson, *Masters and Journeymen: A Prehistory of Industrial Relations, 1717–1800*, Croom Helm, 1980, pp. 117, 145–6.
56. Chambers and Mingay, op. cit., p. 118.
57. M. K. Ashby, *The Changing English Village*, Roundwood Press, Kineton, 1974, p. 275.
58. W. Davies, *General View of the Agriculture of South Wales*, Nicol, 1814, I, p. 136; idem, *General View of the Agriculture of North Wales*, Phillips, 1810, p. 82. On the subject generally, see M. W. Barley, *The English Farmhouse and Cottage*, Routledge and Kegan Paul, 1961 and G. E. Fussell, *The English Rural Labourer*, Batchworth Press, 1949, ch. V.
59. *Annals of Agriculture*, 1784, vol. II, p. 332; 1785, vol. IV, p. 52; 1787, vol. VIII, p. 350; Essex R.O. D/P 88/18/9. Census of Wakes Colne, 1809.
60. A. Young, *Agriculture of Lincolnshire*, pp. 39–41; J. A. Perkins, 'Working Class Housing in Lindsey, 1780–1870', *Lincolnshire History and Archaeology*, 1975, vol. X, pp. 50, 52.
61. A. Young, *General View of the Agriculture of the County of Norfolk*, 1804, reprinted David and Charles, Newton Abbot, 1969, p. 24; J. A. Perkins, 'The Housing of the Working Class in Lindsey, 1790–1850', *Lincolnshire History and Archaeology*, 1977, vol. XII, pp. 65–6.
62. C. B. Andrews, ed., *The Torrington Diaries*, Methuen, 1938, I, p. 278, II, p. 238.
63. H. Mills, ed., *George Crabbe: Tales, 1812 and other Selected Poems*, Cambridge, 1967, p. 149; Robinson and Summerfield, op. cit., pp. 67, 70.
64. Hasbach, op. cit., p. 178.
65. Young, *Agriculture of Norfolk*, p. 484.
66. Kussmaul, op. cit., pp. 123–4.
67. J. Mavor, *General View of the Agriculture of Berkshire*, Phillips, 1813, p. 416; *Communications to the Board of Agriculture*, V, Pt. I, Nicol, 1808, pp. 225–6.
68. *Gentleman's Magazine*, 1823, vol. XCIII, p. 213.
69. Ernle, op. cit., p. 211.

Chapter 3, pp. 61–87

1. Lord Ernle, *English Farming, Past and Present*, 5th edition, Longmans, Green, 1936, pp. 317, 319.
2. Board of Agriculture, *The Agricultural State of the Kingdom, 1816*, ed. G. E. Mingay, Adams and Dart, Bath, 1970, pp. 3, 4.
3. L. P. Adams, *Agricultural Depression and Farm Relief in England, 1813–52*, P. and S. King,

1932, p. 69; P.P. 1817, vol. VI. *Select Committee on the Petitions of Watchmakers of Coventry*, Mins. of Evidence, p. 19.

4. Rousseaux' index of prices for agricultural products, in B. R. Mitchell and P. Deane, *Abstract of British Historical Statistics*, Cambridge, 1962, p. 471; J. D. Chambers and G. E. Mingay, *The Agricultural Revolution, 1750–1880*, Batsford, 1966, p. 129.
5. E. J. T. Collins, 'Harvest Technology and Labour Supply in Britain, 1790–1870', *Economic History Review*, 2nd series, 1969, vol. XXII, p. 457.
6. W. Marshall, *Review and Abstract of the County Reports to the Board of Agriculture*, 1818, reprinted David and Charles, Newton Abbot, 1969, IV (*Midlands*), p. 637.
7. G. E. Fussell and M. Compton, 'Agricultural Adjustments after the Napoleonic Wars', *Economic History*, 1939, vol. IV, pp. 188, 197; E. L. Jones, *The Development of English Agriculture, 1815–73*, Macmillan, 1968, pp. 13–16; C. S. Davies, *Agricultural History of Cheshire*, Chetham Society, Manchester, 1960, p. 47; F. M. L. Thompson, *English Landed Society in the Nineteenth Century*, Routledge and Kegan Paul, 1963, p. 231.
8. P. Deane and W. A. Cole, *British Economic Growth, 1688–1959*, Cambridge, 1962, p. 172, though see the comments in N. F. R. Crafts, *British Economic Growth during the Industrial Revolution*, Clarendon, Oxford, 1985, pp. 41–2; Jones, op. cit., p. 13.
9. Chambers and Mingay, op. cit., pp. 130–1.
10. A. Kussmaul, *Servants in Husbandry in Early Modern England*, Cambridge, 1981, p. 171.
11. B. Short, 'The Decline of Living-in Servants in the Transition to Capitalist Farming: a Critique of the Sussex Evidence', *Sussex Archaeological Collections*, 1984, vol. CXXII, pp. 161, 163.
12. See e.g. M. Turner, *Enclosures in Britain, 1750–1830*, Macmillan, 1984, pp. 69–70.
13. J. R. Wordie, 'Social Change on the Leveson-Gower Estates, 1714–1832', *Economic History Review*, 2nd series, 1974, vol. XXVII, p. 596; B. A. Holderness, 'The Victorian Farmer' in G. E. Mingay, ed., *The Victorian Countryside*, Routledge and Kegan Paul, 1981, I, p. 230.
14. B. A. Holderness, '"Open" and "Close" Parishes in England in the Eighteenth and Nineteenth Centuries', *Agricultural History Review*, 1972, vol. XX, p. 135; D. Mills, *Lord and Peasant in Nineteenth Century Britain*, Croom Helm, 1980, p. 85.
15. See S. Banks, 'Open and Close Parishes in Nineteenth Century England', Ph.D. thesis, University of Reading, 1982. As yet, none of the findings of this valuable study have been published.
16. E. A. Wrigley, 'Men on the Land and Men in the Countryside: Employment in Agriculture in Early Nineteenth Century England' in L. Bonfield, R. M. Smith and K. Wrightson, eds., *The World We have Gained: Histories of Population and Social Structure*, Blackwell, Oxford, 1986, p. 332. His figures include farmers.
17. Based on the counties listed in chapter 1, footnote 78, and the population figures calculated for 1815 in W. A. Armstrong, 'La Population de l'Angleterre et du Pays de Galles', *Annales de Démographie Historique*, 1965, vol. II, p. 186, and Mitchell and Deane, op. cit., p. 20.
18. Wrigley, op. cit., pp. 300, 302, 335.
19. Board of Agriculture, *State of the Kingdom*, pp. xv, 86, 146, 185, 228, 298.
20. E. J. Hobsbawm and G. Rudé, *Captain Swing*, Lawrence and Wishart, 1969, p. 73.
21. S. W. Amos, 'Social Discontent and Agrarian Disturbances in Essex, 1795–1850', M.A. thesis, University of Essex, 1971, p. 102; Bedfordshire R.O. P. 30/12/10–12. Surplus Labour Accounts for the Parish of Ampthill. (My figures are based on comparisons of names listed at any time between 9 December 1826 and 3 March 1827 with those appearing between 3 January and 21 February 1829 and 9 January and 27 February 1830).
22. A. F. Cirket, 'The 1830 Riots in Bedfordshire. Background and Events', *Bedfordshire Historical Record Society*, 1978, vol. LVII, pp. 77–8; N. Agar, *The Bedfordshire Farm Worker in the Nineteenth Century*, Bedfordshire Historical Record Society, 1981, vol. LX, p. 78; J. Thirsk and J. Imray, eds., *Suffolk Farming in the Nineteenth Century*, Suffolk Record Society, 1958, vol. I, pp. 134–5.
23. C. Thomas, 'Agricultural Employment in Nineteenth Century Wales: a New Approach', *Welsh History Review*, 1972, vol. VI, p. 151.
24. J. D. Marshall, 'The Lancashire Rural Labourer in the Early Nineteenth Century', *Transactions of the Lancashire and Cheshire Antiquarian Society*, 1965, vol. LXXI, p. 110; W. H. Long,

'Facets of Farm Labour and Wages, mainly in the Eighteenth and Nineteenth Centuries', *Journal of the Royal Agricultural Society*, 1975, vol. CXXXVI, p. 49.

25. Marshall, 'Lancashire Rural Labourer', p. 107; idem, 'Nottinghamshire Labourers in the Early Nineteenth Century', *Transactions of the Thoroton Society*, 1960, vol. LXIV, p. 61.
26. Agar, op. cit., p. 56.
27. Bedfordshire R.O. Correspondence, Bedford Settled Estates. R 3/35–74. Letter from E. Crocker to W. G. Adams dated 2 January, 1831.
28. R. M. Bacon, *Letter to the Rt. Hon. Edward Lord Suffield upon the Distress of the Labourers and its Remedy*, Hachard, London and Norwich, 1831, pp. 48–9; J. Richardson, *Letter to the Rt. Hon. Henry Lord Brougham and Vaux ... on an Alteration in the Poor Laws*, 2nd edition, Hachard, London, 1831, pp. 38, 44.
29. Agar, op. cit., p. 72.
30. Mitchell and Deane, op. cit., p. 349; M. W. Greenslade and D. A. Johnson, eds., *Victoria County History. A History of the County of Stafford*, VI, Oxford, 1979, p. 120.
31. M. Roake, 'The Camer Estate, 1716–1852', M.A. thesis, University of Kent, 1969, p. 263; J. E. Archer, 'Rural Protest in Norfolk and Suffolk, 1830–70', Ph.D. thesis, University of East Anglia, 1982, pp. 39–40; J. H. Kent, *Remarks on the Injuriousness of the Consolidation of Small Farms ... [and] on the Past and Present State of the Agricultural Labourers*, Gedge and Parker, Bury St Edmunds, 1844, p. 74.
32. J. Marriage, *Letters on the Distressed State of the Agricultural Labourers*, 4th edition, Meggy and Chalk, Chelmsford, 1832, p. 17.
33. See, e.g., P.P. 1833, vol. V. *Select Committee on Agriculture, Mins. of Evidence*, pp. 481, 489; J. R. McCulloch, *A Dictionary, Practical, Theoretical and Historical of Commerce*, new edition, Longman, Brown, Green, 1844, pp. 512–13, 635.
34. J. H. Clapham, *An Economic History of Modern Britain*, I, *The Early Railway Age*, 2nd edition, Cambridge, 1930, pp. 127–8.
35. E.g. T. L. Richardson, 'The Standard of Living Controversy, 1790–1840 with Special Reference to Agricultural Labourers in Seven English Counties', Ph.D. thesis, University of Hull, 1977; B. Eccleston, 'A Survey of Wage Rates in Five Midland Counties, 1750–1834', Ph.D. thesis, University of Leicester, 1977.
36. M. W. Flinn, 'Trends in Real Wages, 1750–1850', *Economic History Review*, 2nd series, 1974, vol. XXVII, p. 403; P. H. Lindert and J. G. Williamson, 'English Workers' Living Standards during the Industrial Revolution', *Economic History Review*, 2nd series, 1983, vol. XXXVI, pp. 12–13.
37. Clapham, op. cit., p. 128.
38. Davies, op. cit., p. 86.
39. Marshall, 'Nottinghamshire Labourers', p. 60; idem, 'Lancashire Rural Labourers', pp. 100, 116.
40. P. H. J. H. Gosden, *The Friendly Societies in England, 1815–75*, Manchester University Press, 1961, but relating the data given on p. 22 to the adult (20+) male populations (scaled up for omissions) for the various counties in P.P. 1822, vol. XV. *Census of Great Britain, Abstract of Answers and Returns, Enumeration Abstract*. Note that there is no way of allowing for multiple membership.
41. Marshall, 'Nottinghamshire Labourers', p. 73.
42. P.P. 1833, vol. V. *S.C. on Agriculture, Mins. of Evidence*, p. 531.
43. K. D. M. Snell, *Annals of the Labouring Poor. Social Change and Agrarian England, 1660–1900*, Cambridge, 1985, p. 54.
44. J. Glyde, *Suffolk in the Nineteenth Century*, Simpkin and Marshall, 1856, p. 364; M. A. Havinden, 'The South-west: a Case of De-Industrialisation' in M. Palmer, ed., *The Onset of Industrialisation*, University of Nottingham, Department of Adult Education, 1977, p. 10; W. T. Thornton, *Overpopulation and its Remedy*, Longman, Brown, Green, 1846, p. 236.
45. O. Seito, 'Who Worked Where: Life-time Profiles of Labour-Force Participation in Cardington and Corfe Castle in the Late Eighteenth and Mid-Nineteenth Centuries', *Local Population Studies*, 1979, No. 22, pp. 22, 25.
46. D. C. Barnett, 'Allotments and the Problem of Rural Poverty, 1780–1840' in E. L. Jones and

G. E. Mingay, eds., *Land, Labour and Population in the Industrial Revolution*, Edward Arnold, 1967, pp. 167, 175.

47. *The Labourer's Friend*, Labourers' Friend Society, London, 1835, pp. 189–90; Anon., 'The Condition of the English Peasantry', *Quarterly Review*, 1829, vol. XLI, p. 263.
48. *The Labourer's Friend*, p. 213.
49. Barnett, op. cit., pp. 163, 171–2.
50. J. B. Huzel, 'The Labourer and the Poor Law' in G. E. Mingay, ed., *The Agrarian History of England and Wales*, VI, *1750–1850*, Cambridge, forthcoming.
51. D. A. Baugh, 'The Cost of Poor Relief in South-East England, 1790–1834', *Economic History Review*, 2nd series, 1975, vol. XXVIII, p. 62.
52. H. J. M. Johnson, *British Emigration Policy, 1815–30: 'Shovelling out Paupers'*, Clarendon, Oxford, 1972, pp. 100–1; M. F. Davies, *Life in an English Village*, Fisher Unwin, 1910, p. 80.
53. Glyde, op. cit., p. 169.
54. M. Blaug, 'The Myth of the Old Poor Law and the Making of the New', *Journal of Economic History*, 1963, vol. XXIII, pp. 178–9.
55. S. G. and E. O. A. Checkland, eds., *The Poor Law Report of 1834*, Penguin, 1974, pp. 337–9.
56. P. Horn, *The Rural World, 1780–1850*, Hutchinson, 1980, p. 108; Bedfordshire R.O. Correspondence, Bedford Settled Estates. R3/3830. Letter from T. Bennett to W. G. Adams dated 18 November 1834; E. Billinge, 'Rural Crime and Protest in Wiltshire, 1830–75', Ph.D. thesis, University of Kent, 1984, p. 62.
57. J. Rowe, *Cornwall in the Age of the Industrial Revolution*, Liverpool University Press, 1953, p. 239; Horn, op. cit., p. 105.
58. Essex R.O. D/P 207/11/7. Pebmarsh Labour Rate, 1832–3.
59. Cirket, op. cit., pp. 79, 85–6.
60. S. G. and E. O. A. Checkland, op. cit., p. 165.
61. E. Weber, *Peasants into Frenchmen. The Modernization of Rural France, 1870–1914*, Chatto and Windus, 1977, p. 51.
62. Glyde, op. cit., p. 116; Hobsbawm and Rudé, op. cit., p. 77.
63. P.P. 1826–7, vol. VI. *Select Committee on Criminal Commitments and Convictions*, p. 4.
64. P.P. 1826–7, vol. VIII. (Lords) *Select Committee on the Game Laws, Mins. of Evidence*, p. 32.
65. P.P. 1828, vol. VI. *Select Committee on Criminal Commitments and Convictions*, p. 31; P. B. Munsche, *Gentlemen and Poachers. The English Game Laws, 1671–1831*, Cambridge, 1981, pp. 138–9, 148–9.
66. E.g. Hobsbawm and Rudé, op. cit., p. 16.
67. A. J. Peacock, *Bread or Blood. The Agrarian Riots in East Anglia, 1816*, Gollancz, 1965, pp. 76, 78, 102, 111–12, 114–15, 127, 132, 164–5; and see A. Charlesworth, 'A Comparative Study of the Spread of the Agricultural Disturbances of 1816, 1822 and 1830 in England', *Peasant Studies*, 1984, vol. XI, pp. 92–8.
68. A. Charlesworth, *An Atlas of Rural Protest in Britain, 1548–1900*, Croom Helm, 1983, pp. 148–51; idem, 'Comparative Study', pp. 92–104; P. Muskett, 'The East Anglian Agrarian Riots of 1822', *Agricultural History Review*, 1984, vol. XXXII, pp. 1–13.
69. East Suffolk R.O. HA 247/5/85. Edgar Family Papers. Letters to Col. Edgar dated 1 March 1822, 7 March 1822; HA 24: 50/19/4.4 (1). Suffolk Magistrates' Resolutions re. Labour, 1822–30. Declaration dated 20 April 1822.
70. Hobsbawm and Rudé, op. cit., pp. 85–6.
71. D. W. Howell, *Land and People in Nineteenth Century Wales*, Routledge and Kegan Paul, 1978, p. 109.
72. E.g. Archer, thesis, p. 411 suggests that the figures given by Hobsbawm and Rudé for Norfolk and Suffolk underestimate the number of villages affected and machinery destroyed.
73. Hobsbawm and Rudé, op. cit., p. 82.
74. Snell, op. cit., pp. 222–3.
75. Muskett, op. cit., p. 11; Billinge, thesis, pp. 167–8; Amos, thesis, pp. 59, 81, 99–101.
76. Hobsbawm and Rudé, op. cit., pp. 188–9.
77. Kent R.O. U 951.C177/36. Knatchbull MSS. Letter from G. Gipps to E. Knatchbull dated 24 October 1830.

78. A. Charlesworth, *Social Protest in a Rural Society*, Historical Geography Research Series, No. 1, Geo Abstracts Ltd, Norwich, 1979, pp. 7, 28, 37–9, 44.
79. Hobsbawm and Rudé, op. cit., p. 245.
80. ibid., p. 152; and for Wiltshire see Billinge, thesis, pp. 175, 177.
81. Hobsbawm and Rudé, op. cit., p. 101.
82. H. G. Mundy, ed., *The Journal of Mary Frampton*, Sampson Low, 1885, pp. 361–2, 365–6; W. H. Parry Okeden, 'The Agricultural Riots in Dorset in 1830', *Proceedings of the Dorset Natural History and Archaeological Society*, 1930, vol. LII, quoting a letter from C. B. Wollaston to the author's grandfather, a Dorset magistrate.
83. Mundy, op. cit., p. 361; Dorset R.O. P175/VE1. Sturminster Newton Vestry Minutes, 2 December 1830, 31 December 1830.
84. E. Richards, '"Captain Swing" in the West Midlands', *International Review of Social History*, 1974, vol. XIX, pp. 93, 94, 98.
85. Bedfordshire R.O. Correspondence, Bedford Settled Estates. R3/3567. Letters from E. Crocker to W. G. Adam dated 17 November 1830; R3/3579, Crocker to Adam, 26 February 1831; R3/2879, Adam to Crocker, 19 November 1830.
86. Dorset R.O. O.P.I. Letters and Printed Circulars relative to Dorset Agricultural Riots. Excerpt of letter written by Revd J. Moon.
87. Hobsbawm and Rudé, op. cit., pp. 247, 262.
88. For a more detailed account see J. Marlow, *The Tolpuddle Martyrs*, Andre Deutsch, 1971.
89. Amos, thesis, pp. 152–3.
90. Dorset R.O. D29/X4. J. Frampton's MS Account of the Dorset Yeomanry Cavalry from its Reformation in 1830 to 1845, p. 31; H. Fearn, 'Chartism in Suffolk' in A. Briggs, ed., *Chartist Studies*, Macmillan, 1962, p. 172; but see also D. Thompson, *The Chartists. Popular Politics in the Industrial Revolution*, Maurice Temple Smith, 1984, pp. 173–9, who suspects that the strength of Chartist sentiment in the countryside has been underestimated.
91. East Suffolk R.O. HA 11/B5/25. Petition from Agricultural Labourers in Wickham Market and other Parishes re. the Poor Law Amendment Act; Amos, thesis, p. 134; Archer, thesis, pp. 116–18.
92. N.C. Edsall, *The Anti-Poor Law Movement 1834–44*, Manchester University Press, 1971, pp. 116–18; J. Godber, 'Some Documents Relating to Riots', *Bedfordshire Historical Record Society*, 1970, vol. XLIX, p. 150. And see Charlesworth, *Atlas*, pp. 155–61.
93. R.A. Lewis, 'William Day and the Poor Law Commissioners', *University of Birmingham Historical Journal*, 1964, vol. IX, p. 183.
94. See *First Annual Report of the Poor Law Commissioners*, HMSO, 1835, esp. pp. 318, 324.
95. A. Redford, *Labour Migration in England, 1800–50*, 2nd edition, Manchester University Press, 1964, pp. 105–8.
96. See S. Pollard, 'Labour in Great Britain' in P. Mathias and M. M. Postan, eds., *Cambridge Economic History of Europe*, VII (Pt. I), Cambridge, 1978, pp. 141–2.
97. Redford, op. cit., pp. 109–10.
98. Mitchell and Deane, op. cit., p. 410.
99. Glyde, op. cit., pp. 183–4; J. S. Henslow, *Some Suggestions towards an Enquiry into the Present Condition of the Labouring People in Suffolk*, 1844, quoted in Archer, op. cit., pp. 128–9.
100. Agar, op. cit., pp. 97–9.
101. P.P. 1843, vol. XII. *Employment of Women and Children in Agriculture. Reports of Special Assistant Poor Law Commissioners*, pp. 16, 228, 231, 307, 312–13, 371.
102. ibid., pp. 224–5.
103. Adams, op. cit., pp. 132–3; F. M. L. Thompson, 'The Second Agricultural Revolution, 1815–50', *Economic History Review*, 2nd series, 1968, vol. XXI, p. 67; E. J. T. Collins, 'The Age of Machinery' in Mingay, ed., *Victorian Countryside*, I, p. 202; Ernle, op. cit., p. 362.
104. Thirsk and Imray, op. cit., pp. 138–40; *Agricultural Gazette*, 1 May 1847 quoted in E. J. T. Collins, 'Harvest Technology and Labour Supply in Britain, 1790–1870', Ph.D. thesis, University of Nottingham, 1970, p. 185.
105. T. Coleman, *The Railway Navvies*, Hutchinson, 1965, p. 25; E. L. Jones, 'The Agricultural

Labour Market in England, 1793–1872', *Economic History Review*, 2nd series, 1964, vol. XVII, pp. 327–8; Collins, thesis, p. 190.

106. Buckinghamshire R.O. D/X 610/1. Papers of the South Bucks. Friendly Society, 1838–66.
107. Gosden, op. cit., pp. 31, 42, 47–8, using data on the counties listed in ch. 1, footnote 78 above; Marshall, 'Nottinghamshire Labourers', p. 73.
108. Public Record Office. MH 32/71. Correspondence of Assistant Commissioner Tufnell dated 1 March 1842. I owe this reference to Dr B. Wojciechowska-Kibble.
109. P.P. 1847, vol. XI. *Select Committee on Settlement and Poor Removal*, 6th Report, *Mins. of Evidence*, p. 95; H. Tanner, 'The Farming of Devonshire', *Journal of the Royal Agricultural Society*, 1848, vol. IX, p. 490; W. Bearn, 'On the Farming of Northamptonshire', ibid., 1852, vol. XIII, p. 89.
110. P.P. 1843, vol. XII. *Women and Children in Agriculture*, pp. 233, 302–6.
111. Huzel, op. cit. (see footnote 50).
112. A. Digby, 'The Labour Market and the Continuity of Social Policy after 1834: the Case of the Eastern Counties', *Economic History Review*, 2nd series, 1975, vol. XXVIII, pp. 71–4; Howell, op. cit., pp. 102–3.
113. Huzel, op. cit. (see footnote 50).
114. Bedfordshire R.O. PUAR 5/2. Application and Report Books, Ampthill Poor Law Union.
115. P. E. Razzell and R. W. Wainwright, eds., *The Victorian Working class: Selections from the Morning Chronicle*, Cass, 1972, p. 11.
116. Glyde, op. cit., pp. 130–1.
117. Hobsbawm and Rudé, op. cit., pp. 285, 288; and for Wiltshire see Billinge, thesis, p. 214.
118. A. Peacock, 'Village Radicalism in East Anglia' in J. P. D. Dunbabin, ed., *Rural Discontent in Nineteenth Century Britain*, Faber and Faber, 1974, pp. 30–2.
119. Case instanced in D. Jones, 'Thomas Campbell Foster and the Rural Labourer: Incendiarism in East Anglia in the 1840s', *Social History*, 1976, vol. I, p. 20.
120. Archer, thesis, p. 163.
121. Glyde, op. cit., p. 185; Jones, 'Thomas Campbell Foster', p. 27.
122. Jones, 'Thomas Campbell Foster', p. 20.
123. ibid., pp. 38–9.
124. J. Caird, *English Agriculture in 1850–1*, 2nd edition, Cass, 1968, p. 518.
125. Jones, 'Thomas Campbell Foster', pp. 38–9.
126. A. Armstrong, *Stability and Change in an English County Town. A Social Study of York, 1801–51*, Cambridge, 1974, p. 106.
127. S. F. Surtees, *Emigrants' Letters from Settlers in Canada and South Australia collected in the Parish of Banham, Norfolk*, Jarrold, London and Norwich, 1852, pp. 3, 4, 7.
128. Account based on material in Wiltshire R.O. W.R.O.9. Severnake Papers. Wiltshire Emigration Association.
129. Calculations based on P.P. 1844, vol. XXVII. *Census of Great Britain, 1841, Occupation Abstract*.
130. E. Robinson and G. Summerfield, eds., *Clare: Selected Poems and Prose*, Oxford, 1966, p. 193.
131. P.P. 1843, vol. XII. *Women and Children in Agriculture*, p. 77.
132. E.g. H. Perkin, *The Origins of Modern English Society, 1780–1880*, Routledge and Kegan Paul, 1969, pp. 183–95.
133. East Suffolk R.O. HA 11/A14/4. Papers re. Strike of Agricultural Labourers in 1874 (includes letter from E. Weekes to Lord Stradbroke dated 10 September, 1853).
134. G. Crewe, *A Word for the Poor*, 1843, quoted in Snell, op. cit., p. 9.
135. Humberside R.O., Beverley. DDGR 43/40. Letter from C. Collyer to T. Grimston of Kilnwick, dated 8 January, 1820; Berkshire R.O. D/ES v (B) F.16. Copy letter from Lambert to T. Stevens dated 28 October 1837.
136. Hobsbawm and Rudé, op. cit., p. 61; Razzell and Wainwright, op. cit., p. 51.
137. W. Cobbett, *Rural Rides*, Everyman edition, 1957, I, p. 152; II, pp. 9, 34, 71.
138. G. E. Evans, *Ask the Fellows who cut the Hay*, Faber and Faber, 1965 edition, p. 101 and see R. Cobbold's novel, *Margaret Catchpole*, first published in 1845; Mrs Cobden Unwin, *The Hungry Forties. Life under the Bread Tax*, Fisher Unwin, 1904, p. 143.

139. Amos, thesis, p. 142.
140. J. A. Venn, *Foundations of Agricultural Economics*, Cambridge, 1923, p. 108.
141. Peacock, *Bread or Blood*, pp. 60, 61.
142. Hobsbawm and Rudé, op. cit., p. 287.
143. E.g. J. D. Gay, *The Geography of Religion in England*, Duckworth, 1971, p. 111; D. M. Thompson, 'The Churches and Society in Nineteenth Century England: a Rural Perspective' in G. J. Cumsing and D. Baker, eds., *Popular Belief and Practice*, Studies in Church History, No. 8, Cambridge, 1972, pp. 269–70; A. M. Everitt, *The Pattern of Rural Dissent: the Nineteenth Century*, Department of English Local History, Occasional Papers, 2nd series, No. 4, Leicester University Press, 1974, pp. 20, 22, 27–30; Mills, op. cit., pp. 125–6.
144. Razzell and Wainwright, op. cit., pp. 288–91.
145. A. D. Gilbert, 'The Land and the Church' in Mingay, ed., *Victorian Countryside*, I, pp. 44–6.
146. These calculations cover the registration districts of Hoo (Kent), Alton, Hartley Wintney (Hants.), Pewsey, Amesbury, Wilton (Wilts.), Biggleswade (Beds.), Rochford (Essex), Royston (Cambs.), and Docking (Norfolk). They are explained more fully in my contribution to G. E. Mingay, ed., *Agrarian History of England*, VI, *1750–1850*, Cambridge, forthcoming.
147. Hobsbawm and Rudé, op. cit., p. 287.

Chapter 4, pp. 88–109

1. Unless otherwise stated, all price data cited in this chapter rest on the Rousseaux index and the Gazette wheat price series given in B. R. Mitchell and P. Deane, *Abstract of British Historical Statistics*, Cambridge, 1962, pp. 471–3, 488–9.
2. J. Oxley Parker, *The Oxley Parker Papers*, Benham, Colchester, 1964, p. 142; A. Briggs, *Victorian People*, Penguin, 1965, p. 30.
3. E. L. Jones, *The Development of English Agriculture 1815–73*, Macmillan, 1968, pp. 19–25.
4. F. M. L. Thompson, *English Landed Society in the Nineteenth Century*, Routledge and Kegan Paul, 1963, pp. 240; idem, 'Free Trade and the Land' in G. E. Mingay, ed., *The Victorian Countryside*, Routlege and Kegan Paul, 1981, I, p. 106.
5. Duke of Bedford, *A Great Agricultural Estate*, 3rd edition, Murray, 1897, pp. 226–7, 283–9.
6. J. R. Bellerby, 'National and Agricultural Income, 1851', *Economic Journal*, 1959, vol. LXIX, p. 103.
7. Thompson, 'Free Trade and Land', p. 106.
8. S. W. Martins, *A Great Estate at Work*, Cambridge, 1980, p. 113 et seq., and see photographs, pp. 148–9; D. W. Howell, *Land and People in Nineteenth Century Wales*, Routledge and Kegan Paul, 1978, p. 34.
9. E. L. Jones, 'The Agricultural Labour Market in England, 1793–1872', *Economic History Review*, 2nd series, 1964, vol. XVII, p. 338; Thompson, 'Free Trade and Land', p. 104.
10. J. Caird, *English Agriculture in 1850–51*, 2nd edition, Cass, 1968, p. 468; J. Archer, 'Rural Protest in Norfolk and Suffolk, 1830–70', Ph.D. thesis, University of East Anglia, 1982, pp. 252, 286; W. L. Burn, *The Age of Equipoise*, Unwin, 1968, pp. 17, 331.
11. R. Samuel, ed., *Village Life and Labour*, History Workshop Series, Routledge and Kegan Paul, 1975; O. R. MacGregor, introduction to Lord Ernle, *English Farming, Past and Present*, 6th edition, Heinemann, 1961, p. cxviii.
12. F. Clifford, 'The Labour Bill in Farming', *Journal of the Royal Agricultural Society*, 2nd series, 1875, vol. XI, p. 117.
13. E. H. Hunt, *Regional Wage Variations in Britain, 1850–1914*, Clarendon, Oxford, 1973, pp. 56–7.
14. Caird, op. cit., pp. 510–14.
15. Using the data given in Hunt, op. cit., pp. 62–3 which relates to earnings including payments in kind.
16. G. H. Wood, 'Real Wages and the Standard of Comfort since 1850', *Journal of the Royal Statistical Society*, 1909, vol. LXXIII, reprinted in E. M. Carus Wilson, ed., *Essays in*

Economic History, III, Edward Arnold 1962. Wood described the provenance of his index in very general terms, and characterized it as 'frankly experimental'.

17. C.G. Spence, *God Speed the Plow*, University of Illinois Press, Urbana, Illinois, 1960, pp. 63, 81, 106, 123–6.
18. E.J.T. Collins, 'The Age of Machinery' in Mingay, ed., *Victorian Countryside*, I, pp. 205, 206; idem, 'Harvest Technology and Labour Supply in Britain, 1790–1870', *Economic History Review*, 2nd series, 1969, vol. XXII, p. 458.
19. Archer, thesis, pp. 228–9; N. Agar, *The Bedfordshire Farm Worker in the Nineteenth Century*, Bedfordshire Historical Record Society, 1981, vol. LX, pp. 107–8.
20. Clifford, op. cit., pp. 72–3; J.C. Morton, *Handbook of Farm Labour*, new edition, Cassell, Petter and Galpin, 1868, p. 70.
21. Note however the recent work of E. A. Wrigley, 'Men on the Land and Men in the Countryside: Employment in Agriculture in Early Nineteenth Century England', in L. Bonfield, R.M. Smith, and K. Wrightson, eds., *The World We Have Gained: Histories of Population and Social Structure*, Blackwell, Oxford, 1986. A careful comparison of successive censuses causes him to conclude that employment in agriculture was only 6 per cent higher in 1851 than in 1821, so that the figure for the latter year looks more like the edge of a plateau than a commanding peak (pp. 304, 329, 322).
22. P.P. 1852–3, vol. LXXXVIII. *Census of Great Britain. Population Tables* II, *Ages, Civil Condition, Occupations and Birth Places*, vol. I, pp. lxxviii–lxxix.
23. In particular, there is uncertainty over whether or not employers included indoor servants in the numbers they claimed to employ, and this may have varied from one district to another. Compare, e.g. J.A. Sheppard, 'East Yorkshire's Agricultural Labour Force in the Mid-Nineteenth Century', *Agricultural History Review*, 1961, vol. IX, pp. 45–6; P.M. Tillott and G.S. Stevenson, *North-West Lindsey in 1851*, University of Sheffield, Department of Extra-Mural Studies, 1970, pp. 6–9; S. Thomas, 'The Agricultural Labour Force in some South-West Carmarthenshire Parishes in the Mid-Nineteenth Century', *Welsh History Review*, 1966, vol. III, pp. 65–7; C. Thomas, 'Rural Society in Nineteenth Century Wales: South Cardiganshire in 1851', *Ceredigion*, 1971, vol. VI, pp. 396–8.
24. P.P. 1873, vol. LXXI. *Census of England and Wales, 1871*, IV, *General Report*, pp. xlvi–xlvii.
25. J.A. Banks, *Prosperity and Parenthood*, Routledge and Kegan Paul, 1954, pp. 81, 85.
26. Wrigley, op. cit., pp. 307, 309; W.S. Shepperson, *British Emigration to North America*, Blackwell, Oxford, 1957, p. 35.
27. Agar, op. cit., p. 173; E. Grey, *Cottage Life in a Hertfordshire Village*, 2nd edition, Harpenden and District Local History Society, Harpenden, 1977, pp. 58–9.
28. J.P.D. Dunbabin, 'The Incidence and Organisation of Agricultural Trades Unionism in the 1870s', *Agricultural History Review*, 1968, vol. XVI, pp. 123–4; Howell, op. cit., p. 94; A. Kussmaul, *Servants in Husbandry in Early Modern England*, Cambridge, 1981, p. 23.
29. S. Caunce, 'East Riding Hiring Fairs', *Oral History*, 1975, vol. III, p. 45; Cumbria R.O. DX 192/28. Extracts from the Journal, Recollections and Experiences of Thomas Irving, pp. 6–16.
30. F.W. Garnett, *Westmorland Agriculture, 1800–1900*, Wilson, Kendal, 1912, p. 95; P. Horn *The Victorian Country Child*, Roundwood Press, Kineton, 1974, p. 83.
31. P. Horn, *Labouring Life in the Victorian Countryside*, Gill and Macmillan, Dublin, 1976, p. 70; D. Hudson, *Munby, Man of Two Worlds*, John Murray, 1972, pp. 287–8.
32. K.D.M. Snell, *Annals of the Labouring Poor. Social Change and Agrarian England, 1660–1900*, Cambridge, 1985, pp. 51, 56, 66, 125.
33. P.P. 1867–8, vol. XVII. *Royal Commission on Employment of Children, Young Persons and Women in Agriculture, First Report*, Appendix, Pt. I, *Repts. of Assistant Commissioners* (Fraser), p. 9; Pt. II, *Mins. of Evidence*, pp. 31, 36, 61, 77; Agar, op. cit., pp. 16–18.
34. R. Samuel, 'Comers and Goers' in H.J. Dyos and P. Wolff, eds., *The Victorian City: Images and Realities*, Routledge and Kegan Paul, 1972, I, pp. 123–53.
35. E.J.T. Collins, 'Harvest Technology and Labour Supply in Britain, 1790–1870', Ph.D. thesis, University of Nottingham, 1970, pp. 87, 92, 114–15, 132; idem, 'Harvest Technology and Labour Supply in Britain, 1790–1870', *Economic History Review*, 2nd series, 1969, vol. XXII,

pp. 468, 470–2, and 'Migrant Labour in British Agriculture in the Nineteenth Century', *Economic History Review*, 2nd series, 1976, vol. XXIX, pp. 48–51.

36. Collins, 'Harvest Technology' (art. cit.), p. 470; M. C. F. Morris, *The British Workman, Past and Present*, Oxford, 1928, p. 80.
37. C. Thomas, 'Seasonality in Agricultural Labour Patterns: Examples from Estates in the Vale of Clwyd', *Publications of the Flintshire Historical Society*, 1974, vol. XXVI, pp. 111–13.
38. Grey, op. cit., pp. 99, 109, 113, 186–8.
39. The comparison thus excludes the 'dregs' of society on the one hand and highly paid skilled workers in the advanced sectors of the economy on the other.
40. J. Burnett, 'Country Diet' in Mingay, ed., *Victorian Countryside*, II, p. 560.
41. T. C. Barker, D. J. Oddy and J. Yudkin, *The Dietary Surveys of Dr Edwin Smith, 1862–3*, Department of Nutrition, Queen Elizabeth College, University of London, Occasional Paper No. 1, Staples Press, 1970, pp. 42–5.
42. Grey, op. cit., p. 27.
43. H. Ratcliffe, *Observations on the Rate of Mortality and Sickness ... calculated from the experience of ... the Manchester Unity of Oddfellows*, Manchester, 1850, p. 50; R. Wall, introduction to the reprint of Ratcliffe in *Mortality in Mid-Nineteenth Century Britain*, Gregg International, Farnborough, 1976 (unpaginated), footnote 44.
44. Grey, op. cit., pp. 31, 33, 35–7.
45. P. Laslett, K. Oosterveen and R. M. Smith, eds., *Bastardy and its Comparative History*, Edward Arnold, 1980, p. 109; Snell, op. cit., pp. 348, 354.
46. Laslett, Oosterveen and Smith, op. cit., p. 30.
47. Anon., 'The Life of a Farm Labourer', *Cornhill Magazine*, 1864, vol. IX, p. 179.
48. *Census of England and Wales, 1911*, vol. XIII. *Fertility of Marriage*, Pt. II, HMSO, 1923, pp. xcii, civ. Note that the source does not cover the ages of bridegrooms, but data from the 1861 census suggests that the mean marriage age in agricultural areas characterized by a high proportion of labourers was 26, i.e., nearly two years younger than in districts where highly 'traditional' small-scale agriculture survived. See M. Anderson, 'Marriage Patterns in Victorian Britain. An Analysis based on Registration District Data for England and Wales, 1861', *Journal of Family History*, 1976, vol. I, p. 65.
49. Garnett, op. cit., p. 95; Grey, op. cit., p. 66.
50. Anon., 'Life of a Farm Labourer', pp. 181–3; Snell, op. cit., pp. 344, 345.
51. A. Digby, 'The Rural Poor', in Mingay, ed., *Victorian Countryside*, II, pp. 598–600.
52. R. Fletcher, ed., *The Biography of a Victorian Village: Richard Cobbold's Account of Wortham, Suffolk, 1860*, Batsford, 1977, pp. 125–7.
53. A. Digby, *Pauper Palaces*, Routledge and Kegan Paul, 1978, pp. 109–13.
54. Cited in G. E. Mingay, *Rural Life in Victorian England*, Futura Publications, 1979, pp. 54–5.
55. Thompson, *Landed Society*, p. 210. Note that the percentages relate only to outlays recorded in estate accounts and would tend to exclude spontaneous acts of charity.
56. E. L. Jones, 'Agricultural Labour Market', p. 331.
57. A. Jessop, *Arcady: For Better for Worse*, Fisher Unwin, 1887, p. 4.
58. M. K. Ashby, *Joseph Ashby of Tysoe, 1859–1919*, Cambridge, 1961, pp. 46, 129; Burn, op. cit., p. 118.
59. See, e.g., E. Chadwick, *Report on the Sanitary Condition of the Labouring Population of Great Britain, 1842*, ed. M. W. Flinn, Edinburgh University Press, 1965, pp. 82–8, 155–9, 190–1, 329–31.
60. W. G. Savage, *Rural Housing*, Fisher Unwin, 1915, p. 19.
61. Caird, op. cit., p. 474; Martins, op. cit., p. 237; B. Kerr, 'Dorset Cottages', *Proceedings of the Dorset Natural History and Archaeological Society*, 1964, vol. LXXXVI, p. 199.
62. Agar, op. cit., pp. 37, 149.
63. Martins, op. cit., pp. 221–4, 235; and see J. H. Clapham, *An Economic History of Modern Britain*, II, *Free Trade and Steel*, Cambridge, 1932, pp. 509–10.
64. Clapham, op. cit., p. 287; Grey, op. cit., pp. 52–4.
65. J. Glyde, *Suffolk in the Nineteenth Century*, Simpkin and Marshall, 1856, pp. 239–30, 236–7,

247–8; J. Grey, 'A View of the Past and Present State of Agriculture in Northumberland', *Journal of the Royal Agricultural Society*, 1841, vol. II, p. 190.

66. R. Sellman, *Devon Village Schools in the Nineteenth Century*, David and Charles, Newton Abbot, 1967, p. 25; F. M. L. Thompson, 'Landowners and the Rural Community' in Mingay, ed., *Victorian Countryside*, II, p. 466.
67. J. Obelkevich, *Religion and Society: South Lindsey 1825–75*, Clarendon Press, Oxford, 1976, p. 79.
68. See, e.g., R. C. Russell, *The Foundation and Maintenance of Schools for the Poor*, Lindsey County Council Education Committee, Lincoln, 1965, pp. 22–35.
69. Martins, op. cit., pp. 194–5; F. M. L. Thompson, 'Landowners and the Rural Community', p. 468.
70. L. M. Springall, *Labouring Life in Norfolk Villages*, Allen and Unwin, 1936, p. 75; R. E. Brown, *The Book of the Landed Estate*, Blackwood, Edinburgh, 1869, pp. 289–90; C. B. Freeman, *Mary Simpson of Boynton Vicarage: Teacher of Ploughboys and Critic of Methodism*, East Yorkshire Local History Series, No. 28, 1972, pp. 13–27.
71. See, e.g., Obelkevich, op. cit., pp. 147–50; B. Bushaway, *By Rite: Custom, Ceremony and Community in England 1700–1880*, Junction Books, 1982, pp. 53–6.
72. Bushaway, op. cit., pp. 265–72; S. F. Surtees, *Banham Harvest Home*, Jarrold, London and Norwich, 1855.
73. P.P. 1867–8, vol. XVII. *R.C. on Children and Women in Agriculture, First Rept.*, Appendix, Pt. I, *Repts. of Assistant Commissioners* (Fraser), p. 44; G. Cresswell, *Norfolk and its Squires, Clergy, Farmers and Labourers*, Simpkin and Marshall, London, 1875, p. 23.
74. C. Phythian-Adams, 'Rural Culture' in Mingay, ed., *Victorian Countryside*, II, pp. 617, 623; and see Obelkevich, op. cit., ch. VI.
75. Obelkevich, op. cit., pp. 195, 202-3, 220–1, 238–9.
76. ibid., pp. 139–41; P.P. 1867–8, vol. XVII. *R.C. on Children and Women in Agriculture. First Rept.*, Appendix, Pt. I, *Repts. of Assistant Commissioners* (Portman), p. 100; and see A. D. Gilbert, 'The Land and the Church', in Mingay, ed., *Victorian Countryside*, I, pp. 50–6.
77. M. A. Havinden, *Estate Villages*, Lund Humphries, 1966, p. 64; W. M. Williams, *A West Country Village: Ashworthy*, Routledge and Kegan Paul, 1963, p. 123; J. Robin, *Elmdon. Continuity and Change in a North-West Essex Village, 1861–1964*, Cambridge, 1980, pp. 25, 76.
78. Snell, op. cit., pp. 123, 334, 336, 337–8.
79. B. Kerr, 'The Dorset Agricultural Labourer, 1750–1850', *Proceedings of the Dorset Natural History and Archaeological Society*, 1962, vol. LXXXIV, pp. 175–6; J. D. Chambers and G. E. Mingay, *The Agricultural Revolution, 1750–1880*, Batsford, 1966, p. 188.
80. A. K. Cairncross, *Home and Foreign Investment, 1870–1914*, Cambridge, 1953, pp. 76, 78; G. B. Longstaff, 'Rural Depopulation', *Journal of the Royal Statistical Society*, 1893, vol. LVI, pp. 385–6.
81. *The Times*, 1 April 1867, letter of William Smith of Woolston; Robin, op. cit., p. 78.
82. Lloyd Jones's editorial in *The Beehive*, January 1872, quoted in R. Groves, *Sharpen the Sickle*, new edition, Merlin Press, 1981, p. 36.
83. P. Horn, *Joseph Arch, 1826–1919. The Farm Workers Leader*, Roundwood Press, Kineton, 1971, p. 18; F. Carlton, '"A Substantial and Sterling Friend to the Labouring Man": the Kent and Sussex Labourers' Union 1872–95', M.Phil. thesis, University of Sussex, 1977, pp. 45–9.
84. Horn, *Joseph Arch*, pp. 19–20, 44–5.
85. Notably in E. Selley, *Village Trade Unions in Two Centuries*, Allen and Unwin, 1919; Groves, op. cit.; and most recently and carefully in Horn, *Joseph Arch*.
86. Horn, *Joseph Arch*, p. 79.
87. W. Hasbach, *History of the English Agricultural Labourer*, P. and S. King, 1908, p. 284; Horn, *Labouring Life*, p. 132.
88. See the exchange of views between D. H. Aldcroft and J. P. D. Dunbabin in *Past and Present*, 1964, No. 27, pp. 109–13 following the publication of Dunbabin, 'The Revolt of the Field: The Agricultural Labourers' Movement in the 1870s', *Past and Present*, 1963, No. 26, pp. 68–97.

Chapter 5, pp. 110–33

1. W. W. Rostow, *British Economy of the Nineteenth Century*, Oxford, 1948, p. 81.
2. Lord Ernle, *English Farming Past and Present*, 5th edition, Longmans, Green, 1936, pp. 379, 383; E. L. Jones, *Seasons and Prices. The Role of the Weather in English Agricultural History*, Allen and Unwin, 1964, pp. 173–7; P. J. Perry, ed., *British Agriculture, 1875–1914*, Methuen, 1973, p. xviii.
3. B. R. Mitchell and P. Deane, *Abstract of British Historical Statistics*, Cambridge, 1962, pp. 489, 496; C. S. Orwin and E. Whetham, *History of British Agriculture, 1846–1914*, Longmans, Green, 1964, pp. 258–9.
4. ibid, pp. 258–60; Perry, op. cit., pp. xiv–xvii.
5. S. W. Martins, *A Great Estate at Work*, Cambridge, 1980, p. 93; Duke of Bedford, *A Great Estate*, 3rd edition, John Murray, 1897, pp. 1–2, 67, 115–23; J. Oxley Parker, *The Oxley Park Papers*, Benham, Colchester, p. 153.
6. Perry, op. cit., pp. xliii, 96–8.
7. T. W. Fletcher, 'The Great Depression of English Agriculture, 1873–96', *Economic History Review*, 2nd series, 1961, vol. XIII, pp. 418–21, 423, 425–30.
8. Perry, op. cit., pp. 131, 133, 141.
9. M. W. Ashby, *Joseph Ashby of Tysoe, 1859–1919*, Cambridge, 1961, p. 146.
10. P. A. Graham, *The Rural Exodus*, Methuen, 1892, p. 113.
11. H. R. Haggard, *Rural England*, 2nd edition, Longmans, Green, 1906, II, p. 99.
12. H. R. Haggard, *A Farmer's Year: Being his Common Place Book for 1898*, Longmans, Green, 1906, p. 223.
13. E. J. T. Collins, 'The Age of Machinery' in G. E. Mingay, ed., *The Victorian Countryside*, Routledge and Kegan Paul, 1981, I, p. 204; B. Kerr, *Bound to the Soil. A Social History of Dorset*, John Baker, 1968, p. 242; J. Ashby and B. King, 'Statistics of some Midland Villages', *Economic Journal*, 1893, vol. III, p. 6; C. G. Spence, *God Speed the Plow. The Coming of Steam Cultivation to Great Britain*, University of Illinois Press, Urbana, Illinois, 1960, p. 165.
14. G. E. and F. R. Fussell, *Farming Techniques from Prehistoric to Modern Times*, Oxford, 1966, pp. 198–9; and see the discussion in D. H. Morgan, *Harvesters and Harvesting, 1840–1900*, Croom Helm, 1982, pp. 20–1.
15. J. D. Dent, 'The Present Position of the Agricultural Labourer', *Journal of the Royal Agricultural Society*, 1871, 2nd series, vol. VII, p. 348.
16. Museum of English Rural Life, Reading University. D71/8. Reminiscences of Charles Slater, II, p. 46.
17. J. C. Morton, *The Labour on the Farm*, new edition, Broadbury Agnew, 1887, p. 75.
18. R. Jefferies, *Hodge and his Masters*, Smith Elder, 1880, II, p. 115; Morton, op. cit., p. 108; P.P. 1893–4 (C.6894–VI), vol. XXXV. *Royal Commission on Labour*. Rept. of E. Wilkinson on Derbys., Lincs., Staffs., Yorks., p. 9.
19. D. J. Davies, 'The Condition of the Rural Population in England and Wales, 1870–1928', Ph.D. thesis, University of Wales, 1931, p. 51.
20. Based on tables in Orwin and Whetham, op. cit., pp. 251, 252, 267, 268.
21. F. D. W. Taylor, 'United Kingdom: Numbers in Agriculture', *Farm Economist*, 1955, vol. VIII, p. 38, using his category 'Contract Workers on Farms'.
22. ibid.; and see R. Lawton, 'Rural Depopulation in Nineteenth Century England' in D. Mills, ed., *English Rural Communities: the Impact of a Specialized Economy*, Macmillan, 1973, pp. 210–11.
23. Graham, op. cit., p. 9.
24. T. Hardy, 'The Dorsetshire Labourer', *Longman's Magazine*, 1883, quoted in H. Orel, ed., *Thomas Hardy: Personal Writings*, Macmillan, 1967, p. 188; Ashby, op. cit., p. 161.
25. R. Heath, *The English Peasant*, Fisher Unwin, 1893, p. 91.
26. Haggard, *Farmer's Year*, p. 460.
27. F. Thompson, *Lark Rise to Candleford*, World's Classics edition, Oxford, 1954, p. 163; D. C. Pedder, 'Service and Farm Service', *Contemporary Review*, 1903, vol. LXXXIII, pp. 271–3.
28. Haggard, *Farmer's Year*, pp. 75–6.

29. A. Jessop, *Arcady: for Better for Worse*, Fisher Unwin, 1887, p. 117.
30. P.P. 1893–4 (C.6894–IV), vol. XXXV. *R.C. on Labour*. Rept. of R. C. Richards on Cheshire, Derbys., Gloucs., Herefs., Mon., Northants., Warwicks., p. 109; P.P. 1884–5 (C.4402–I), vol. XXV. *Royal Commission on the Housing of the Working Classes*, II, *Mins. of Evidence*, p. 449.
31. P.P. 1906 (C.3273), vol. XCVI. Board of Agriculture and Fisheries, *Report on the Decline in the Agricultural Population of Great Britain, 1881–1906*, p. 31; P.P. 1893–4 (C. 6894–I), vol. XXXV. *R.C. on Labour*. Rept. of W. E. Bear on Beds., Hants., Hunts., Leics., Notts., Sussex, p. 114.
32. P.P. 1893–4 (C.6894–XIV), vol. XXXVI. *R.C. on Labour*. Rept. of D. L. Thomas on Wales, p. 8.
33. ibid., p. 9; Haggard, *Farmer's Year*, p. 75; N. Agar, *The Bedfordshire Farm Worker in the Nineteenth Century*, Bedfordshire Historical Record Society, 1981, vol. LX, p. 28.
34. Mitchell and Deane, op. cit., pp. 20–2, 24–5; D. Sherry, 'Socio-economic Changes in some Dorset Villages 1871–1974 with reference to Rural Planning', Ph.D. thesis, Unviersity of Manchester, 1975, pp. 11, 14.
35. D. Baines, *Migration in a Mature Economy. Emigration and Internal Migration in England and Wales, 1861–1900*, Cambridge 1985, pp. 78, 192. For the loss of the *Cospatrick* see R. Arnold, *The Farthest Promised Land. English Villagers, New Zealand Immigrants of the 1870s*, Victoria University Press, Wellington, New Zealand, 1981, pp. 131–2.
36. P. Horn, *Joseph Arch, 1826–1919. The Farm Workers' Leader*, Roundwood Press, Kineton, 1971, pp. 88, 91–8; Arnold, op. cit., pp. 79–91.
37. ibid., p. 70; Agar, op. cit., p. 198.
38. Arnold, op. cit., p. 348.
39. Baines, op. cit., pp. 63, 76, 77, 78, 117, 192.
40. E.g. Jessop, op. cit., pp. 111–12, who opined in the mid-1880s that emigration from Norfolk was much less in fashion, instancing the suspicions of one labourer: 'They none of 'em comes back. They writes for a time and then we never hear no more ... Fares as if they mos' of 'em goes up country, and they tell me as when they've got 'em they has to work till they drops, and they kangarous eats 'em'.
41. Baines, op. cit., pp. 194, 205; and see A. K. *Cairncross, Home and Foreign Investment*, Cambridge, 1953, p. 75.
42. Baines, op. cit., p. 238. See table 8.9.
43. See, e.g., A Wykehamist, *The Agricultural Labourer* (reprint from *Fraser's Magazine*, 1873), p. 108.
44. Agar, op. cit., p. 140.
45. R. Arnold, 'English Rural Unionism and the Taranaki Immigration, 1871–6', *New Zealand Journal of History*, 1972, vol. VI, p. 36; M. A. Havinden, *Estate Villages*, Lund Humphries 1966, p. 119.
46. Norfolk R.O. WLS/40/34. Letter from E. Levy to Lord Walsingham dated 21 May 1873.
47. Arnold, *Farthest Promised Land*, pp. 159–60, 161–2.
48. Suffolk R.O. HA 11/A14/4. Letter from Carus-Wilson to Lady Stradbroke, dated 4 April 1874; G. C. Brodrick, *English Land and English Landlords*, Cassell, Petter and Galpin, 1881, p. 225; P.P. 1893–4 (C.6894–I), vol. XXXV. *R.C. on Labour*. Rept of W. E. Bear, pp. 92, 149.
49. Jessop, op. cit., p. 106; Little's view is quoted in A. Wilson Fox, 'Agricultural Wages in England during the Last Half Century', *Journal of the Royal Statistical Society*, 1903, vol. LXVI, reprinted in W. E. Minchinton, ed., *Essays in Agrarian History*, David and Charles, Newton Abbot, 1968, II. See p. 166.
50. F. Clifford, 'The Labour Bill in Farming', *Journal of the Royal Agricultural Society*, 2nd series, 1875, vol. XI, pp. 97–8.
51. Jefferies, op. cit., II, p. 78; Thompson, op. cit., p. 46.
52. H. Aronson, *The Land and the Labourer*, Melrose, 1914, p. 63, quoting evidence to the *Select Committee on the Housing of the Working Classes Amendment Bill*, 1906.
53. E.H. Hunt, 'Labour Productivity in English Agriculture, 1850–1914', *Economic History Review*, 2nd series, 1967, vol. XX, p. 286.

54. See D. Metcalf, 'Labour Productivity in English Agriculture 1850–1914', *Economic History Review*, 2nd series, 1969, vol. XXII, p. 118, and P. A. David, 'Labour Productivity in English Agriculture, 1850–1914: Some Quantitative Evidence on Regional Differences', *Economic History Review*, 2nd series, 1970, vol. XXIII, pp. 504–5.
55. P.P. 1893–4 (C.6894–XXV), vol. XXXVII–Pt. II. *R.C. on Labour*. General Rept. of W.C. Little, pp. 33–4; W. Hasbach, *A History of the English Agricultural Labourer*, P. and S. King, London, 1908, p. 341.
56. P.P. 1895 (C.7684–I), vol. XIV. *Royal Commission on Aged Poor, Mins. of Evidence*, p. 239; P.P. 1893–4 (C.6894–VI), vol. XXXV. *R.C. on Labour*. Rept. of E. Wilkinson, p. 68.
57. Wilson Fox, in Minchinton, op. cit., pp. 173–80.
58. Clifford, op. cit., p. 120; P. Horn, *Labouring Life in the Victorian Countryside*, Gill and Macmillan, Dublin, 1976, pp. 207–8.
59. D.W. Howell, *Land and People in Nineteenth Century Wales*, Routledge and Kegan Paul, 1978, p. 101; Wilson Fox in Minchinton, op. cit., p. 139.
60. Museum of English Rural Life, Reading University. Slater Reminiscences, II, p. 45.
61. Clifford, op. cit., p. 84. Such increases were general in East Anglia according to Jessop, op. cit., pp. 243–4. See also D.H. Morgan, op. cit., pp. 94, 102.
62. P.P. 1882 (C.3309–I), vol. XIV. *Royal Commission on Agriculture*, III, *Mins. of Evidence*, p. 40; P.P. 1893–4 (C.6894–II), vol. XXXV. *R.C. on Labour*. Rept. of C.M. Chapman on Berks., Bucks., Cambs., Cornwall, Devon, Hants., Oxon., Shropshire, p. 45.
63. Wilson Fox, in Minchinton, op. cit., p. 140.
64. Clifford, op. cit., p. 121.
65. P.P. 1893–4 (C.6894–V), vol. XXXV. *R.C. on Labour*. Rept. of A.J. Spencer on Dorset, Essex, Kent, Somerset, Surrey, Wilts., Worcs., p. 76.
66. I have departed from the Bowley index relied on in chs. 3 and 4 because the material tabulated in tables 5.2 and 5.3 is better suited to the purpose in hand.
67. P.P. 1893–4 (C.6894–XXV), vol. XXXVII–Pt. II. *R.C. on Labour*. Rept. of W.C. Little, pp. 58, 84; Wilson Fox, in Minchinton, op. cit., p. 138, supported the view that earnings were ordinarily 18–20 per cent higher than weekly wages.
68. The same impression is given by Bowley's index given in Mitchell and Deane, op. cit., pp. 348–50, the relevant averages for England and Wales being 93.4 (1866–70), 115.3 (1871–7) and 98.4 (1892–6).
69. ibid., pp. 343–4, 348–50. Wood's index of retail prices registers a fall from 122 (1873) to 83 (1896), while the wage index moves from 117 to 98 over these years.
70. J. Burnett, *Plenty and Want. A Social History of Diet in England from 1815 to the Present Day*, Nelson, 1966, p. 129; K. Stephens, *Book of the Farm*, 4th edition, Blackwood, Edinburgh, 1891, III, p. 500.
71. P.P. 1893–4 (C.6894–II), vol. XXXV. *R.C. on Labour*. Rept. of C.M. Chapman, p. 45.
72. ibid., pp. 57, 83.
73. ibid., p. 45; P.J. Perry, 'Working Class Isolation and Mobility in Rural Dorset, 1837–1936: a Study of Marriage Distances', *Transactions of the Institute of British Geographers*, 1969, vol. XXXXVI, pp. 125, 131–4.
74. P.P. 1893–4 (C.6894–II), vol. XXXV. *R.C. on Labour*. Rept. of C.M. Chapman, p. 45; R. Heath, *English Peasant*, p. 215; E. Grey, *Cottage Life in a Hertfordshire Village*, new edition, Harpenden and District Local History Society, Harpenden, 1977, pp. 232–3; Jessop, op. cit., p. 18.
75. Ashby op. cit., p. 147.
76. Ashby and King, op. cit., p. 208; W.E. Bear, 'The Farm Labourers of England and Wales', *Journal of the Royal Agricultural Society*, 3rd series, 1893, vol. IV, p. 676; Agar, op. cit., p. 45.
77. P.P. 1893–4 (C.6994–XXV), vol. XXXVII–Pt. II. *R.C. on Labour*. Rept. of W.C. Little, p. 92.
78. B. Weber's data, in J. Parry Lewis, *Building Cycles and Britain's Growth*, Macmillan, 1965, pp. 331–2.

79. J.C. Thresh, *The Housing of the Labouring Classes in the Chelmsford and Maldon Rural Sanitary Districts*, Chelmsford and Maldon Sanitary Authorities, Chelmsford, 1891, pp. 3, 4, 8–9, 21–2.
80. Jessop, op. cit., p. 22.
81. Martins, op. cit., p. 242; K. Jackson, 'Housing Standards of the English Working Classes, 1837–1914', Ph.D. thesis, University of Kent, 1978, p. 79.
82. P.P. 1893–4 (C.6894–VI), vol. XXXV. *R.C. on Labour*. Rept. of E. Wilkinson, p. 112.
83. D. Bythell, *The Sweated Trades. Outwork in Nineteenth Century Britain*, Batsford, 1978, pp. 118, 147; P. Horn, 'Worker's Cottage Industries' in Mingay, ed., *Victorian Countryside*, I, p. 348; G.F.R. Spenceley, 'The English Pillow Lace Industry 1840–80: A Rural Industry in Competition with Machinery', *Business History*, 1977, vol. XIX, pp. 69, 79, 82.
84. Agar, op. cit., p. 31.
85. Taylor, op. cit., p. 38; Thompson, op. cit., p. 49; Jessop, op. cit., p. 18; P.P. 1893–4 (C.6894–III), vol. XXXV. *R.C. on Labour*. Rept. of A. Wilson Fox, on Cumberland, Lancs., Norfolk, Northumberland, Suffolk, p. 104.
86. E. Hostettler, 'Gourlay Steel and the Sexual Division of Labour', *History Workshop*, 1977, No. 4, pp. 95–100.
87. P.P. 1893–4 (C.6894–XIV), vol. XXXVI. *R.C. on Labour*. Rept. of D.L. Thomas, p. 11.
88. T.M. Devine, ed., *Farm Servants and Labour in Lowland Scotland, 1770–1914*, John Donald, Edinburgh, 1984, pp. 113–14, 119–20.
89. P.P. 1893–4 (C.6894–II), vol. XXXVI. *R.C. on Labour*. Rept. of C.M. Chapman, p. 16.
90. C. Miller, 'The Hidden Workforce: Female Fieldworkers in Gloucestershire, 1870–1901', *Southern History*, 1984, vol. VI, pp. 143, 145, 148.
91. R. Heath, *English Peasant*, pp. 113–14.
92. Warwickshire R.O. C 114 A/765. Correspondence re. Agricultural Children's Act. Letter from James Taplin to the Marquess of Hertford dated 6 January 1876.
93. P. Horn, *The Victorian Country Child*, Roundwood Press, Kineton, 1974, pp. 52, 64.
94. Morgan, op. cit., p. 72; Horn, *Victorian Country Child*, p. 64.
95. Graham, op. cit., p. 73.
96. B.J. Davey, *Ashwell, 1830–1914. The Decline of a Village Community*. Department of English Local History, Leicester University, Occasional Papers, 3rd series, No. 5, Leicester University Press, 1980, p. 49. The proportion of English and Welsh brides and bridegrooms signing the marriage registers with marks was reduced to 3 per cent by 1900, according to the tables in C.M. Cipolla, *Literacy and Education in the West*, Penguin, 1969, pp. 121–5.
97. J.P.D. Dunbabin, 'The Incidence and Organization of Agricultural Trades Unionism in the 1870s', *Agricultural History Review*, 1968, vol. XVI, p. 117, who, however, thinks the true membership of NALU to have been 10 per cent lower than the figure claimed.
98. ibid., p. 122.
99. R.F. Wearmouth, *Some Working Class Movements of the Nineteenth Century*, Epworth Press, 1949, pp. 317–20; E.J. Hobsbawm, *Primitive Rebels*, Manchester University Press, 1959, pp. 137–9; N. Scotland, *Methodism and the Revolt of the Field. A Study of the Methodist Contribution to Agricultural Trade Unionism in East Anglia, 1872–96*, Alan Sutton, Gloucester, 1981, pp. 58, 83.
100. H. Gurden, 'Trade Unionism, Education and Religion: Aspects of the Social History of Warwickshire Agricultural Labourers in the 1870s', M.Phil. thesis, University of Warwick, 1975, pp. 55–7.
101. The following account is based mainly on R. Groves, *Sharpen the Sickle*, new edition, Merlin Press, 1981, Pt. I, ch. IV and Horn, *Joseph Arch*, pp. 102–9.
102. The controversy aroused by the Bishop may be followed in *The Times* newspaper and his correspondence with the Countess of Stradbroke (Suffolk R.O. HA 11/A 14/4. Papers re. Strike of Agricultural Labourers in 1874).
103. Suffolk R.O. 9. S9. J. Glyde, *The Autobiography of a Suffolk Farm Labourer*, pp. 56–7. (Xerox of newspaper cuttings from the *Suffolk Mercury*, 1894).
104. Groves, op. cit., p. 78; Horn, *Joseph Arch*, p. 109.
105. ibid., p. 108; Dunbabin, 'Incidence and Organization', p. 133.

106. ibid., p. 118; Groves, op. cit., Pt. II, ch. V.
107. Horn, *Joseph Arch*, p. 137.
108. ibid, pp. 114–17; Groves, op. cit., pp. 80, 82.
109. A. Howkins, *Poor Labouring Men. Rural Radicalism in Norfolk, 1870–1923*, History Workshop Series, Routledge and Kegan Paul, 1985, pp. 71–4.
110. E. Selley, *Village Trade Unions in Two Centuries*, Allen and Unwin, 1919, p. 75; Groves, op. cit., pp. 82–3.
111. Glyde, op. cit., p. 58; Selley, op. cit., p. 88; Horn, *Joseph Arch*, p. 72.
112. Howkins, op. cit., pp. 69, 71; Arnold, *Farthest Promised Land*, pp. 196–7.
113. Suffolk R.O. HA 11/A14/4. Copy letter from Stradbroke to S. Morley dated 16 May 1874; Glyde, op. cit., p. 56; Agar, op. cit., p. 179.
114. See *The Life and Experience of a Warwickshire Labourer with his own Thoughts and Opinions on the Strike, as told by Himself*, Routledge, 1872, pp. 21–6, which according to Gurden, thesis, p. 94, needs to be viewed with caution, since the publishers have no record of it and it was distributed from the office of the *Leamington Courier*, a Tory paper.
115. E.g. *Farmer and Labourer. A Letter from Mr Mark Phillips upon the Agricultural Labour Question* (Extracts from the *Leamington Courier*, 4 April 1872, in Suffolk R.O. HA 11/A 14/4. Papers re. Strike of Agricultural Labourers); *A Farmer's Views on the Agricultural Labour Question, by One of Them*, Norwich, 1873, pp. 5, 13–14.
116. Arnold, op. cit., pp. 200–1, 206; Agar, op. cit., p. 179.
117. Dunbabin, 'Incidence and Organization', p. 133.
118. R. C. Russell, *The Revolt of the Field in Lincolnshire: The Origins and Early History of Farm Workers' Trade Unions*, Lincolnshire County Committee of the NUAW, Louth, 1956, pp. 112, 124–5.
119. Norfolk R.O. WLS LXVIII/40/16. Newspaper cutting from the *Norwich Mercury*, 8 March 1873. Letter from the Rector of Brandiston.
120. J. A. Venn, *Foundations of Agricultural Economics*, Cambridge, 1923, p. 207.
121. D. Read, *England 1868–1914. The Age of Urban Democracy*, Longman, 1979, pp. 309–10.
122. Horn, *Joseph Arch*, pp. 170–1; H. Pelling, *Social Geography of British Elections, 1885–1910*, Macmillan, 1967, pp. 97–8.
123. See J. Collings, *Land Reform. Occupying Ownership, Peasant Proprietary and Rural Education*, 3rd edition, Longmans, Green, 1908, pp. 176, 179.
124. E.g. Jefferies, *Hodge*, II, p. 230; Brodrick, op. cit., pp. 236, 439–40; Graham, op. cit., pp. 137–8, 140–1.
125. Hasbach, op. cit., p. 316.
126. ibid.; and see J. Frome Wilkinson, 'Pages in the History of Allotments', *Contemporary Review*, 1894, vol. LXV p. 534 who, however, thought that progress was far too slow.
127. Collings, op. cit., pp. 212–13, who discusses at length the most successful experiment at Catshill, Worcs.
128. Graham, op. cit., p. 114; Jessop, op. cit., p. xvii; P.P. 1893–4 (C.6894–VI), vol. XXXV. *R.C. on Labour*. Rept. of E. Wilkinson, p. 29.
129. J. G. O'Leary, ed., *The Autobiography of Joseph Arch*, MacGibbon and Kee, 1966, p. 138; Ashby, op. cit., p. 114.
130. Jessop, op. cit., p. xviii; Museum of English Rural Life, Reading University. Slater Reminiscences, II, p. 11.
131. P. Horn, 'Rural Unionism in the 1890s: The Berkshire Agricultural and General Workers Union', *Local Historian*, 1979, vol. XIII, p. 354.
132. Russell, op. cit., pp. 152, 154; J. A. Mollett, 'An Economic Study of the Supply of Agricultural Labour in Buckinghamshire', M.Sc. thesis, University of Reading, 1949, p. 161.
133. Horn, 'Rural Unionism', pp. 355, 357; Selley, op. cit., p. 77; P. Horn, 'The Warwickshire Agricultural and General Workers Union, 1893–7', *Midland History*, 1972, vol. I, pp. 27, 30.
134. F. Carlton, '"A Substantial and Sterling Friend to the Working Man": The Kent and Sussex Labourers' Union, 1872–95', M.Phil. thesis, University of Sussex, 1977, p. 135; O. J. Dunlop. *The Farm Labourer: The History of a Modern Problem*, Fisher Unwin, 1913, pp. 170–2; Horn, *Joseph Arch*, p. 195.

135. Norfolk R.O. WLS LXVIII/40/46. Agricultural Union Agitation in Norfolk. Press-cutting from *The Argus*, Norwich, 22 November 1890; WLS LXVIII/40. Letter from W. Herring to Lord Walsingham, 24 January 1891.
136. Mollett, thesis, p. 161.
137. Horn, *Joseph Arch*, pp. 205–6; G. Edwards, *From Crow-Scaring to Westminster*, Labour Publishing Co., 1922, pp. 90, 93.
138. Dunlop, op. cit., p. 187.
139. Jessop, op. cit., pp. 4, 18, 241.
140. E.g. C.S. Orwin, 'A Century of Wages and Earnings in Agriculture', *Journal of the Royal Agricultural Society*, 1931, vol. XCII, p. 244, qualifies the advance of real wages in this way. The argument is taken to extremes in Davey, op. cit., p. 53.
141. Arnold, *Farthest Promised Land*, p. 141; Martins, op. cit., p. 28, citing H. Overman's evidence to the *Royal Commission on Agriculture*, 1881.
142. Ashby, op. cit., p. 146.

Chapter 6, pp. 134–55

1. W.E. Bear, 'The Farm Labourers of England and Wales', *Journal of the Royal Agricultural Society*, 3rd series, 1893, vol. IV, p. 677.
2. B.R. Mitchell and P. Deane, *Abstract of British Historical Statistics*, Cambridge, 1962, pp. 472–3; R. Lennard, *Economic Notes on English Agricultural Wages*, Macmillan, 1914, p. 52.
3. C.S. Orwin and P. Whetham, *History of British Agriculture, 1846–1914*, Longmans, Green, 1964, pp. 347, 350, 356, 374; A.R. Hall, *A Pilgrimage of British Farming, 1910–12*, John Murray, 1912, p. 431; R.E. Prothero (Lord Ernle), *English Farming, Past and Present*, Longmans, Green, 1912, p. 382.
4. F.M.L. Thompson, *English Landed Society in the Nineteenth Century*, Routledge and Kegan Paul, 1963, pp. 317, 320–2. For a more detailed account of Liberal policies in relation to the land see A. Offer, *Property and Politics, 1870–1914*, Cambridge, 1981, chs. 19–22.
5. M. Girouard, *Life in the English Country House*, Penguin, 1980, p. 298.
6. A.L. Bowley, 'Rural Population in England and Wales: a study of the Changes of Density, Occupations and Ages', *Journal of the Royal Statistical Society*, 1914, vol. LXXXVII, p. 618.
7. P.P. 1910 (Cd. 5068), vol. XLIX. *Royal Commission on the Poor Laws*. Appendix J, p. 729; H. Rider Haggard, *Rural England*, 2nd edition, Longmans, Green, 1906, I, pp. 268–9, 427 and II, pp. 565–6.
8. Haggard, op. cit., I, p. 206; P.P. 1906 (Cd. 3273), vol. XCVI. Board of Agriculture and Fisheries, *Report on the Decline in the Rural Population of Great Britain, 1881–1906*, p. 34.
9. H. Aronson, *The Land and the Labourer*, Melrose, 1914, p. 19; E.N. Bennett, *Problems of Village Life*, Williams and Norgate, n.d., p. 93; Board of Agriculture and Fisheries, *Report on Migration from Rural Districts in England and Wales*, HMSO, 1913, pp. 10, 19, 22, 25.
10. Haggard op. cit., II, pp. 285–7; F. Kitchen, *Brother to the Ox*, Dent, 1940, pp. 45, 49, 71; H. Reffold, *Pie for Breakfast*, Hutton Press, Beverley, 1984, pp. 104–5.
11. Lennard, op. cit., p. 42.
12. Haggard, op. cit., II, pp. 443, 449, 467.
13. Bowley, op. cit., p. 616.
14. Lennard, op. cit., pp. 63–4, 86, 95, 109; Hall, op. cit., p. 153.
15. E.H. Hunt, *Regional Wage Variations in Britain, 1850–1914*, Oxford, 1973, p. 60. For food consumption see J. Burnett, 'Country Diet' in G.E. Mingay, ed., *The Victorian Countryside*, Routledge and Kegan Paul, 1981, II, pp. 563–4.
16. F.E. Green, *The Tyranny of the Countryside*, Fisher Unwin, 1913, pp. 249–50; Bennett, op. cit., p. 160.
17. A. Wilson Fox, 'Agricultural Wages in England and Wales during the last Fifty Years', *Journal of the Royal Statistical Society*, 1903, vol. LXVI, reprinted in W.E. Minchinton, ed., *Essays in Agrarian History*, David and Charles, 1968, II, p. 182; *The Land. The Report of the Land Enquiry Committee*, I, *Rural*, Hodder and Stoughton, 1913, p. 9.

18. Mitchell and Deane, op. cit., p. 478.
19. *The Land*, pp. 10–12.
20. E.g. D. H. Morgan, *Harvesters and Harvesting, 1840–1900. A Study of the Rural Proletariat*, Croom Helm, 1982, pp. 118, 187.
21. The cost of living indexes quoted in *The Land*, p. 11 and those cited in Mitchell and Deane (see footnote 18) are founded largely on London prices. No satisfactory cost of living series based on rural retail prices weighted to suit the farmworker's pattern of expenditure is available. If it were, it is possible that price trends as distinct from levels would be similar, though this was strongly contested in Land Agents' Society, *Facts about the Land*, John Murray, 1916, pp. 17–24, a publication which was likewise critical of the wage and earnings data used in *The Land*. On balance, the conclusion of J. H. Clapham, *An Economic History of Modern Britain*, III, *Machines and National Rivalries, 1887–1914*, Cambridge, 1938, p. 100, that 'there was a certain stagnation in rural well-being after the sharp upward motion of the late Victorian age' seems amply justified.
22. G. Sturt, *The Bettesworth Book*, 2nd edition, Caliban, Firle, 1978, p. 295; idem, *Lucy Bettesworth*, 2nd edition, Caliban, Firle, 1978, p. 85; E. Grey, *Cottage Life in a Hertfordshire Village*, Harpenden Local History Society, Harpenden, 1977, p. 231. And see M. S. Gretton, *A Corner of the Cotswolds through the Nineteenth Century*, Methuen, 1914, p. 209 – although the labourer's condition had improved it was 'not better relative to his increased needs and desires'.
23. J. R. Bellerby, 'The Distribution of Farm Income in the United Kingdom, 1867–1938', *Journal of Proceedings of the Agricultural Economics Society*, 1953, vol. X, p. 135.
24. P. H. Mann, 'Life in an Agricultural Village in England', *Sociological Review*, 1904, vol. I, esp. pp. 176, 184–5, 188, 192. For York see B. S. Rowntree, *Poverty. A Study of Town Life*, 2nd edition, Macmillan, 1902, pp. 111, 117.
25. M. F. Davies, *Life in an English Village*, Fisher Unwin, 1910, esp. pp. 146–7, 285–7.
26. B. S. Rowntree and M. Kendall, *How the Labourer Lives*, Nelson, 1913, esp. pp. 31, 38, 45, 61, 75, 123, 201, 224, 257, 303–4 and table facing p. 36. E. M. Martin, *The Shearers and the Shorn*, Routledge and Kegan Paul, 1965, pp. 91–5, has some useful material on the extension of credit by village shopkeepers in Devonshire.
27. Lennard, op. cit., p. 91.
28. B. S. Rowntree, *The Human Needs of Labour*, new edition, Longmans, Green, 1937, pp. 71–2, himself suggested a standard of 3,400 calories and 100 gms. of protein as against 3,500 and 125 respectively in 1899, for men on moderate work.
29. Gretton, op. cit., p. 208.
30. P. Horn, *The Victorian Country Child*, Roundwood Press, Kineton, 1974, pp. 178–9.
31. A. Newsholme, *The Elements of Vital Statistics*, new edition, Allen and Unwin 1923, p. 318; P.P. 1912–13 (Cd. 6578) vol. XII. *Registrar-General of Births, Deaths and Marriages, 74th Annual Report* (for 1911), pp. xli, xliii, 73–87.
32. C. Holdenby, *Folk of the Furrow*, Smith Elder, 1913, p. 150.
33. P.P. 1919 (Cmd. 24), vol. IX. Board of Agriculture and Fisheries, *Wages and Conditions of Employment in Agriculture*, I, *General Report*, p. 64.
34. C. Booth. *The Aged Poor in England and Wales. Condition*, Macmillan, 1894, pp. 321, 339, 348, 506.
35. P. A. Graham, *The Rural Exodus*, Methuen, 1892, p. 184; Museum of English Rural Life, Reading University. D71/8. Reminiscences of Charles Slater, II, pp. 77–8.
36. E.g. Davies, op. cit., p. 189; A. Williams, *A Wiltshire Village*, Duckworth, 1912, p. 87.
37. G. Sturt, *Memorials of a Surrey Labourer*, 2nd edition, Caliban, Firle, 1978, pp. 212–13, 246, 255–6, 259.
38. F. Thompson, *Lark Rise to Candleford*, World's Classics edition, Oxford, 1954, p. 94; H. Aronson, 'Liberalism in the Village', *Nation*, 18 May 1912, quoted in B. B. Gilbert, *The Evolution of National Insurance in Great Britain*, Michael Joseph, 1966, pp. 226–7.
39. G. C. Cuttle, *The Legacy of the Rural Guardians*, Heffer, Cambridge, 1934, pp. 57–8.
40. On gleaning see Morgan, op. cit., pp. 151–7 and A. Randell, *Fenland Memories*, Routledge and Kegan Paul, 1969, p. 15.

41. D. W. Howell, *Land and People in Nineteenth Century Wales*, Routledge and Kegan Paul, 1978, p. 94; Hall, op. cit., pp. 249, 256.
42. A. Tweedy, 'Recollections of a Farm Worker', *Bulletin of the Cleveland and Teesside Local History Society*, 1973, No. 21, p. 6; R. Blythe, *Akenfield*, Penguin, 1972, pp. 40–1.
43. Kitchen, op. cit., p. 98; S. Caunce, 'East Riding Hiring Fairs', *Oral History*, 1975, vol. II, pp. 46–50.
44. A. Howkins, 'In the Sweat of thy Face: the Labourer and Work', in Mingay, ed., *Victorian Countryside*, II, pp. 506–8; F. G. Heath, *British Rural Life and Labour*, P. and S. King, 1911, pp. 2–8; P.P. 1919 (Cmd. 24), vol. IX. *Wages and Conditions in Agriculture*, I, p. 65.
45. Hall, op. cit., p. 114; W. R. Mitchell, 'The Irish Connection', *The Dalesman*, 1984, vol. XXXXV, pp. 1,001–5.
46. W. Page ed., *Victoria History of the County of Kent*, I, Constable, 1908, p. 466; M. Lewis, ed., *Old Days in the Kent Hop Gardens*, West Kent Federation of Women's Institutes, Maidstone, 1981, pp. 29, 32, 33, 35, 39, 40, 48, 49. However, the most thorough academic discussion of hop-picking may be found in C. Baker, 'Home-Dwellers and Foreigners: the Seasonal Labour Force in Kentish Agriculture', M.Phil. thesis, University of Kent, 1979.
47. G. E. Evans, *Where Beards Wag All*, Faber and Faber, 1970, pp. 246–76, 283–7, deals with this subject in detail.
48. ibid., pp. 117–25, esp. 77, 121, 123, 124, 203, 209. For Lord Ongley see G. Darley, *Villages of Vision*, Architectural Press, 1975, p. 32.
49. M. A. Havinden, *Estate Villages*, Lund Humphries, 1966, pp. 113–15.
50. Cf. A. Briggs, *Victorian Cities*, Odhams, 1963, p. 32.
51. *Census of Great Britain, 1911, General Report*, quoted in J. Saville, *Rural Depopulation in England and Wales, 1851–1951*, Routledge and Kegan Paul, 1957, pp. 62–3.
52. W. G. Savage, *Rural Housing*, Fisher Unwin, 1915, pp. 113, 129; *The Land*, pp. 110–11.
53. *The Land*, p. 132.
54. J. C. Thresh, *Housing of the Agricultural Labourer with special reference to the County of Essex*, Rural Housing and Sanitation Association, Adelphi, 1919, p. 73; Sturt, *Lucy Bettesworth*, p. 264; idem, *Change in the Village*, Readers Library edition, 1920, p. 6; Hall, op. cit., pp. 33–4; W. W. Crotch, *The Cottage Homes of England*, 3rd edition, Industrial Publishing Co., 1908, pp. 40–4.
55. Savage, op. cit., pp. 153–4; Land Agents' Society, *Facts about the Land*, John Murray, 1916, pp. 81–3.
56. See, e.g. A. Jessop, *Arcady: For Better for Worse*, Fisher Unwin, 1887, pp. 112, 233, 234; Graham, op. cit., pp. 69–70, 104; Williams, op. cit., pp. 233–4.
57. Williams, op. cit., p. 234; T. E. Kebbel, *The Agricultural Labourer*, new edition, Swann Sonenschein, 1907, pp. 134–5.
58. Horn, *Victorian Country Child*, p. 159; Randell, op. cit., pp. 16–17, 53 et seq.
59. M. French, *A Victorian Village*, Glasney Press, Falmouth, 1977, pp. 83–9, 96.
60. E.g. R. Malcolmson, 'Leisure', in Mingay, ed., *Victorian Countryside*, II, pp. 611–13.
61. M. C. F. Morris, *The British Workman, Past and Present*, Oxford, 1928, pp. 93, 98; Cumbria Record Office. DX 192/28. Extracts from the Journal, Recollections and Experiences of Thomas Irving, pp. 21, 23, 31, 38–45; Museum of English Rural Life, Reading University. Reminiscences of Charles Slater, I, p. 55–81.
62. Quoted in L. M. Springall, *Labouring Life in Norfolk Villages 1834–1914*, Allen and Unwin, 1936, p. 103.
63. Davies, op. cit., p. 260.
64. Lennard, op. cit., pp. 57–9.
65. Orwin and Whetham, op. cit., p. 335.
66. Offer, op. cit., p. 359; W. Sutherland, *Rural Regeneration in England*, Methuen, 1913, pp. 55–6.
67. Among several commentators using this expression, see A. H. D. Acland, introduction to *The Land*, p. xxxiv.
68. Among many sources attesting to the way in which farmworkers were critical observers of the standards of each other's work, see G. Sturt, *Bettesworth Book*, p. 277; Evans, *Where Beards*

Wag All, pp. 64–7; and the Reminiscences of Frederick Swaffield (Dorset R.O. 459/1) unpaginated: 'what yarns we used to hear if a carter had ploughed a field with a crooked furrow', etc.

69. R. Groves, *Sharpen the Sickle*, new edition, Merlin, 1981, p. 95.
70. The following account is based on Groves, op. cit., pp. 115–22; G. Edwards, *From Crow-scaring to Westminster*, Labour Publishing Co., 1922, pp. 137–67; the Eastern Counties Agricultural Labourers' and Smallholders' Union, *Fourth Annual Report* (for 1910), and St Faith's branch Minute Book for 1906–11, both held at the Museum of English Rural Life, Reading University. A more detailed account of the St Faith's strike may be found in A. Howkins, *Poor Labouring Men. Rural Radicalism in Norfolk, 1870–1923*, History Workshop Series, Routledge and Kegan Paul, 1985, pp. 94–100.
71. Groves, op. cit., pp. 124–5; Howkins, *Poor Labouring Men*, pp. 103, 109–10.
72. ECALSU, *Fifth Annual Report* (for 1911).
73. E. Selley, *Village Trade Unions in Two Centuries*, Allen and Unwin, 1919, pp. 134–5; Groves op. cit., pp. 127–8.
74. My account of the Ormskirk strike is based on Groves, op. cit., pp. 140–1 and A. Mutch, 'Lancashire's "Revolt of the Field": the Ormskirk Farmworkers' Strike of 1913', *North West Labour History Society*, 1982, Bulletin No. 8, pp. 56–67.
75. Selley, op. cit., pp. 128–30; F. E. Green, *A History of the English Agricultural Labourer, 1870–1920*, P. and S. King, 1920, pp. 214–19; Clapham, op. cit., p. 98.
76. *The Times*, 6 March 1914, quoted in Selley, op. cit., p. 138.
77. Mutch, op. cit., pp. 64–5.
78. Green, *Agricultural Labourer*, p. 123; Bennett, op. cit., p. 119.
79. Green, *Tyranny*, pp. 124–44.
80. Groves, op. cit., pp. 151–60.
81. G. E. Evans, *Ask the Fellows Who Cut the Hay*, Faber and Faber, 1965 edition, p. 209; B. J. Davey, *Ashwell 1830–1914. The Decline of a Village Community*, Department of English Local History, Occasional Papers, 3rd series, No. 5, Leicester University Press, 1980, pp. 51–2.
82. R. J. Olney, *Rural Society and County Government in Nineteenth Century Lincolnshire*. History of Lincolnshire, vol. X, History of Lincolnshire Committee, Lincoln, 1979, p. 184.
83. H. Pelling, *Social Geography of British Elections, 1885–1910*, Macmillan, 1967, p. 428.
84. W. H. Hudson, *A Shepherd's Life*, Everyman edition, Dent, 1936, p. 79; Bennett, op. cit., p. 114.
85. Pelling, op. cit., p. 428; Sturt, *Bettesworth Book*, p. 274. And see Holdenby, op. cit., p. 226.
86. See, e.g., Sturt, *Change in the Village*, p. 174; Evans, *Where Beards Wag All*, pp. 181, 183.
87. P. Horn, *Labouring Life in the Victorian Countryside*, Gill and Macmillan, Dublin, 1976, pp. 227–8; Kebbel, op. cit., p. 110; F. M. L. Thompson, 'Landowners and the rural Community' in Mingay, ed., *Victorian Countryside*, II, p. 461.
88. W. Sullivan, *Alcoholism*, 1906, quoted in D. J. Davies, 'The Condition of the rural Population in England and Wales, 1870–1928', Ph.D. thesis, University of Wales, 1931, p. 156; Land Agents' Society, *Facts about Land*, p. 76.
89. Howkins, *Poor Labouring Men*, p. xiii.
90. Holdenby, op. cit., pp. 226–7. My italics.
91. Sturt, *Change in the Village*, p. 105. I return to the issue of class in Chapter 11.
92. Lennard, op. cit., p. 153.
93. B. S. Rowntree, *The Labourer and the Land*, Brother Richard's Bookshelf Library, 1914, esp. p. 57. For the general context see A. Briggs, *Social Thought and Social Action. A Study of the Work of Seebohm Rowntree 1871–1954*, Longmans, 1961, pp. 64–78, and Offer, op. cit., ch. XXII.
94. P. Adeane and E. Savill, *The Land Retort*, John Murray, 1914, p. 152. The Land Agents' Society's *Facts about Land*, cited several times in this chapter, was not published until 1916 and has been neglected by historians. According to Offer, op. cit., p. 383, the text was compiled by R. Prothero (Lord Ernle).

Chapter 7, pp. 156–72

1. M. Olson, *The Economics of the Wartime Shortage*, Duke University Press, Durham, North Carolina, 1963, p. 73.
2. E. Whetham, *The Agrarian History of England and Wales*, VIII, *1914–1939*, Cambridge, 1978, p. 70.
3. T. Carew, *The Vanished Army*, Kimber, 1964, p. 48; P.P. 1919 (Cmd. 25), vol. IX. Board of Agriculture and Fisheries, *Wages and Conditions of Employment in Agriculture*, II, *Reports of Investigators*, p. 382; *Beverley Guardian*, 18 September 1920.
4. P. Horn, *Rural Life in England in the First World War*, Gill and Macmillan, Dublin, 1984, pp. 27–8. Dr Horn's study has been drawn on only sparingly but is by far the most comprehensive account of its subject, offering a wealth of illustrations of points made in this chapter.
5. H. Reffold, *Pie for Breakfast*, Hutton Press, Beverley, 1984, p. 7.
6. A. L. Bowley, *Prices and Wages in the United Kingdom, 1914–20*, Carnegie Endowment for International Peace, Economic and Social History of the World War, Clarendon Press, Oxford, 1921, pp. 8–9; S. Pollard, *The Development of the British Economy, 1914–50*, Edward Arnold, 1962, pp. 46–7.
7. Condensed account based on Olson, op. cit., pp. 82–6, 94–7 and J. Burnett, *Plenty and Want. A Social History of Diet in England from 1815 to the Present Day*, Nelson, 1966, pp. 216–18.
8. These committees derived from the agricultural committees of county councils, whose prewar business has been confined chiefly to matters arising from legislation on smallholdings, etc.
9. Olson, op. cit., p. 108; P. E. Dewey, 'Farm Labour in Wartime; the Relationship between Agricultural Labour Supply and Food Production in Great Britain during 1914–18 with International Comparisons', Ph.D. thesis, University of Reading, 1978, pp. 50–5, whose calculations on the calorific value of UK agricultural output suggest a significant dip by 1916 (92 on the base 1909–13 = 100), but a recovery by 1918 to 101.
10. Burnett, op. cit., pp. 222–3.
11. Dewey, thesis, pp. 307–8.
12. Whetham, op. cit., pp. 106–7; P. E. Dewey, 'Agricultural Labour Supply in England and Wales during the First World War', *Economic History Review*, 2nd series, 1975, vol. XXVIII, p. 109.
13. Reffold, op. cit., p. 78.
14. Dewey, thesis, pp. 122–3.
15. ibid., p. 82.
16. Reffold, op. cit., pp. 25, 81, 83.
17. Dewey, thesis, p. 128.
18. Whetham, op. cit., p. 71, citing the *Journal of the Ministry of Agriculture* and *Hansard*. However, see PE. Dewey, 'Agricultural Labour Supply', pp. 101–2, 109–10 who shows that the statistical basis for all such estimates is fragile.
19. J. M. Winter, 'Britain's "Lost Generation" of the First World War', *Population Studies*, 1977, vol. XXXI, p. 454.
20. Whetham, op. cit., pp. 80, 99–100, 112; Cumbria R.O. CC1/39/2. War Agric. Cttee. Mins., May–June, 1917.
21. Cumbria R.O. CC1/39/2. War Agric. Cttee. Copy letter dated 13 August 1918.
22. Whetham, op. cit., p. 71.
23. P.P. 1919 (Cmd. 25), vol. IX. *Wages and Conditions in Agriculture*, II, pp. 13, 14, 177, 260, 372.
24. ibid., p. 223; E. J. Mejer, *Agricultural Labour in England and Wales*, Part I, *1900–20*, University of Nottingham, Department of Agricultural Economics, 1949, pp. 22–3.
25. Warwickshire R.O. C.630 War (p). War Agric. Cttee., *Report of the Agricultural Survey of the County*, 1917, esp. pp. 3, 4, 17, 37, 49, 59, 60.
26. F. E. Green, *A History of the English Agricultural Labourer, 1870–1920*, P. and S. King, 1920, p. 1.

27. P.P. 1919 (Cmd. 24), vol. IX. Board of Agriculture and Fisheries, *Wages and Conditions of Employment in Agriculture*, I, *General Report*, pp. 58, 59.
28. ibid., p. 93.
29. Reffold, op. cit., pp. 39, 100; Dewey, 'Agricultural Labour', p. 103.
30. Dewey, thesis, p. 239; Green, op. cit., pp. 224–5.
31. P.P. 1919 (Cmd. 24), vol. IX. *Wages and Conditions in Agriculture*, I, pp. 48, 50.
32. ibid., p. 49.
33. Reffold, op. cit., pp. 72, 73, 75.
34. Nottinghamshire R.O. CC/21/2/4. War Agric. Cttee. Labour Cttee. Mins., 18 November 1918.
35. Cumbria R.O. CC1/39/2. War Agric. Cttee. Mins., 12 June 1918; and see P.E. Dewey, 'Government Provision of Farm Labour in England and Wales, 1914–18', *Agricultural History Review*. 1979, vol. XXVII, pp. 112–14.
36. Cumbria R.O. CC1/39/3. War Agric. Cttee. Mins., 10 February 1919; Horn, op. cit., p. 157.
37. Wiltshire R.O. County Council Records. War Agric. Cttee. Mins., 8 January 1919.
38. Horn, op. cit., pp. 153, 159; Nottinghamshire R.O. CC 21/2/4. War Agric. Cttee. Mins., 11 March 1919.
39. F. G. Wolseley, *Women and the Land*, Chatto and Windus, 1916, pp. 30, 38–42, 63, 66, 180.
40. Horn, op. cit., p. 115.
41. Wiltshire R.O. War Agric. Cttee. Mins., 14 July 1916.
42. Dewey, thesis, p. 267, quoting the Secretary of the Women's Branch of the Board of Agriculture; Mejer op. cit., p. 20.
43. P.P. 1919 (Cmd. 24), vol. IX. *Wages and Conditions in Agriculture*, I,p. 189.
44. ibid., p. 53.
45. A. Marwick, *The Deluge. British Society and the First World War*, Macmillan, 1965, p. 91; Mejer, op. cit., p. 20.
46. Mejer, op. cit., p. 55.
47. Horn, op. cit., p. 170.
48. E. Selley, *Village Trade Unions in Two Centuries*, Allen and Unwin 1919, pp. 139–40, 144.
49. Horn, op. cit., p. 177.
50. Cumbria R.O. CC1/39/2. War Agric. Cttee. Mins., 17 June 1918; Museum of English Rural Life, Reading University. Reminiscences of Charles Slater, III, pp. 34–5.
51. Dewey, 'Agricultural Labour Supply', p. 106.
52. Dewey, thesis, p. 300. His article, 'Government Provision' considers the role of each category of replacement labour in detail.
53. P.P. 1919 (Cmd. 24), vol. IX. *Wages and Conditions in Agriculture*, I, pp. 88, III; Mejer, op. cit., pp. 45–6.
54. Whetham, op. cit., p. 80; *Hereford Times*, 27 February 1915, quoted in Selley, op. cit., p. 142.
55. A. L. Bowley, op. cit., p. 170.
56. Mejer, op. cit., pp. 50–1; P.P. 1919 (Cmd. 24), vol. IX. *Wages and Conditions in Agriculture*, I, pp. 125–6.
57. E. J. Mejer, *Agricultural Labour in England and Wales*, Part II, *1917–1951*, University of Nottingham, Department of Agricultural Economics, 1951, p. 10.
58. P.P. 1919 (Cmd. 24), vol. IX. *Wages and Conditions in Agriculture*, I, p. 178; Mejer, op. cit., II, p. 11.
59. S. W. Benusan, *Latterday Rural England, 1927*, Benn, 1928, p. 24. N.B. The speaker had three sons, all earning a wage equal to his own.
60. Bowley, op. cit., pp. 170–2.
61. Mejer, op. cit., II, p. 13.
62. C. S. Orwin and B. I. Felton, 'A Century of Wages and Earnings in Agriculture', *Journal of the Royal Agricultural Society*, 1931, vol. XCII, pp. 252–3, quoting from P.P. 1919 (Cmd. 76), vol. VIII. Agricultural Wages Board, *Financial Results of the Occupation of Land and the Cost of Living of Rural Workers*.
63. P.P. 1919 (Cmd. 24), vol. IX. *Wages and Conditions in Agriculture*, I, p. 166.
64. ibid., pp. 177–8.
65. ibid., p. 159.

66. P.P. 1919 (Cmd. 25), vol. IX. *Wages and Conditions in Agriculture*, II, pp. 21, 130, 232.
67. M. Madden, 'The National Union of Agricultural Workers, 1906–1956', B. Litt. thesis, University of Oxford, 1956, p. 37; and see A. Howkins, *Poor Labouring Men. Rural Radicalism in Norfolk, 1870–1923*, History Workshop Series, Routledge and Kegan Paul, 1985, p. 117.
68. G. Edwards, *From Crow-Scaring to Westminster*, Labour Publishing Co., 1922, pp. 191, 193–6; Madden, op. cit., p. 38.
69. H. Newby, *The Deferential Worker*, Allen Lane, 1977, p. 216, citing estimates made by Madden and Hyman; Green, op. cit., p. 127.
70. Whetham, op. cit., p. 129.
71. Madden, op. cit., pp. 65–6.
72. Nottinghamshire R.O. CC3/21/2/4. War Agric. Cttee. Labour Cttee. Mins., 30 September 1918; 11 November 1918; 3 February 1919; 11 March 1919.
73. Newby, op. cit., pp. 218, 228. These estimates can be regarded as only rough approximations. See the note accompanying table 8.1 below.
74. Reffold, op. cit., p. 79; Selley, op. cit., p. 166.
75. R. Groves, *Sharpen the Sickle*, new edition, Merlin Press, 1981, p. 166.
76. P. E. Dewey, 'British Farming Profits and Government Policy during the First World War', *Economic History Review*, 2nd series, 1984, vol. XXXVII, pp. 378, 379, 386; idem, 'Government Provision', p. 110.
77. Dewey, 'British Farming Profits', p. 386.
78. A. G. Street, *Farmer's Glory*, 23rd impression, Faber and Faber, 1947, p. 142.
79. Horn, op. cit., pp. 78, 79, 83; Reffold, op. cit., p. 42.
80. Horn, op. cit., p. 62.
81. ibid., p. 28, instancing the Duke of Bedford and the Marquis of Lincolnshire; F. M. L. Thompson, *English Landed Society in the Nineteenth Century*, Routledge and Kegan Paul, 1963, pp. 328, 330.
82. Winter, 'Britain's "Lost Generation"', pp. 459–61, 464; C. F. G. Masterman, *England after the War*, Hodder and Stoughton, 1922, pp. 31–2.
83. Thompson, op. cit., pp. 329, 332.
84. M. French, *A Victorian Village*, Glasney Press, Falmouth, 1977, pp. 6–10.
85. Whetham, op. cit., p. 45, table 8.
86. Mejer, op. cit., II, p. 13, table 2.
87. P.P. 1917–18 (Cd. 8668), vol. XV. *Commission of Enquiry into Industrial Unrest. Wales and Monmouth*, p. 38.
88. That is, taking the figure cited by Whetham (footnote 22) and applying to it the casualty rates advanced in Winter, 'Britain's "Lost Generation"', p. 450.
89. Horn, op. cit., pp. 189, 248.
90. G. E. Evans, *Where Beards Wag All*, Faber and Faber, 1970, pp. 103–4; R. Blythe, *Akenfield*, Allen Lane, 1969, pp. 46, 56.
91. See, e.g., Green, op. cit., p. 329; J. W. Robertson Scott, *England's Green and Pleasant Land*, Cape, 1925, p. 35; Blythe, op. cit., pp. 46–7; Reffold, op. cit., pp. 41–95.
92. P.P. 1919 (Cmd. 25), vol. IX. *Wages and Conditions in Agriculture*, II, p. 462; Nottinghamshire R.O. CC3 21/2/4. Labour Cttee. Mins., 25 March 1919; Cumbria R.O. CC 1/39/4. War Agric. Cttee. Mins., 28 April 1919, 5 May 1919.

Chapter 8, pp. 173–201

1. A. G. Street, *Farmer's Glory*, 23rd impression, Faber and Faber, 1947, pp. 130, 138, 144–5, 162.
2. E. Whetham, *The Agrarian History of England and Wales,* VIII, *1914–39*, Cambridge, 1978, p. 230.
3. E. M. Ojala, *Agriculture and Economic Progress*, Oxford, 1952, p. 67.
4. S. Pollard, *The Development of the British Economy, 1914–50*, Edward Arnold, 1962, p. 136.
5. Viscount Astor and B. S. Rowntree, *British Agriculture*, Longmans, Green, 1938, p. 36.

6. Pollard, op. cit., p. 141.
7. See, e.g. Astor and Rowntree, op. cit., pp. xii–xiii.
8. Based on F. D. W. Taylor, 'United Kingdom: Numbers in Agriculture', *Farm Economist*, 1955, vol. V, pp. 38–40.
9. A. W. Ashby and I. L. Evans, *The Agriculture of Wales and Monmouthshire*, University of Wales Press, Cardiff, 1944, p. 231.
10. Whetham, op. cit., pp. 304–5.
11. R. P. Askew, 'The Future Changes in the Number of Horses in England and Wales', *Farm Economist*, 1937, vol. II, pp. 129–30; W. H. Pedley, *Labour on the Land*, King and Staples, 1942, p. 6.
12. D. J. Davies, 'The Condition of the Rural Population in England and Wales, 1870–1914', Ph.D. thesis, University of Wales, 1931, p. 53.
13. Pedley, op. cit., p. 6; J. H. Smith, 'The Supply and Use of Farm Labour in Wales, 1921–41', *Farm Economist*, 1942, Vol. IV, pp. 7, 9.
14. Pedley, op. cit., p. 5.
15. J. A. Mollett, 'An Economic Study of the Supply of Labour in Buckinghamshire', M.Sc. thesis, University of Reading, 1949, p. 65.
16. Pedley, op. cit., p. 5; Mollett, thesis, pp. 49, 54.
17. Ministry of Agriculture and Fisheries, *Report on Proceedings under the Agricultural Wages (Regulation) Act, 1924, for the two years ending 30 September 1931*, HMSO, 1931, p. 116.
18. Ashby and Evans, op. cit., p. 80.
19. W. Irons, 'Agriculture in Warwickshire', *Journal of the Royal Agricultural Society*, 1930, vol. XCI, p. 48; MAF, *Rept. of Proceedings, etc.*, 1931, p. 116; Mollett, thesis, p. 50.
20. J. W. Robertson Scott, *The Dying Peasant*, Williams and Norgate, 1926, p. 150.
21. A. W. Ashby, 'Some Human and Social Factors in the Depression', *Journal of Proceedings of the Agricultural Economics Society*, 1928, vol. I, p. 94.
22. D. K. Britton and J. H. Smith, 'Farm Labour: Problems of Age-Composition and Recruitment', *Farm Economist*, 1947, vol. V, p. 206.
23. Museum of English Rural Life, Reading University. D69/97/1–2. Press Cuttings of A. G. Stratton (clippings from *The Wiltshire Gazette*, n.d.); *The Land Worker*, November 1921. Subsequent references to *The Land Worker*, a monthly publication, are mostly worked into the text.
24. F. G. Thomas, *The Changing Village*, Nelson, 1939, pp. 19–20.
25. Robertson Scott, op. cit., pp. 246–59.
26. Pedley, op. cit., p. 65; Mollett, thesis, p. 67.
27. Robertson Scott, op. cit., pp. 251, 255. See p. 118 above.
28. O. J. Beilby, 'Comparative Labour Efficiency in Agriculture', *Empire Journal of Experimental Agriculture*, 1947, vol. IX, pp. 139–40.
29. Pedley, op. cit., p. 29.
30. ibid., pp. 29–30, and see E. J. Mejer, *Agricultural Labour in England and Wales*, Part II, *1917–51*, University of Nottingham, Department of Agricultural Economics, 1951, pp. 26–9. These are the chief sources used in the following account of changes in statutory wage-fixing machinery.
31. Liberal Land Committee, *The Land and the Nation*, Hodder and Stoughton, 1925, p. 69.
32. R. Henderson, 'Some Sociological Aspects of Farm Labour in North Northumberland', *Journal of Proceedings of the Agricultural Economics Society*, 1937, Vol. IV, pp. 301–2; R. M. Carslaw and P. E. Graves, 'Labour Bill and Output on Arable Farms', *Journal of the Royal Statistical Society*, 1935, Vol. XCVIII, p. 605.
33. A. W. Ashby and J. H. Smith, 'Agricultural Labour in Wales Under Statutory Regulation of Wages, 1924–37', *Welsh Journal of Agriculture*, 1938, Vol. XIV, p. 28; Pedley, op. cit., pp. 42–3.
34. Pedley, op. cit., p. 42; and see Mejer, op. cit., p. 60.
35. G. Henderson, *The Farming Ladder*, Faber and Faber, 1944, p. 107.
36. Pedley, op. cit., pp. 51–4; Ashby and Smith, op. cit., p. 20.
37. These comments were made in a discussion following J. Orr's paper, 'The Economic Basis of

the Minimum Wage in Agriculture', *Journal of Proceedings of the Agricultural Economics Society*, 1930, vol. I, p. 17.
38. J. F. Duncan, 'Organizing Farm Workers', *Journal of Proceedings of the Agricultural Economics Society*, 1936, vol. IV, pp. 256–7; Pedley, op. cit., pp. 63–4.
39. P.P. 1923 (Cmd. 1842), vol. IX. *Agricultural Tribunal of Investigation, First Interim Report*, p. 9.
40. Pedley, op. cit., p. 44, and Appendix II. These comparisons exclude Lancashire where (in part of the committee's area) the minimum remained as high as 38s 6d, but for a sixty hour week.
41. Mejer, op. cit., p. 44; Pedley, op. cit., p. 37.
42. Pedley, op. cit., p. 38.
43. Mejer, op. cit., pp. 48–51; Pedley, op. cit., p. 39.
44. M. Madden, 'The National Union of Agricultural Workers, 1906–1956', B.Litt. thesis, University of Oxford, 1956, pp. 262, 277.
45. ibid., pp. 113, 115.
46. R. Hyman, *The Workers' Union*, Clarendon Press, Oxford, 1971, p. 148.
47. Robertson Scott, op. cit., p. 57; Pedley, op. cit., p. 168.
48. Thomas, op. cit., p. 72.
49. M. C. F. Morris, *The British Workman Past and Present*, Oxford, 1928, p. 107.
50. The following account is based primarily upon R. Groves, *Sharpen the Sickle*, new edition, Merlin Press, 1981, Part IV, chs. III–IV; Madden, thesis, pp. 69–81; H. Newby, *The Deferential Worker*, Allen Lane, 1977, pp. 221–6, and the recent work of A. Howkins, *Poor Labouring Men. Rural Radicalism in Norfolk, 1870–1923*, History Workshop Series, Routledge and Kegan Paul, 1985, chs. VII and VIII, which deals most thoroughly with the topic. Extensive use has also been made of *The Land Worker* and the valuable NUAW book of press-cuttings entitled 'The Norfolk Dispute, 1923' in the Museum of English Rural Life, Reading University. D.II.8.
51. Newby, op. cit., p. 224. Howkins, op. cit., p. 160 puts the numbers on strike as 7,102, basing himself on Lunnon's report of the strike, and stresses that the turn-out was as high as 90 per cent in some districts. However, both authorities agree that no more than a quarter of Norfolk's agricultural labour force was on strike, at the peak.
52. Madden, thesis, p. 81.
53. *The Land Worker*, April 1932.
54. Museum of English Rural Life, Reading University, D.II.8. 'Norfolk Dispute' press-cutting book.
55. Madden, thesis, pp. 286–7.
56. ibid., pp. 145–51, 154; Newby, op. cit., pp. 235–6, 238–9.
57. Pedley, op. cit., p. 35.
58. R. G. Carslaw, and P. E. Graves, 'The Farmer's Labour Bill', *Farm Economist*, 1935, vol. I, p. 203.
59. Robertson Scott, op. cit., p. vii.
60. M. K. Ashby, 'Recent Social Changes as they affect the Younger Generation', *Journal of Proceedings of the Agricultural Economics Society*, 1933, vol. II, p. 229.
61. Pedley, op. cit., p. 94; P. Ambrose, *The Quiet Revolution. Social Change in a Sussex Village, 1871–1971*, Chatto and Windus, 1974, p. 60.
62. M. Chamberlain, *Fenwomen*, Virago, 1975, pp. 74, 77.
63. J. W. Innes, 'Class Birth Rates in England and Wales, 1921–31', *Millbank Memorial Fund Quarterly*, 1941, vol. XIX, p. 87.
64. Whetham, op. cit., p. 239.
65. A. W. Ashby, 'Farm Workers' Budgets', *Journal of the Ministry of Agriculture*, December 1924; January and February 1925. These comments are based on the summary in Mejer, op. cit., pp. 68–9.
66. J. R. E. Phillips, 'Agricultural Workers' Budgets', *Welsh Journal of Agriculture*, 1940, vol. XVI, pp. 61–3, 65, 68. Note that the average size of the households was 4.27 and that cases with supplementary wage earners were screened out. Hence the conclusions contrast unfavourably with those from table 8.5 below.

67. Pedley, op. cit., pp. 58–9.
68. *The Land Worker*, February 1931.
69. Pedley, op. cit., p. 56.
70. *The Land Worker*, May 1921.
71. Dorset R.O. D466/28. *Dorset Rural Insurance Society. Report for 1930.*
72. Davies, thesis, pp. 106–7.
73. According to the Registrar-General's data for 1930–2, the standardized mortality ratio from suicide (deaths as a percentage of all males from this cause) was for farmers and their relatives, 142; for agricultural and gardeners' labourers, 84.
74. See p. 233 below.
75. Pedley, op. cit., pp. 107–8.
76. ibid., pp. 101, 104; B. S. Bosanquet, 'The Quality of the Rural Population', *Eugenics Review*, 1950, vol. XLII, p. 81.
77. See pp. 246–7 below.
78. Liberal Land Committee, op. cit., pp. 71, 151.
79. See G. Orwell, *The Road to Wigan Pier*, Penguin, 1962, pp. 68–9. Orwell's book, first published in 1937, contains one of the most insightful discussions of the dole standard, in all its aspects.
80. Pedley, op. cit., p. 10.
81. ibid., pp. 20–1.
82. G. Henderson, op. cit. See especially pp. 5, 14, 112, 117.
83. Ashby and Evans, op. cit., p. 84. These data were gathered in 1925.
84. E. J. Mejer, *Agricultural Labour in England and Wales,* Part I, *1900–20*, University of Nottingham, Department of Agricultural Economics, 1949, p. 38.
85. R. Henderson, op. cit., pp. 304, 306–12, 317.
86. Thomas, op. cit., p. 54.
87. Britton and Smith, op. cit., p. 208.
88. F. Kitchen, *Brother to the Ox*, Dent, 1940, p. 220; Museum of English Rural Life, Reading University. D71/8. Reminiscences of Charles Slater, I, p. 44.
89. G. Henderson, op. cit., p. 107; R. Blythe, *Akenfield*, Allen Lane, 1969, p. 100.
90. Based on a comparison of the overall extent of the decline of wage employment, 1930–9 (Table 8.1) with data given for 'contract workers on farms' and 'others', 1851–1931, in Taylor, op. cit., pp. 38, 40.

Chapter 9, pp. 202–21

1. K. A. H. Murray, *Agriculture*. History of the Second World War, United Kingdom, Civil Series, HMSO, 1955, p. 39; Ministry of Agriculture, Fisheries and Food, *A Century of Agricultural Statistics*, HMSO, 1968, p. 91.
2. M. Olson, *The Economics of the Wartime Shortage*, Duke University Press, Durham, North Carolina, 1963, p. 118.
3. Murray op. cit., pp. 59–60; E. H. Whetham, *Agrarian History of England and Wales,* VIII, *1914–39*, Cambridge, 1978, p. 333.
4. Olson, op. cit., p. 119.
5. Rationing schemes are discussed in J. Burnett, *Plenty and Want. A Social History of Diet in England from 1815 to the Present Day*, Nelson, 1966, ch. 13 and at greater length in R. J. Hammond, *Food.* History of the Second World War, United Kingdom Civil Series, 1951, vol. I.
6. M. Bruce, *The Coming of the Welfare State*, Batsford, 1961, p. 262.
7. E. S. Turner, *The Phoney War on the Home Front*, Michael Joseph, 1961, pp. 157–8.
8. MAFF, *Century of Agricultural Statistics*, pp. 95–101, 122–4, 126, 128.
9. N. Longmate, *How We Lived Then*, Hutchinson, 1971, p. 234.
10. W. H. Long, 'Agricultural Labour and its problems in War Time', *Journal of the Yorkshire Agricultural Society*, 1940, Vol. XLIV, pp. 44–7; J. H. Smith, 'The Labour Requirements of the Ploughing-Up Campaign in Wales', *Welsh Journal of Agriculture*, 1940, vol. XVI, pp. 21–6.

11. Murray, op. cit., p. 82.
12. F. G. Sturrock, 'Movement of Agricultural Workers on 157 Farms in the Eastern Counties during the First Year of War', *Farm Economist*, 1941, vol. III, pp. 161–2.
13. The course of farm wages during the war is discussed below, pp. 213–16.
14. Murray, op. cit., p. 331.
15. *The Kent Farmers' Journal*, March 1941, pp. 80–1; April 1941, p. 106.
16. Shropshire R.O. 207/26–27. War Agricultural Executive. Labour Sub-Cttee. Mins., 16 October 1941; 5 February 1942; 19 February 1942; 26 November 1940; 26 March 1942.
17. V. Sackville-West, *The Women's Land Army*, Michael Joseph, 1944, pp. 10, 12, 17–21.
18. 'They Served the Land: A Tribute to the Work of the Women's Land Army, 1939–50', *Agriculture*, 1950, vol. LVII, p. 404.
19. Murray, op. cit., pp. 126, 159, 188, 210.
20. Sackville-West, op. cit., pp. 27, 38.
21. Longmate, op. cit., pp. 240–1.
22. Sackville-West, op. cit., p. 42; P. W. Cox, 'Front-Line Farming: Kent's Wartime Effort', *Agriculture*, 1944, vol. LI, p. 121.
23. Murray, op. cit., pp. 125, 159, 189, 210.
24. Longmate, op. cit., pp. 480–1.
25. ibid., p. 239; Murray, op. cit., pp. 126, 209 (these figures relate to GB); J. V. Measures, 'Leicestershire School Children help the Farmers', *Agriculture*, 1943, vol. L, pp. 84–8.
26. Shropshire R.O. Labour Sub-Cttee. Mins. 13 August 1942.
27. MAFF, *Century of Agricultural Statistics*, p. 62; Ministry of Agriculture, Fisheries and Food, *Report of Proceedings under the Agricultural Wages Acts, 1937–50*, HMSO, 1952, p. 20.
28. H. T. Williams, 'Changes in the Productivity of Labour in British Agriculture', *Journal of Agricultural Economics*, 1954, vol. IX, p. 334. These 'relative efficiencies', based on a scrutiny of post-war earnings, were as follows: regular males, 21 and over 1.0, or under 21, 0.63; females and WLA 0.66; casual and part-time males 21 and over 0.70, or under 21, 0.46; casual and part-time females and WLA 0.50; prisoners of war 0.65 (billeted) and 0.40 (not billeted).
29. S. Pollard, *The Development of the British Economy 1914–1950*, Edward Arnold, 1962, p. 316.
30. D. R. Bamford, 'Making the Most of Farm Labour', *Agriculture*, 1942, vol. XLVIII, p. 221.
31. Murray, op. cit., pp. 127, 161, 199, 277; R. Bennett Jones, 'Yorkshire Farmers are buying more Tractors', *Farm Economist*, 1941, vol. III, pp. 148–9.
32. In 1944 there were 295,247 agricultural holdings in England and Wales excluding those under five acres or consisting exclusively of rough grazing.
33. Murray, op. cit., pp. 242–3. These figures relate to the UK.
34. Williams, op. cit., p. 338; A. W. Ashby and J. H. Smith, 'Labour Organisation on Farms', *Journal of Proceedings of the Agricultural Economics Society*, 1948, vol. VI, pp. 358–9. Note that the latter estimates include farmers.
35. E. J. Mejer, *Agricultural Labour in England and Wales*, Part II, *1917–51*, University of Nottingham, Department of Agricultural Economics, 1951, pp. 89–90.
36. ibid., pp. 74–6: M. Madden, 'The National Union of Agricultural Workers, 1906–1956', B.Litt. thesis, University of Oxford, 1956, p. 269.
37. Dorset R.O. D466/E11–16. Wages Books of H. J. Smith.
38. L. G. Bennett, 'The Relation Between an Increase in the Legal Minimum Rate of Wages and the Farmers' Wage Bill', *Farm Economist*, 1942, vol. IV, pp. 34–6.
39. MAFF, *Century of Agricultural Statistics*, pp. 67–8.
40. Mejer, op. cit., pp. 80, 84.
41. J. H. Smith, 'Changes of Wages and Costs of Labour on Farms in Wales, 1939–43', *Welsh Journal of Agriculture*, 1945, vol. XVIII, pp. 150–5.
42. Ministry of Health, *Rural Housing: Second Report of the Rural Housing Sub-Committee of the Central Housing Advisory Committee*, HMSO, 1937, pp. 5–9.
43. Ministry of Health, *Rural Housing: Third Report of the Rural Housing Sub-Committee*, HMSO, 1944, pp. 12–16, 30–1. Whereas English private enterprise had to that date constructed houses equivalent to 41 per cent of the 1919 stock, the Welsh had built 19.3; and

whilst English District Councils had constructed a number equivalent to 9.1 per cent of the stock in 1919, the corresponding Welsh figure was 6.6 per cent.

44. ibid., p. 48.
45. W. H. Pedley, *Labour on the Land*, King and Staples, 1942, pp. 113, 117.
46. Turner, op. cit., pp. 82–3. The significance of evacuation schemes as a factor in shaping social policy is discussed in R. M. Titmuss, *Problems in Social Policy*. History of the Second World War, United Kingdom, Civil Series, HMSO, 1950, and more critically, in T. L. Crosby, *The Impact of Civilian Evacuation in the Second World War*, Croom Helm, 1986.
47. Longmate, op. cit., pp. 55–6.
48. 'Summertime' was extended to 19 November in 1939 and re-introduced in February to last for the rest of the war. 'Double summer time', whereby the clocks were put forward a further hour, was introduced from May–August 1941 and thereafter every spring down to and including 1945.
49. Longmate, op. cit., pp. 87, 418–19.
50. Murray, op. cit., p. 353.
51. P.P. 1942–3 (Cmd. 6404), vol. VI. *Report on Social Insurance and Allied Services*, pp. 61–3.
52. Murray, op. cit., p. 339.
53. ibid., pp. 379, 289–91. UK figures.
54. Longmate, op. cit., p. 235.
55. ibid., pp. 237, 313.
56. Madden, thesis, p. 155.
57. H. Newby, *The Deferential Worker*, Allen Lane, 1977, p. 228.
58. E. G. Gooch, 'The Farm Worker – Past, Present and Future' *Journal of the Farmers' Club*, 1941, Part 4, pp. 77–86. The ensuing discussion is reported on pp. 86–94.
59. E. G. Gooch, 'The Worker and Post-War Agriculture' *Journal of the Farmers' Club*, 1944, Part 3, pp. 25–33 and discussion on pp. 33–40.

Chapter 10, pp. 222–51

1. Quoted in J. K. Bowers, 'British Agricultural Policy since the Second World War', *Agricultural History Review*, 1985, vol. XXXIII, p. 66.
2. Ministry of Agriculture, Fisheries and Food, *A Century of Agricultural Statistics*, HMSO, 1968, p. 62.
3. E. J. Mejer, *Agricultural Labour in England and Wales*, Part II, *1917–1951*, University of Nottingham, Department of Agricultural Economics, 1951, pp. 94, 104–5; J. A. Mollett, 'An Economic Study of the Supply of Agricultural Labour in Buckinghamshire', M.Sc. thesis, University of Reading, 1949, pp. 192–3.
4. MAFF, *Century of Agricultural Statistics*, pp. 71, 129.
5. Quoted in M. Shoard, *The Theft of the Countryside*, Temple Smith, 1980, p. 11.
6. Ministry of Agriculture, Fisheries and Food, *Studies in Urban Household Diets, 1944–9. Second Report of the National Food Survey Committee*, HMSO, 1956, pp. 62–5.
7. J. W. Hobson and E. Henry, *The Rural Market. A Compilation of Facts Related to the Agricultural Industry and Rural Standards of Living and Purchasing Habits*, Hulton Press, 1948, pp. 85, 86, 93, 100, 103, 104, 110–13, 121.
8. *The Hop Pocket*, October 1949. This monthly newsletter, and the *West Riding Bulletin* cited below, were kindly made available to me by the NUAW District Organizer at Maidstone in 1982.
9. Mejer, op. cit., p. 108.
10. K. Cowling and D. Metcalf, 'Labour Transfer from Agriculture: A Regional Analysis', *Manchester School*, 1968, vol. XXXVI, p. 85; P. J. Lund, T. G. Morris, J. D. Temple and J. M. Watson, *Wages and Employment in Agriculture: England and Wales, 1960–80*, Government Economic Service Working Paper No. 52, Ministry of Agriculture, Fisheries and Food, 1982, Appendix X, p. 50.
11. B. A. Holderness, *British Agriculture since 1945*, Manchester University Press, 1985, pp. 134–

5; and see R. Gasson, *Mobility of Farm Workers*, University of Cambridge, Department of Land Economy, Occasional Paper No. 2, 1974, p. 32.
12. R. Body, *Agriculture: The Triumph and the Shame*, Temple Smith, 1982, p. 124; see also Holderness, op. cit., pp. 106–7.
13. G. Sharp and C. W. Capstick, 'The Place of Agriculture in the National Economy', *Journal of Agricultural Economics*, 1966, vol. XVII, p. 5; R. Gasson, 'Resources in Agriculture: Labour' in A. Edwards and A. Rogers, eds., *Agricultural Resources*, Faber and Faber, 1974, p. 130; Body, op. cit., p. 124.
14. MAFF, *Century of Agricultural Statistics*, p. 71.
15. G. H. Peters, 'Recent Trends in Farm Real Estate Values in England and Wales', *Farm Economist*, 1966, vol. XI, p. 46; Body, op. cit., p. 31.
16. Holderness, op. cit., pp. 126–8, 140.
17. The exception to this statement is small specialist livestock producers whose numbers have fallen significantly, partly as a result of the heavy cost of feeding compounds. See Body, op. cit., p. 4.
18. Bowers, op. cit., pp. 69–72; Holderness, op. cit., pp. 21–4.
19. Body, op. cit., p. 27, who also points out that these benefits were very unevenly distributed.
20. Gasson, 'Resources in Agriculture', p. 130.
21. H. Newby, *Green and Pleasant Land? Social Change in Rural England*, Penguin, pp. 209–10.
22. Holderness, op. cit., pp. 116–17.
23. Newby, op. cit., pp. 210–11; Shoard, op. cit., pp. 34, 49 et seq.; Bowers, op. cit., p. 75.
24. ibid., p. 76; Body, op. cit., p. 128.
25. H. Newby, *The Deferential Worker*, Allen Lane, 1977, p. 200; J. S. Nalson, *Mobility of Farm Families*, Manchester University Press, 1968, p. 120.
26. Newby, *Green and Pleasant Land*, pp. 85–95, describes these changes more fully.
27. G. E. Evans, *Ask the Fellows Who Cut the Hay*, Faber and Faber, 1965 edition, esp. pp. 221–37; idem, *Where Beards Wag All*, Faber and Faber, 1970, esp. pp. 159–92.
28. Evans, *Ask the Fellows*, p. 239; Newby, *Deferential Worker*, p. 292.
29. E.g. Evans, *Ask the Fellows*, p. 16; Newby, *Green and Pleasant Land*, p. 129.
30. Newby, *Deferential Worker*, p. 289.
31. Ministry of Agriculture, Fisheries and Food, *The Changing Structure of the Agricultural Labour Force in England and Wales. Number of Workers, Hours and Earnings, 1945–65*, HMSO, 1967, pp. 25, 27.
32. A. K. Giles and W. J. G. Cowie, *The Farm Worker: His Training, Pay and Status*, University of Bristol, Department of Agricultural Economics, 1964, pp. 4–5, 9, 11, 14, 16.
33. Gasson, 'Resources in Agriculture', p. 113; Newby, *Green and Pleasant Land*, p. 98.
34. M. Black, 'Agricultural Labour in an Expanding Economy', *Journal of Agricultural Economics*, 1968, vol. XIX, p. 69.
35. W. Mackenzie, 'Notes on Systems of Payment of Agricultural Workers', *Farm Economist*, 1949, vol. VI, p. 76.
36. Concurrently, a New Entrant (Apprenticeship) Training Scheme was introduced which was run by the Agricultural Training Board. This involved a three-year period of practical training on the farm, integrated with part-time further education. Successful apprentices would receive the Board's craftsman certificate.
37. Newby, *Deferential Worker*, p. 169; Lund, Morris, Temple and Watson, op. cit., appendix IV, p. 43.
38. ibid., p. 10.
39. See MAFF, *Changing Structure of the Agricultural Labour Force*, p. 72 for minimum wages and total weekly earnings. The official retail price index used is from B. R. Mitchell and H. G. Jones, *Second Abstract of British Historical Statistics*, Cambridge, 1971, pp. 191–2. N.B. The weights attached to different components (food, clothing, fuel and light, rent and rates, durable goods, services, drink and tobacco) were changed from time to time (1952, 1956) and need not reflect the farmworker's pattern of expenditure very closely.
40. *West Yorkshire Bulletin*, June 1960.
41. M. A. Havinden, *Estate Villages*, Lund Humphries 1966, p. 176; *The Hop Pocket*, September 1959.

42. Havinden, op. cit., p. 176; H. E. Brady, *English Rural Life*, Routledge and Kegan Paul, 1959, p. 239.
43. *West Yorkshire Bulletin*, November 1966; *The Hop Pocket*, September 1972.
44. M. Brown and S. Winyard, *Low Pay on the Farm*, Low Pay Unit, Pamphlet No. 3, 1975, p. 14. 97 out of 110 farmworkers contacted through the Jimmy Young radio show for the purpose of this survey possessed a car by this date.
45. ibid, pp. 5–6, 13–14, 21.
46. MAFF, *Changing Structure of the Agricultural Labour Force*, pp. 19–20; Newby, *Deferential Worker*, p. 170.
47. J. D. Hughes, 'A Note on the Decline in Numbers of Farm Workers in Great Britain', *Farm Economist*, 1957, vol. VIII, p. 35; Newby, *Deferential Worker*, p. 172.
48. See Lund, Morris, Temple and Watson, op. cit., appendix X, p. 50.
49. W. J. G. Cowie and A. K. Giles, *An Inquiry into Reasons for The Drift from the Land*, University of Bristol, Department of Economics, Selected Papers in Agricultural Economics, 5, No. 3, 1957, pp. 85–6, 103–4; Gasson, *Mobility of Farm Workers*, p. 47.
50. Cowie and Giles, op. cit., pp. 86–7, 103–4.
51. MAFF, *Changing Structure of the Agricultural Labour Force*, p. 5; Gasson, 'Resources in Agriculture', p. 121.
52. R.J. Green and J.B. Ayton, *Changes in the Pattern of Rural Settlements*, 1967, quoted in Gasson, *Mobility of Farm Workers*, p. 48; Newby, *Deferential Worker*, pp. 161, 195.
53. Gasson, 'Resources in Agriculture', p. 128.
54. J.E. Bessell, *The Younger Worker in Agriculture*, National Economic Development Office, 1972, pp. 18, 20, 25, 27, 39.
55. R. Blythe, *Akenfield*, Penguin, 1972, pp. 112–15.
56. See Gasson, *Mobility of Farm Workers*, p. 53.
57. ibid., pp. 25–6, 66–7. She notes that it is important to distinguish between *rates* of turnover, which might be greater near towns, and *net* losses which need not be so (p. 29).
58. ibid., p. 79.
59. ibid., p. 90 (table A.4.2); Newby, *Deferential Worker*, pp. 160–1.
60. G.F. Keatinge and R. Littlewood, 'The Agricultural Worker', *The Lancet*, 21 August 1948, p. 283.
61. Mollett, thesis, pp. 222–6.
62. Ministry of Agriculture, Fisheries and Food, *Report on Safety, Health, Welfare and Wages in Agriculture, 1 January to 31 December 1975*, HMSO, 1977, pp. 14–15; Health and Safety Executive, *Health and Safety Statistics, 1980*, HMSO, 1982, pp. 5, 41.
63. *The Land Worker*, May 1981; June 1981.
64. Office of Population Censuses and Surveys, *Occupational Mortality: The Registrar-General's Decennial Supplement for England and Wales, 1970–2*, HMSO, 1978, pp. 77, 191. Expectation of life of a farmworker aged 15 was 55.7 further years.
65. The average rates of unemployment in the economy as a whole were 1.52 per cent (1961–70) and 4.19 (1971–80), but in agriculture, 2.84 and 7.18 respectively. Lund, Morris, Temple and Watson, op. cit., appendix X, p. 50.
66. Black, op. cit., p. 70; Gasson, *Mobility of Farm Labour*, pp. 41–3, 52.
67. ibid., p. 54; Newby, *Deferential Worker*, p. 163.
68. See Lund, Morris, Temple and Watson, op. cit., appendix X, p. 50.
69. Havinden, op. cit., pp. 173–5.
70. P. Fletcher, 'The Agricultural Housing Problem', *Social and Economic Administration*, 1969, vol. III, p. 160.
71. Newby, *Green and Pleasant Land*, pp. 185–9, points out that in 1974 district councils provided only 20 per cent of the rural housing stock (compared with 31 per cent elsewhere) and, while recognizing that local authorities' hands are tied by centralized control of their expenditure and strict planning controls, quite fairly points out that landlords and farmers in their role as councillors have often given priority to keeping rates down.
72. MAFF, *Changing Structure of the Agricultural Labour Force*, p. 26; R. Gasson, *Provision of*

Tied Cottages, University of Cambridge, Department of Land Economy, Occasional Paper No. 4, 1975, p. 61.

73. ibid., pp. 81–2; Newby, *Deferential Worker*, pp. 189–90.
74. A. K. Jones, *Rural Housing: The Agricultural Tied Cottage*, Occasional Papers on Social Administration, No. 25, Bell and Sons, 1975, discusses the political background to these steps. He found that in practice suspensions tended to be short and that the attitude of rural district councils to re-housing farmworkers was very variable. All were wary of collusion between employer and employee, designed to force their hand (Newby, *Deferential Worker*, p. 180).
75. Gasson, *Provision of Tied Cottages*, p. 90; Newby, *Green and Pleasant Land*, p. 138.
76. Fletcher, op. cit., pp. 164–5.
77. Newby, *Deferential Worker*, pp. 183–4, 194.
78. P. Ambrose, *The Quiet Revolution. Social Change in a Sussex Village, 1871–1971*, Chatto and Windus, 1974, pp. 2, 66, 67, 116. The Registrar-General's social classes I and II, comprise chiefly professional and managerial persons.
79. D. Sherry, 'Socio-Economic Changes in some Dorset Villages, 1871–1974, with reference to Rural Planning', Ph.D. thesis, University of Manchester, 1975, p. 56.
80. Humberside R.O. (Beverley). SLB. Seaton Ross and Huggate Admissions Registers; Sherry, thesis, table 22, following p. 35.
81. Cowie and Giles, *Drift from the Land*, p. 79.
82. Giles and Cowie, *The Farm Worker*, p. 6.
83. *John Betjeman's Collected Poems*, 2nd edition, John Murray, 1962, p. 238. His poem, 'The Dear Old Village', is nevertheless a perspicacious if heavily value-laden evocation of village life about 1950.
84. Blythe, op. cit., pp. 275–6.
85. Cowie and Giles, *The Farm Worker*, p. 31.
86. I. Emmett, *A North Wales Village. A Social Anthropological Study*, Routledge and Kegan Paul, 1964, p. 11.
87. Newby, *Deferential Worker*, pp. 316, 328–9, 339, 429.
88. ibid., p. 330.
89. Blythe, op. cit., p. 92; Newby, *Deferential Worker*, p. 375.
90. ibid., pp. 333–4, 371, 378, 388, 391.
91. F. D. Mills, 'The National Union of Agricultural Workers', *Journal of Agricultural Economics*, 1964, vol. XVI, p. 231.
92. *The Land Worker*, February 1981; March 1982.
93. *The Hop Pocket*, April 1968; M. W. Greenslade and D. A. Johnson, eds., *Victoria County History. A History of Staffordshire*, VI, Oxford, 1979, p. 146; Newby, *Deferential Worker*, pp. 254–5.
94. Museum of English Rural Life, University of Reading. NUAW Records. Tuttington Branch Minutes, 17 December 1948; Mills, op. cit., p. 231; Newby, *Deferential Worker*, pp. 261–2.
95. *The Hop Pocket*, January 1974.
96. Newby, *Deferential Worker*, pp. 260–3.
97. ibid., pp. 264–5, 268–71.
98. P. Self and H. J. Storing, *The State and the Farmer*, Allen and Unwin, 1962, p. 164.
99. See, e.g., *The Hop Pocket*, April 1947, March 1948; *West Yorkshire Bulletin*, June 1959, when the district organizer asked for details which would be passed onto the Inland Revenue.
100. M. Madden, 'The National Union of Agricultural Workers, 1906–1956', B.Litt. thesis, University of Oxford, 1956, pp. 246–7, 251–2; E. G. Gooch, 'Farm Labour since 1894', *Agriculture*, 1954, vol. LXI, p. 275.
101. Self and Storing, op. cit., pp. 168–9.
102. ibid., p. 164.
103. Copy letter from W. H. Pearson, County Organizer (Kent) to A. C. Dann, General Secretary of NUAW, dated 13 September 1948, and reply (Correspondence held at NUAW office, Maidstone, in 1982).
104. *The Land Worker*, January 1981.
105. ibid., issues of June–October 1981.

106. This significant point was made in a letter to *The Land Worker* in March 1982.

Chapter 11, pp. 244–52

1. E.g. G.E. Mingay, introduction to *The Victorian Countryside*, Routledge and Kegan Paul, 1981, I, pp. 3–16; W.M. Williams, *A West Country Village: Ashworthy*, Routledge and Kegan Paul, 1963, pp. xviii, 138–9, 208–13.
2. R. Williams, *The Country and the City*, Paladin, St Albans, 1975, pp. 18–22.
3. J. Barrell, *The Dark Side of the Landscape*, Cambridge, 1980, pp. 17, 52, 133.
4. J.W. Robertson Scott, *The Dying Peasant*, Williams and Norgate, 1926, p. 63; G. Henderson, *The Farming Ladder*, Faber and Faber, 1944, p. 107.
5. J.A. Venn, *Foundations of Agricultural Economics*, Cambridge, 1923, p. 228.
6. E.N. Bennett, *Problems of Village Life*, Williams and Norgate, n.d., p. 68; Venn, op. cit., pp. 232–3.
7. J.R. Bellerby, 'Comparison of Skill, Endurance, and Experience Required in Agriculture and Industry', *Farm Economist*, 1952, vol. XII, p. 13. His enquiry was based on a questionnaire addressed to men who had worked in both, who were asked to give a point-rating (on a scale 0–4) to various characteristics of the work involved, including skill, responsibilities, strains and stresses.
8. The words of Edward David, a leading socialist theorist quoted in P.P. 1924 (Cmd. 2145), vol. VII. *Agricultural Tribunal of Investigation, Final Report*, pp. 230–1 remain relevant today: 'The worker becomes not the servant but the director.... No agricultural machine chains the labourer to itself as industrial machines do. What is continuous is change ... at the same time the machine is moving, and the man with it, in the open air.'
9. Robertson Scott, op. cit., p. 142, quoting the view of Sir Henry Rew, who among many other public appointments and offices was Deputy-Chairman of the Central Agricultural Wages Board, 1917–21.
10. ibid., p. ix.
11. P.P. 1924 (Cmd. 2145), vol. VII. *Agricultural Tribunal*, p. 35.
12. E. Weber, *Peasants into Frenchmen. The Modernization of Rural France, 1870–1914*, Chatto and Windus, 1977, pp. 140–1, 154. For Britain, see, *inter alia*, P.P. 1919 (Cmd. 504), vol. XXVI. *Ministry of National Service, 1917–19. Report* (vol. I) *on the Physical Examination of Men of Military Age by National Service Medical Boards from 1 November 1917–31 October 1918*, pp. 17, 18, showing that agriculturalists, along with miners, provided 'a good class of recruit'.
13. L. E. Howard, *Labour in Agriculture: an International Survey*, Royal Institute of International Affairs, Oxford, 1935, pp. 133, 135–6, 148–50, 162, 181–3, 204; F. Wunderlich, *Farm Labour in Germany, 1810–1945*, Princeton University Press, Princeton, New Jersey, 1961, p. 354.
14. T. Devine, ed., *Farm Servants and Labour in Lowland Scotland*, John Donald, Edinburgh, 1984, pp. 252–3.
15. E.W. Martin, *The Shearers and the Shorn*, Routledge and Kegan Paul, 1965, p. 135.
16. R.E. Prothero (Lord Ernle), *English Farming, Past and Present*, Longmans, Green, 1912, p. 413.
17. A.H. Baverstock, *The English Agricultural Labourer*, Vineyard Press, 1912, p. 1.
18. Various studies are discussed in B. Bosanquet, 'The Quality of the Rural Population', *Eugenics Review*, 1950, vol. XLII, pp. 75–92. On intelligence testing see G. Sutherland, 'The Magic of Measurement; Mental Testing and English Education 1900–40', *Transactions of the Royal Historical Society*, 5th series, 1977, vol. XXVIII, pp. 135–53.
19. Bennett, op. cit., p. 37; L.M. Springall, *Labouring Life in Norfolk Villages, 1834–1914*, Allen and Unwin, 1936, p. 133.
20. H. Newby, *The Deferential Worker*, Allen Lane, 1977, pp. 368, 380–1.
21. Howard, op. cit., pp. 45–6.
22. See A. Briggs, 'The Language of "Class" in Early Nineteenth Century England' in A. Briggs and J. Saville, eds., *Essays in Labour History*, Macmillan, 1960, pp. 43–73.

23. R. Quinault and J. Stevenson, *Popular Protest and Public Order*, Allen and Unwin, 1974, pp. 24, 48.
24. E. J. Hobsbawm and G. Rudé, *Captain Swing*, Lawrence and Wishart, 1969, p. 47.
25. E.g. R. A. E. Wells, 'The Development of the English Rural Proletariat and Social Protest, 1700–1850', *Journal of Peasant Studies*, 1979, vol. VI, p. 131; R. Samuel, foreword to B. Reaney, *The Class Struggle in Nineteenth Century Oxfordshire*, History Workshop pamphlets, No. 3, 1970, p. iii; A. Charlesworth, *Social Protest in a Rural Society*, Historical Geography Research Series, No. 1, Geo Abstracts Ltd, Norwich, 1979, p. 46.
26. Hobsbawm and Rudé, op. cit., pp. 16, 19.
27. J. Obelkevich, *Religion and Rural Society: South Lindsey, 1825–75*, Oxford, 1976, ch. II.
28. H. Perkin, *The Origins of Modern English Society, 1780–1880*, Routledge and Kegan Paul, 1969, chs. VI–IX.
29. For an elaboration of these distinctions see H. H. Gerth and C. Wright Mills, *From Max Weber. Essays in Sociology*, Routledge and Kegan Paul, 1948, esp. pp. 68–9, 180–95.
30. W. H. Pedley, *Labour on the Land*, King and Staples, 1942, p. 148, gives a figure of 328,000 members for the Women's Institutes. If we assume, arbitrarily, that as few as one-fifth were farmworkers' wives this would result in a figure nearly three times as high as contemporary membership of NUAW (see table 8.3 above).
31. A. Howkins, 'The Norfolk Farm Labourer, 1900–23', *Society for the Study of Labour History*, Bulletin No. 33, 1976, pp. 7–9; idem, 'Structural Conflict and the Farm Worker: Norfolk, 1900–20', *Journal of Peasant Studies*, 1977, vol. IV, pp. 217–29; and *Poor Labouring Men. Rural Radicalism in Norfolk, 1870–1923*, History Workshop Series, Routledge and Kegan Paul, 1985, p. 28.
32. F. Thompson, *Lark Rise to Candleford*, World's Classics edition, Oxford, 1954, pp. 53–4, 261, 268–9, 278, 284, 321, 473. Another writer conscious of vast social differences yet also holding that discontent was 'foreign to the cottage proper' was R. Jefferies, *Hodge and his Masters*, Smith Elder, 1880, I, pp. 82–3, 281, and II, pp. 10, 206–7.
33. F. E. Green, *A History of the English Agricultural Labourer, 1870–1920*, P. and S. King, 1920, p. 224; G. Sturt, *Change in the Village*, Readers Library edition, 1920, pp. 103–5, 161.
34. On Flora Thompson see B. English, 'Lark Rise and Juniper Hill: A Victorian Community in Literature and History', *Victorian Studies*, 1985, vol. XXIX, esp. pp. 32–4; and on Jefferies, the comments in K. D. M. Snell, *Annals of the Labouring Poor. Social Change and Agrarian England, 1660–1900*, Cambridge, 1985, p. 388.
35. M. K. Ashby, *Joseph Ashby of Tysoe, 1859–1919*, Cambridge, 1961, p. 258.
36. Green, op. cit., p. 282; P. Ambrose, *The Quiet Revolution. Social Change in a Sussex Village 1871–1971*, Chatto and Windus, 1974, p. 56.
37. M. Winstanley, 'Voices from the Past: Rural Kent at the Close of an Era' in Mingay, *Victorian Countryside*, II, pp. 633–4.
38. F. Kitchen, *Brother to the Ox. The Autobiography of a Farm Labourer*, Dent, 1940, pp. 81, 83.
39. 'The Wagoners', BBC Radio 4, 6 April 1982.
40. Newby, op. cit., pp. 335–6, 361, 387–8, 391–5, 408.
41. Museum of English Rural Life, Reading University. D71/8. Reminiscences of Charles Slater, II, pp. 60–1.
42. This tradition is examined in detail by A. Howkins, *Poor Labouring Men*. See, however, the important reservations on p. xiii.
43. P.P. 1893–4 (C.6894–III), vol. XXXV. *Royal Commission on Labour*. Rept. of A. Wilson Fox on Cambs., Lancs., Norfolk, Northumberland, Suffolk, p. 23.
44. D. W. Howell, *Land and People in Nineteenth Century Wales*, Routledge and Kegan Paul, 1978, pp. 93–4. Like Howell, Wunderlich, op. cit., pp. 15–16 has associated the presence of farm servants with absence of class feeling in the Germany of the 1920s.
45. Jefferies, op. cit., I, p. 199.
46. Howkins, *Poor Labouring Men*, p. 177.
47. Newby, op. cit., pp. 335–40, 352, 378–80.
48. H. Orel, ed., *Thomas Hardy: Personal Writings*, Macmillan, 1967, p. 172.
49. For example, the misleading observations about enclosures, nineteenth century real wages and

sundry other matters in the background chapter to H. E. Bracey, *English Rural Life*, Routledge and Kegan Paul, 1959, pp. 7–9; or A. Jones, *Rural Housing. The Agricultural Tied Cottage*, Occasional Papers in Social Administration, No. 6, Bell and Sons, 1975 who suggests in a cursory introduction, p. 14, that the enclosure movement was 'replacing the old system of agriculture'.

50. This suggestion is to be developed in H. Perkin, *The Rise of Professional Society: England since 1880*, Routledge and Kegan Paul, forthcoming.

Further reading

N. Agar, *The Bedfordshire Farm Worker in the Nineteenth Century*, Bedfordshire Historical Record Society, 1981, vol. LX.

R. Arnold, *The Farthest Promised Land. English Villagers, New Zealand Immigrants of the 1870s*, Victoria University Press, Wellington, New Zealand, 1981.

M. K. Ashby, *Joseph Ashby of Tysoe, 1859–1919*, Cambridge, 1961.

D. C. Barnett, 'Allotments and the Problem of Rural Poverty', in E. L. Jones and G. E. Mingay, eds., *Land, Labour and Population in the Industrial Revolution*, Edward Arnold, 1967.

R. Blythe, *Akenfield*, Allen Lane, 1969.

B. S. Bosanquet, 'The Quality of the Rural Population', *Eugenics Review*, 1950, vol. XLII.

M. Brown and S. Wingard, *Low Pay on the Farm*, Low Pay Unit, Pamphlet No. 3, 1975.

A. Charlesworth, *An Atlas of Rural Protest in Britain, 1548–1900*, Croom Helm, 1983.

A. Charlesworth, 'A Comparative Study of the Spread of the Agricultural Disturbances of 1816, 1822 and 1830 in England', *Peasant Studies*, 1984, vol. XI.

E. J. T. Collins, 'Harvest Technology and Labour Supply in Britain, 1790–1870', *Economic History Review*, 2nd series, 1969, vol. XXII.

E. J. T. Collins, 'Migrant Labour in British Agriculture in the Nineteenth Century', *Economic History Review*, 2nd series, 1976, vol. XXIX.

W. J. G. Cowie and A. K. Giles, *An Inquiry into Reasons for the Drift from the Land*, University of Bristol, Department of Economics, Selected Papers in Agricultural Economics, 5, No. 3, 1957.

P. E. Dewey, 'Agricultural Labour Supply in England and Wales during the First World War', *Economic History Review*, 2nd series, 1975, vol. XXVIII.

P. E. Dewey, 'Government Provision of Farm Labour in England and Wales, 1914–18', *Agricultural History Review*, 1979, vol. XXVII.

J. P. D. Dunbabin, ed., *Rural Discontent in Nineteenth Century Britain*, Faber and Faber, 1974.

G. Edwards, *From Crow-scaring to Westminster*, Labour Publishing Co., 1922.

G. E. Evans, *Ask the Fellows who Cut the Hay*, new edition, Faber and Faber, 1965.

G. E. Evans, *Where Beards Wag All*, Faber and Faber, 1970.

G. E. Fussell, *The English Rural Labourer*, Batchworth Press, 1949.

R. Gasson, 'Resources in Agriculture: Labour', in A. Edwards and A. Rogers, eds., *Agricultural Resources*, Faber and Faber, 1974.

R. Gasson, *Mobility of Farm Workers*, University of Cambridge, Department of Land Economy, Occasional Paper No. 2, 1974.

E. Gilboy, 'Labour at Thornborough: an Eighteenth Century Estate', *Economic History Review*, 1st series, 1932, vol. III.

A. K. Giles and W. J. G. Cowie, *The Farm Worker: His Training, Pay and Status*, University of Bristol, Department of Agricultural Economics, 1964.

F. E. Green, *A History of the English Agricultural Labourer, 1870–1920*, P. and S. King, 1920.

R. Groves, *Sharpen the Sickle*, Porcupine Press, 1949, reprinted Merlin Press, 1981.

J. L. and B. Hammond, *The Village Labourer*, new edition, Longman, 1978.

W. Hasbach, *A History of the English Agricultural Labourer*, P. and S. King 1908, reprinted Cass, 1966.

M. A. Havinden, *Estate Villages*, Lund Humphries, 1966.

F. G. Heath, *British Rural Life and Labour*, P. and S. King, 1911.

E. J. Hobsbawm and G. Rudé, *Captain Swing*, Lawrence and Wishart, 1969, reprinted Penguin Books, 1985.

B. A. Holderness, *British Agriculture since 1945*, Manchester University Press, 1985.

P. Horn, *Joseph Arch, 1826–1919. The Farm Workers' Leader*, Roundwood Press, Kineton, 1971.

P. Horn, *Labouring Life in the Victorian Countryside*, Gill and Macmillan, Dublin, 1976.

P. Horn, *The Rural World, 1780–1850. Social Change in the English Countryside*, Hutchinson, 1980.

P. Horn, *Rural Life in England in the First World War*, Gill and Macmillan, Dublin, 1984.

L. E. Howard, *Labour in Agriculture: an International Survey*, Royal Institute of International Affairs, Oxford, 1935.

D. W. Howell, *Land and People in Nineteenth Century Wales*, Routledge and Kegan Paul, 1978.

A. Howkins, *Poor Labouring Men. Rural Radicalism in Norfolk, 1870–1923*, History Workshop series, Routledge and Kegan Paul, 1985.

E. H. Hunt, 'Labour Productivity in English Agriculture, 1850–1914', *Economic History Review*, 2nd series, 1967, vol. XX.

D. Jones, 'Thomas Campbell Foster and the Rural Labourer: Incendiarism in East Anglia in the 1840s', *Social History*, 1976, vol. I.

E. L. Jones, 'The Agricultural Labour Market in England, 1793–1872', *Economic History Review*, 2nd series, 1964, vol. XVII.

B. Kerr, 'The Dorset Agricultural Labourer, 1750–1850', *Proceedings of the Dorset Natural History and Archaeological Society*, 1962, vol. LXXXIV.

A. Kussmaul, *Servants in Husbandry in Early Modern England*, Cambridge, 1981.

Land Agents' Society, *Facts about the Land*, John Murray, 1916.

R. Lennard, *Economic Notes on English Agricultural Wages*, Macmillan, 1914.
R. W. Malcolmson, *Life and Labour in England, 1700–1780*, Hutchinson, 1981.
J. Marlow, *The Tolpuddle Martyrs*, Andre Deutsch, 1971.
J. D. Marshall, 'Nottinghamshire Labourers in the Early Nineteenth Century', *Transactions of the Thoroton Society*, 1960, vol. LXIV.
J. D. Marshall, 'The Lancashire Rural Labourer in the Early Nineteenth Century', *Transactions of the Lancashire and Cheshire Antiquarian Society*, 1965, vol. LXXI.
E. J. Mejer, *Agricultural Labour in England and Wales*, I, *1900–20* and II, *1917–1951*, University of Nottingham, Department of Agricultural Economics, 1949, 1951.
C. Miller, 'The Hidden Workforce: Female Fieldworkers in Gloucestershire, 1870–1901', *Southern History*, 1984, vol. VI.
D. Mills, *Lord and Peasant in Nineteenth Century Britain*, Croom Helm, 1980.
G. E. Mingay, ed., *The Victorian Countryside*, 2 vols., Routledge and Kegan Paul, 1981.
G. E. Mingay, ed., *The Agrarian History of England and Wales*, VI, *1750–1850*, Cambridge, forthcoming.
D. H. Morgan, *Harvesters and Harvesting, 1840–1900. A Study of the Rural Proletariat*, Croom Helm, 1982.
K. A. H. Murray, *Agriculture*. History of the Second World War, United Kingdom, Civil Series, HMSO, 1955.
A. Mutch, 'Lancashire's "Revolt of the Field": the Ormskirk Farmworkers' Strike of 1913', *North West Labour History Society*, 1982, Bulletin No. 8.
H. Newby, *The Deferential Worker*, Allen Lane, 1977.
J. Obelkevich, *Religion and Society: South Lindsey, 1825–75*, Clarendon Press, Oxford, 1976.
C. S. Orwin, 'A Century of Wages and Earnings in Agriculture', *Journal of the Royal Agricultural Society*, 1931, vol. XCII.
C. S. Orwin and E. Whetham, *History of British Agriculture, 1875–1914*, Longmans, Green, 1964, reprinted David and Charles, Newton Abbot, 1971.
W. H. Pedley, *Labour on the Land*, King and Staples, 1942.
T. L. Richardson, 'The Agricultural Labourer's Standard of Living in Kent, 1790–1840' in D. J. Oddy and D. Miller, eds., *The Making of the Modern British Diet*, Croom Helm, 1976.
J. Robin, *Elmdon. Continuity and Change in a North-West Essex Village, 1861–1964*, Cambridge, 1980.
B. S. Rowntree and M. Kendall, *How the Labourer Lives*, Nelson, 1913.
V. Sackville-West, *The Women's Land Army*, Michael Joseph, 1944.
R. Samuel, ed., *Village Life and Labour*, History Workshop series, Routledge and Kegan Paul, 1975.
N. Scotland, *Methodism and the Revolt of the Field. A Study of the Methodist Contribution to Agricultural Trade Unionism in East Anglia, 1872–96*, Alan Sutton, Gloucester, 1981.
B. Short, 'The Decline of Living-in Servants in the Transition to Capitalist Farming: a Critique of the Sussex Evidence', *Sussex Archaeological Collections*, 1984, vol. CXXII.

K. D. M. Snell, *Annals of the Labouring Poor. Social Change and Agrarian England, 1660–1900*, Cambridge, 1985.

L. M. Springall, *Labouring Life in Norfolk Villages*, Allen and Unwin, 1936.

G. Sturt, *Change in the Village*, Duckworth, 1912, reprinted 1920 (Readers Library edition), 1955.

The Land. The Report of the Land Enquiry Committee, I, *Rural*, Hodder and Stoughton, 1913.

C. Thomas, 'Agricultural Employment in Nineteenth Century Wales: a New Approach', *Welsh History Review*, 1972, vol. VI.

C. Thomas, 'Seasonality in Agricultural Labour Patterns: Examples from Estates in the Vale of Clwyd'. *Publications of the Flintshire Historical Society*, 1974, vol. XXVI.

E. Whetham, *The Agrarian History of England and Wales*, VIII, *1914–39*, Cambridge, 1978.

H. T. Williams, 'Changes in the Productivity of Labour in British Agriculture', *Journal of Agricultural Economics*, 1954, vol. IX.

A. Wilson-Fox, 'Agricultural Wages in England during the Last Half Century', *Journal of the Royal Statistical Society*, 1903, vol. LXVI, reprinted in W. E. Michinton, ed., *Essays in Agrarian History*, David and Charles, Newton Abbot, 1968, II.

E. A. Wrigley, 'Men on the Land and Men in the Countryside: Employment in Agriculture in Early Nineteenth Century England' in L. Bonfield, R. M. Smith and K. Wrightson, eds., *The World We have Gained: Histories of Population and Social Structure*, Blackwell, Oxford, 1986.

Index

NOTE: Villages and minor towns are indexed separately only where significant research findings exist; otherwise, the appropriate county headings have been extended to cover them. Individual persons are included on a selective basis and, in the case of writers and authors, where their works or opinions are cited in the text.